AN ARTIST IN TWO FIELDS

Christopher Thistlethwaite

A sketchbook glimpse into half a century of livestock farming in a bygone age

First published in 2003 by Christopher Thistlethwaite
Formerly of 28 Knighton Rise, Oadby, Leicester LE2 2RE

All sketches, drawings, linocuts and lithographs included in this book are the work of the author, except one (on page 11) which is by his son, Jeremy.

Christopher offers his gratitude for the following sources of inspiration - some going back to the 19th Century.

Lucy Kemp Welch

"Black Beauty" by Anna Sewell

"Country Crafts"

"Soper's Horses" by Paul Heiney

"Both Sides of the Road" by Charles Tunnicliffe

"The Thistlethwaite Family" and

"The Bax Family" - both books by my father, Bernard Thistlethwaite

Some original linocuts shown in the book may be purchased.
They are printed on hand-made paper, and offered at reasonable prices, according to size.

Orders for prints or books to:

223 Dunchurch Road, Rugby CV22 6HP
Email: admin@artistin2fields.co.uk

Printed in Great Britain by

Norwood Press, Cropston Road, Anstey, Leicestershire LE7 7BJ

ISBN: 0-9546084-0-2

FOREWORD

It gives great pleasure to see Christopher's life's work and experience brought to fruition in his book:

'AN ARTIST IN TWO FIELDS'.

For over 50 years, I have had the priviledge of being a colleague of Christopher. We first met when he was studying at Leicester College of Art. Christopher's career has 4 directions: farmer, artist, teacher, parent. The book includes references to his family; all four children, of whom he is justifiably proud, have continued his interests relating to farming and art.

Once, whilst travelling through Northamptonshire, we stopped at an early bale-making machine standing on display: he explored and explained all the functions and complexities of the machine which he knew from experience: the book has similar detailed familiarity with early farming methods and machines, and tells of the way of life in farming during his active involvement in the past.

It is clear that a sketchbook must have been in continuous use, since drawings and prints embellish the text, and the book is a rich combination of the two activities; it is a visual and narrative delight.

Enjoy it as I have

David Howells. ATD.
FELLOW, SOCIETY OF SCRIBES & ILLUMINATORS

Dedication

I dedicate this book to my dear wife,
Elizabeth,
without whom I would never have had the inspirational wherewithal to farm, and the dogged perseverance to continue in the pursuit in spite of all the difficulties encountered along the way.

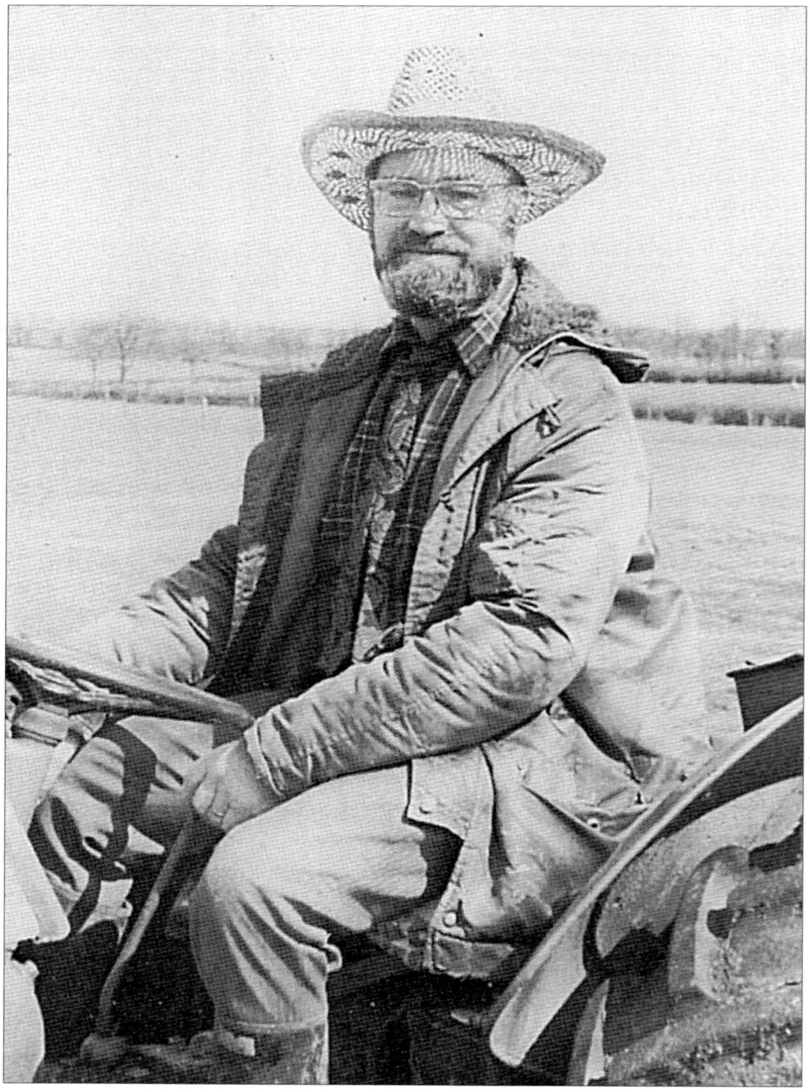

Christopher on his grey Fergie - circa 1980

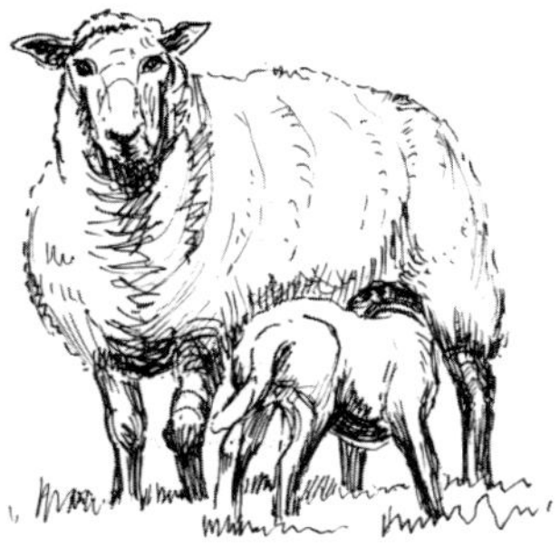

Contents

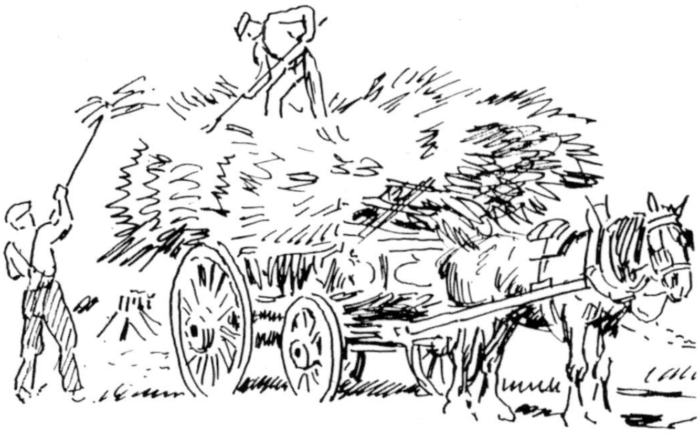

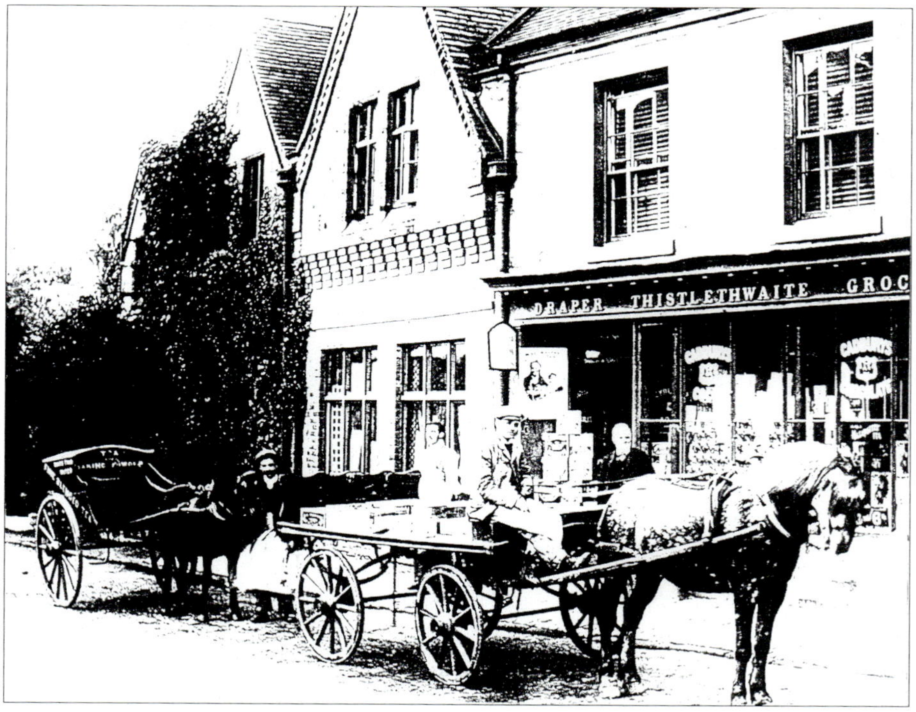

This shows my Quaker great grandfather Jeremiah Thistlethwaite (1826-1910) standing in the doorway of his Grocery and Drapery shop in the village of Great Ayton, Cleveland, North Yorkshire - the birthplace of Captain Cook. My father lived in the house beyond. The houses were designed by the Quaker Architect, Alfred Waterhouse, who also designed the London Natural History Museum. According to Quaker custom, he would open his shop on Christmas Day and he wore no lapels on his jackets.

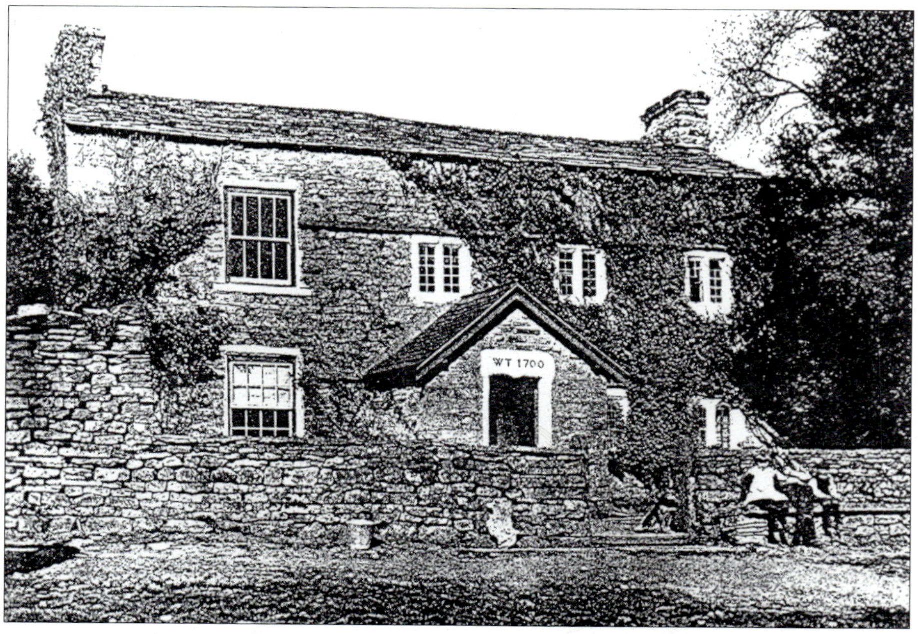

This stone built farmhouse in Upper Dentdale has the initials W.T.1700 incised in the door lintel. It was the family home of my ancestor William Thistlethwaite (1677-1766). See page 229 for an account of the avalanche which took place there in 1752.

Introduction

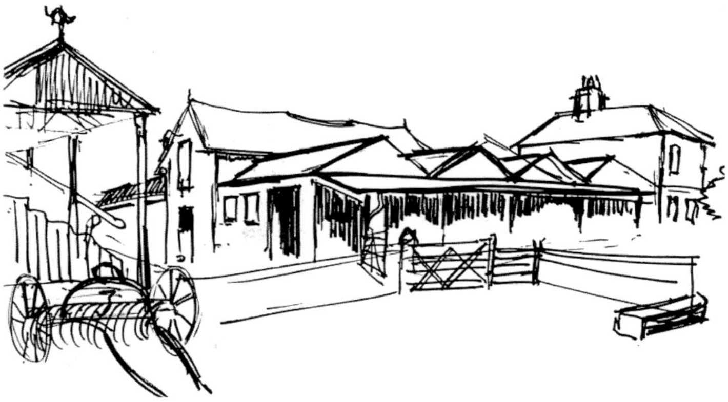

In order to set the scene for anyone bold enough to wish to read my memoirs, it might be useful to indicate briefly my connections with farming.

My Thistlethwaite ancestors were yeomen farmers in Dentdale, on the western side of the Pennine watershed in the North Riding of Yorkshire, where they were sometimes known as statesmen (estatesmen). They can be traced back to 1648, and were quite possibly descended from Vikings. Many of them adopted the Quaker faith soon after its beginnings and suffered persecution for it. There is a place in Dentdale named High Thistlethwaite to be seen on the Ordnance Survey map.

Although I was born in 1920 at Buxton in Derbyshire, my family would spend holidays with my paternal grandparents in the North Riding village of Great Ayton. My great-grandfather, Ralph Dixon, was headmaster of the Great Ayton Quaker School. The school had its own home farm, where in addition to their normal academic work, the boys were taught the rudiments of farming and the girls about dairy management and how to make butter and cheese. We are the proud owners of a silver cup that he won for breeding a champion Cleveland Bay horse, like those which pull the ceremonial royal carriages.

The school farm adjoined my grandfather's house at the foot of the Cleveland Hills. I have fond memories of farming activities and of visiting his Whinstone Mine and its narrow gauge railway. He had two horses for his business. As a small child, I used to sit at the front of the pony trap and drive the pony as it took us to the seaside at Saltburn or Redcar.

In 1929, my father's work took him to Birmingham, where I later attended the Birmingham College of Art in Margaret Street. I spent my school holidays helping on a 100-acre farm on the fringe of the hop and fruit growing area near Tardebigge in Worcestershire. Our farming friends then moved to a much larger farm of 250 acres near Harbury in Warwickshire and I continued to spend all my holidays there, helping with the hay and corn harvest and a large flock of sheep. But this had to end when the farmer was accidentally killed by his bull and the farm was sold. There is more reference to this incident later.

In 1940, I was directed into agriculture and worked on two 300-acre mixed farms near the Fosse Way in Warwickshire. During this time I took a correspondence course in agriculture. Looking back, it seems worth noting that mechanisation was not yet as extensive as one might expect, and one had to learn a great deal about horses. One of these farms had eighteen horses. It was about this time that I spent a year in

Somerset helping a friend to get established on a 70-acre farm in the Quantock Hills where all the work was done by horses.

In 1945, I was approached to become manager of a company farm with 200 acres at Wolvey in Warwickshire and 350 acres seven miles away in Leicestershire. There was a good house and a fair salary, so with the confidence of youth, my wife, Elizabeth, and I took it on. There were about twenty men to organise in their work and a lack of good machinery. Later, when the company sold the farm in lots, we had first refusal of our house, cottage and three sets of fairly dilapidated farm buildings, and so the story begins.

The Home of Christopher and Elizabeth Thistlethwaite

1946-1982

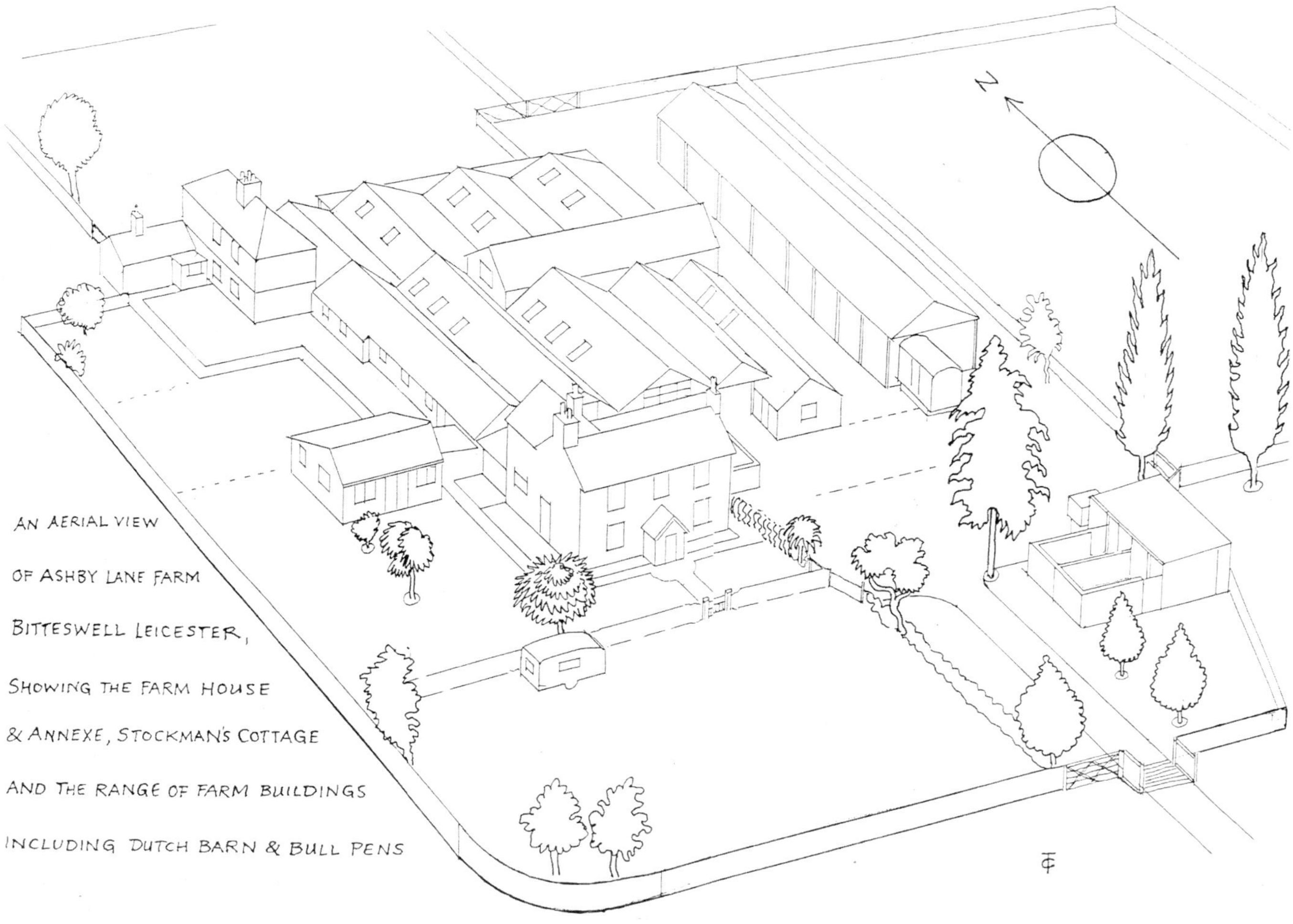

This Plan Shows the Location of Ashby Lane Farm

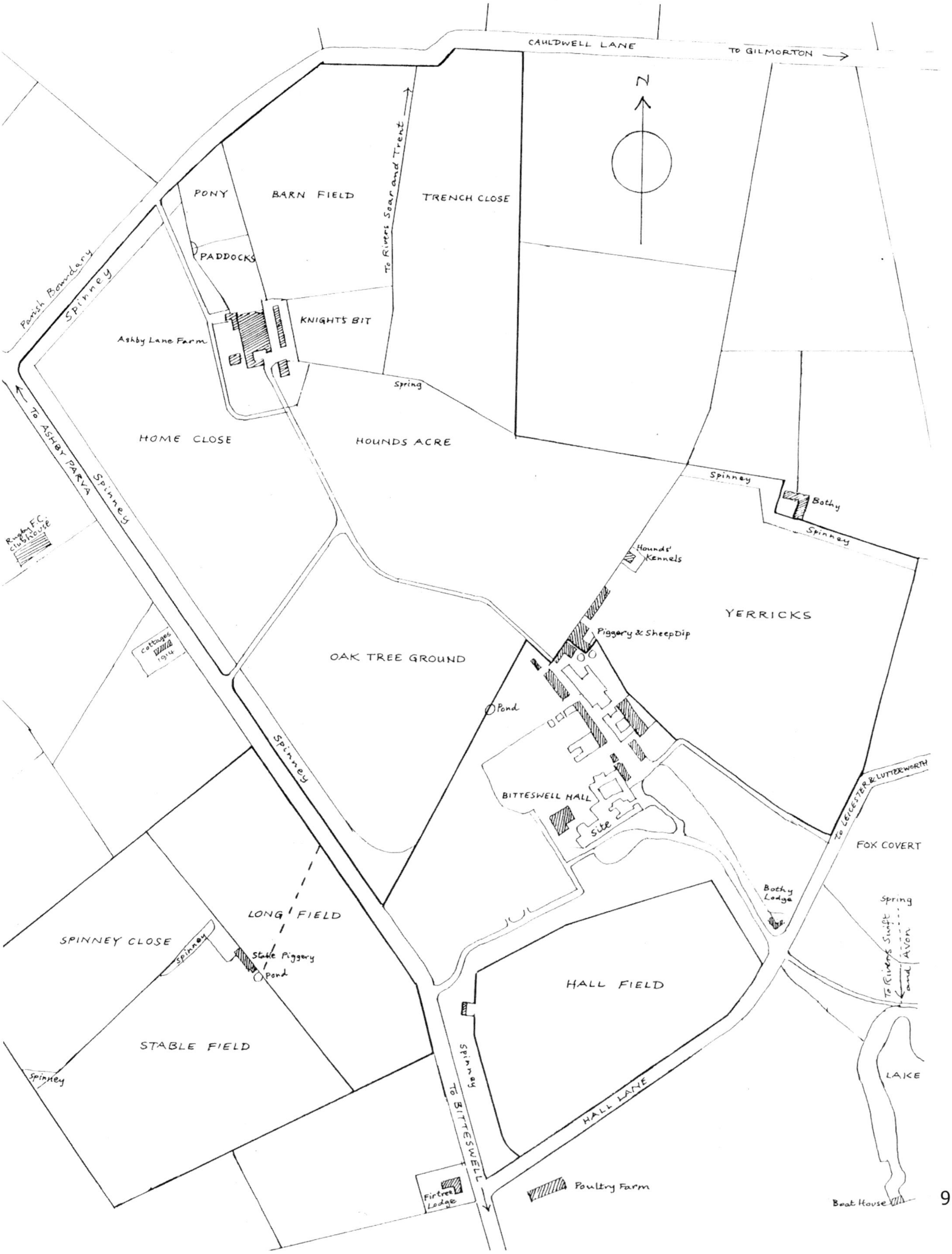

ASHBY LANE FARM HOUSE, COTTAGE AND FARM BUILDINGS
SCHEMATIC PLAN SHOWING THE GENERAL LAYOUT

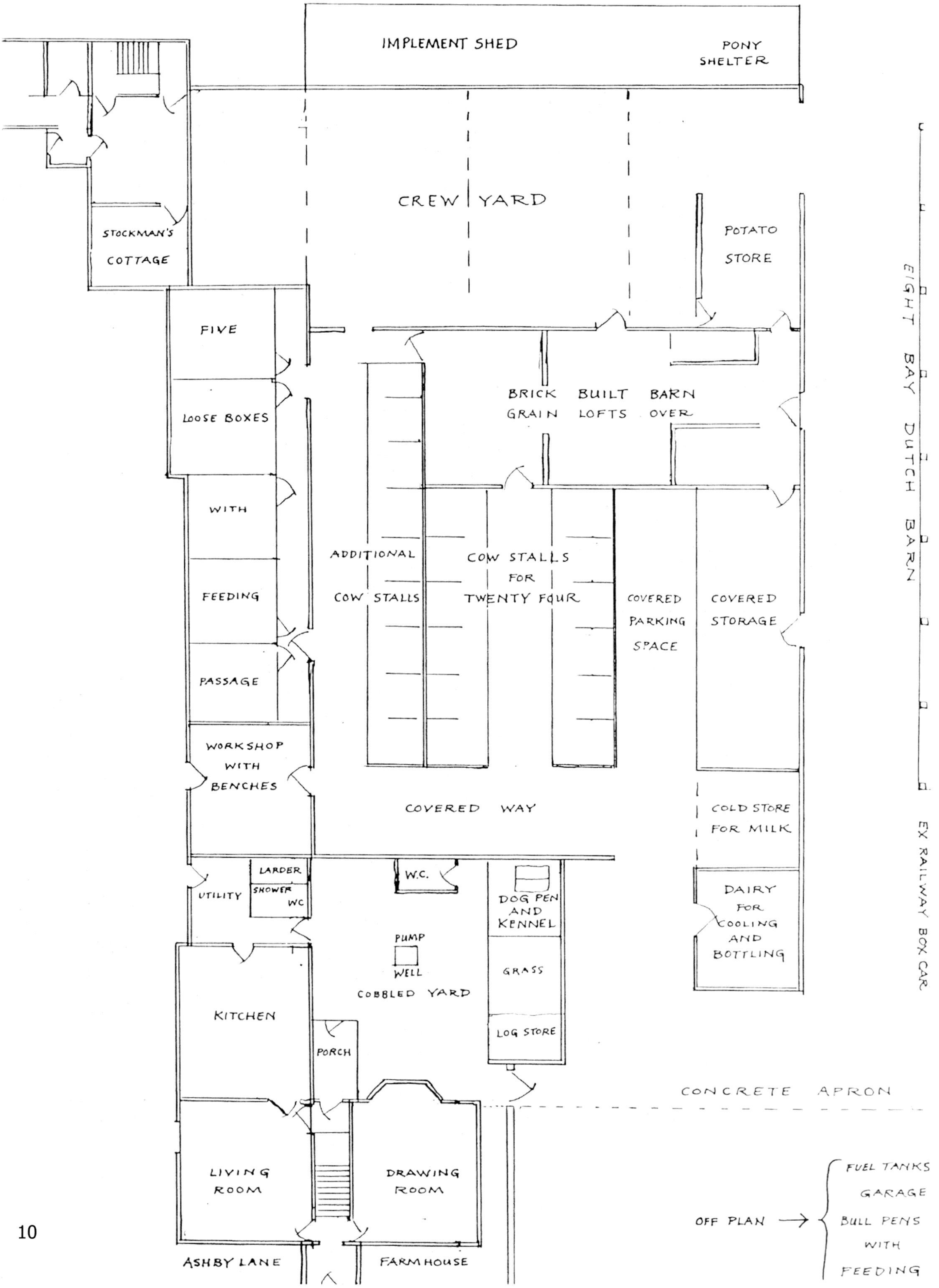

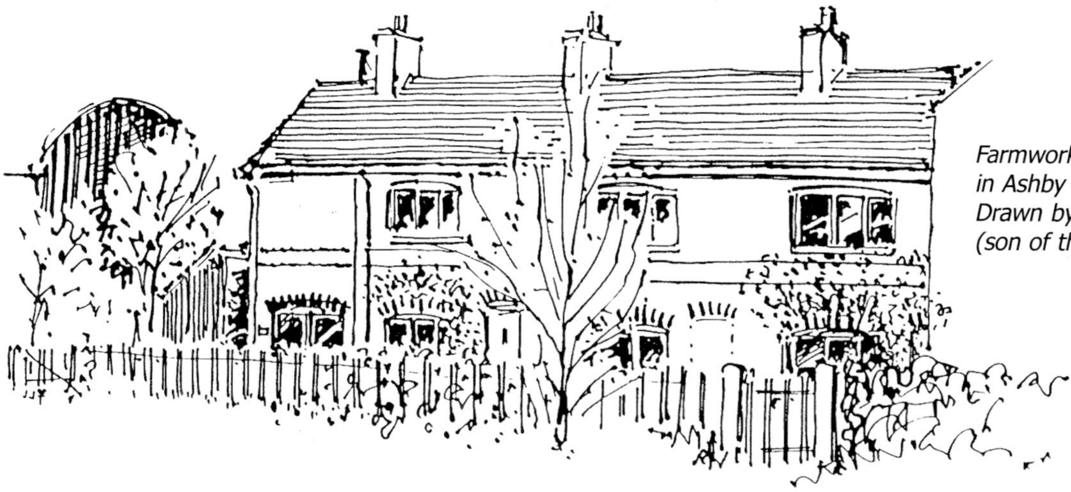

Farmworker's Cottage in Ashby Parva Drawn by Jeremy Thistlethwaite (son of the author)

With the help and encouragement of friends, family and local mentors, in a comparatively short of space of time we had a thriving, small mixed farm partnership employing several people, and the responsibility of a large mortgage (!), a herdsman and his wife, a pig man/general worker, a poultry/dairy maid, a milk-roundsman and a pensioner hedging and ditching as a casual worker.

In considering whether to rent or buy a farm, there are three main factors usually viewed in contrary order by the farmer and his wife. Number 1, the farmhouse; number 2, the buildings; number 3, the land. To my amazement, I had little difficulty in convincing Elizabeth that the land and buildings came first and that the house had potential for improvement later.

In 1946, when we moved into our six-roomed house, it was totally devoid of services and we had very few pieces of furniture and possessions. I soon rigged up a hose-pipe through the window to syphon soft water from a tank. Although it was a very severe winter, we had our love to keep us warm and no plumbing to freeze! The day-old chicks lived in a corner of the kitchen. When we first moved in, Dr. & Mrs. Gateley were both very kind to us and provided many meals and baths. My wife soon learned to cook nourishing meals on a black-leaded range and provisions were delivered along our quarter mile of farm track at regular intervals. It must have been a full two years that we managed without the benefit of electricity, telephone, indoor sanitation or plumbing, yet such were the comforts of wedded bliss that we hardly noticed these privations! This reflects great credit on the devotion and ingenuity of Elizabeth, who has always contrived to make a beautiful, warm, welcoming home, regardless of our financial condition, penniless or otherwise.

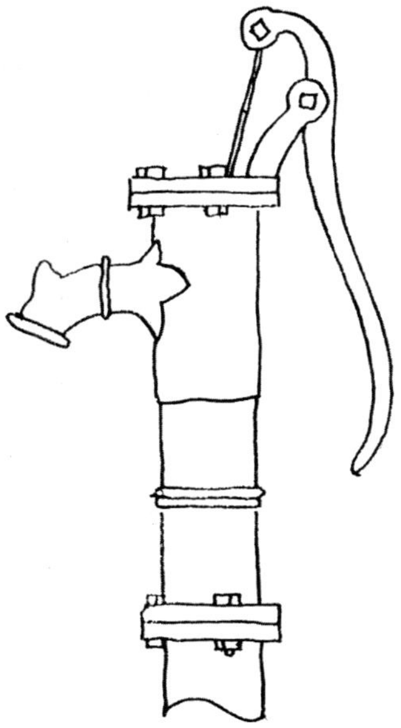

Domestic Cast Iron Water Pump

When hostilities ended, Europe was starving and food production seemed to take priority over picture-making. Ration books persisted until the mid-1950s, years after VE and VJ days. Nevertheless our country people seemed leaner and fitter as a result of a healthier diet, plenty of physical exercise and no central heating.

Starry-eyed Idealism

Our decision to commit ourselves to small-scale farming was not without a measure of starry-eyed religious idealism, in common with many who would aspire to follow 'The Good Life' in one way or another.

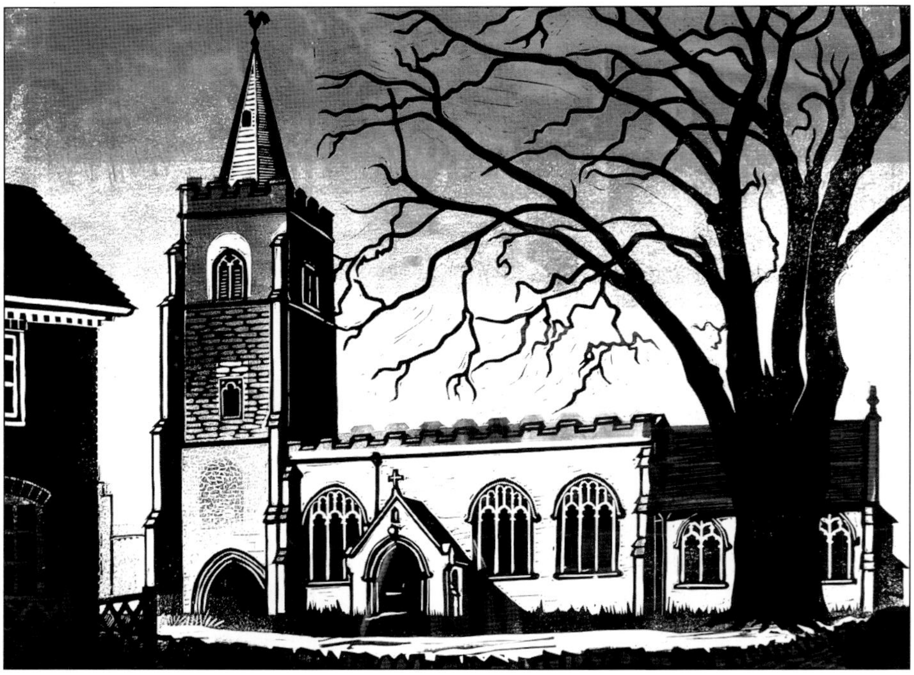

Bitteswell Parish Church
Linocut by Christopher

For many years we used to lay a place at table for the unexpected guest. There was a determination to serve the land in our care with dedication and respect, leaving it better for our husbandry and building up a future reserve for one's family to inherit, and using our skill and knowledge to grow much-needed crops to feed our fellow citizens. By doing this, we hoped to earn their respect and a modest livelihood along the way. Our agricultural ancestors owed a debt of gratitude to the great monastic orders of the past for working at land reclamation and laying the foundations of sound practices in husbandry. Politicians have a short-term view of the world and generally do not understand the needs of agriculture, whereas farmers have always been exhorted to "live as if you will die tomorrow but farm as if you will live forever".

During the 1914-1918 war, because of the intervention of submarines, food was more difficult to import, money was short and all available shipping needed for war materials. The government treated farmers favourably for a short time but all this ceased when the war ended. In my childhood during the twenties and thirties, farming again suffered a great depression due to the imports of foreign food produced by cheap labour in more favourable climates, rendering home production uneconomic.

About this time, my father was devoting much of his spare time and energy to a Midlands Catholic Land Movement: "Back to the Land" (also the title of an album by my third son, Anthony) which was involved with settling young unemployed people on semi-derelict farms in the Midlands. I would accompany him at weekends to see progress and discuss ways and means.

It was tragic but inevitable that the decline in farmers' prosperity had to be passed on to the farm workers, who were either sacked or had their wages cut. In the year of my birth, 1920, working a 50-hour week earned 42 shillings. Only three years later, in 1923, this had been reduced to 25 shillings, which is what it had been about ten years before. In 1938, just prior to the Second World War, wages had crept up to a princely 34 shillings and sixpence for a 50-hour week, still seven shillings and sixpence short of what it had been eighteen years previously!

Life in a Bygone Age

The material presented here opens a doorway onto a lost world, and preserves for future generations a unique and intimate view of life in a bygone age.

We must all be aware of the selectivity of human memory. Given that the lifestyle described here may seem harsh and uncomfortable, most countryfolk would nevertheless say that they had had happy lives in the 'good old days' of their youth. People were more caring then, and more content with their lot. Although aware of the existence of great wealth even within their own communities by the presence of the squire and the big farmers, they did not aspire to emulate their betters, or indeed, see any possibility of doing so. They had to struggle constantly to maintain their standard of life, low as it was. And there was a constant threat of unemployment, so that people were always conscious of the fact that they were lucky to have a job.

Hannah Hauxwell is famous now for her stoic survival on a remote Yorkshire Dales farm, but in the not-too-distant past there must have been thousands like her who accepted their harsh conditions without question.

Midday bait for the horseman and his team

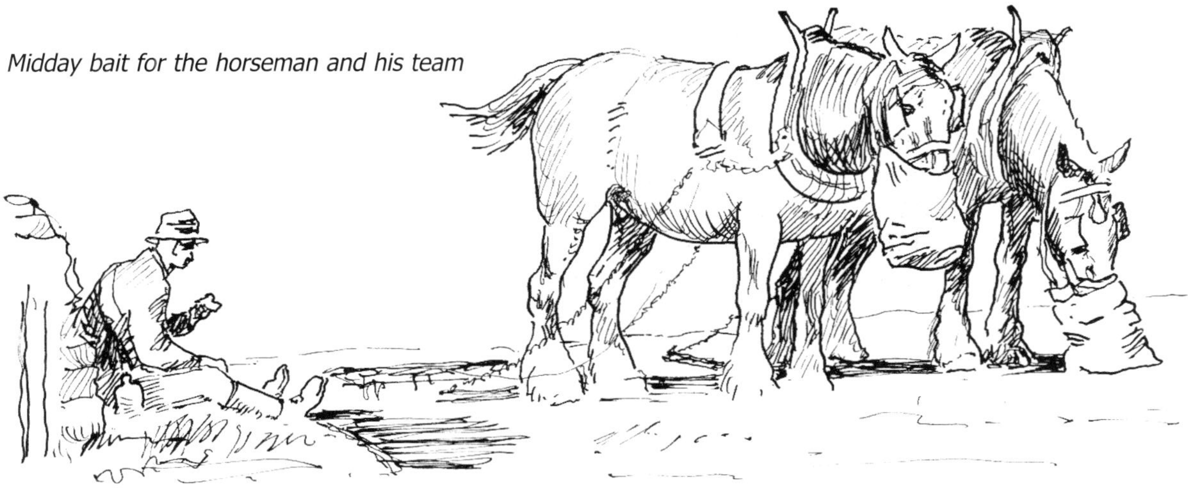

Five Social Classes

Rural society was divided into at least five social classes that were to be found everywhere in the countryside:

1. The gentry: aristocrats, squires and landowners
2. Big farmers
3. Professionals: doctors, lawyers, clergymen
4. Small farmers, shopkeepers, craftsmen
5. Farm workers.

However, there was another factor, social rather than economic, which to some extent cut across this class structure. This was demonstrated in the religious and political allegiance of members of a class. Most villages were divided into the Anglican/Conservatives on one hand and the Non-Conformist/Liberals on the other. The first three of the classes described above tended to be Anglican/Conservative. The fourth class tended to be Non-Conformist/Liberal. The fifth group tended to go to Chapel and to be active trade unionists and supporters of the Labour Party. There was a strong connection between Unionism and Primitive Methodism. I remember well going to hear a local Methodist preacher using his skills as a public orator in support of the Labour Party and workers' rights. He was also an erudite lecturer for the university-sponsored Workers Education Association whose courses on philosophy I attended in the winter evenings.

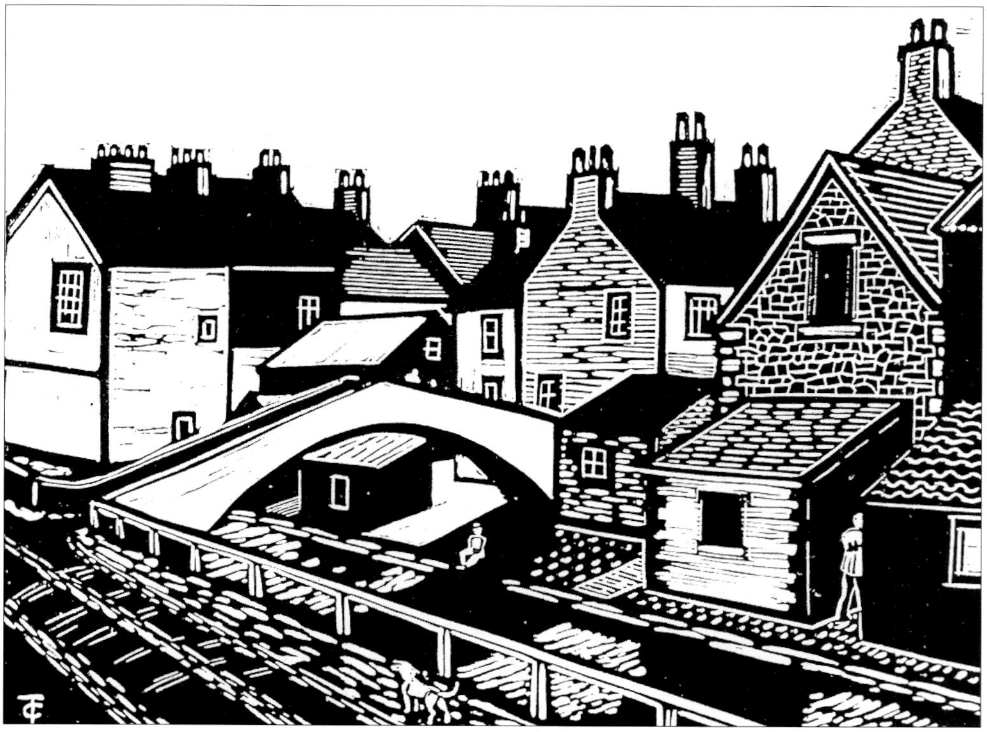

Packhorse Bridge

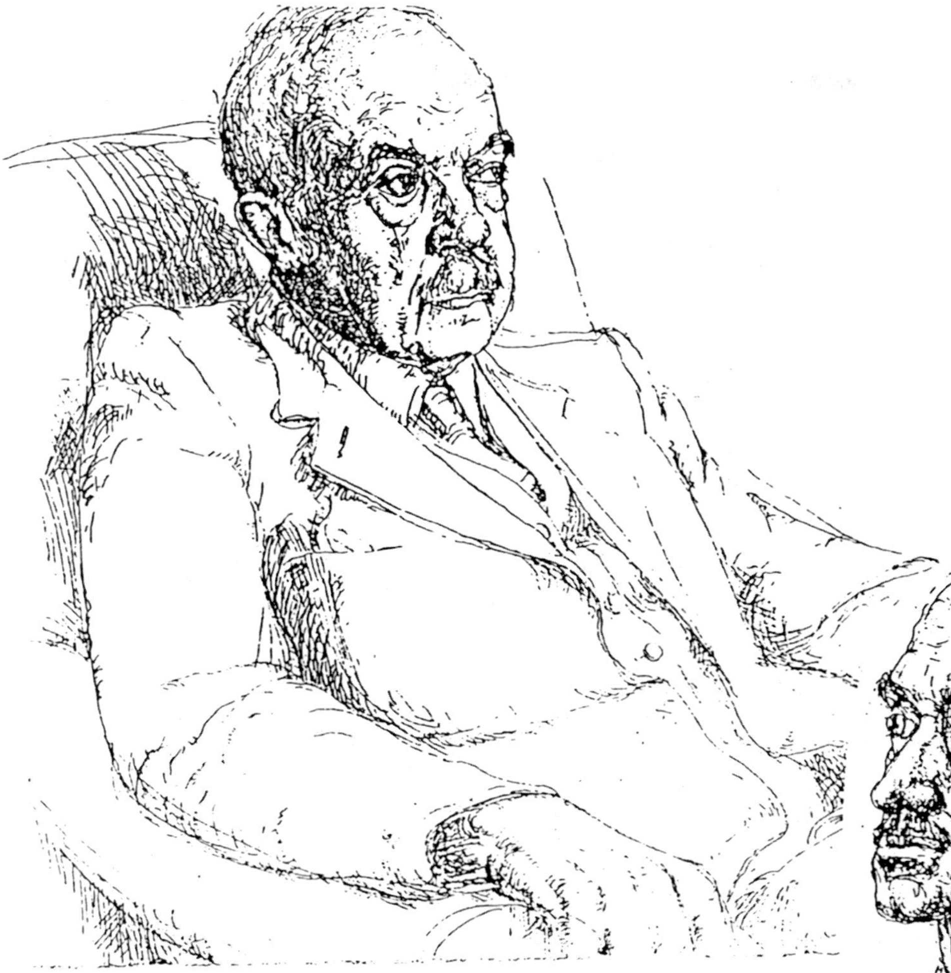

"Wm. Henry Thistlethwaite" my grandfather

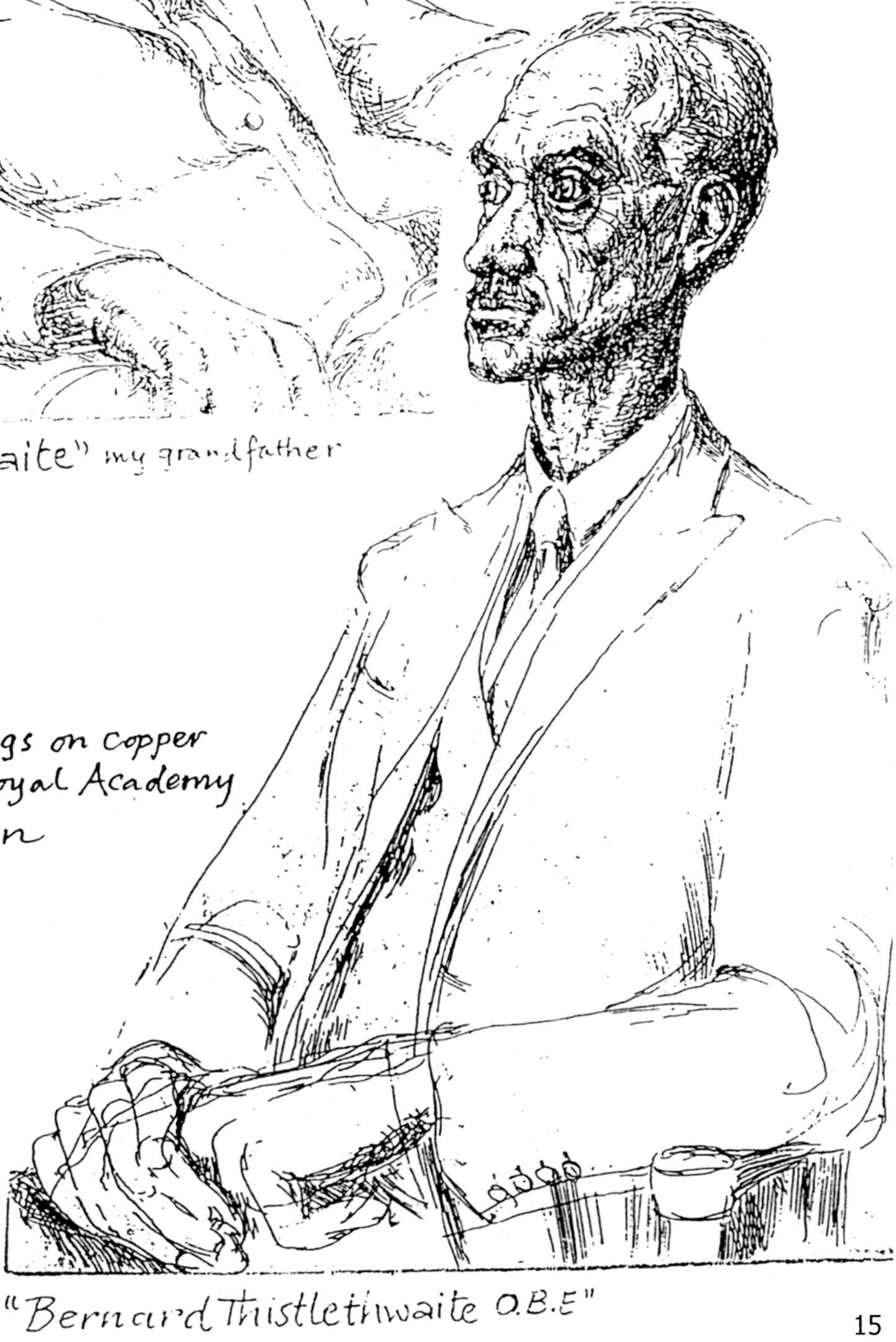

These two portrait etchings on copper were hung in the Royal Academy Summer Exhibition

Bernard Thistlethwaite O.B.E.
(Order of the British Empire)
awarded to him in 1950 for
services to U.N.R.R.A.
(United Nations Relief and
Rehabilitation Association)

Christopher's father "Bernard Thistlethwaite O.B.E"

Imprisoned for His Faith

One of my ancestors, a certain Arthur Thistlethwaite, a small farmer of Carperby in Wensleydale, was imprisoned in 1675 for six years and 29 weeks in York jail for his Quaker beliefs.

When one considers and compares the discomforts offered by York jail in those days with the comforts offered by a modern prison, one begins to realise the certainty of his beliefs and the robustness of his character. He refused to uncover his head and kow-tow to the local magistrate, whom he considered to be just another human being of equal status to himself.

There is a story of another of my ancestors, William Thistlethwaite, born in 1786 at Hobsons Farm in Dentdale who, at a tender age, rode pillion behind his father over hill and dale to attend the famous Quaker school at Ackworth, near Pontefract, a distance of 80 miles. My father treasured the pathetically small wooden box in which William had kept all his worldly possessions. When he returned home, after five years at school with no holidays, his mother completely failed to recognise him!

Job Satisfaction for the Farm Worker

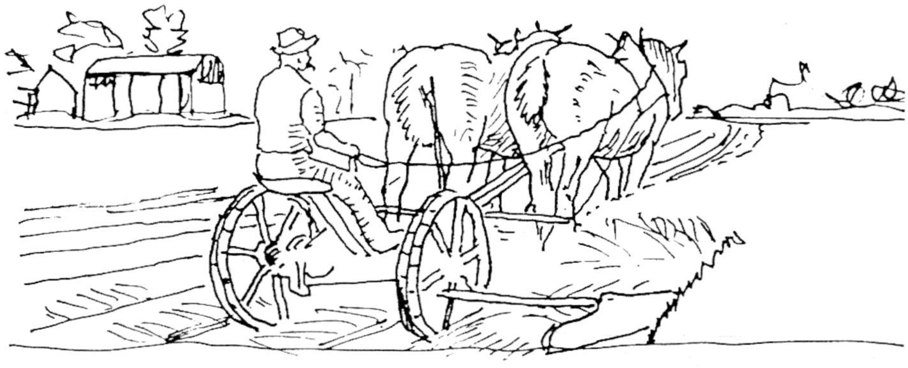

Horseman mowing grass for hay

The farm worker often got great satisfaction from the conditions of his work.

The close contact with animals and the land led to a love of the soil and nature and all wildlife. Unlike the factory worker, who was tied down to one repetitive process, he had to be master of many trades and to be able to turn his hand to anything on the farm. For instance, the horseman was not only in charge of the horses, but was responsible for ploughing, sowing, mowing, reaping, and any other task that involved the use of a horse. He was expected to take care of any horse that was sick or injured, and to act as a midwife when a foal was being born. On some farms he might be expected to help with other jobs, such as fencing and hedge laying.

The worker who could plough the straightest furrow, the rick-builder who could build the best stack, the thatcher who did the finest thatching, and the hedger who could lay the neatest hedge were all greatly admired and even envied by their peers, who gave them extra status in the community according to the quality of their workmanship.

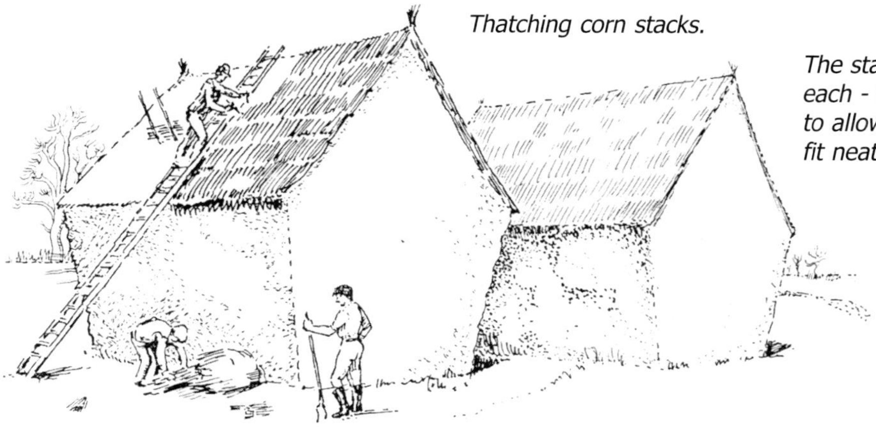

Thatching corn stacks.

The stacks - 5 yards x 10 yards each - were erected side by side to allow the threshing machine to fit neatly in between.

The man near the ladder is Yelming.

Union Membership

I still have my membership card of the National Union of Agricultural Workers, which was numerically weak and carried little clout.

Farmers were prepared to undercut one another rather than co-operate in orderly marketing. The desperate plight of agriculture in the early '30s led to the establishment of marketing boards. The Milk Marketing Board began in 1933 and was the saviour of many small farmers. Many farm and estate workers were afraid to join a union or vote for the 'wrong' party for fear of the sack and eviction from their tied cottages. Unlike many, I reasoned that if I was willing to accept the benefits negotiated on my behalf by the unions, I should pay my dues. Later I supported the National Farmers Union for the same reason.

In the England of those inter-war years of my youth, it was still possible to experience, as I did to some extent, an almost mediaeval lifestyle. Machines were quite rudimentary and the majority of the work was done by hand or horse power. When we moved into our first home in 1946, there were few home comforts. Our house was even denied the advantages of mains water, which did not come until about 1976 when it was needed for the weekly baths of the rugby clubhouse opposite!

Nowadays there need be little difference between the lifestyles of town and country dweller, but in those days, the advent of electricity was regarded as a priceless boon, doing away with oil lamps and candles

for lighting and coal for heating and cooking. Electric motors could now be used for pumping water and powering milking machines and other labour-saving devices.

Poverty is Relative

It would seem to me that the feeling of poverty is relative as to time and place.

Thus, the poor white person from the deep south of the USA no doubt considers himself to be living in abject poverty compared with his wealthy neighbours, yet he drives to collect his 'welfare' in a gas-guzzling pick-up truck, encrusted with rusting chrome and equipped with a noisy radio. He is surrounded in his home by the trappings of western civilised life, TV, refrigerator and washing machine. He regularly over-eats on junk food or burgers, canned 'coke' and cold beer. The impact of his lifestyle on the dwindling resources of this planet must be far in excess of that of a middle-class vegetarian teetotal Asian clerk who cycles to work in Calcutta, feeling thankful that his lifestyle is far superior to that of the millions of coolies and beggars who exist on the streets of that megacity. There is no way that the world's underprivileged populations could ever be raised to enjoy the standards of living of the American poor white.

Whenever I read these memoirs I feel that I must be giving the impression that farming is a violent, dangerous and thankless occupation, misunderstood by the majority of our fellow citizens who demand from us impossible irreconcilable standards. "What is on the credit side?" you may ask, "that keeps you going in spite of crippling adversity?" I have constantly to remind myself that the future belongs to the believers and not to the cynics and the sceptics. I would guess that most of us have developed a peasant-like, dogged optimism - a simple faith in the long-term future that things can only get better, that luck will change and virtue be rewarded. Happiness is a failure to realise how bad things are! Some maintain that there is no such thing as bad luck - only bad management. Too often they are right.

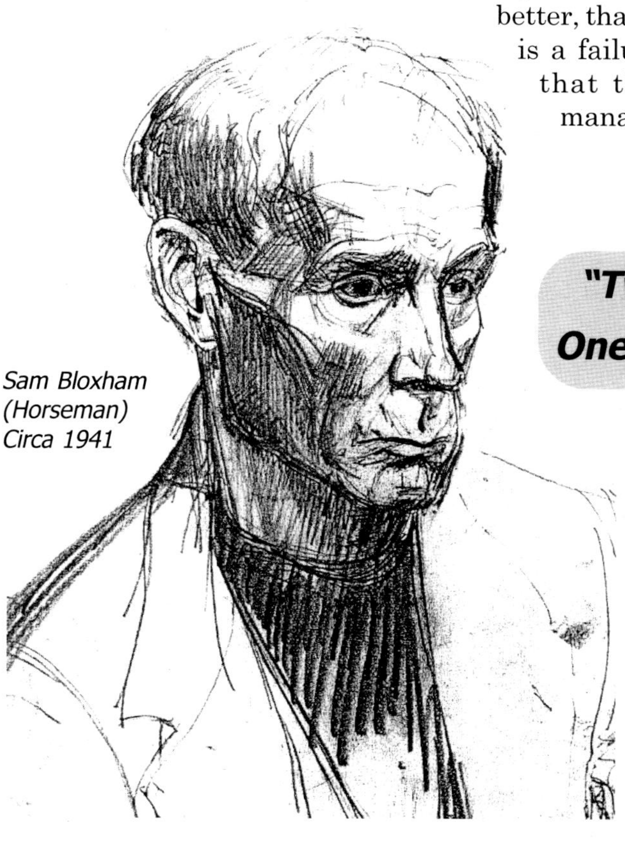

Sam Bloxham (Horseman) Circa 1941

"Two men looked out from prison bars, One saw the mud and the other the stars."

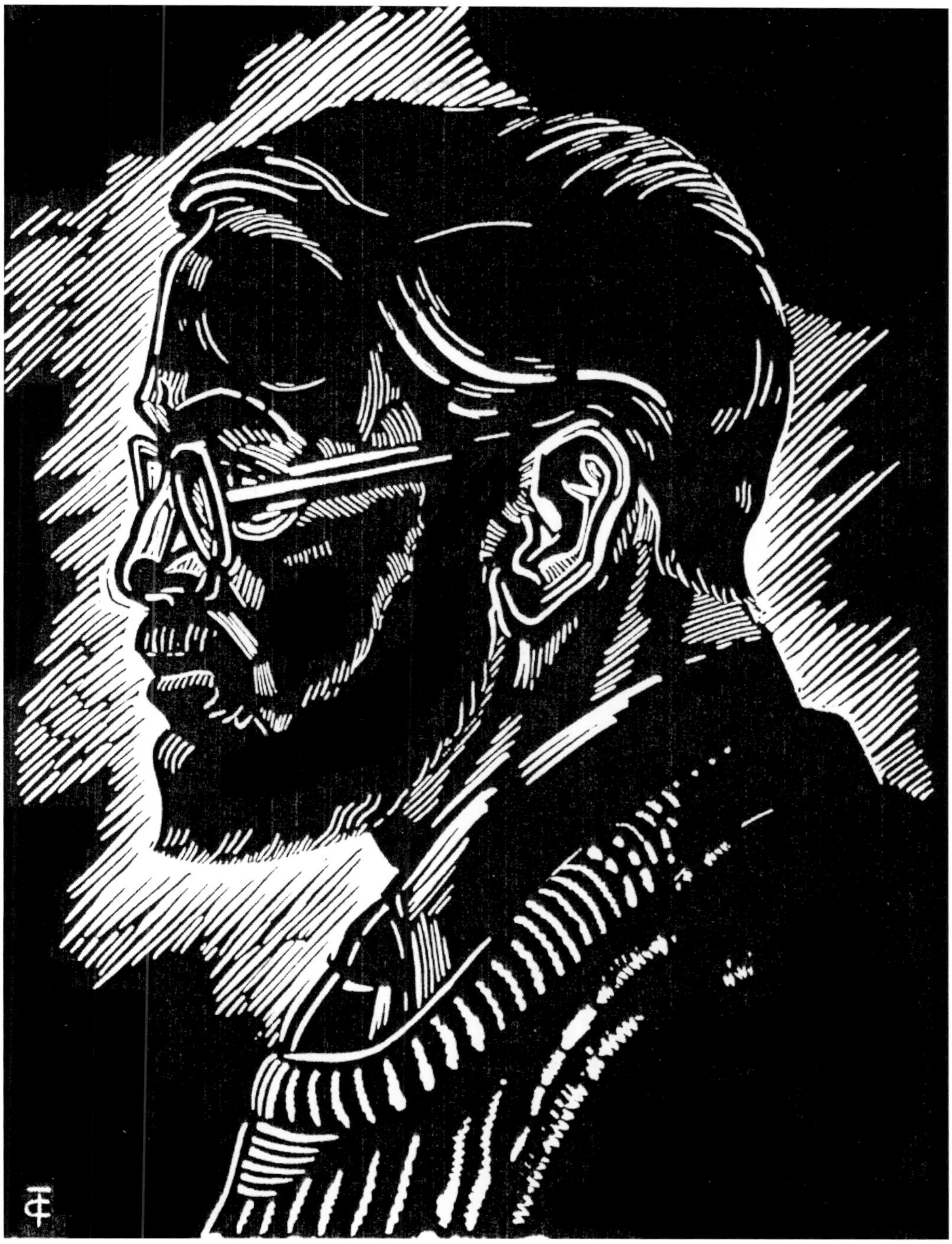

Self-portrait
Linocut by Christopher

"He who can no longer wonder and stand rapt in awe at the glories of creation is as good as dead."

On a clear night, I loved to look at the stars as I did my last rounds of the stockyards to see that all was well. At Christmastide I would reflect on that star so eagerly awaited by the Magi 2000 years ago, which they followed to the humble stable birthplace, and the marvel that wise men still follow Him.

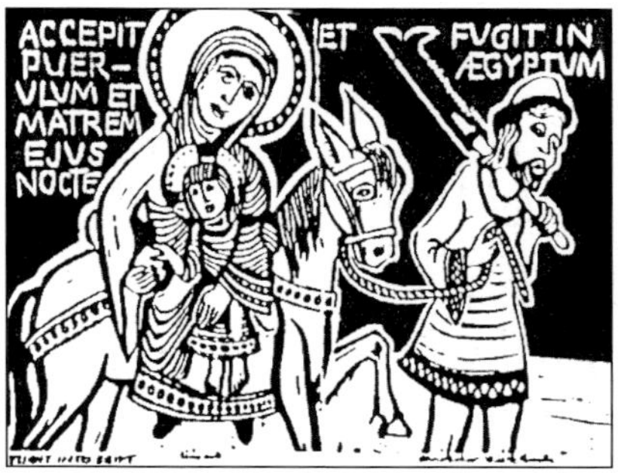

For efficiency and versatility in cultivation, the British farmer and his men need acknowledge no superiors. It is surprising that we seem to care for none of these things, although twice in a lifetime war has shown each one of us how closely farming is connected with our very existence. Apart from times when there are health scares, like the recent ones concerning BSE and salmonella, the mass of people in Great Britain remain uninterested, and though we live in a world perilously balanced over the gulf of war and famine, we seldom give a thought to how we are fed and how we are going to be fed in the uncertain future.

City life has become so remote from the farms that townsfolk tend to forget the direct connection between the soil on the farm and the food on their tables. The daily milk comes in sealed bottles or cartons. Our breakfast cereals are weird and wonderful things that look like dried leaves. Our sugar comes in packets from the grocer or supermarket. Yet the milk has to be *grown* in the form of grass or silage to feed the dairy cows. Those breakfast foods were once growing as wheat, oats, barley or maize, and the crop had to be drilled, harrowed, rolled, sprayed and harvested before being stamped and twisted into the strange shapes in which we eat them. Our sugar comes from an ugly root, like a giant parsnip.

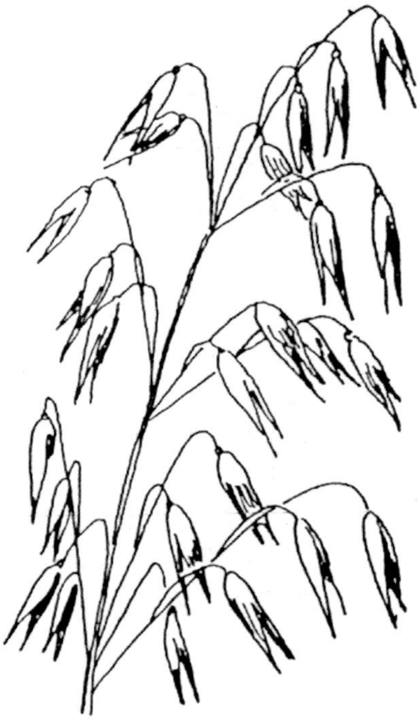

A pannicle of oats

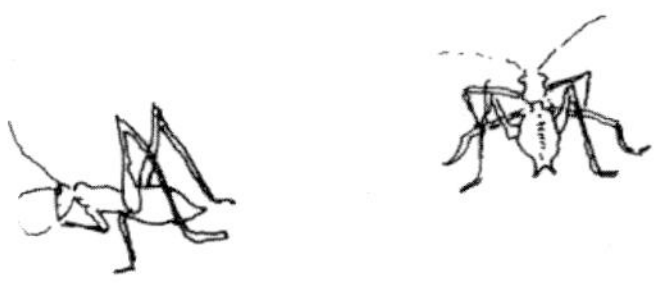

Although it is perhaps understandable that we should forget our daily dependence on the soil, there can be no excuse for such forgetfulness. As we travel by car or train we see the fields on either side of us as they slip past. If we ride the skies in a plane, the farmlands are stretched below in a chequerboard pattern. We seldom give a second's thought to what is growing in those fields, brown in winter, green in spring, and gold and amber as harvest time draws near.

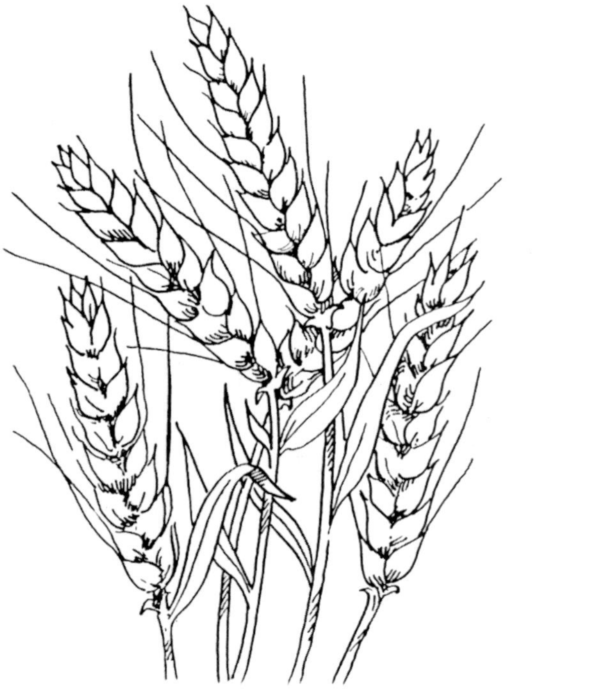

Five ears of corn

Even if we are able to tell the difference between a field of young corn and a pasture of grass, how many of us know what kind of corn it is - wheat, oats or barley - or what quality of grass makes up the pasture, permanent meadow, or temporary ley? When we see cattle grazing, how many of us can tell whether they are bullocks fattened for beef or dairy cows yielding us their milk?

How many of us know or care what the men and women are doing in the fields as they work? The sad truth is that apart from farmers and those who work on the land, we know less about the all-important subject of how our food is grown than we do about any other. For every person who can tell a corn drill from a combine harvester, or name even the common breeds of cattle, like Jerseys, Herefords or Aberdeen Angus, there are many thousands who know how a camera or a computer works, or who can identify at once the different makes of motor car.

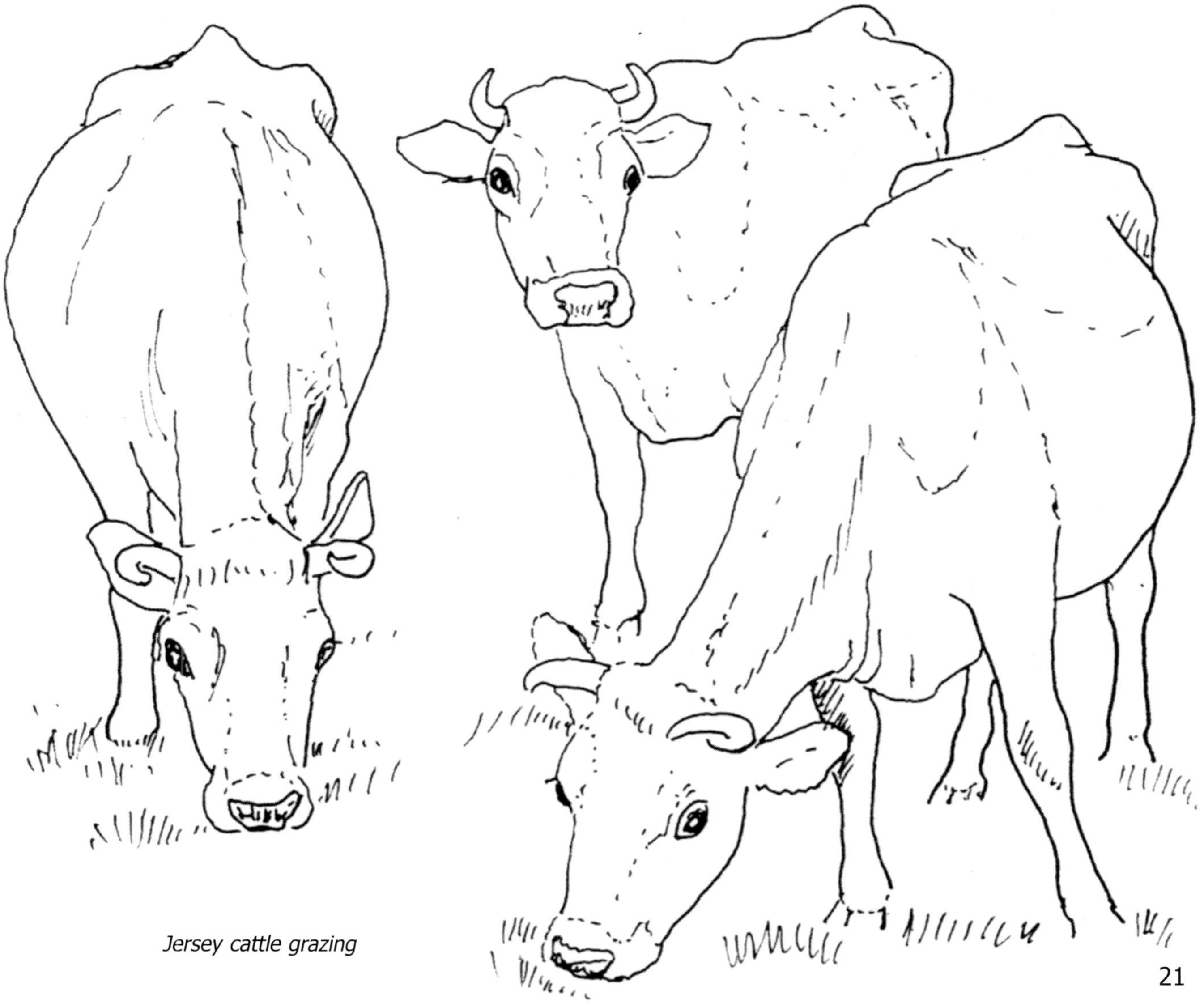

Jersey cattle grazing

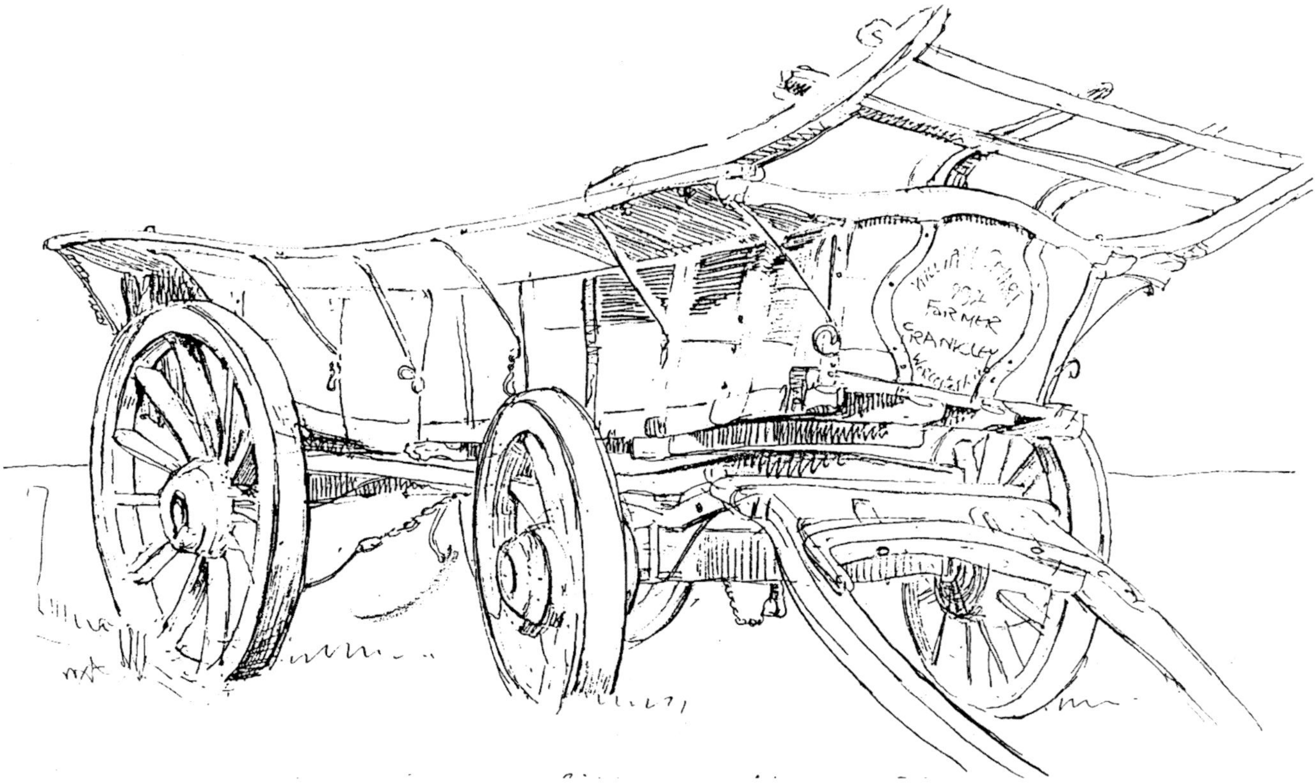

A quarter locking waggon in a field at Frankley, near Birmingham.

These Two Drawings Were Made About 1936, by Christopher - Aged 16 Years.

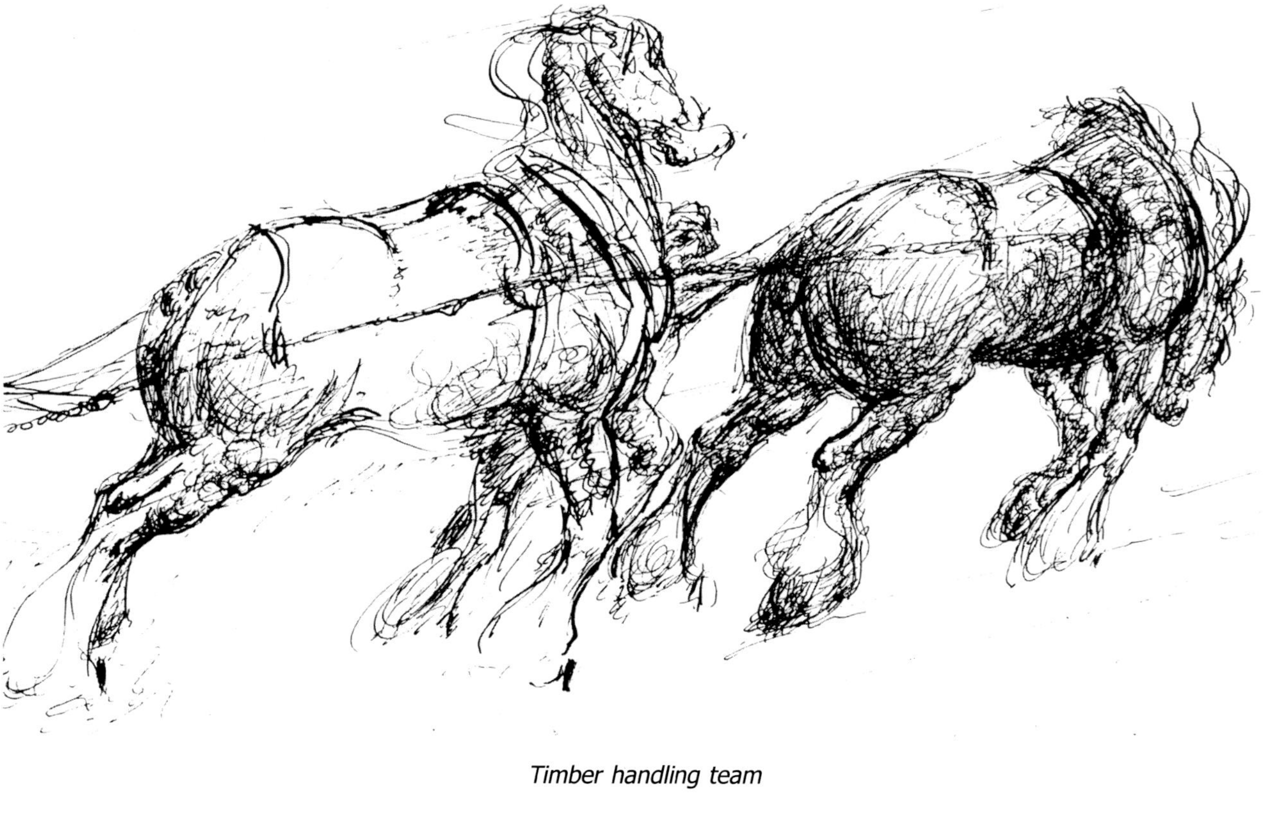

Timber handling team

Notes on the Illustrations

In pre-war years, it was my good fortune to be trained as a fine art draughtsman at the Birmingham College of Art in Margaret Street.

The course covered a wide field of study such as anatomy, perspective, architecture, life drawing, figure composition, portraiture and drawing from moving models.

As I met my future wife Elizabeth there, I suppose I must have learned to apply these subjects in one way or another to my fellow students in learning so as to get along with gifted people from widely different backgrounds! My old mentor, A. G. Street, used to scorn the fashionable habit of calling 'games' by the name of 'sport'. His rigid definition of the word 'sport' involved only activities connected with the pursuit of a quarry such as hunting, shooting and fishing. However, he did make an exception in the case of courting. The pursuit of nubile damsels through the fertile fields of academia must surely be one of the most pleasant sports known to man!

In addition to drawing and painting, I learned other crafts involving modelling small animals in clay and etching on copper plates. I used to practice my growing skills in sketching the moving animals and birds that came to the annual fatstock shows. My love of horses gave me confidence, as a callow youth, to seek entry to the extensive stabling of the railway and canal companies in order to draw the powerful animals at rest in their stalls.

The City of Birmingham had well turned out teams for roadworks and cleansing, but the finest were probably those which advertised the breweries, Mitchells and Butlers of Cape Hill and Ansells at Aston Cross. The strangest sight in the city was a pair of well-matched Hereford bullocks yoked to a covered wagon advertising Atora suet.

Artist in Two Fields

The illustrations for most books are completed in a single set style over a period of only a few months by an artist other than the author himself.

In this case, the author has been described by the BBC as a farmer who is ***'an artist in two fields'***, and it is for the reader to judge how well the illustrations complement the text. As many of the illustrations for these memoirs are taken from sketches made over a period of nearly sixty years, it will be seen that there are changes of mood, style and technique according to the circumstances and instruments available at the time they were executed.

Sketchbooks were filled mainly to record events and objects of interest in odd moments snatched away from the relentless routine of farming chores and family commitments.

Several scenes have had to be reconstructed from memory and others are based on photographic references. Some are plans and diagrams which I felt were relevant to the text, which is not meant to be over-didactic. Strangely, it was the accumulation of drawings that gave me the idea of putting together a farmer's sketchbook, and from that I was encouraged to write explanatory notes which led to these memoirs being written. A classic case of putting the cart before the horse! The illustrations begot the text.

Over the years, we maintained our contacts with former fellow art students and tutors. Our lives were enriched by visits to the farm of groups of students who found a wealth of subject matter to sketch in a place where they would be undisturbed by the public gaze.

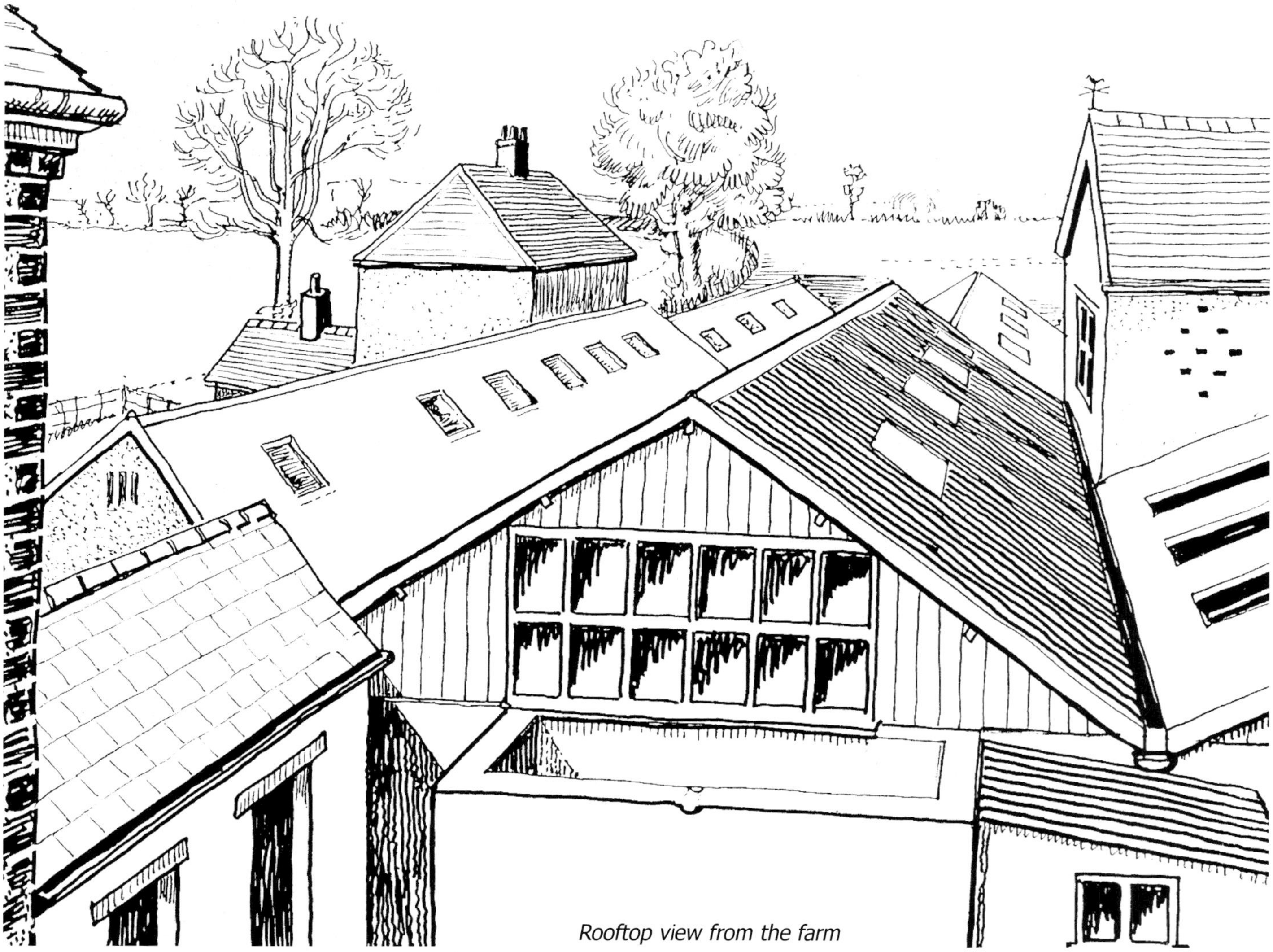

Rooftop view from the farm

Chapter ONE

A Farmer's Character

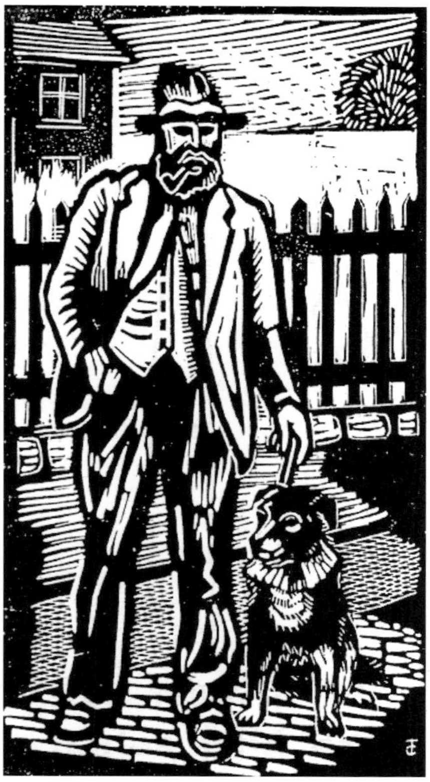

Lakeland farmer and his dog (Linocut)

A Small Farm Implies Livestock Which Forms the Farmer's Character

In order that the reader may form a fairly accurate opinion of the sort of person I am, it is suggested that he or she must do it from the writing.

I am pretty sure that I would not neatly fit anyone's preconception of what a farmer should be - I must be far too inconsistent and illogical. I would soft-heartedly cosset and feed a stray homing-pigeon, yet shoot without compunction the wood-pigeon taking my crops. I would stand in awe and admiration at the skill of a spider or the beauty of a butterfly, yet start up the tractor to spray pesticides on the crops. My mood can swing in an instant from impulsive generosity to parsimonious humility; from elation to depression; from agony to ecstasy.

Outwardly I may appear unemotional and calm but inwardly I may be seething with passionate emotions which I have learned to conceal. A religious boarding school education trains boys to develop a stiff upper lip, presenting this air of inscrutable equanimity at times of disaster. Aggressive instincts are channelled towards worthy ends: the doctor and nurse fight the ravages of disease; the missionary and politician fight for human rights in justice and peace.

There is no doubt in my mind that the type of work a person has to do helps to form his or her character. Livestock farming calls for great patience, compassion and commitment to living creatures.

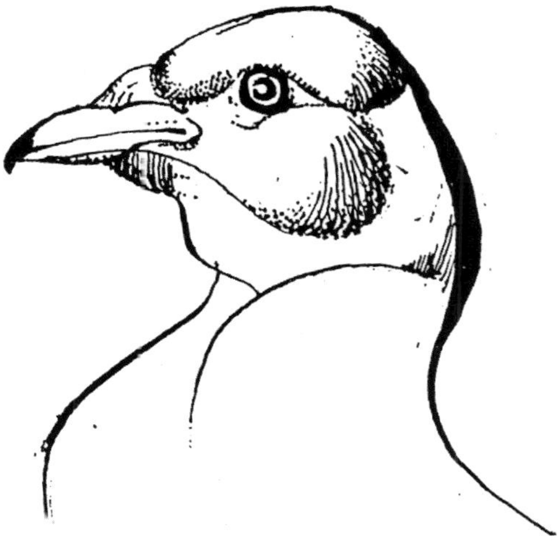

Wood pigeon

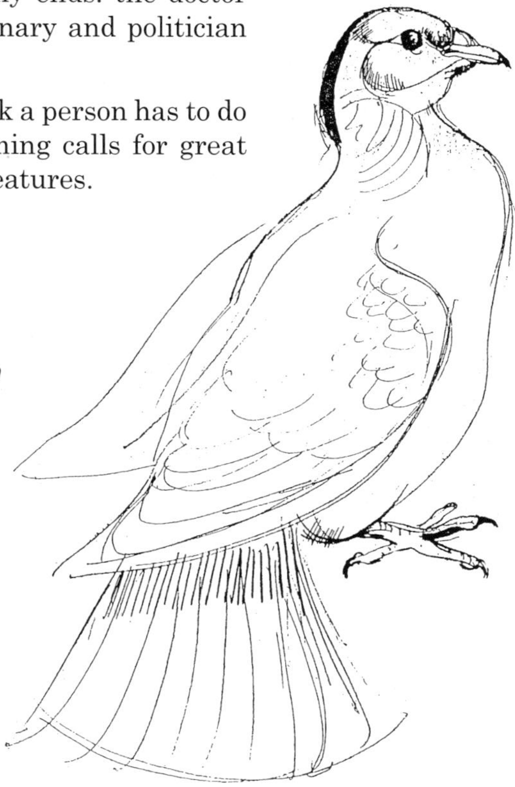

Is There a Typical Farmer?

Does the person exist who is everyone's stereotype of a farmer?

If you heard it said by an acquaintance, "My friend Jack Dawkins from Yorkshire is a farmer", does it conjure up an image in your mind? "Your daughter's friend, Elizabeth, is going to marry a farmer"; do you immediately think of her riding to hounds every other day in immaculate white breeches and shiny black boots?

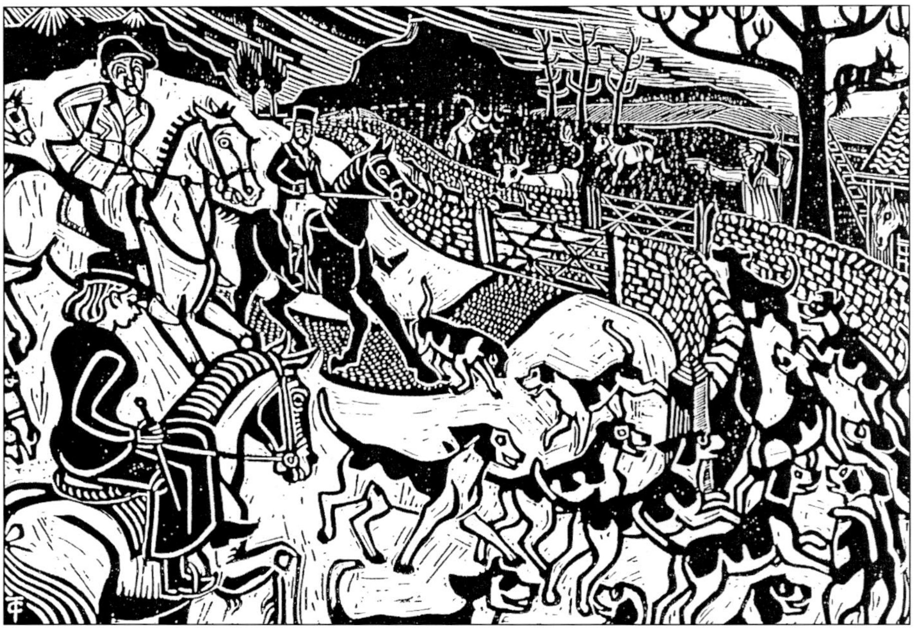

Linocut bought by Leicester Museum & Art Gallery

Or do you see her in muddy boots, climbing a steep hillside through a snowstorm to bottle-feed sickly lambs?

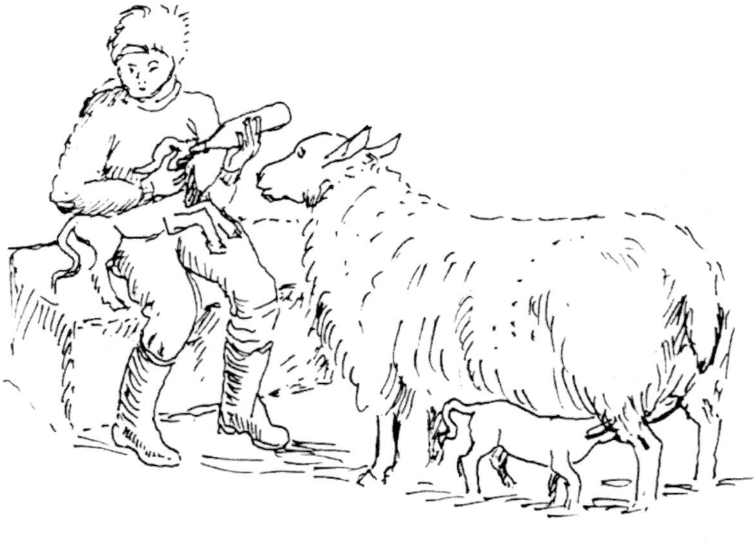

I guess that you would soon be asking for more information upon which to feed your imagination. "Is he a barley-baron from East Anglia, a flock master from Swaledale or a dairy farmer from Cheshire? Is he making his living by intensive pigs or poultry? Does he live in a rambling stone eighteenth century mansion or a modern bungalow? How many men does he employ? Does he have a farm manager or bailiff?" Eventually you will be sure to ask, "How many acres does he farm and is he a tenant or an owner farmer?"

Acreage is a Poor Gauge for Measuring Prosperity

12 tennis courts	=	1 acre	=	0.4047 hectares
1 hockey field	=	1.25 acres	=	0.51 hectares
1 rugby field	=	1.75 acres	=	0.71 hectares

A square acre	is about 70 yards x 70 yards (64 x 64 metres)
A long acre	is 220 yards x 22 yards (201 meters x 20.1 metres)
A square ten acre field	is 220 yards x 220 yards (201 metres x 201 metres)
A square mile	is 640 acres (2.59 square kilometres = 259 hectares)
A hectare	is 2.471 acres

Taken alone, the number of acres farmed is a very poor yardstick by which to gauge the prosperity and activity of a farming business. A hill farmer in marginal, mountainous, less favoured areas may have 80 acres of 'in by' land - small stonewalled grass fields for lambing and haymaking. He may also have access to 2,000 acres of grazing rights over non-nutritious gorse, bracken and ling. He could be regarded as farming over 2,000 acres but his disposable income from the farm could be so low that he must also have another job to survive.

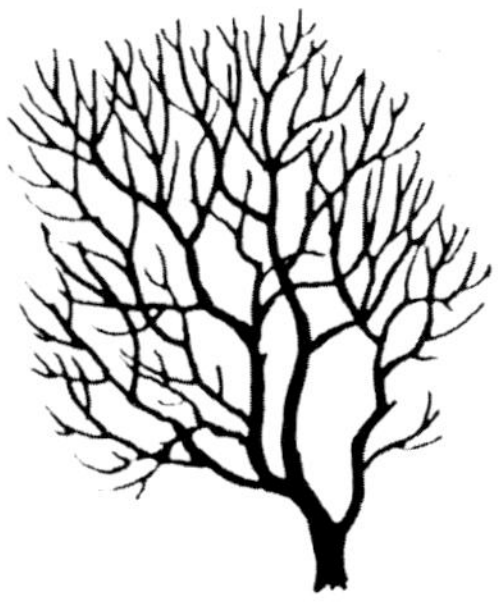

Erosion and the Grain Drain

A persuasive case can be made for vegetarianism.

It has been estimated that livestock, most typically pigs and poultry, are fed more than one-third of the world's grain harvest, whilst 500 million humans remain severely malnourished and undernourished. Farm animals compete with us for food, often wasting the food value of their rations as they inefficiently convert grain into meat.

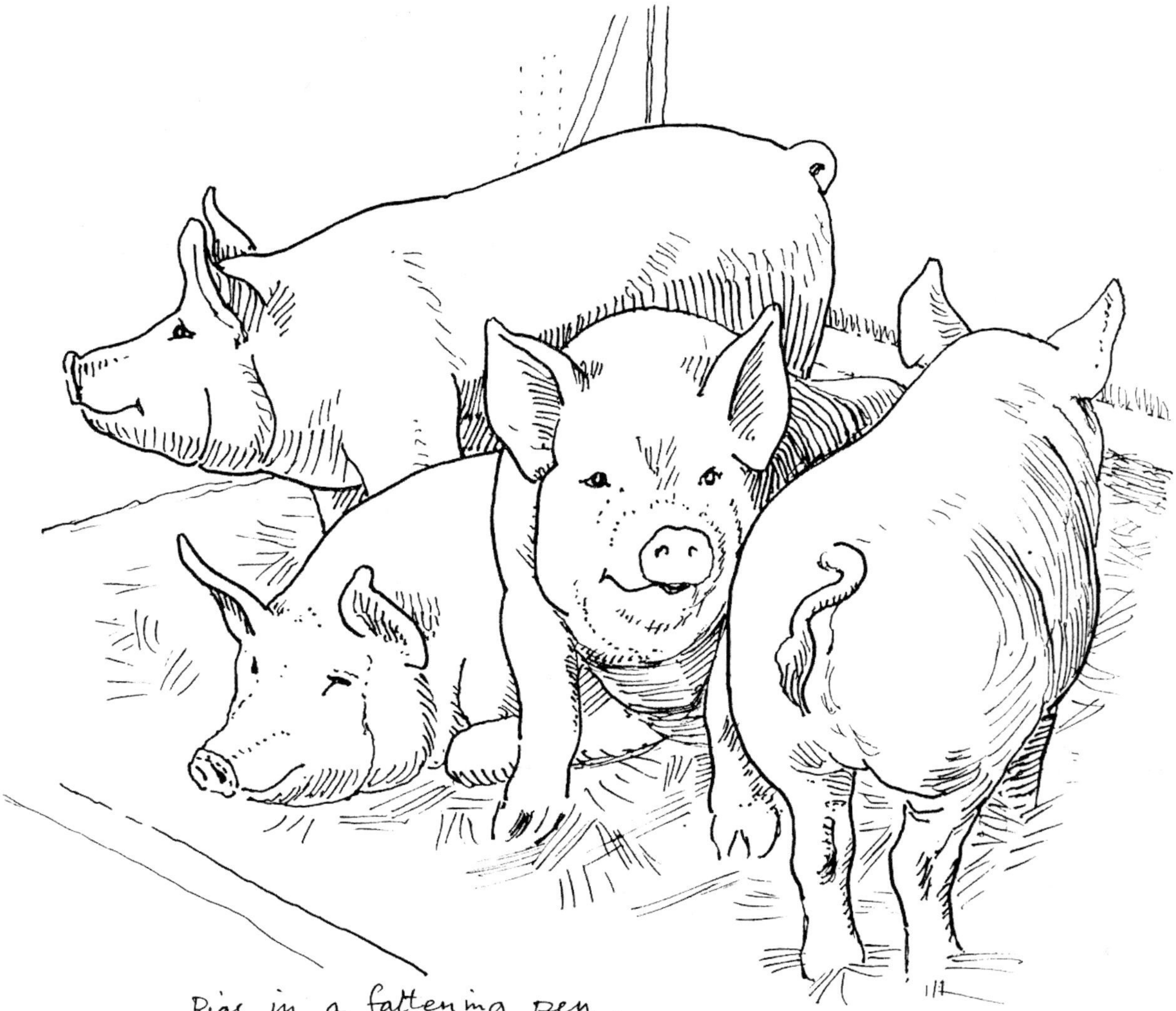

Pigs in a fattening pen.

The world's fertile soils are being shamefully exploited, eroded and degraded. Ten acres of fertile land (the area of about five football pitches with surrounds) would support about 60 people growing soya, or 25 people growing wheat or 10 people growing maize. The same area might support only two or three people growing cattle.

Small is Beautiful and Small Farms Mean Livestock

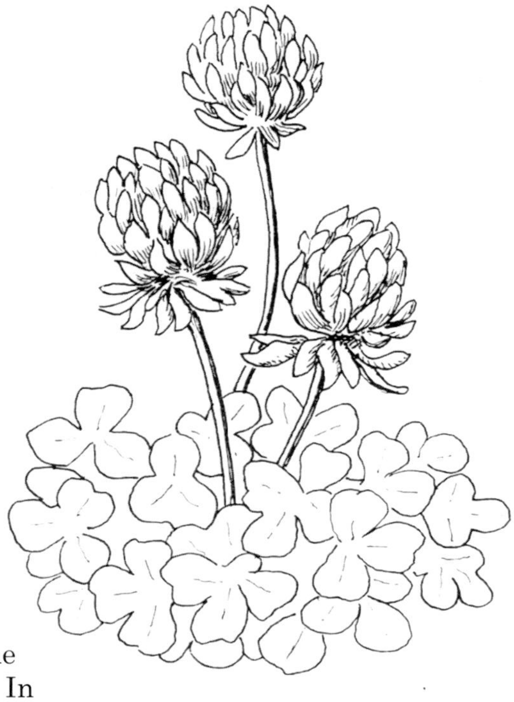

Wild White Clover
A useful plant to incorporate into a grassed ley. Like peas it collects nitrogen from the air to fix in the soil which then becomes available as plant food to other kinds of crops.

Small farms, unless they are entirely horticultural, inevitably entail livestock production and, in pre-war years, the number of animals was largely restricted to that which the farm could support by the grass and crops grown thereon.

Nowadays, however, the compounders of animal feeding stuffs will supply carefully balanced rations for each class of stock. The bulk of this will be made from grain and miller's offals imported from around the world, with fish and bone meal and oilseed products added in smaller quantities. In former years, the feed bags had to be labelled to show only the percentages of protein, oil and fibre. (Likewise, fertiliser bags had to be labelled to show the percentages of plant foods, nitrogen, phosphates and potassium in the contents.)

It was soon discovered that dairy and beef cattle could be managed on 'zero-grazing' with silage and green stuff cut and brought to them. Fattening pigs had nearly always been confined in concrete-floored pens and poultry lived quite happily in deep litter houses, their beaks being cut to discourage cannibalism and egg-eating! Battery cages were soon invented to cut out these vices and ensure clean eggs. They also enabled the operator to see which birds laid fewer or no eggs at all, assuming one bird to a cage.

Thus it was that small farms, by investing in capital equipment and buildings, could remain viable by feeding their animals on feeding stuffs produced elsewhere. The town dwellers could have the doubtful benefit of even cheaper food so that their disposable income could be spent in pubs and wine bars or on clothes, TV and foreign holidays.

In the last twenty-five years the amount spent on food has dropped from one-third to one-fifth of the average family income.

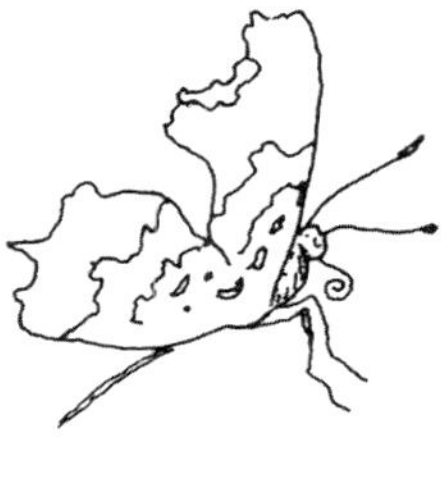

One of the ironies of the intensive methods described is that, as the livestock have disappeared indoors, so have the farmer and his assistants, so that the conventional archetype with thick-set frame and jovial, ruddy complexion is now much more likely to have a slender build and sickly pallor, suffering from farmer's lung and stomach ulcers as he wheezes his way from one dimly lit shed to another!

But never let us forget it is all in the interest of cheap food for the masses and there is no going back to the good old inefficient days which romantic people *say* they want but certainly are not prepared to pay for!

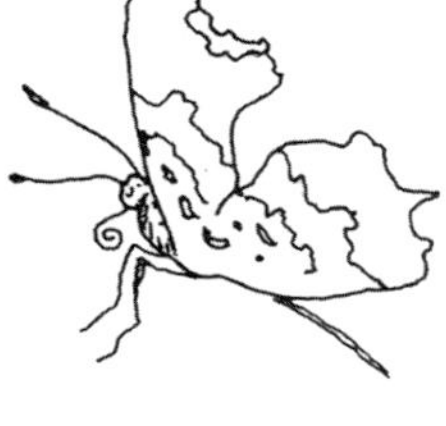

Sadly, Picturesque Means Inefficient

This romantic longing is shown by which kind of place people like to visit for a day out in the car or a holiday abroad.

They do not wish to see a hundred acre flat field of straight rows of sugar beet in Norfolk, or a modern farmyard with enormous sheds and silos sheltering gigantic, efficient machines and surrounded by acres of clean-swept concrete.

So they go down to Devon or the Yorkshire Dales. They make for the most picturesque, inefficient areas where things are of 'human scale': twisting lanes, overgrown hedges, thatched cottages, tumble-down crumbling buildings covered in thistles, nettles and briars, and small, muddy farmyards with pumps and duck-ponds. (Ponds have all been filled in as unhygienic, and everyone knows ducks' eggs are rich in salmonella!)

Tourists will make for the pocket-handkerchief-sized fields in Switzerland where the cows are led out and tethered and the yodelling yokels go out with scythes to mow the impossibly steep hillsides for tiny stacks of hay. Ironically, people will stop to admire a pair of white oxen pulling a stone roller, but they curse if they are forced to follow in their car a mighty, efficient combine proceeding slowly from field to field.

From the start, because of the small size of our farming enterprise, it was inevitable that most of our activities would involve the care of livestock. The following are some of my memories of dealing with the five main categories, namely, horses, cattle, sheep, pigs and poultry, or 'mixed farming' as it was then known.

In this type of farming it was thought one could avoid the dangers of specialisation by not having all your eggs in one basket.

In the descriptions that follow, I could have given more detailed descriptions of the production of all the classes of livestock mentioned, but I felt it would be too repetitious and technical. Therefore, I have only described at some length and in greater detail the production of prime lamb from a lowland flock.

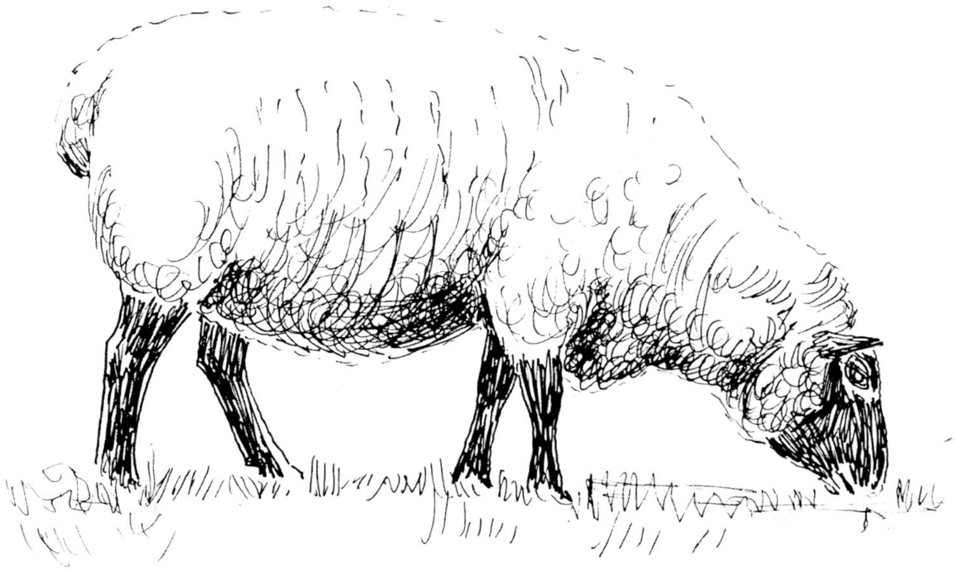

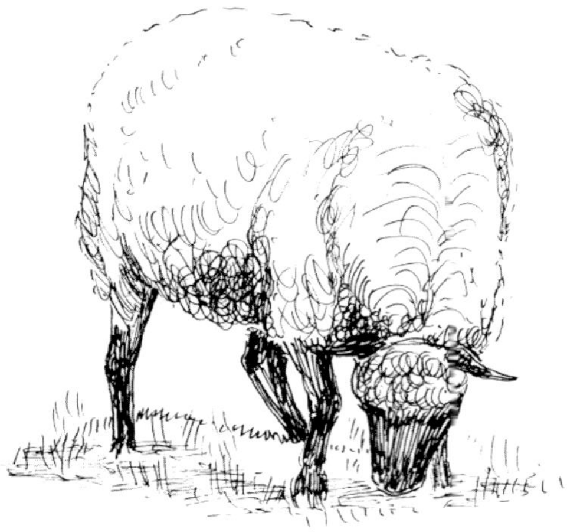

Suffolk sheep

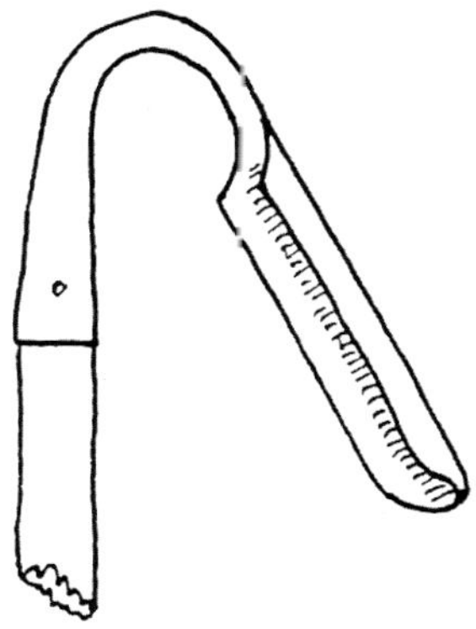

Swan Neck Scoop
for laying field drains

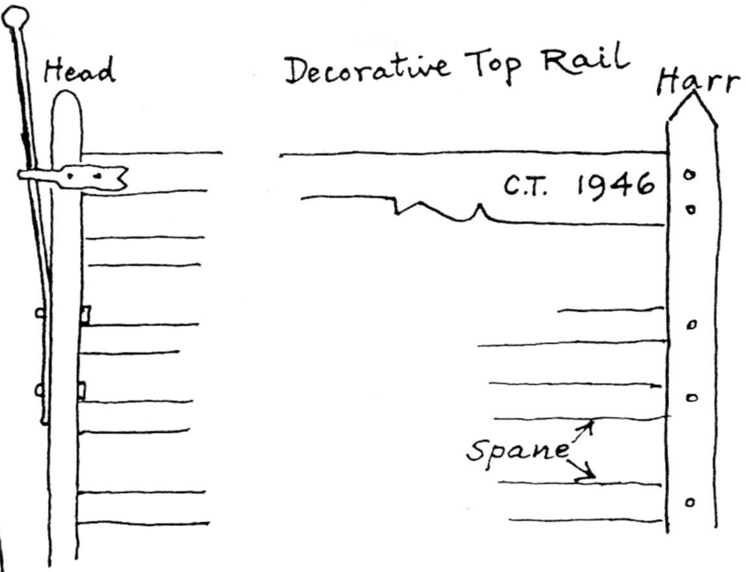

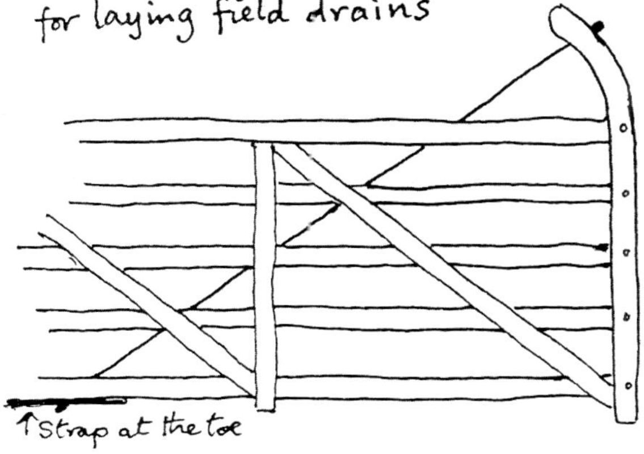

A Gloucester gate
with an iron brace

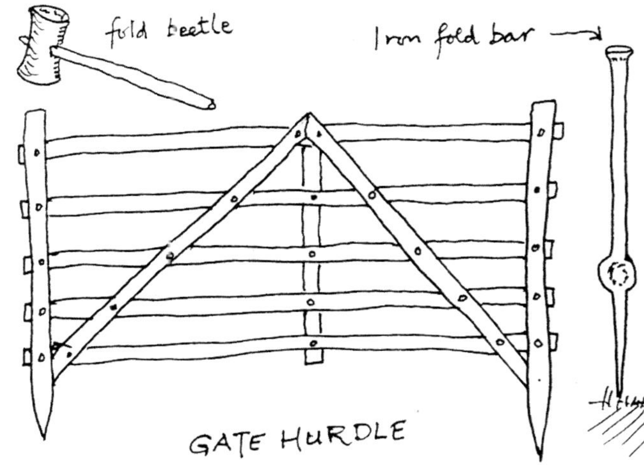

GATE HURDLE

A LAMB CREEP

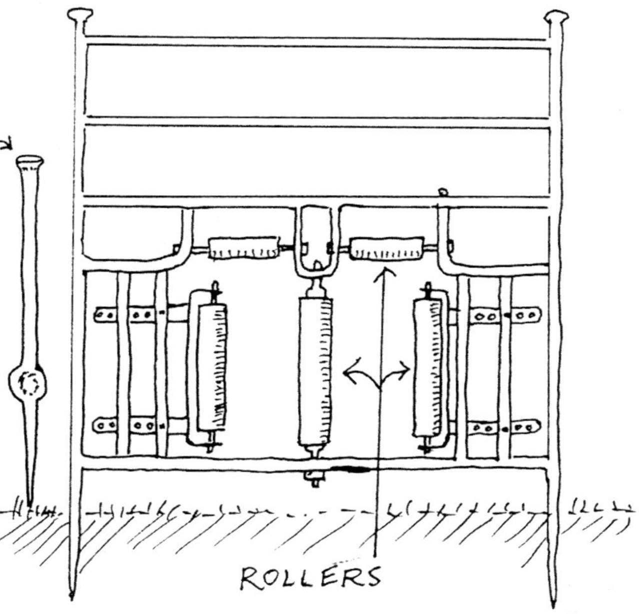

This was set into a line of hurdles or wire netting to allow lambs to get a first bite on clean new grazing.

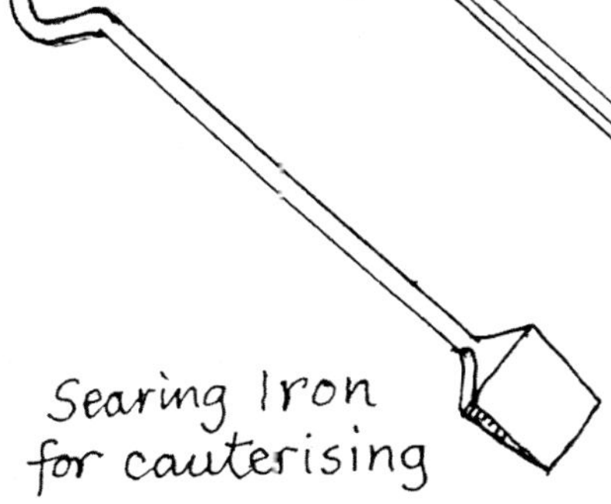

Searing Iron
for cauterising

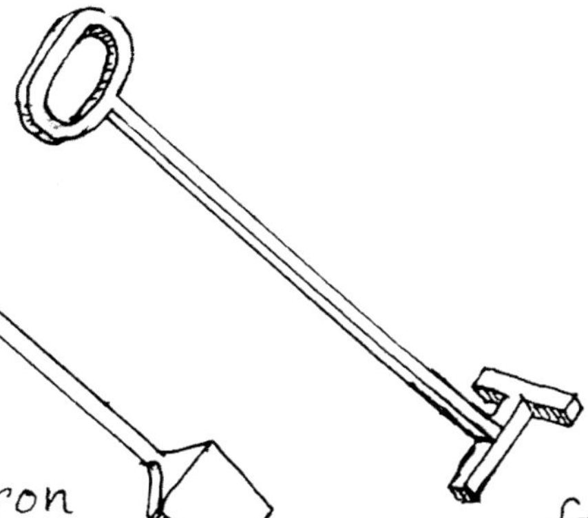

Branding Iron
for paint-marking sheep

Chapter TWO

Horses

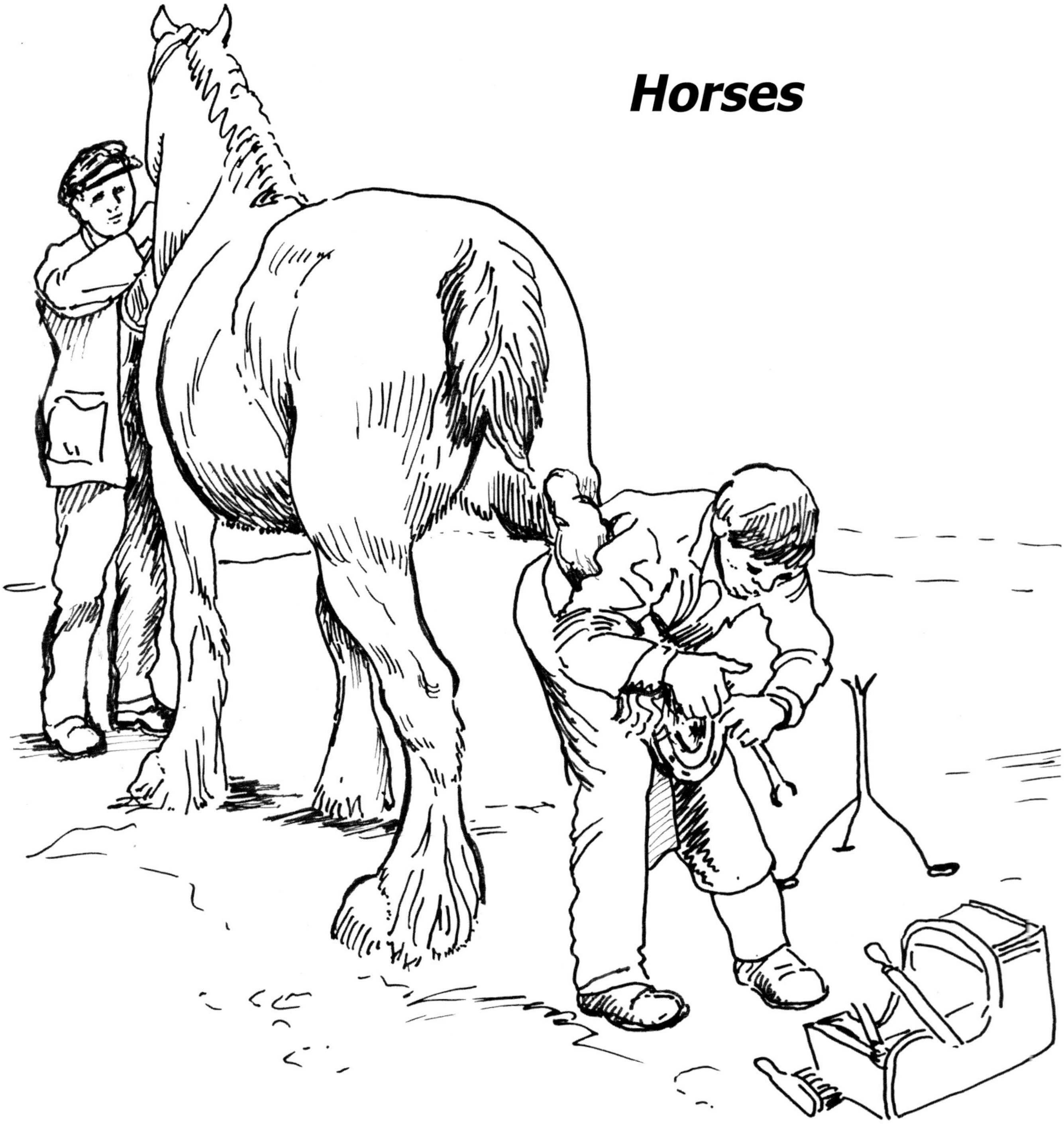

Billy Bryan at his blacksmith shop at Frolesworth

The Village Blacksmith

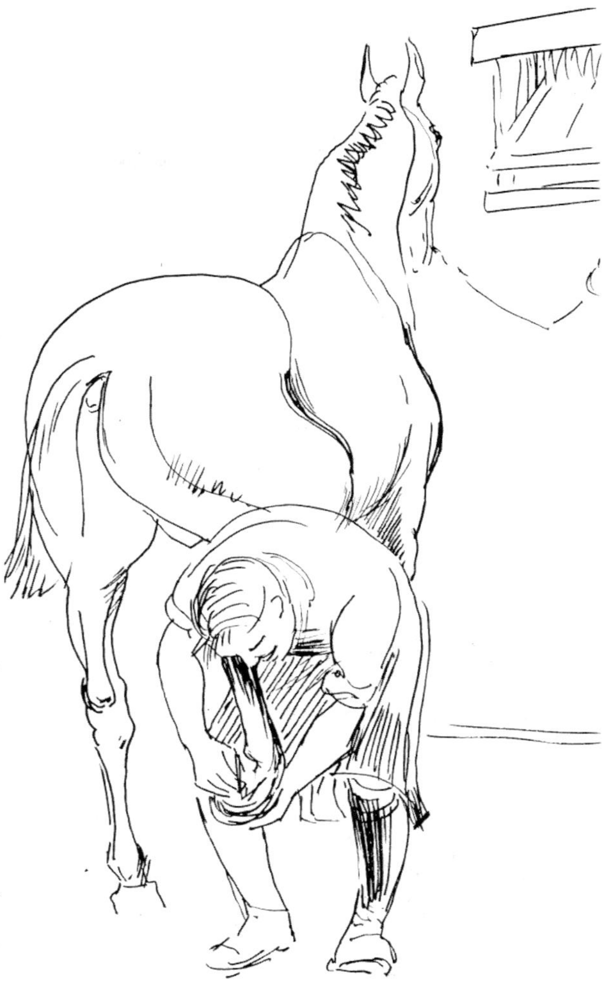

The younger farrier had great difficulty in writing and he explained that he had had very little schooling.

The reason was that the village school adjoined his father's smithy and when a farming customer unexpectedly sent his men with four great Shire work-horses to be shod, the anxious old blacksmith would tap on the schoolroom door and plead with the schoolmaster to release young Billy to help with the work. The courteous old man stood barely five feet tall, had legs well-bowed from rickets, and wore thick pebble glasses. But he had the heart of a lion. When one considers that a Shire or Clydesdale horse can weigh 2,000 pounds (907kg) and stand six foot high (18 hands) (1.8m) at the withers, it requires great courage to work on their steel-shod hooves, the size of dinner plates, knowing that at any time the animal could literally kick your brains out.

If a horse were to show signs of being ever so slightly fidgety, the diminutive old man would strike its ribs vigorously with the flat side of his hammer while uttering dire threats in a guttural voice, assuming that attack was the best sort of defence! In his case, it would have the desired effect, as invariably after this treatment the horse knew who was boss and stood patiently for its shoes to be fitted. Hairy-legged horses were apt to become infected with a greasy condition caused by infestation of itchy mites. Such horses would stamp and rub their heels on gates and fences, aggravating the condition so that it became almost impossible to handle the lower legs. The treatment was to shave the legs and swab them with blue vitriol.

When a man deals with a horse, which may weigh twenty times more than he does, he is apt to forget how much he relies on the horse's good will. The sound of a low-flying plane, a nearby gunshot, or even a bag flapping or a newspaper blowing in the wind can make the horse forget his years of training in good manners. The consequences can be dire, and there is little the man can do.

The flavour of honey is much enhanced if the bees have access to flowering heather. With this in mind, when the heather was in bloom, my grandfather used to take his beehives up onto the North Yorkshire moors in a waggonette drawn by two horses. One sad day, the horses took fright in a thunderstorm and bolted. This upset the hives and the angry bees only further terrified the already distraught horses!

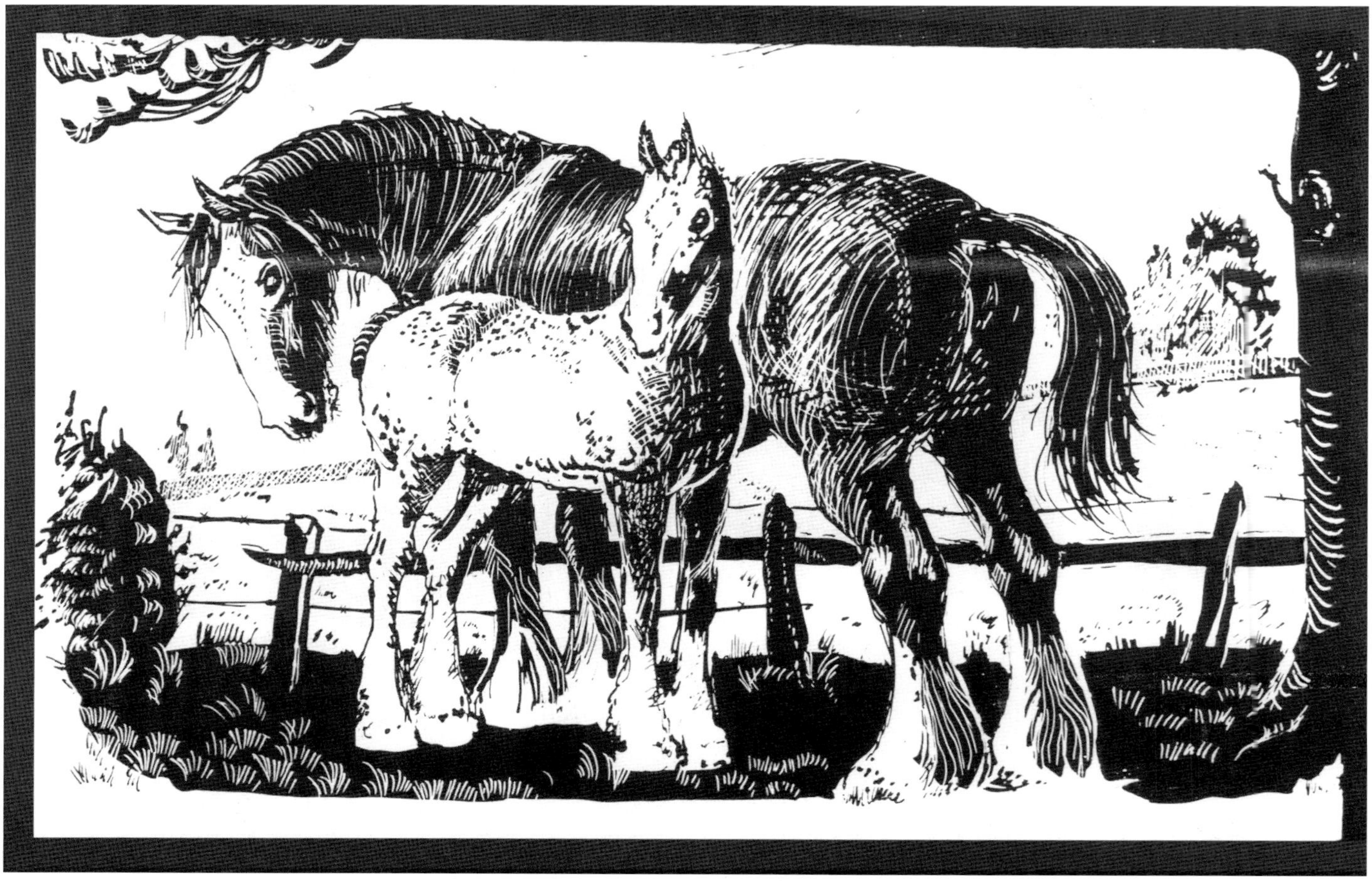

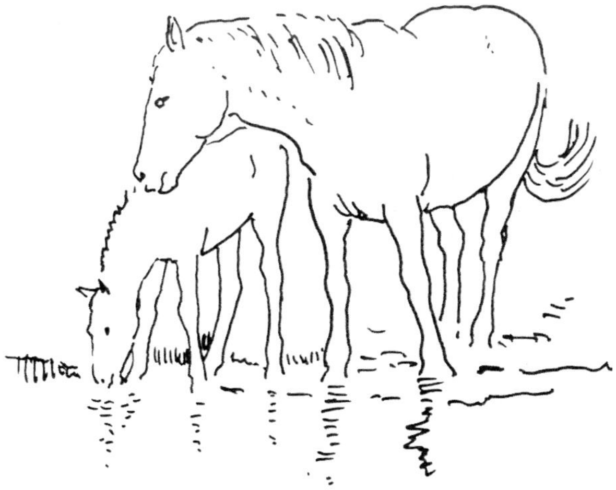

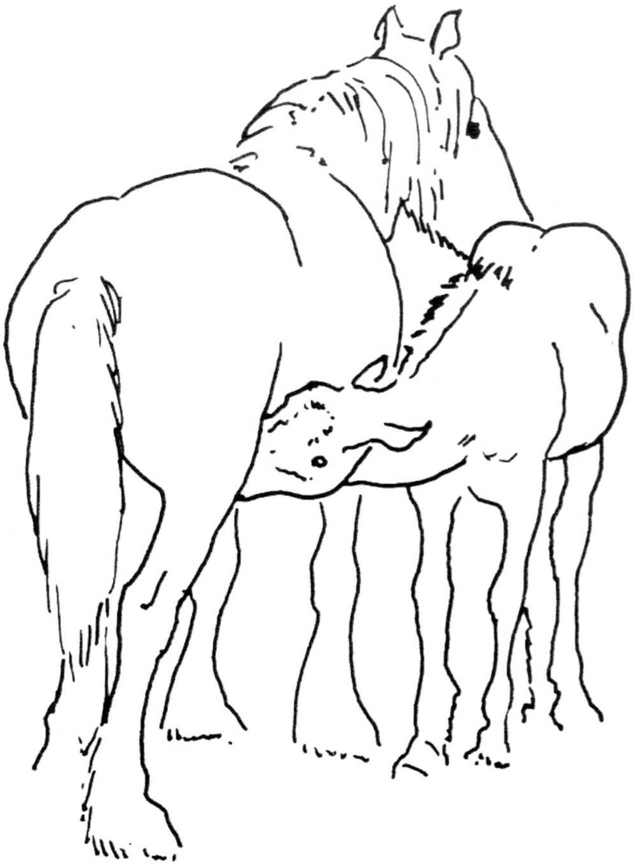

Our Shire Mare, Jessica, and her colt, Jason

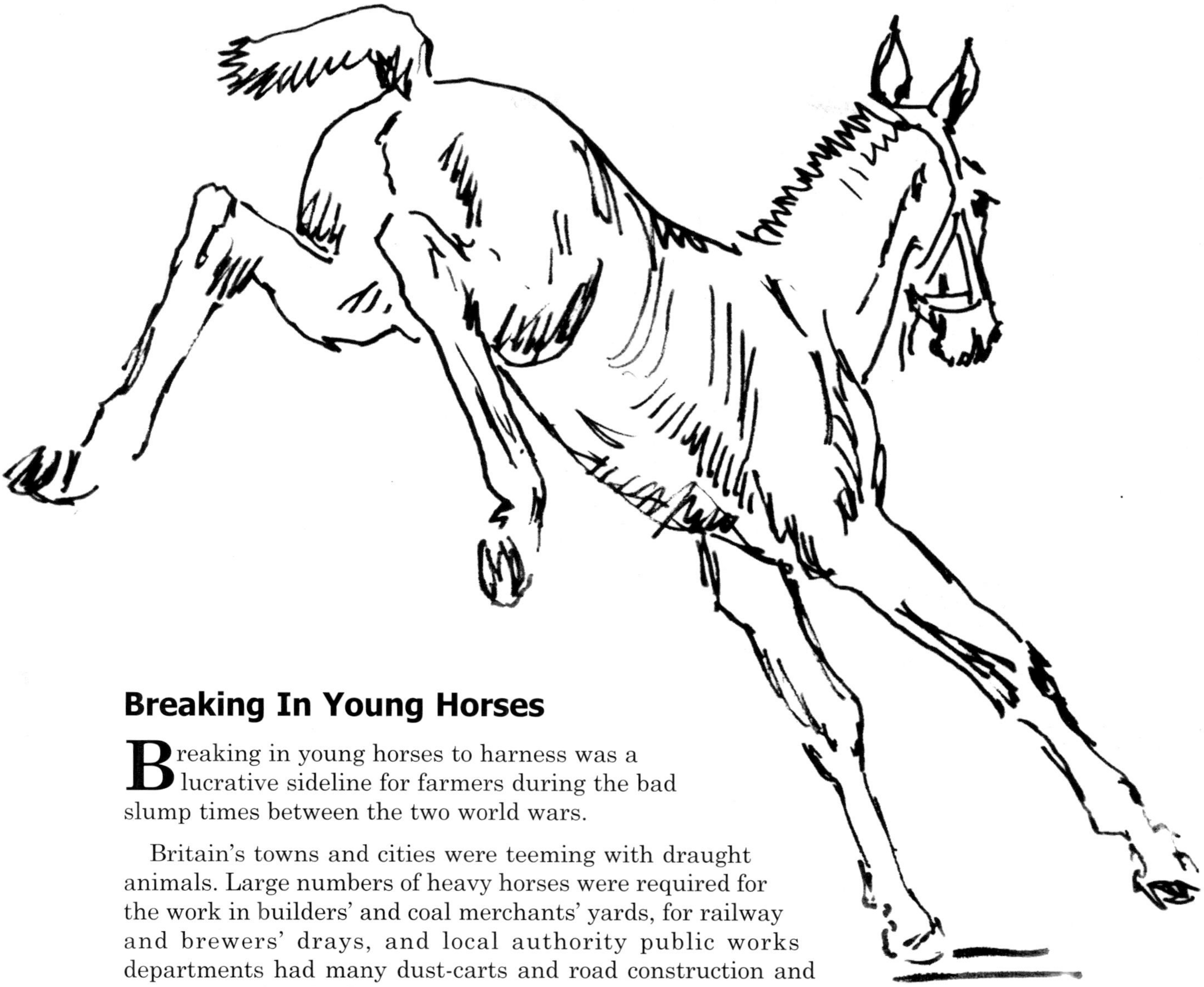

Breaking In Young Horses

Breaking in young horses to harness was a lucrative sideline for farmers during the bad slump times between the two world wars.

Britain's towns and cities were teeming with draught animals. Large numbers of heavy horses were required for the work in builders' and coal merchants' yards, for railway and brewers' drays, and local authority public works departments had many dust-carts and road construction and repair vehicles. Lighter horses, or 'vanners', were needed for delivering parcels and laundry, bread and milk, and fruit and vegetables. By tradition, butchers had showy, high-stepping, fast-trotting ponies.

Firstly, the young horse would have to be fitted with a head collar, then the bridle with blinkers and bit. It would usually show its resentment at the loss of freedom and discomfort with much show of protestation - rearing and biting, even striking forwards with its front hooves. Great patience had to be exercised by the horseman, who would be more than a little apprehensive of being injured by a terrified colt or filly as it plunged about.

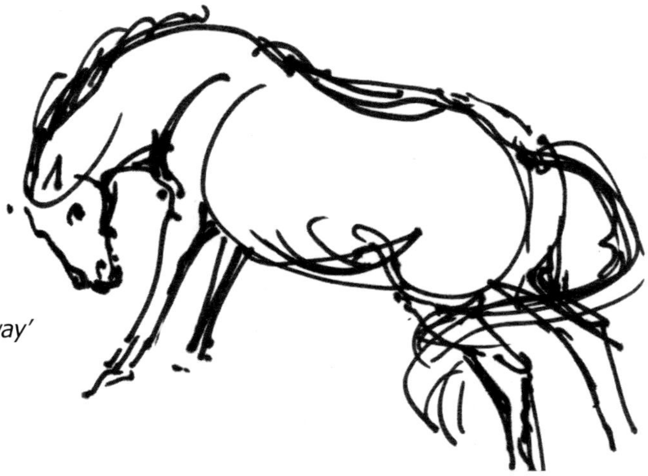

Warning signal to 'Keep Away'

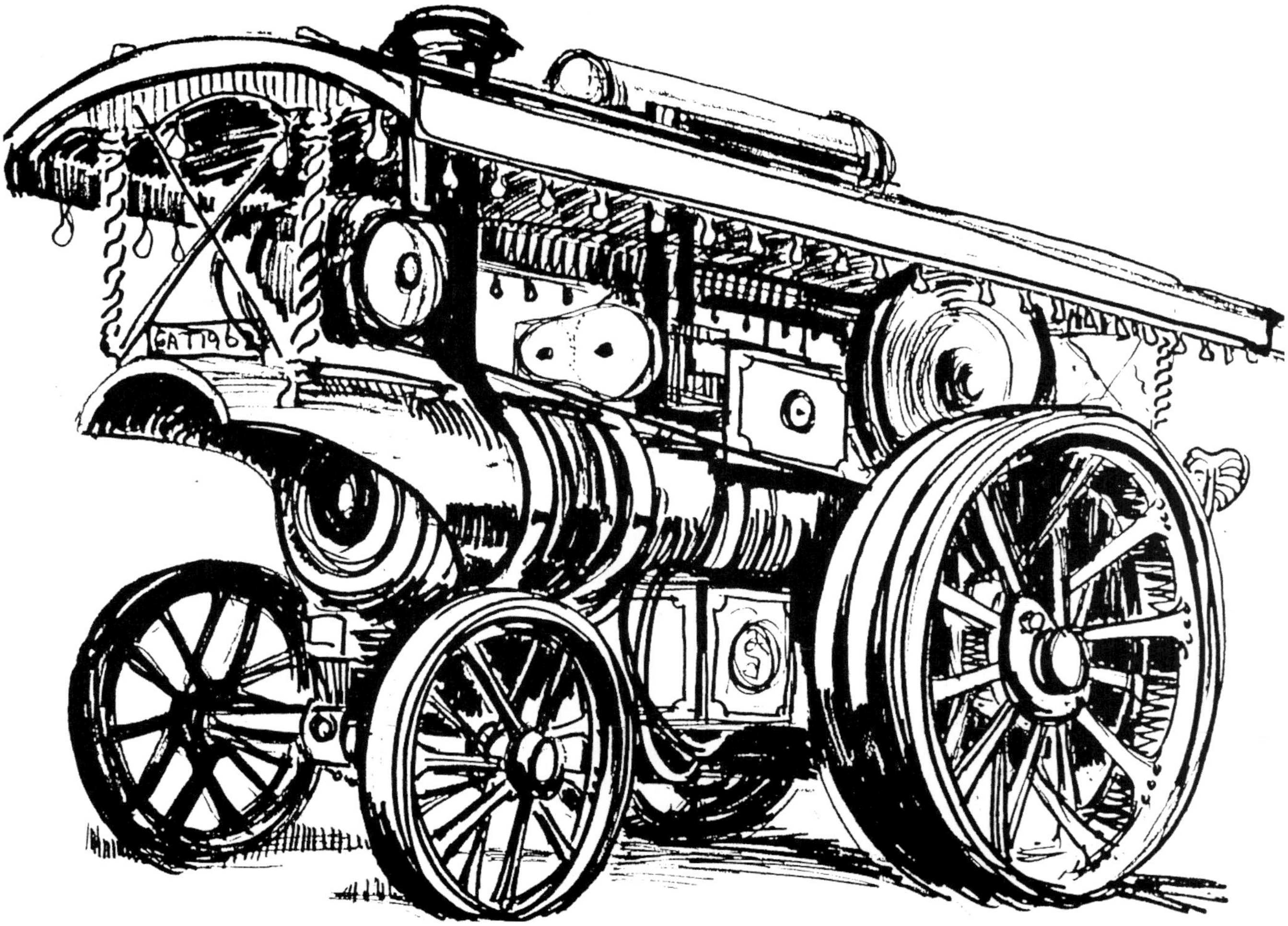

Burrell Showman's Road Locomotive

Horses always reacted very badly to the sinister puffing and hissing sounds emitted by steam engines. Road traction engines, steam rollers and railway trains must have caused many a horse to bolt out of control. Sometimes a runaway horse could be stopped by a brave or foolhardy person standing in its path with outstretched flapping arms.

During visits to the big cities of Manchester and Birmingham in my youth it was not unusual to have the added excitement of seeing a driverless runaway horse careering along, terrified by some unexpected circumstance. Its load would be shed to right and to left as it ploughed into other vehicles, leaving a trail of destruction until it was brought up sharply and fell with a sickening thud onto the unyielding granite sets of the road. Possibly a leg would be fractured or a broken shaft might penetrate the thorax like a spear, in which case a quick despatch by means of a humane killer was indicated. This is a hand gun with a captive bolt which penetrates to the brain and then instantly withdraws into the barrel. When a horse is seen to fall in harness, the heaviest person around should immediately sit on its head as this prevents it struggling to get up while the harness is being released by another helper.

The young horse would spend much time being 'lunged' by the breaker, running in a circle at the end of a single rein, before proceeding to being driven about on long reins. Then, after being fitted with a collar and trace chains, it might be made to pull a large log about in a pasture field. This treatment would occupy a period of several months at odd times after the farmer's normal day's work. The next step then might be to work him alongside an experienced, steady animal at a job like rolling a fallow field where there might be lumps of dry soil as big as your head.

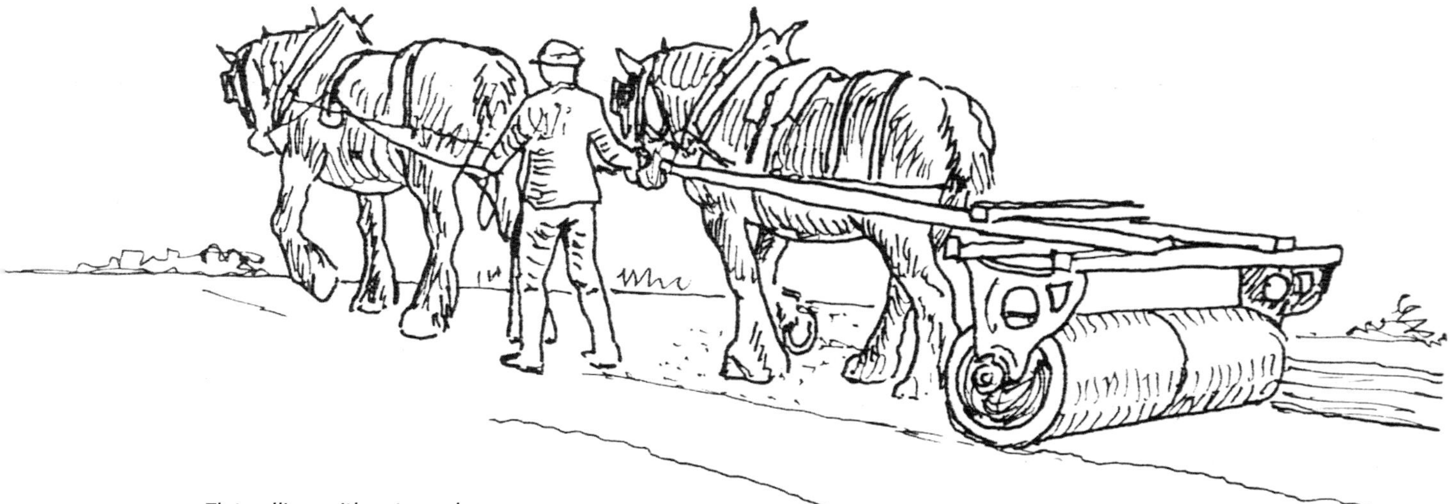

Flat rolling with a trace horse

I was doing this on one occasion when the youngster obviously considered he'd had enough clod-hopping and became truculent, lay down and would not budge.

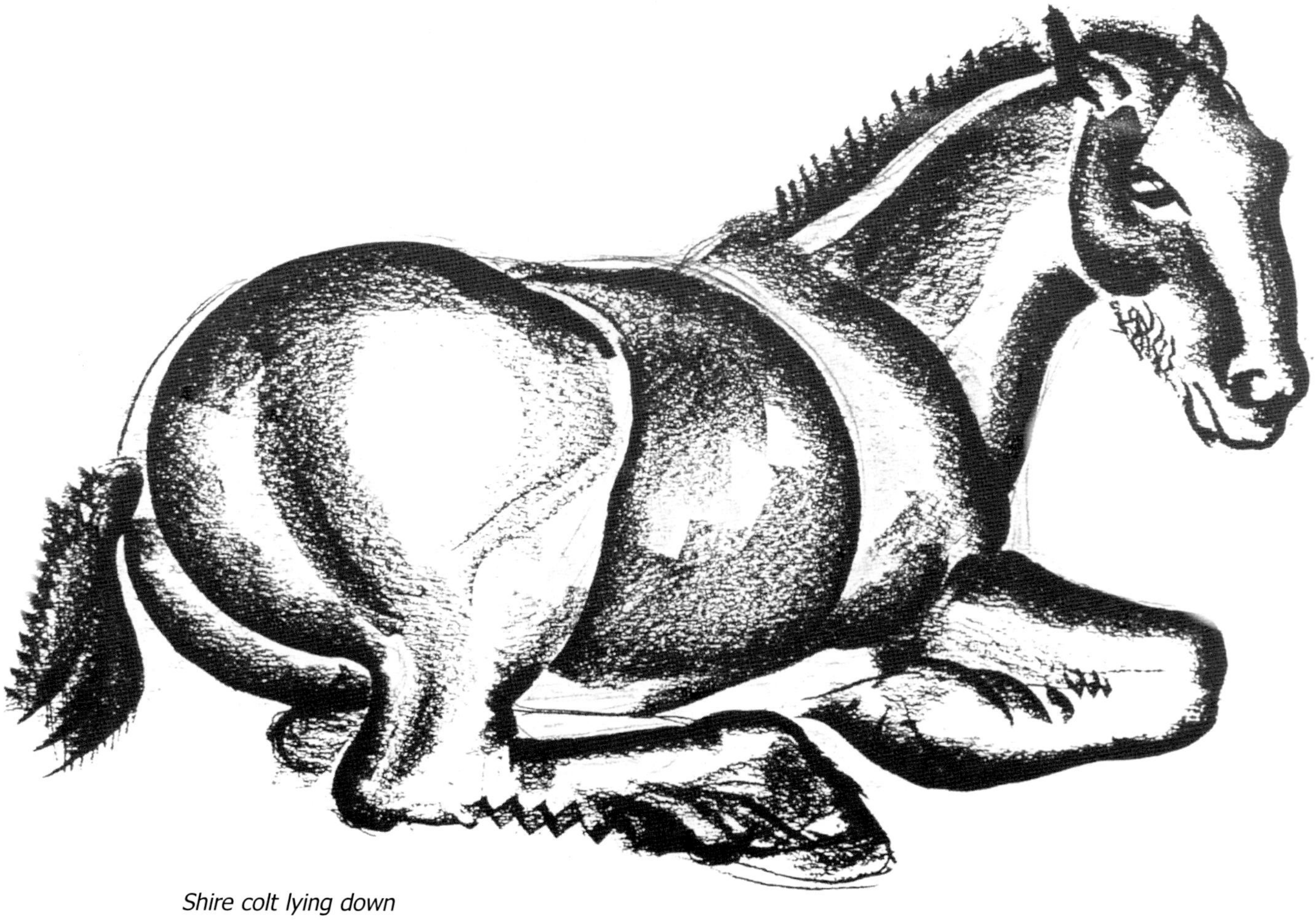

Shire colt lying down

Sam's Solution to a Problem

Old Sam was working nearby with a team hauling a scuffle and, seeing my predicament, came across to investigate.

Ever resourceful, having weighed up the situation between puffs on his pipe, without a word he went across to the hedge bottom and gathered an armful of kindling. After tucking it under the horse's rump, he set fire to it! The colt was up in double quick time and did not lie down again!

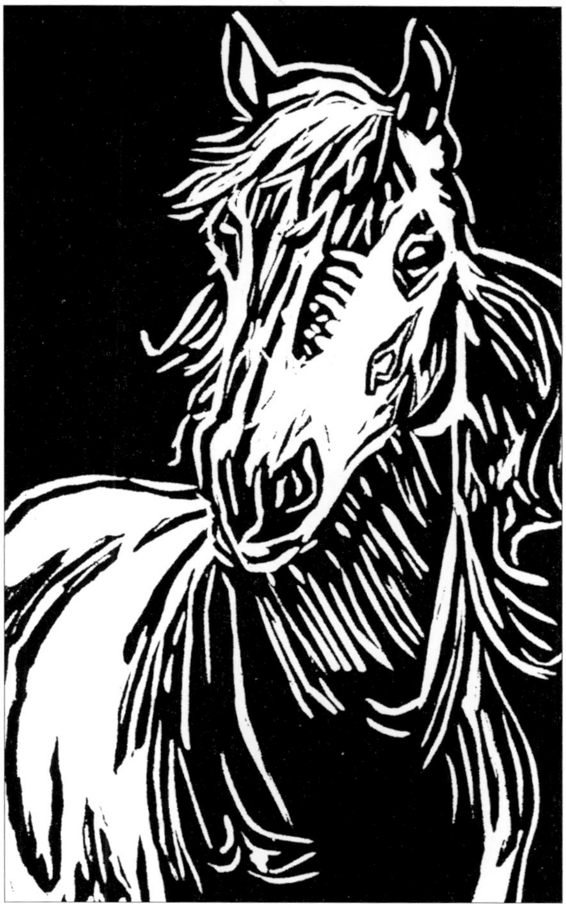

Stallion linocut

A similar effect may be had on recalcitrant animals by peeing in the ear. A tractor driver once told me his machine burst into flames in the centre of a large field. Having no water at hand, the resourceful fellow used a well-directed stream provided by nature to quench the fire. Not to be recommended if there is electricity about!

Young horses worked in chain traces at jobs like harrowing for a considerable time before they were considered fit to wear thiller gear or cart tackle with its 'saddle', girth, belly band and breeching to work between the shafts of a cart or wagon. This involved becoming accustomed to hearing the rumble of the iron shod wheels on the metalled road and to hold back the cart as it tried to over-run down hills. They would also have to learn to reverse it by sitting into the breeching strap.

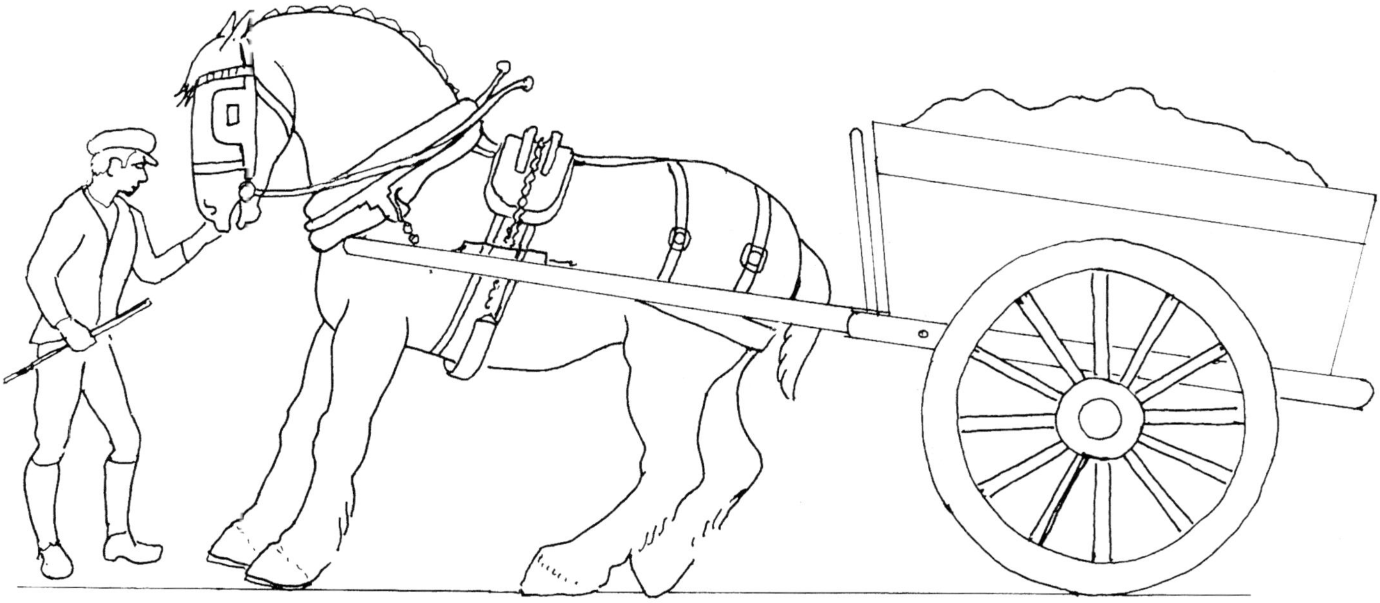

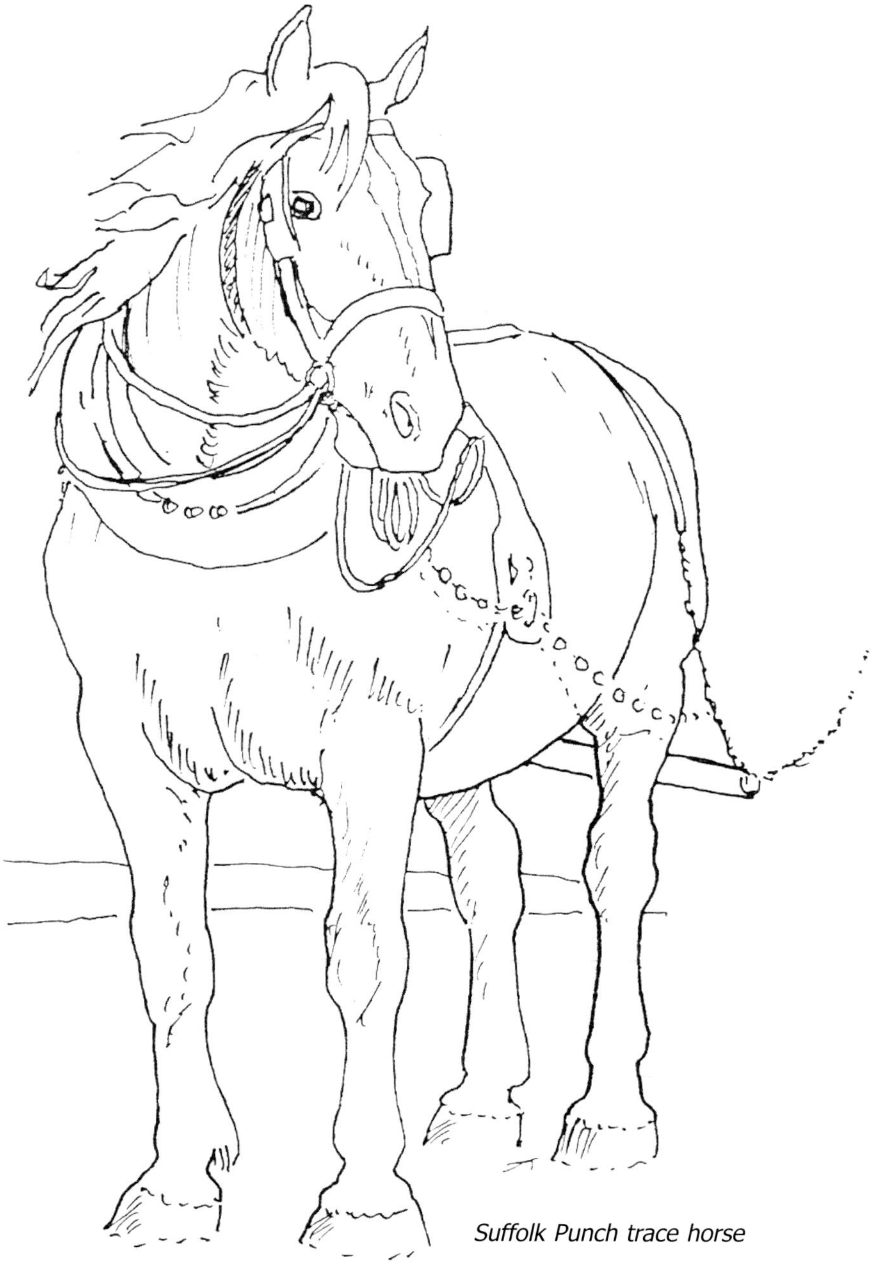

Suffolk Punch trace horse

Old Sam was chain-harrowing one day with a flighty young pair. On hearing the unexpected clatter of the iron harrows as they crossed the road from one field to another, the horses bolted and ran each side of a telegraph pole, breaking one bridle bit clean in half at the joint. Luckily, a cyclist coming the opposite way was able to stop their headlong stampede before much damage was done.

A loose throat strap on a carelessly fitted bridle could cause it to drop off if a horse shook his head. Without the blinkers, he would see the vehicle and load behind him for the first time and take off at great speed, leaving a trail of destruction and broken tackle.

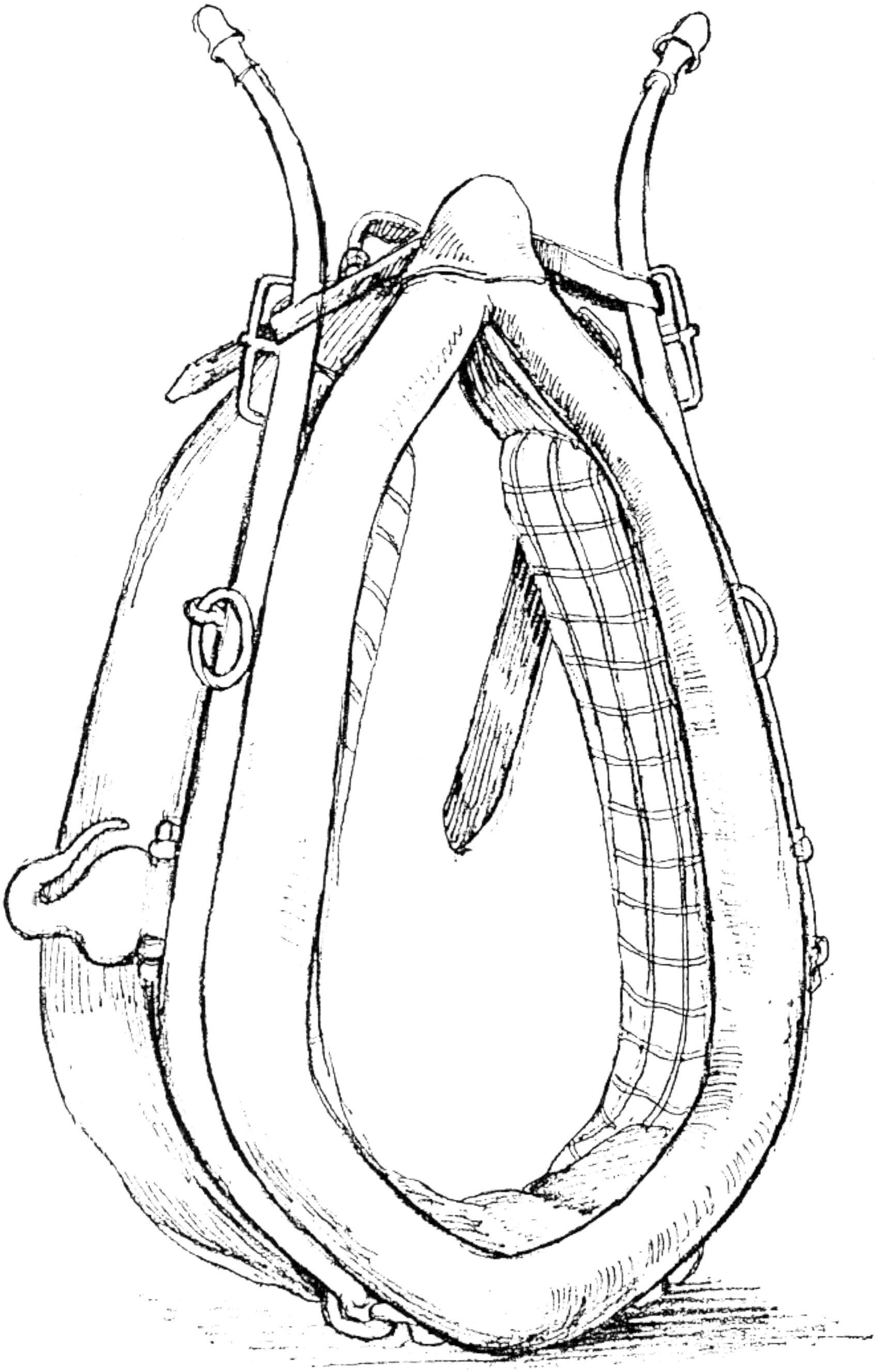

Horse's collar with brass hames

Roy George and the Prince of Wales

Distractions for the horses could come in many ways.

The hunt could be an unwelcome sight for the ploughman - his horses were likely to want to join in the excitement. Even the most docile could become difficult to hold back, and occasionally they did break their traces.

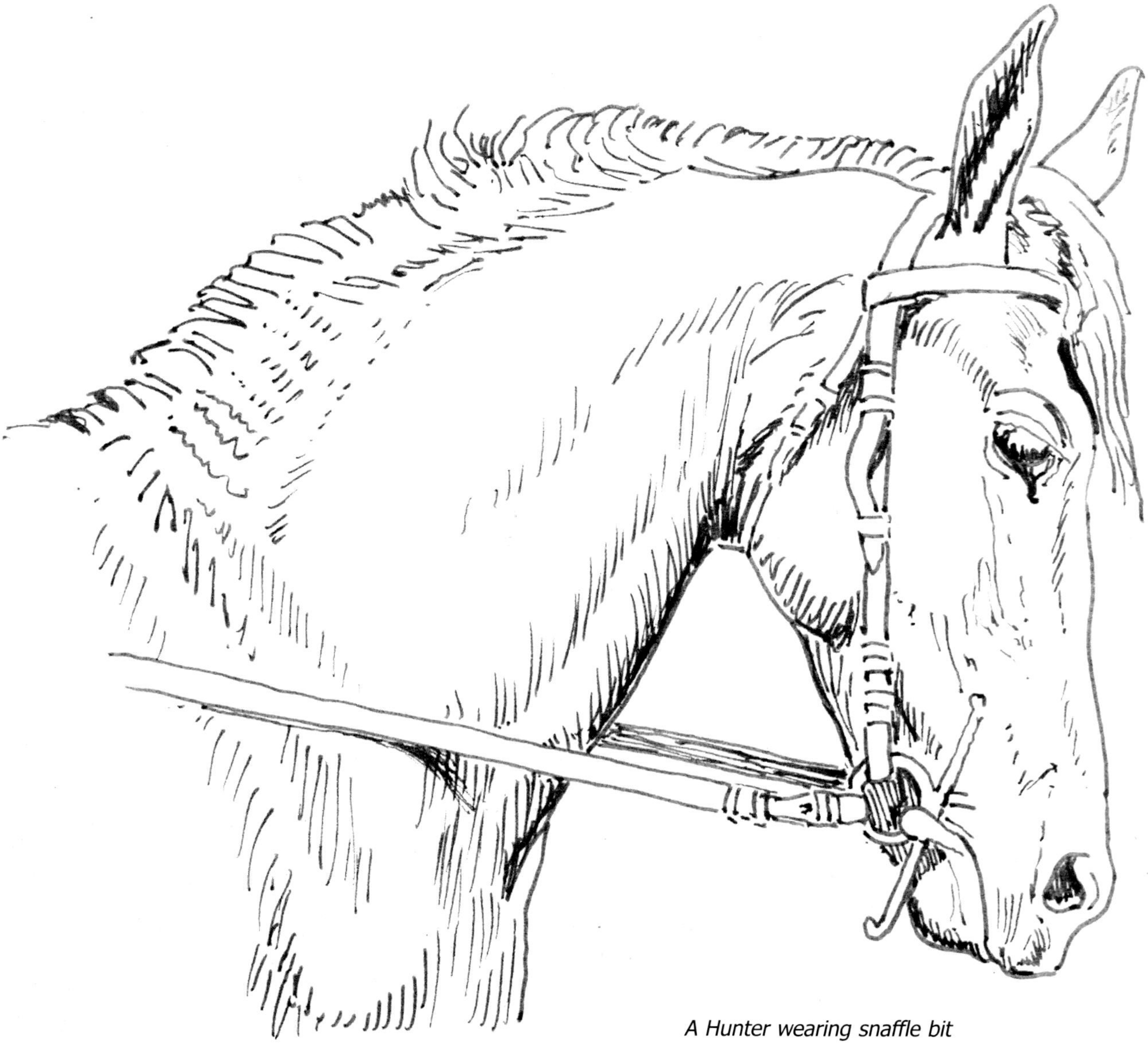

A Hunter wearing snaffle bit

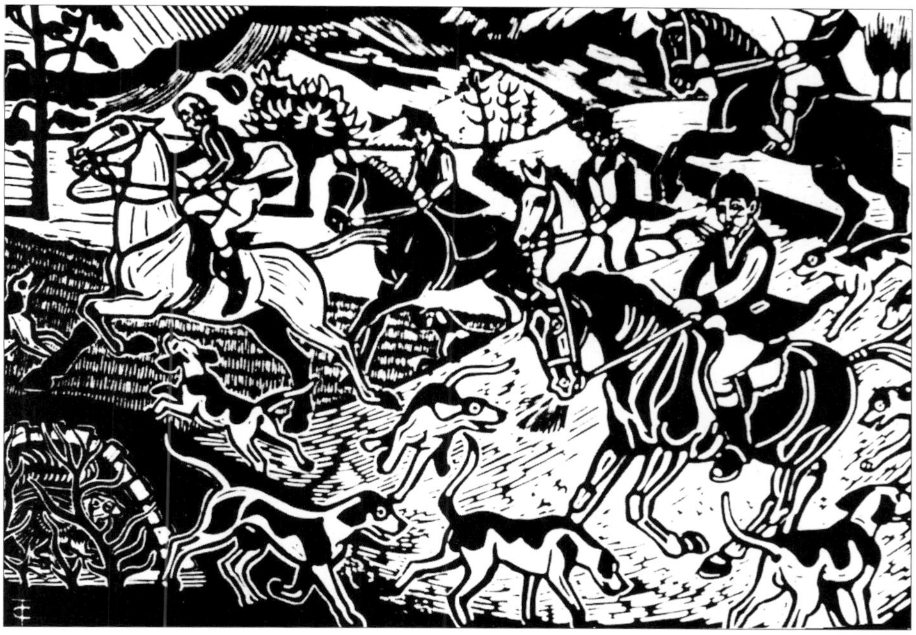

The False Scent (Linocut bought by Leicester Art Gallery)

The five local hunts in the Leicestershire area are: the Quorn, Belvoir, Atherstone, Fernie and Pytchley.

A young Welshman named Roy George farmed in Quorn Hunt territory. One day when ploughing with a team of horses he saw a fox enter the field and make off across his newly-ploughed land, hotly pursued by a pack of hounds. After quickly securing his team he waited by a gap in the hedge for the first rider. When he appeared, Roy George grabbed the mount's reins and told the rider in no uncertain terms to return whence he came and not to trample on his newly ploughed land.

"Do you know who I am?" said the astonished huntsman.

"I don't care if you are the Prince of Wales, you don't ride across this 'yere field, look you!" replied Roy George, knowing full well *...it was the prince,...* who meekly turned and made off another way.

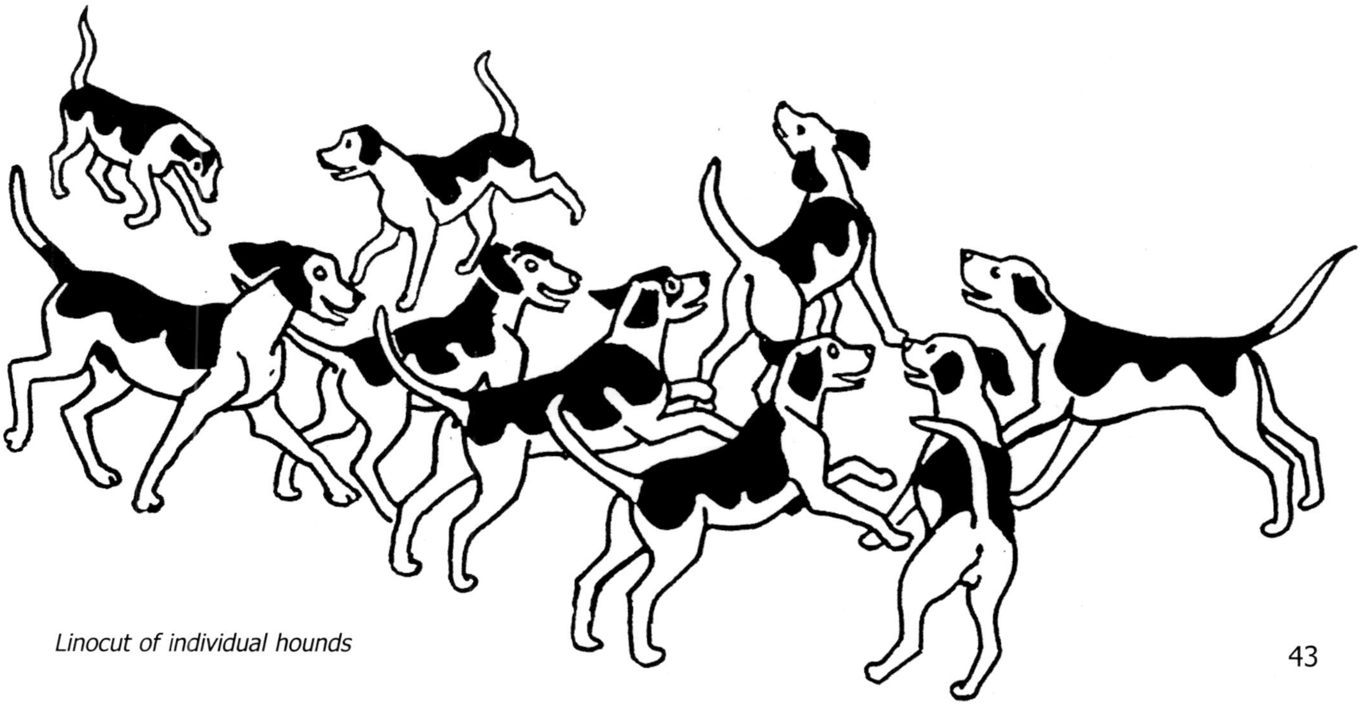

Linocut of individual hounds

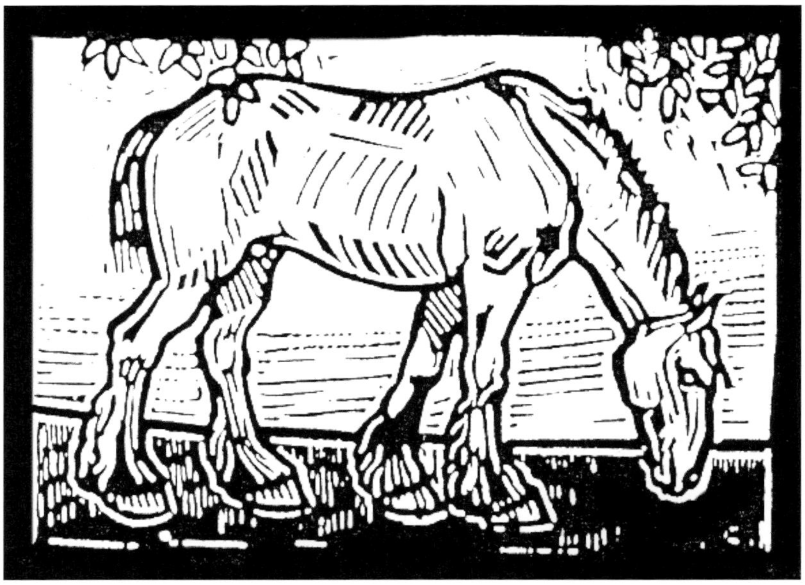

Linocut of Shire Horse grazing

The Horseman's Year

Ploughing was the most intensive task both in terms of the horseman's labour and that of the horses.

The rate of ploughing varied from district to district according to lightness of soil, size, and shape of field, for in a very small field about half the time could be spent turning at the headlands. An acre a day was the standard reckoning for most practical purposes, and that represented walking about 12 to 13 miles (19-21 km) using a 9" wide furrow.

In those areas where 4/5ths of the land would be in tillage, for every 100-acre farm 80 days were in fact taken up by ploughing. This work naturally peaked in autumn with a lesser peak in the spring when some land was being ploughed for late-sown crops such as roots.

The horseman was employed as much for his skills as a ploughman as for his abilities in handling horses, although these usually went hand in hand. He needed only the lightest touch of the reins to keep his horses walking in a perfectly straight line as he marked out the field in landes or stitches.

The common fixed plough, as it goes forward, can only turn the furrow-slice from left to right, the breast or mouldboard being on the right side of the plough and the ploughman walking in the furrow or on the unploughed land on the near, or left, side; the land-handle continuing in line with the beam and the furrow-handle being set out to the right. Hence the ploughman tells his horses to "come" or "go", as he means them to turn left or right.

The ploughman's cries, to turn or stop his horses, though strange and unintelligible to the townsman and often debased to hoarse unarticulated shouts, are instantly understood and obeyed by the team. Some of them are no doubt survivals of respectable antiquity; they are hardly the same in any two parts of the country and several versions of each may be heard in many of those districts from which they have not been finally banished by the unresponsive tractor. The following table, though far from complete, may serve to illustrate their variety:

Ploughman's Cries of Command

Neatness in ploughing was more than a valuable practical skill; it was a matter of pride, a measure of the standards of a horseman's work and indeed of the farm on which he worked.

In particular, fields next to the road had to be perfect, for they were on public view. This was especially so on Sunday afternoons when ploughmen were likely to spend their day off walking the lanes inspecting the work of their neighbours and rivals.

District	To Start	To Stop	To Turn Right	To Turn Left
North Norfolk	go on	whoa	wheesh	cop y olt, cup here
Sussex	-	-	gee wut oot (to hind horse)	tho wut
Isle of Wight	-	-	wut	comeather
Berkshire	-	-	wug off	-
Dorset	-	-	get off	come here
North Devon	come on	we	-	wug
Cornwall	gee up, go on (name of horse)	woa or wey	gee off	way, come here
Scotland	(name of horse)	wo, stand	hupp, gee, haup, hip, weesh	wynd, vane, vine
Yorkshire	gehup	wo-ho	gee, gee-back, gee-ho	wia-beck
Cheshire	-	whoi		come-agin, haw
Gloucestershire	-	wey	height, height	coom-yeh
Kent	-	woa	woot	woi
Hampshire	gee	wey	woot, gee-woot, woag	come hither

The aim was to finish the ploughing by Christmas and the onset of the frost and snow. Then things were a little quieter and the horsemen might be required to assist with threshing and other general work about the steading. There was plenty of work for the horses doing the considerable amount of haulage work connected with agriculture.

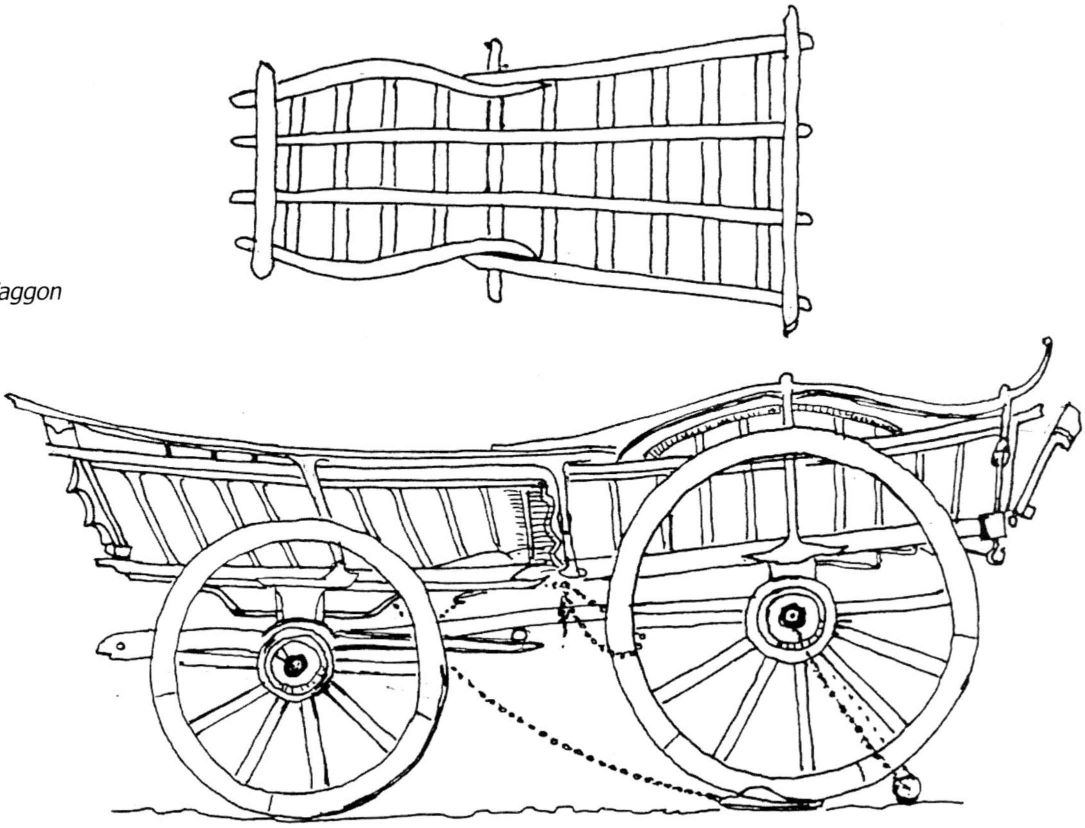

A Hoop-Raved Waggon

The horseman was often known as the waggoner or carter, and he and his team would be required to do all kinds of haulage: taking out muck to be spread on the stubbles; carting crops of potatoes, turnips, mangels, and swedes to clamps. There was kale to be cut and carted for cattle and feed to be taken out to sheep folded on arable land. Bags of seed corn and fertiliser had to be taken out to replenish the drills. During haytime and harvest, the wagons were fully occupied carting to the stacks. And horses had to be well-shod for the amount of hard road work involved in taking produce off the farm and bringing back supplies.

As the stacks were threshed, a little procession of wagons set out to take the corn to the millers, often fetching back-loads of cattle cake and coal from the railway station. As the wagons might carry three or four tons it was often necessary to assign three or four horses to each. These would be well-groomed and plaited up as they were on show to the townsfolk, and more importantly to other horsemen, who would inspect each others' teams wherever they met.

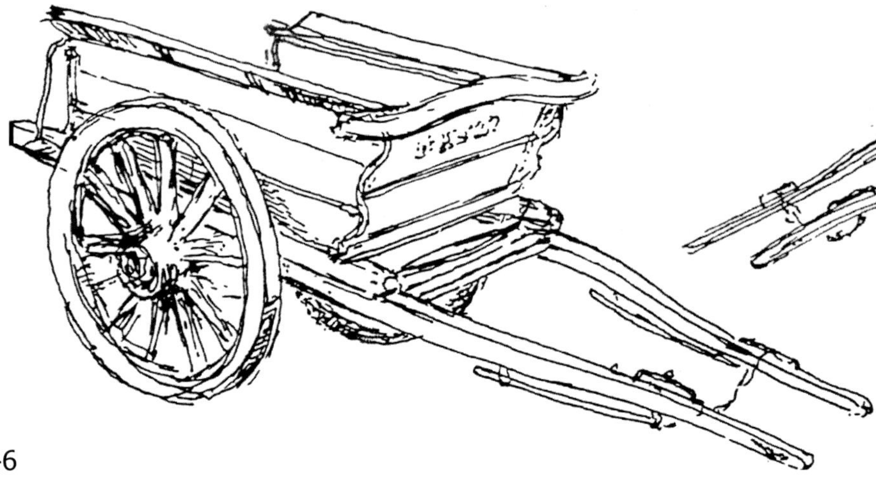

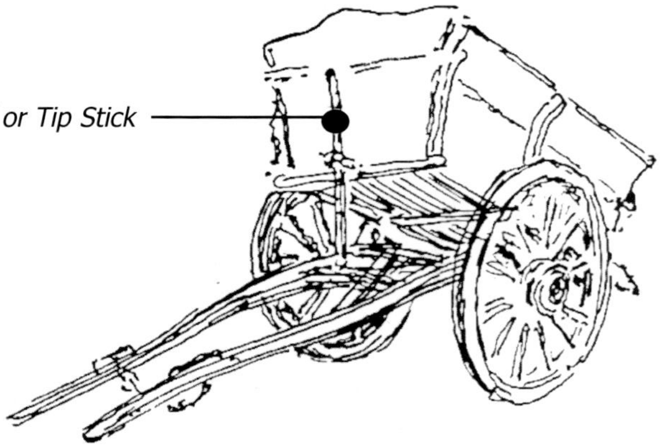

The ubiquitous two-wheeled tipping cart, in Somerset called a Putt

Horses were apt to become unusually excited by the sights, sounds and scents of towns, and carters had to be especially on guard against the horses' being 'spooked' or taking fright from the noise or movement of a steam engine or a double-decker bus; or against the horses' refusing to go under a railway bridge. Bells attached to the lead horse's harness served to give audible warning to others, since two loads could not pass on narrow lanes.

Early morning scene in busy stable with Suffolk horses

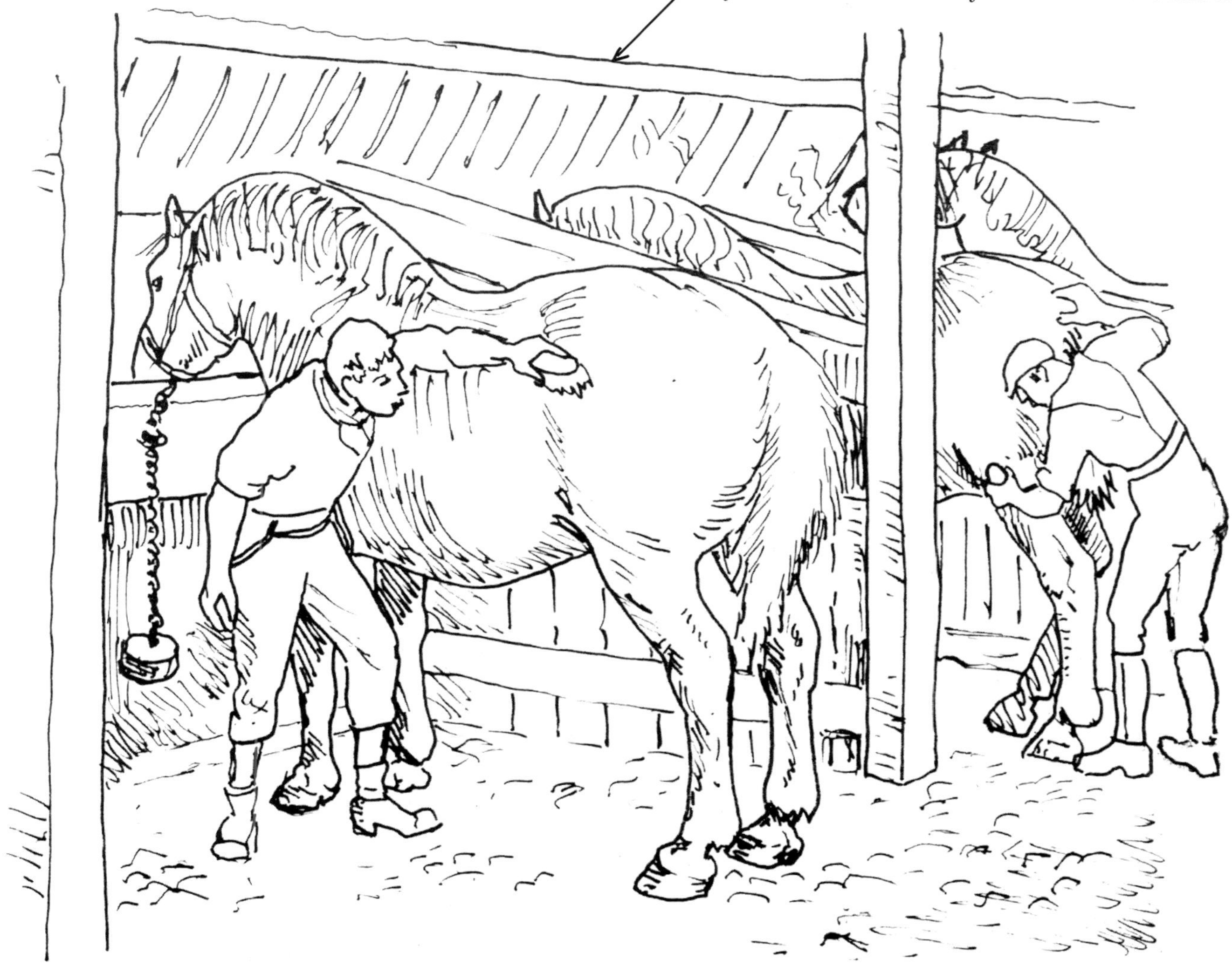

The horsemen rose at 4am and after a quick bite of bread and cheese, hurried to the stable to bait (feed) and groom their horses. They whistled and hissed through their teeth to soothe the horses as they brushed and curry-combed them before turning out to work at 6.30 or 7.00am in winter.
The head horseman was the first baiter and the bait was a carefully measured ration of rolled oats, bran and beans mixed with chopped clover hay and straw known as stover.

Plough Monday

In mediaeval times, Plough Monday was the first Monday after the 12th day of Christmas, when ploughs were blessed and ploughmen returned to work after the days of feasting.

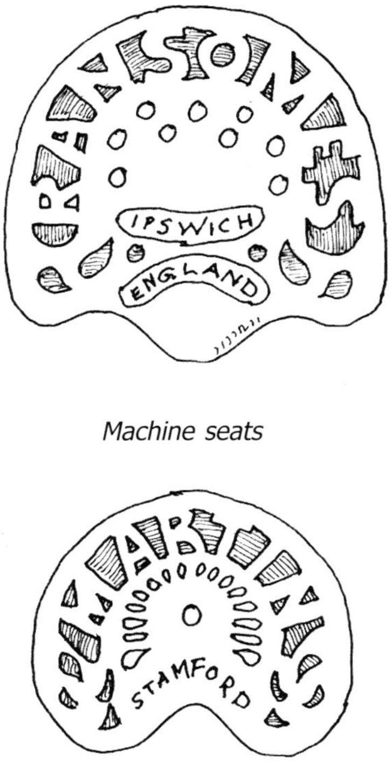

Machine seats

A swarm of bees in May is worth a load of hay,

A swarm of bees in June is worth a tinker's tune.

Seldom does a farmer listen as anxiously to the weather forecasts as when he is hay-making. The best hay is made in June but can be too fiery. If it is stacked too soon into a large rick it may overheat and catch fire by spontaneous combustion. They used to say "better out of season than out of fettle". The saying, "make hay while the sun shines" is true enough, but as the process may take up to a week, the first stage of mowing may be done on dull days leading up to an anticipated sunny spell. Being of a cautious nature, in uncertain weather I would never risk cutting more than 25% of the area of grass until the previous quarter was safe and dry. That has meant that seldom have I been forced to put a match to it as a total write-off.

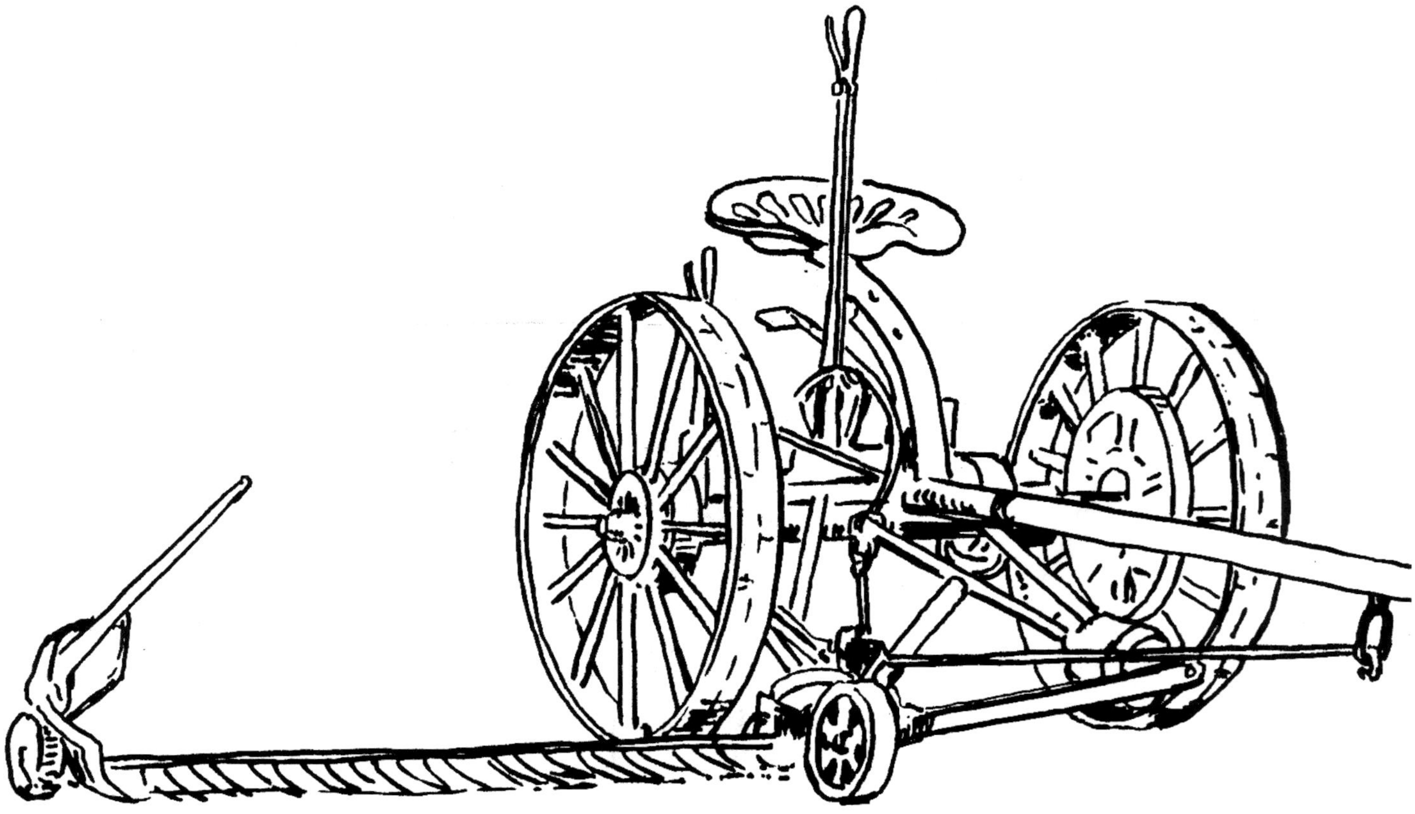

A horse-drawn mowing machine

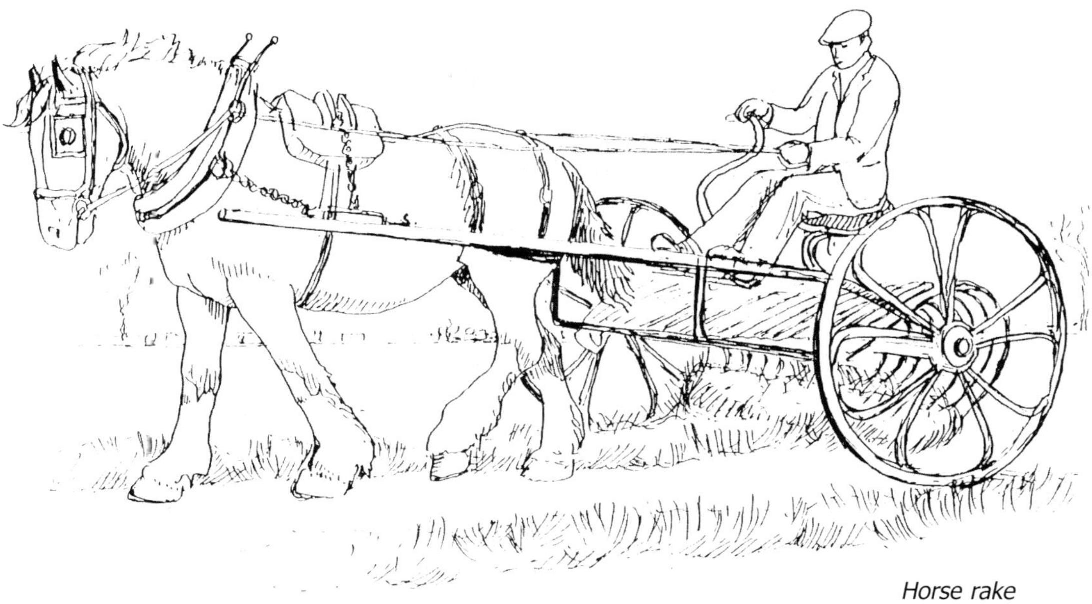

Horse rake

Mowing at Haysel-time

One man and his team went to mow a meadow. The horseman would start early in the morning with his pair hitched each side of the pole of the mowing machine, proceeding round the meadow in a clockwise direction.

Spare knives would be taken as they would need to be changed every hour in a heavy crop. A trestle in the field would grip the five foot knife while a youth with file and stone would sharpen each side of the twenty sections and replace with rivets any section broken by stones and metal objects left by trespassers. Metal tent pegs overlooked by campers can cost the farmer dearly in broken machinery at a busy time.

The youth would also be on hand to rake out the back-swathe so that the final cut could be made anti-clockwise under the hedge bottom. His help would also be needed raking back the loose grass on the triangular 'piking' shape left at the middle of the field. A mower cannot cut through loose grass already severed from the ground.

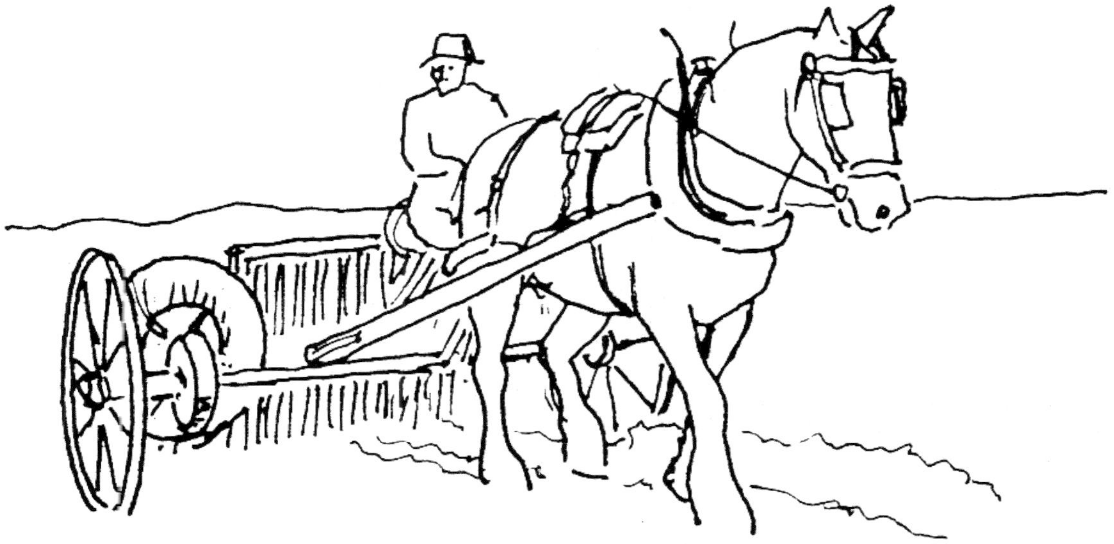

Side rake or swathe-turner for hay making

Danger from the Reciprocating Knife

Such was the nature of the job that in a tall, heavy crop, it was seldom possible to make a complete circuit of the field without frequent stops to reverse and clear the knife and all loose grass in front of it for a fresh start. This operation put one's fingers in dire peril if the horses should start unbidden.

Flattened areas of grass made by thoughtless, trespassing picnickers and lovers' trysts would add to one's exasperation. The reciprocating knife was driven by the wheels' traction on the ground. An area of damp ground would tend to make for an extra lush growth just in the very area where the wheels were more prone to slip and skid, thereby stopping the movement of the knife! To add to our discomfort, the sweating team would be plagued by innumerable flies which rose in clouds from their faces. In some areas, horses were even fitted with little cloth covers for their ears.

When at rest in their pastures, horses thoughtfully stand nose to tail alongside each other so that one's swishing tail can clear the flies off the face of the other. At hay-making time, as a reward during the meal breaks, horses were allowed to eat their fill of new-mown hay and grass on the biblical admonition that "thou shalt not muzzle the ox that treadeth out the corn"!

When the grass had been cut and lain in the swathe for a few sunny days it would be turned and tedded and rowed up and raked. Some would be swept to an elevator and thence made into a stack in the field. Some would be cobbed or piked into conical heaps or hung on tripods to assist the drying process. When driving early horse-drawn hay-making machines, one was forced to spend a fair proportion of the time with a knife cutting away unwanted twists of hay that had been wrapped around and worked into the bearings. It was easy to be injured by restive animals starting off without command while one was working on the machinery. Many a man must have lost a finger that way while clearing a mowing machine knife with the machine still in gear.

I came across a farmer's son who would not on any account be persuaded to work with horses. On enquiring the reason I discovered that in his youth his horse had bolted with a horse rake, causing him to fall off the high seat and pulling him a considerable distance along a narrow lane wrapped in the steel tines. He had not learned his lesson, however, for this same young man and his brother were seen to creep up behind a hedge and fire off their guns to spoil the display as another young man was showing off his horsemanship to his girlfriend in the adjoining field! This irresponsible practical joke could have back-fired tragically. "Pride comes before a fall."

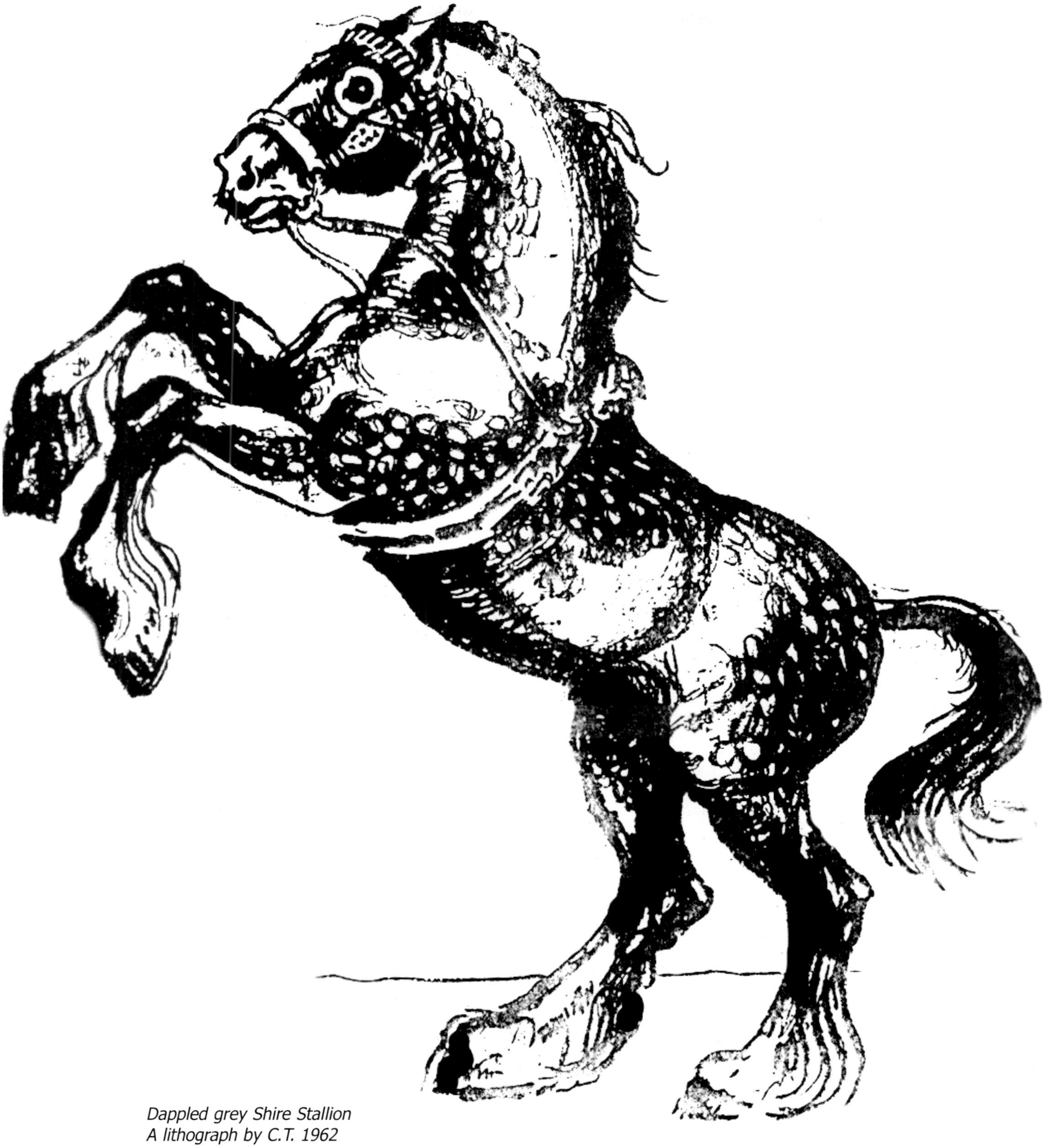

Dappled grey Shire Stallion
A lithograph by C.T. 1962

Shortcomings are Exposed for All to See

Compared with factory production, farming is very much open to the public's scrutiny.

In undulating country one blocked nozzle on the weedkiller spray later proclaims the faulty workmanship to all and sundry many miles away by the colourful strip in the green, growing corn - bright red for poppies or bright yellow for charlock. Likewise, anyone could see if a spout was blocked on the corn seed drill, or that the horse or tractor driver failed to keep straight as an arrow in whatever cultivation he was doing.

As a callow youth, the serpentine marks made by my early attempts at ploughing and working land were subject to appraisal by all and sundry. As I was good at figure drawing, I was accused of having my mind preoccupied by the subtle curves of a woman's form which, come to think of it, may not have been so far from the truth!

In the spring, a young man's fancy may cause his mind to be anywhere but on the job in hand, so it is not surprising that he may have difficulty in steering his horses along the straight and narrow, while he himself is making devious plans about future activities!

Ploughing with Horses

Oft did the harvest to their sickle yield,

Their furrow oft the stubborn glebe has broke;

How jocund did they drive their teams afield!

How bowed the woods beneath their sturdy stroke!

- T. Gray

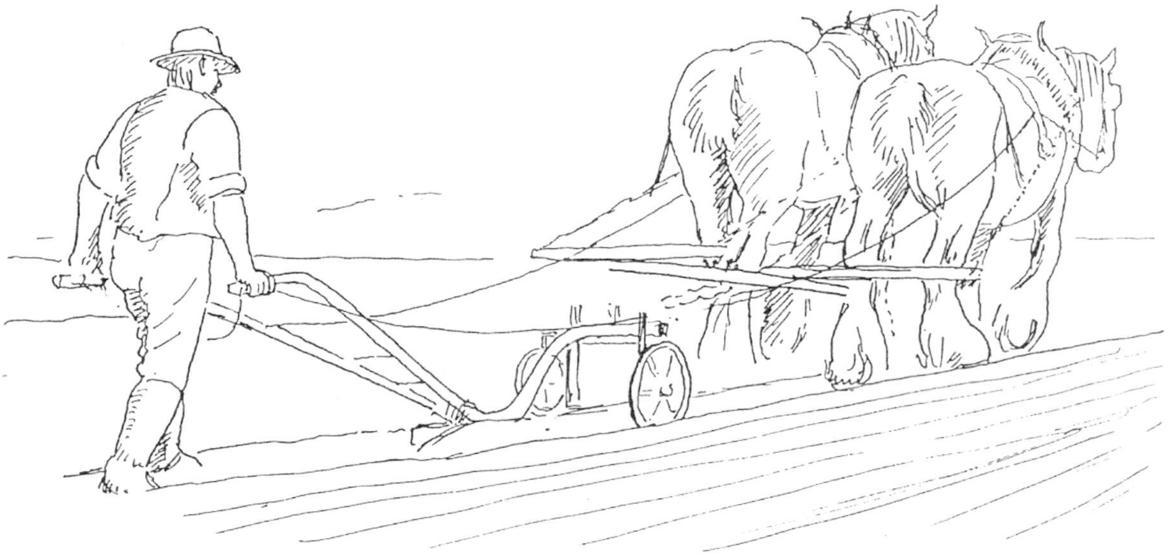

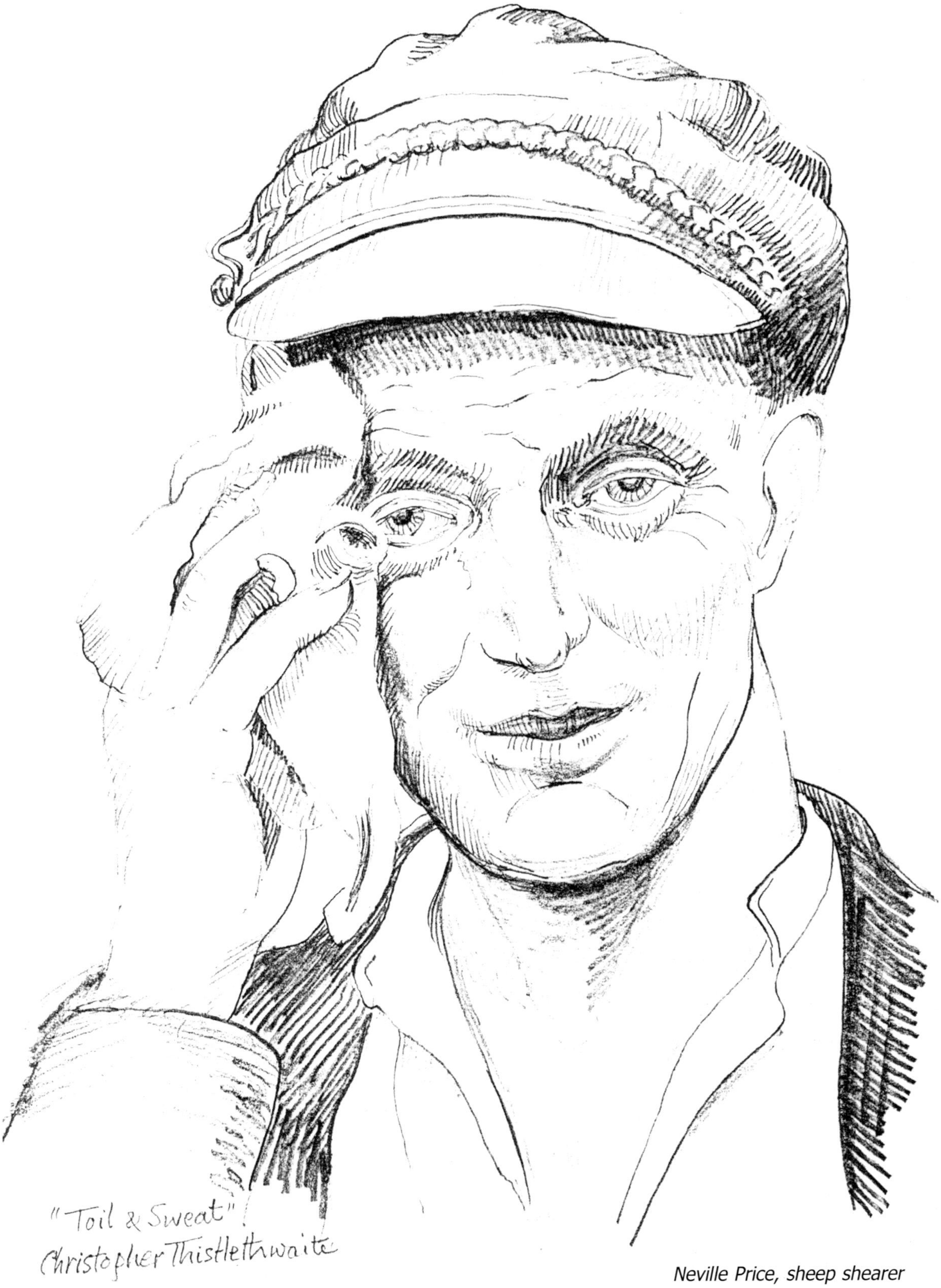

Neville Price, sheep shearer

People will always ask about the great undulations known as ridge and furrow if ploughing is mentioned.

There will soon be few of us left who have actually ploughed with horses and can explain the process from personal experience following 'the painful plough', which was very hard work for man and beast.

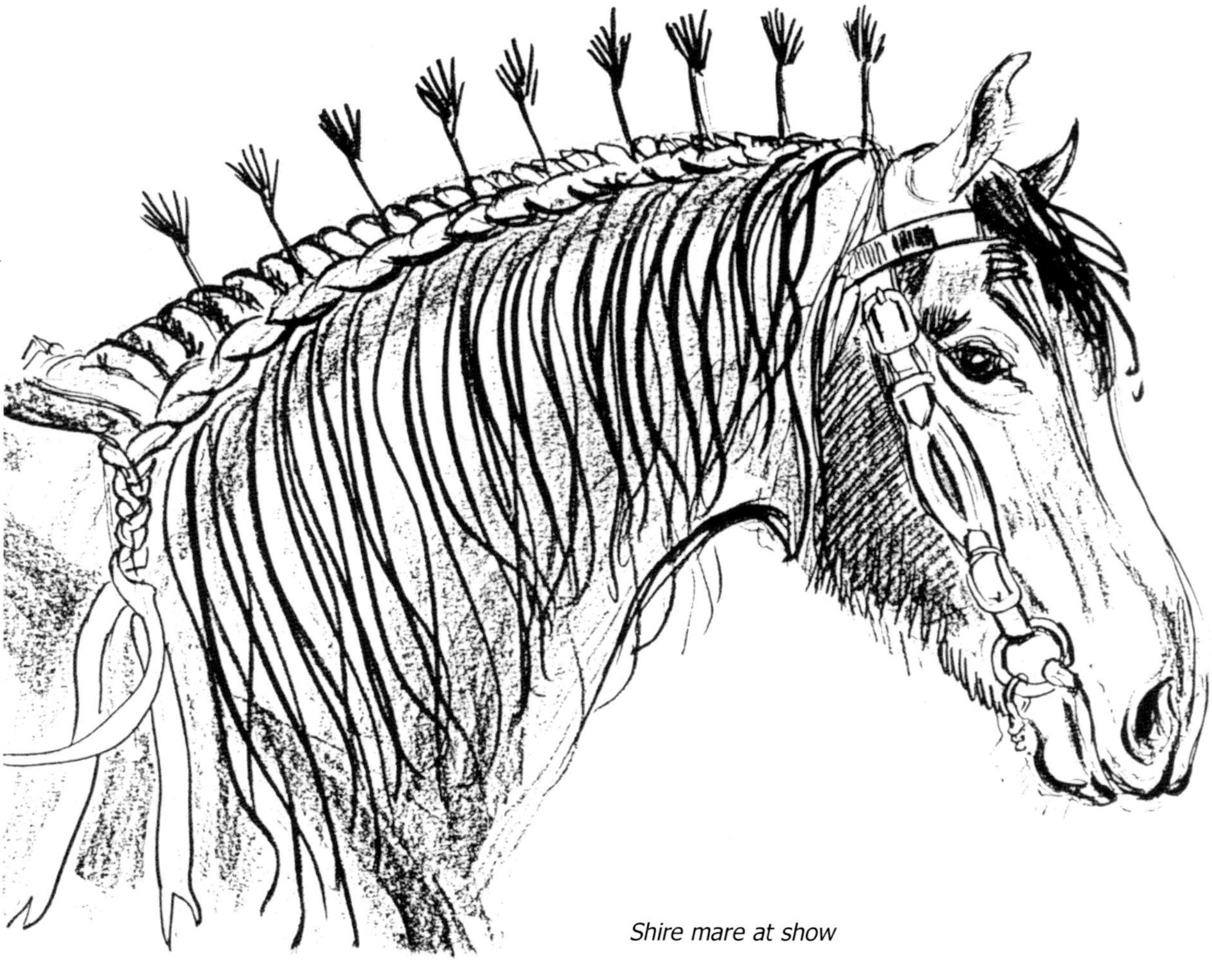

Shire mare at show

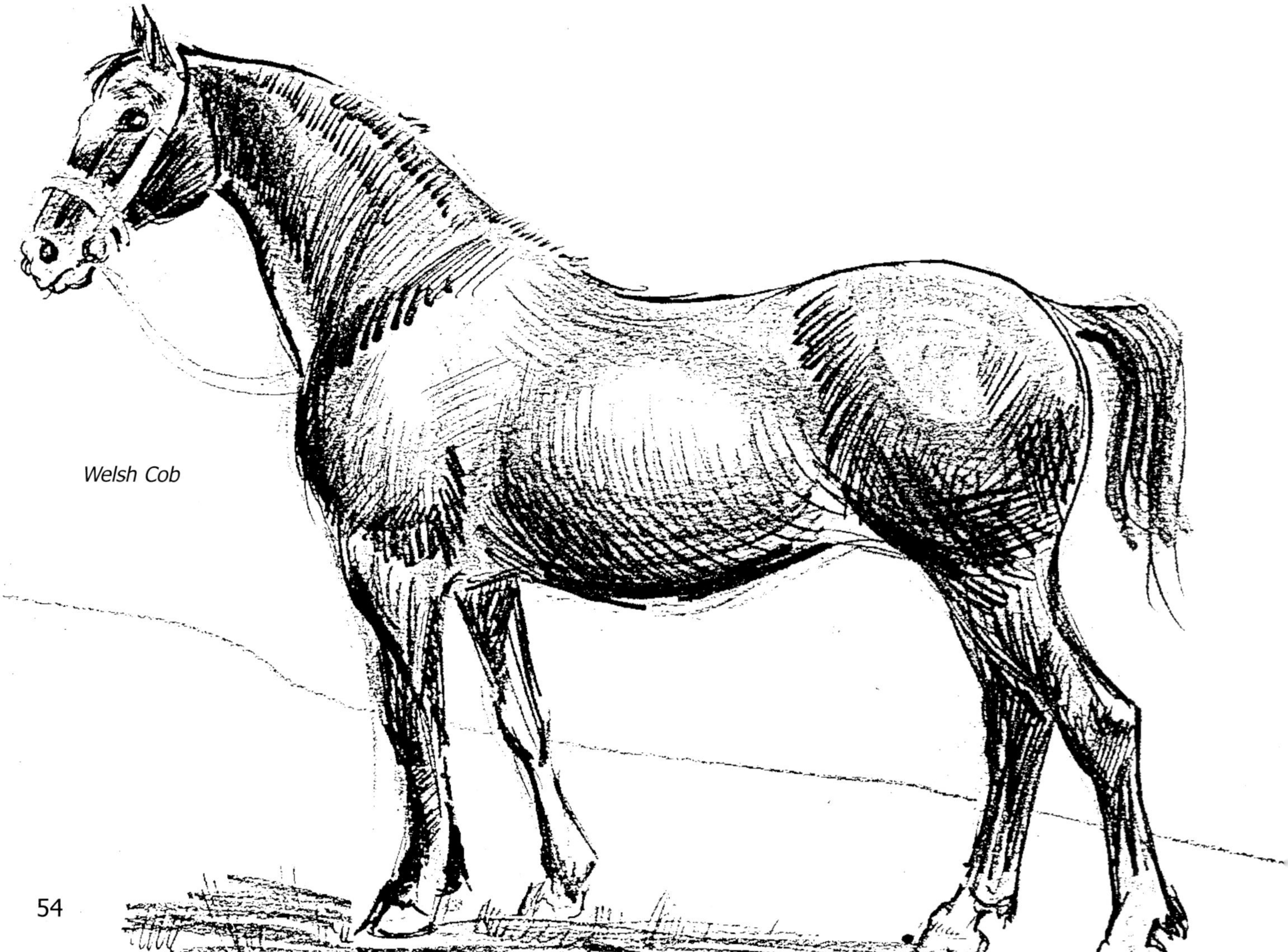

Welsh Cob

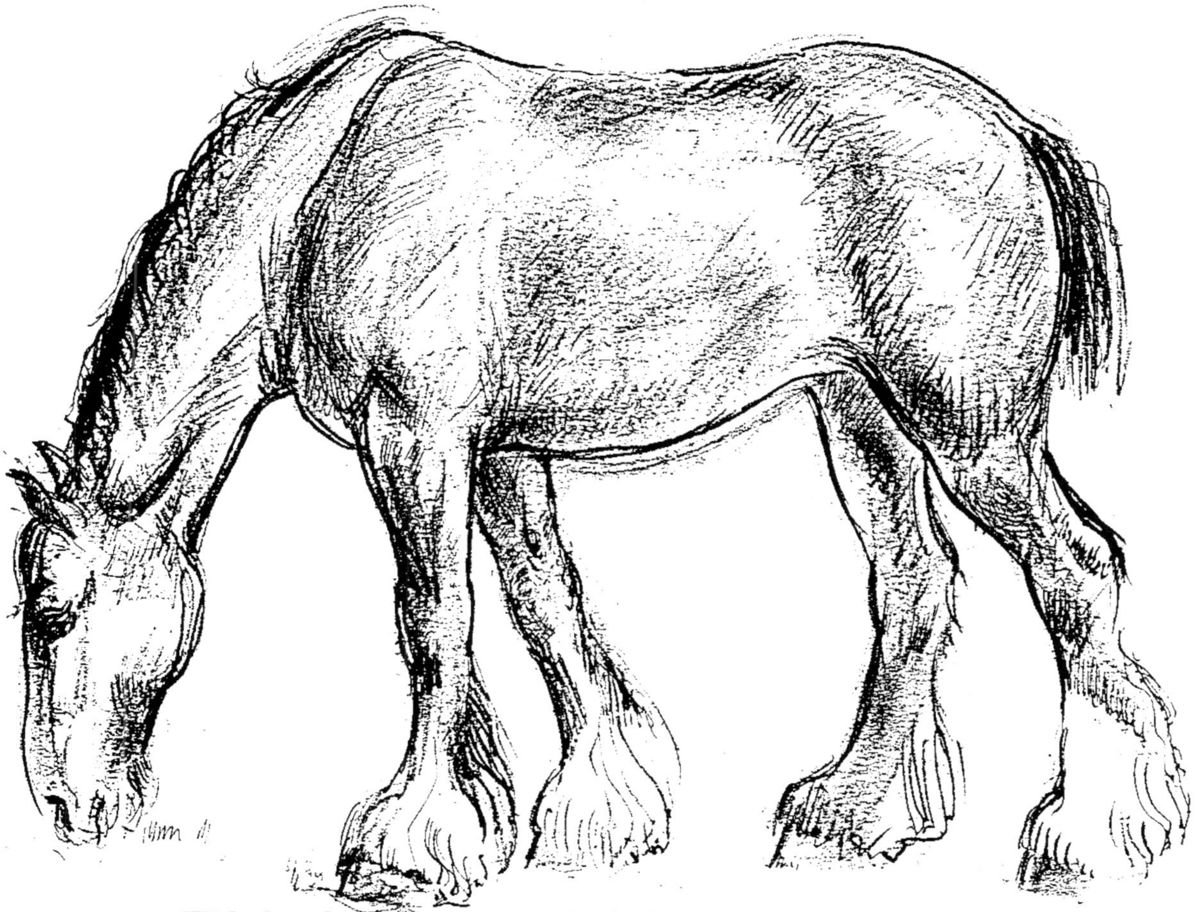

With the advent of tractors to do the heavy duties, I sometimes heard horse-loving people express the wish that they would never see a horse wear a collar again. After a horse had spent five or six years working on hard roads in the city, it might be fortunate enough to spend its remaining years doing light hauling jobs around the farm.

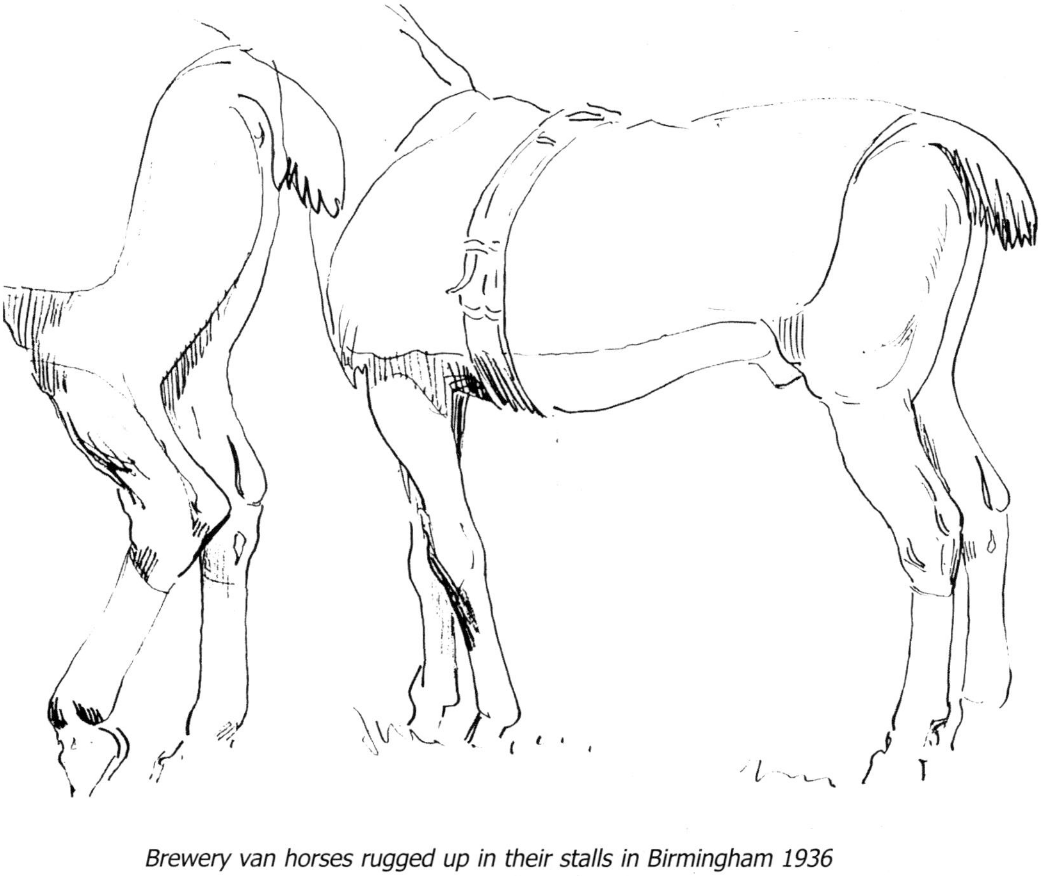

Brewery van horses rugged up in their stalls in Birmingham 1936

Good ploughing was the foundation of all subsequent cultivations and ploughmen took great pride in producing neat, accurate work. Before corn drilling mechanisms were invented, corn would be broadcast by hand to fall in neat rows between high-crested furrows. Then it would be harrowed in.

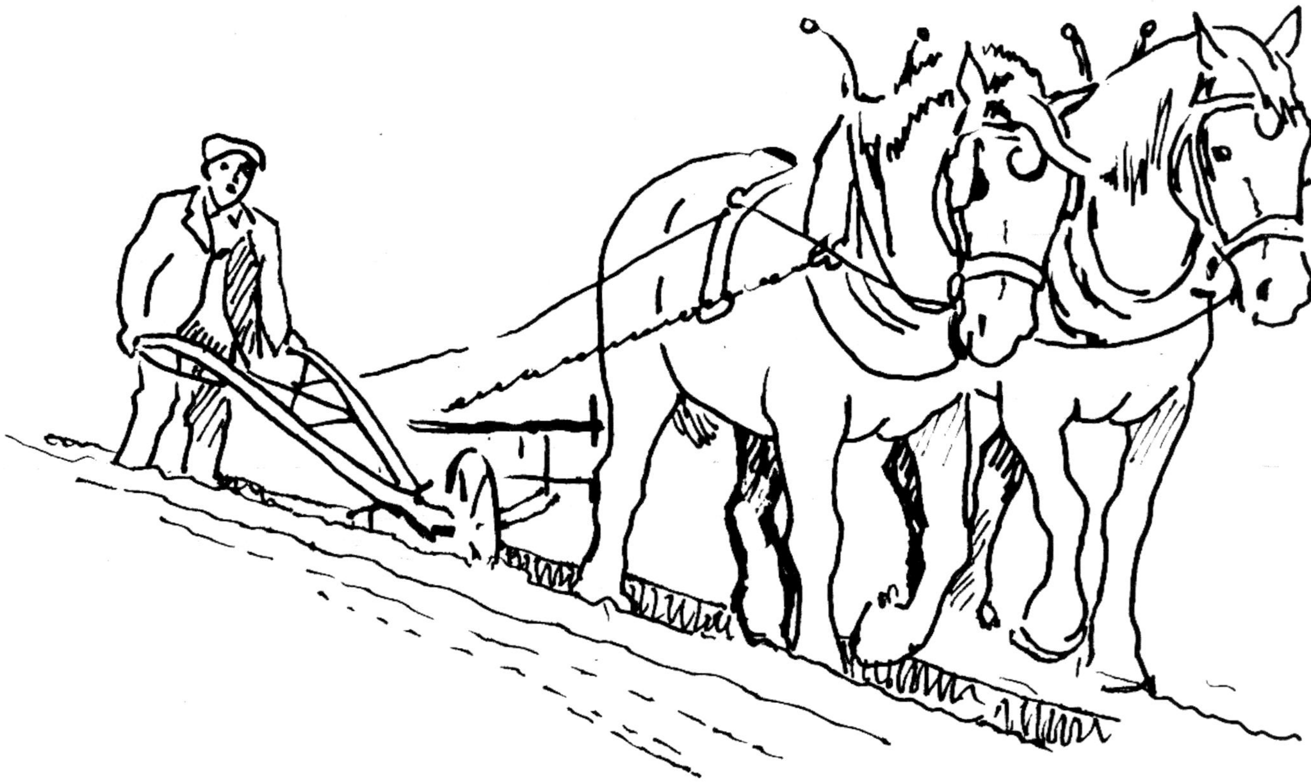

One 'land', the area of land between two open furrows, was usually 1 chain wide (22 yards or 4 poles) (20.1 m). In a square 10 acre field this made the length of furrows 10 chains (220 yards or 1 furlong or 'furrow long') (201 m).

A normal day's work for a man with a team of two horses and a single-furrow plough which threw the soil to the right only, was one acre (10 chains by 1 chain wide). Using this system, idle turning distance on the headlands was kept to a maximum of 11 yards (10 m). The rod or pole of about 5.5 yards (5 m) was the length of the goad for oxen, and therefore was used as a handy measuring tool.

A well-designed HORSE PLOUGH made by Ransome of Ipswich

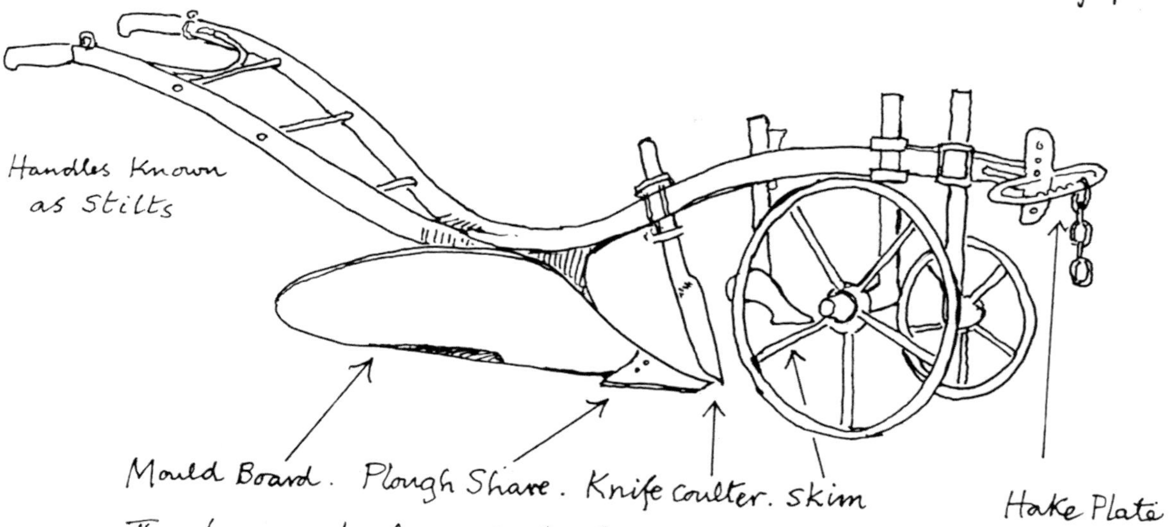

The large wheel ran in the furrow; the small one on the unploughed land.

Robert Ransome son of a Quaker Schoolmaster, with the help of the Gurneys, the Quaker Bankers, started a foundry in Ipswich in 1789.

These are the four essential parts of a plough:

1. The vertical cut is made by a ***knife*** *or* ***disc coulter,*** which precedes the share.

2. The ***ploughshare*** makes the horizontal cut and starts to lift the furrow slice. This takes a great deal of wear and has to be constantly renewed.

3. The ***mould board*** twists and inverts the slice, pressing it neatly against the previous furrow.

4. The ***land slide*** presses against the furrow wall and takes the sideways thrust.

Ploughing the first furrow in setting up a ridge always required great skill in steering the team towards a distant point without the slightest deviation or looking backwards. Thereafter one horse walked in the furrow and the other on the unploughed land.

Ridge and Furrow Patterns

On well-drained arable land the position of the ridges and open furrows were alternated year by year, keeping the field flat.

On wet land, however, if the ridge were to be set up in the same place year on year, great undulations would result from continually moving the soil in the same direction. These can often be seen to this day.

Great importance is attached to straightness and precision in fieldwork. The slightest deviation must be corrected at once; then another will appear, and so on. Keeping an eye fixed on a distant object will sometimes help the driver to keep straight, but with tractor work, one has to be constantly monitoring the machine working behind, so one really needs all-round vision. Hence the quotation from St Luke's Gospel, "He who puts his hand to the plough must never look back." For ploughing matches, three marker sticks with white tops were lined up for setting out the first furrow.

The condition and appearance of hedges, ditches, gates and implements say a good deal about the farm to passers-by. The care of livestock, their quality and condition will not pass unnoticed by the expert eagle eyes of passing farmers.

The unthrifty beast of which you are not so proud will insist on presenting herself at the gate when you are trying to impress your neighbours, while according to Sod's Law her commendably sleek companions remain steadfastly out of sight.

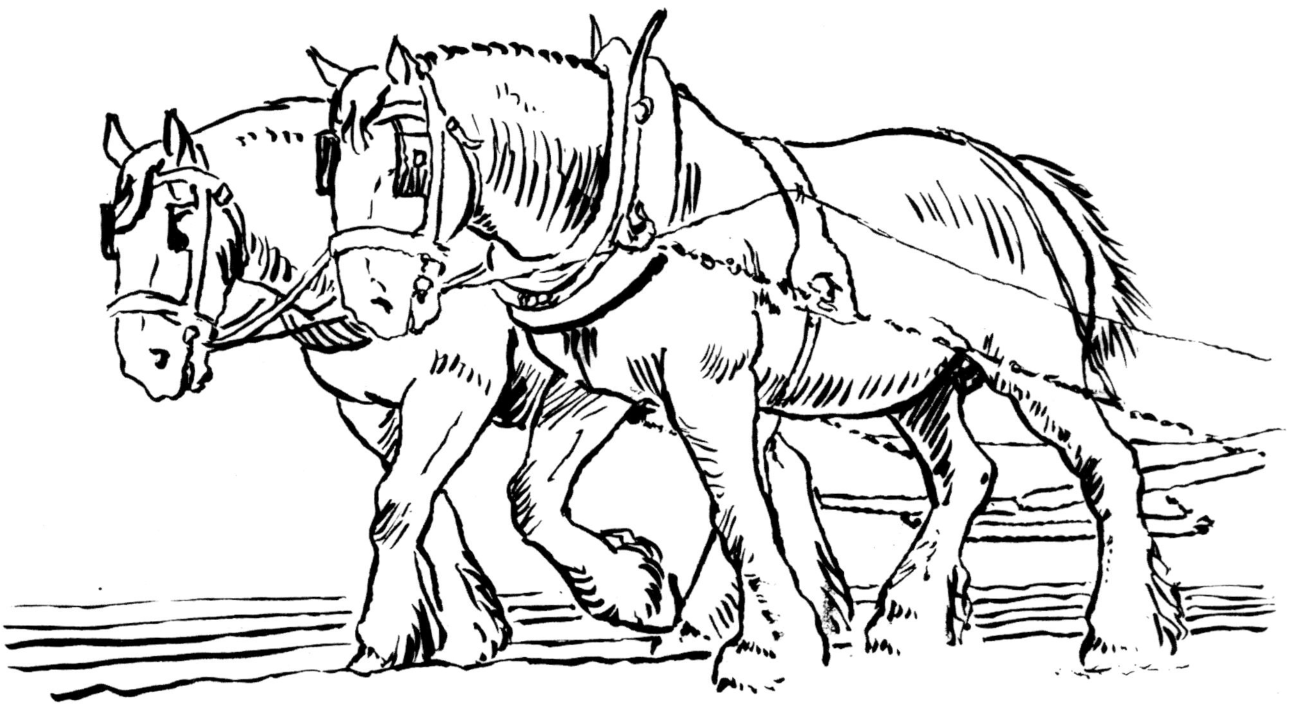

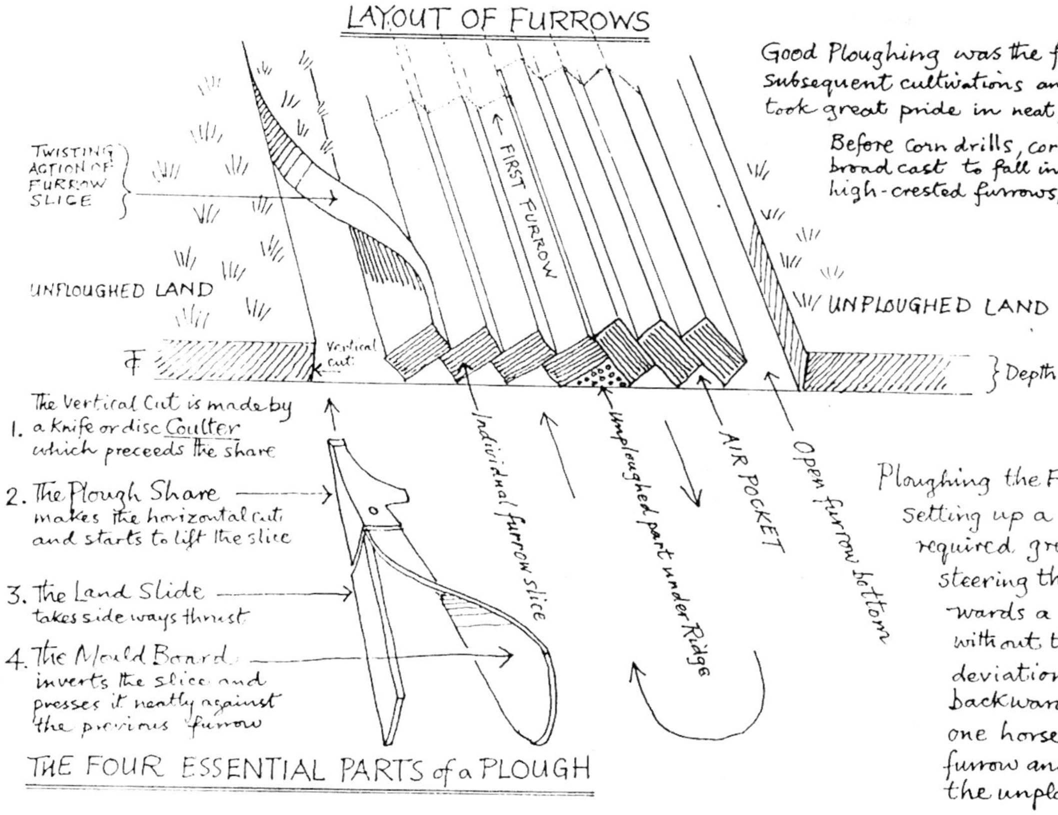

Good Ploughing was the foundation of all subsequent cultivations and ploughmen took great pride in neat, accurate work.

Before corn drills, corn would be hand broadcast to fall in neat rows between high-crested furrows, then harrowed in.

Ploughing the First Furrow in setting up a Ridge always required great skill in steering the team towards a distant point, without the slightest deviation or looking backwards. Thereafter one horse walked in the furrow and the other on the unploughed land.

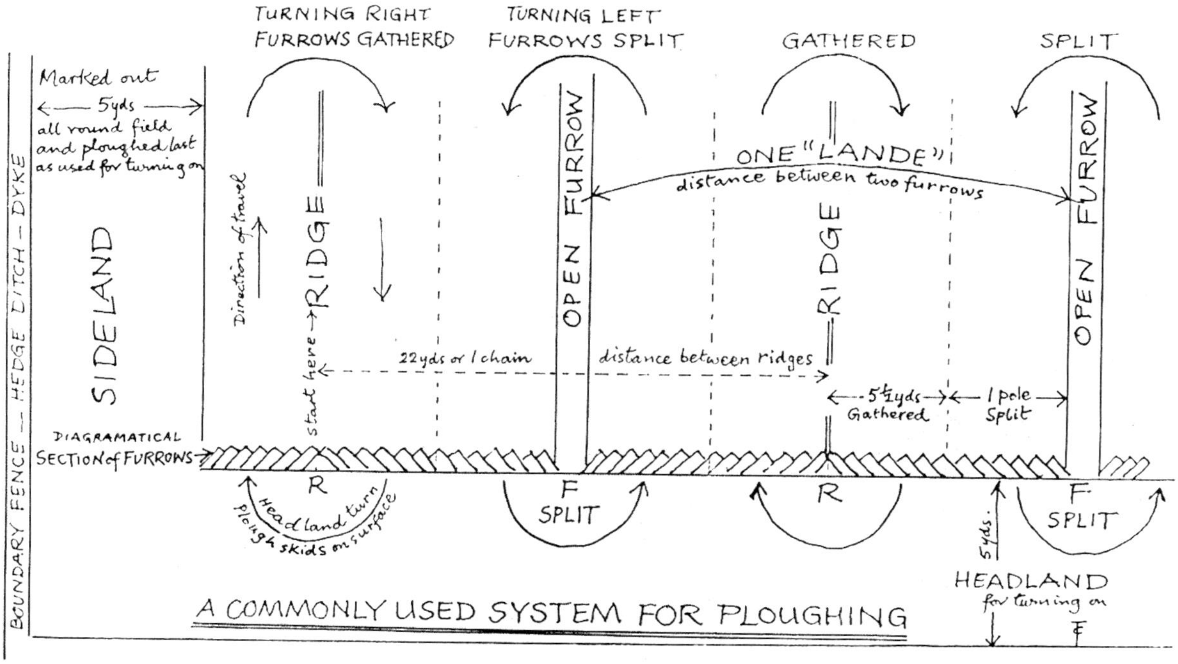

One "land" – the distance between open furrows was usually 1 chain wide – 22 yds or 4 poles. In a square 10 acre field this made length of furrows 10 chains – 220 yds or 1 furlong (furrow long). A normal day's work for a man with a team of 2 horses and single furrow plough which threw the soil to the right was one acre – (10 chains by 1 chain wide). Using this system idle turning distance was kept to a maximum of 11 yds. The Rod or Pole of about 5½ yds was the goad for oxen and therefore was a handy measuring tool.
On well-drained arable land the Ridges and Open Furrows were alternated year by year, keeping the field flat. In wet land, however, if the Ridge were set up in the same place year on year great undulations would result from continually moving the soil in the same direction, as can often be seen today.

Various Designs of Horse Brasses

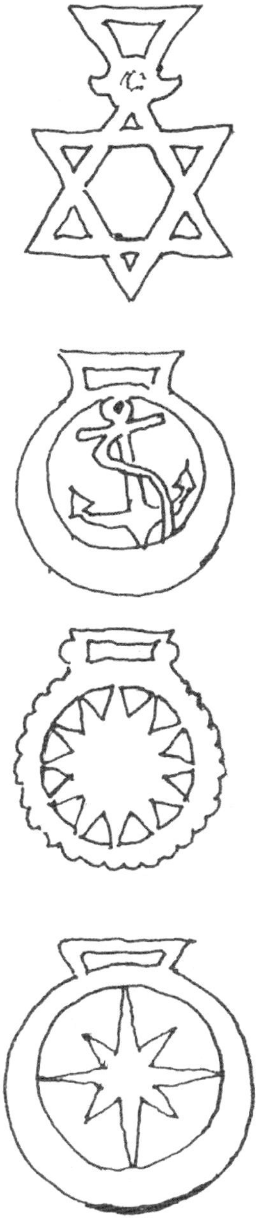

Above: Brasses to ward off the evil eye

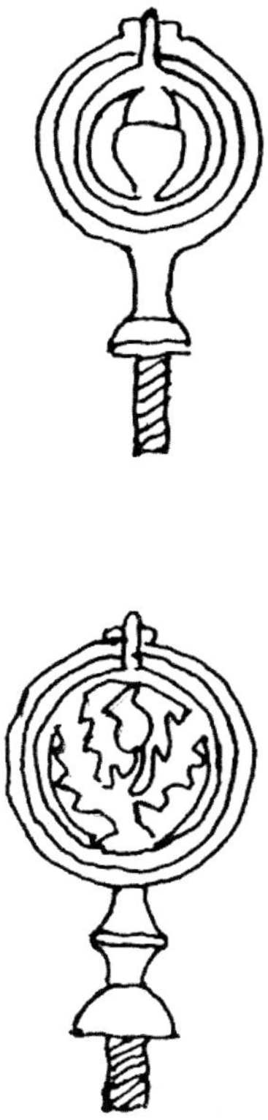

Swingers or Fly Terrets (Positioned between the horse's ears)

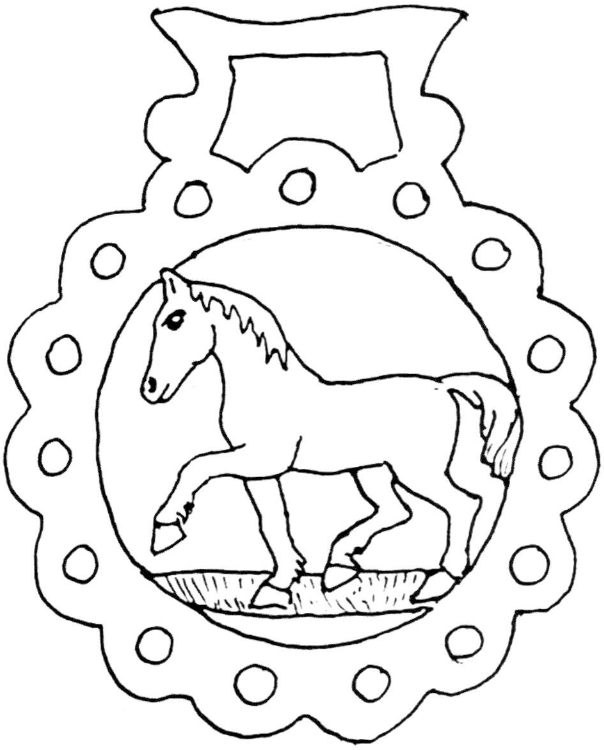

A horse brass or amulet of ancient origin. These are fastened singly at the forehead or in a series to the martingale or breast strap.

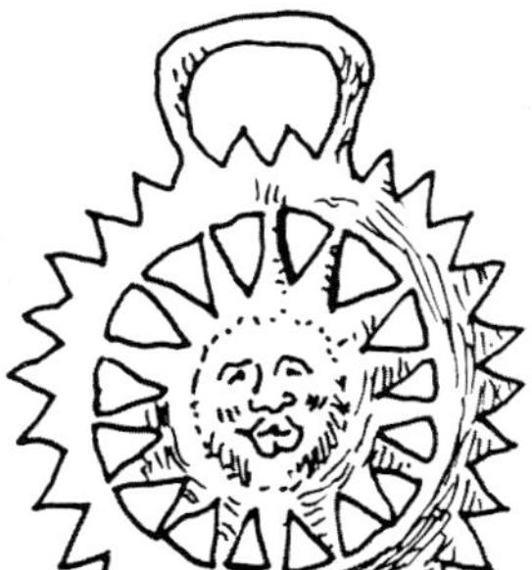

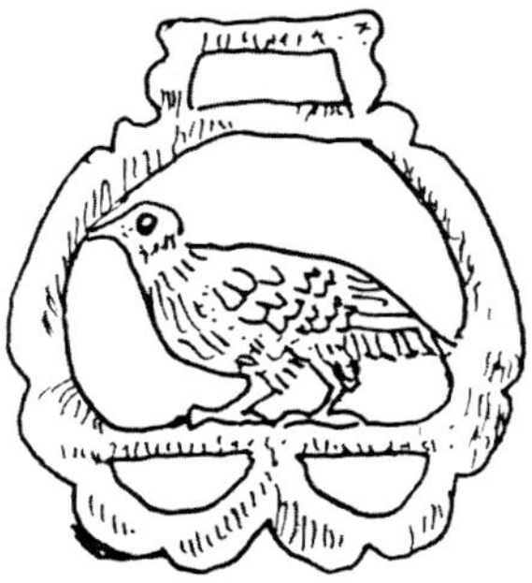

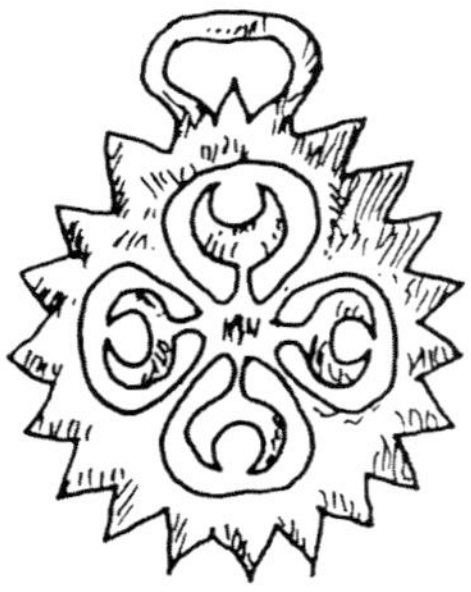

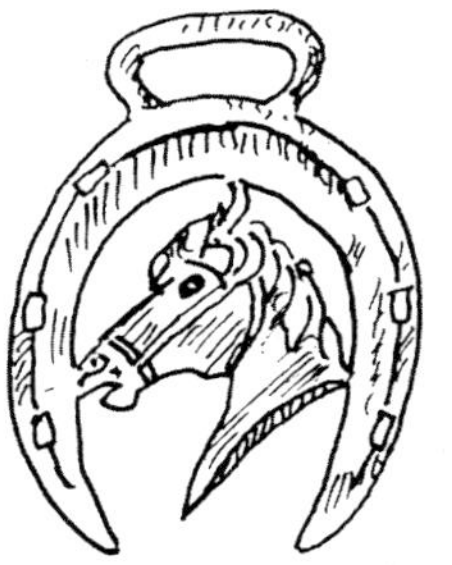

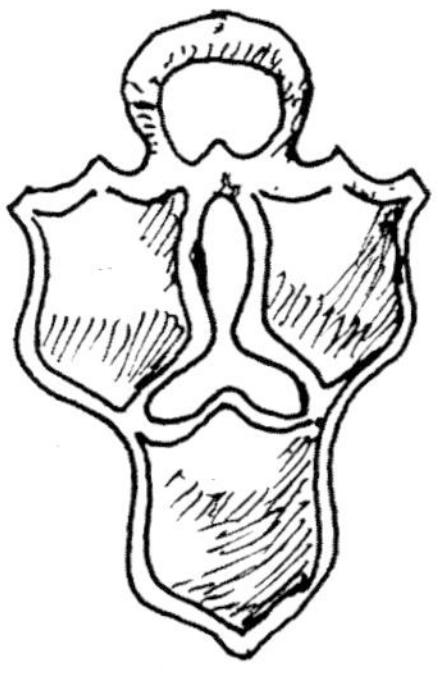

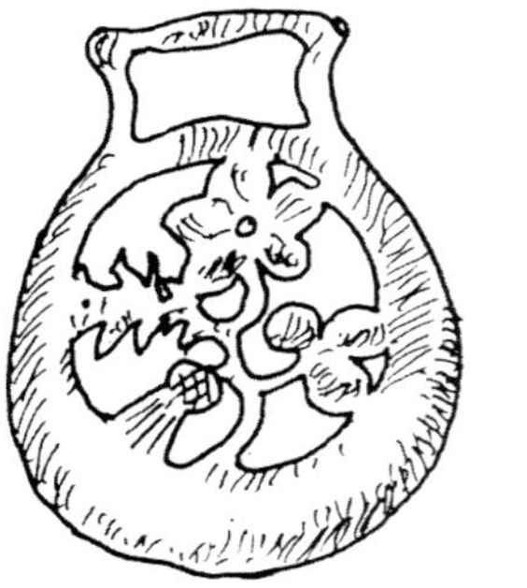

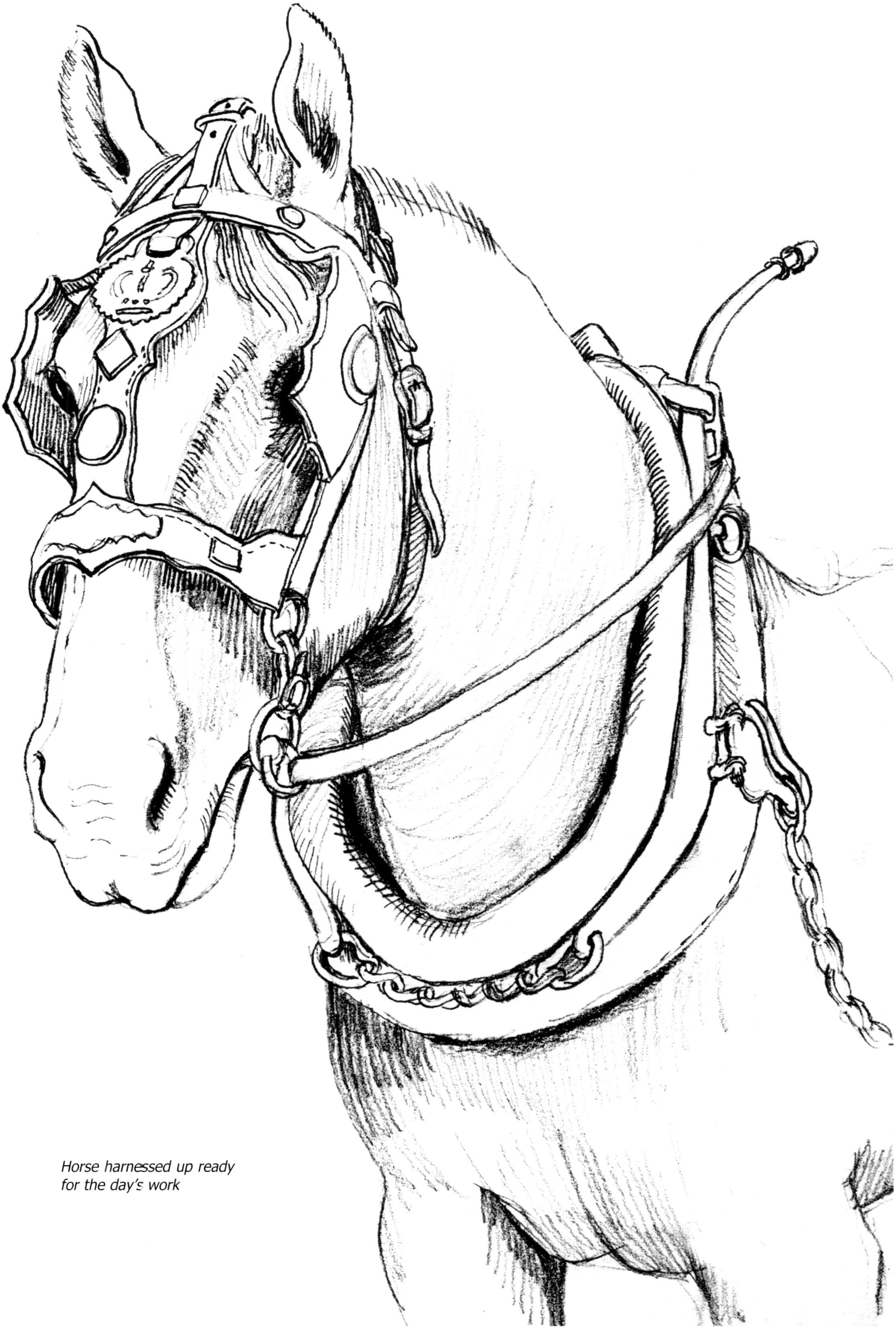

Horse harnessed up ready for the day's work

Stallions

The owner of a pedigree stallion would let it be known that it would be travelling a certain district with its groom at a specified time.

Farmers with brood mares could ask for it to call and service the mare for a certain stud fee. It used to be quite common to come upon a gigantic Shire stallion being led through the leafy lanes from farm to farm by a diminutive groom, who lived a roving life with his potent charge throughout the breeding season.

The stallion would be held, agog with excitement, on one side of a sturdy gate, while the mares and fillies would be paraded one at a time to be introduced to their suitor over the intervening gate. It was soon abundantly clear from the mare's behaviour whether or not she was ready 'in season'. If she was, the gate was opened and mating took place in a few minutes to the accompaniment of ribald remarks about comparative anatomy!

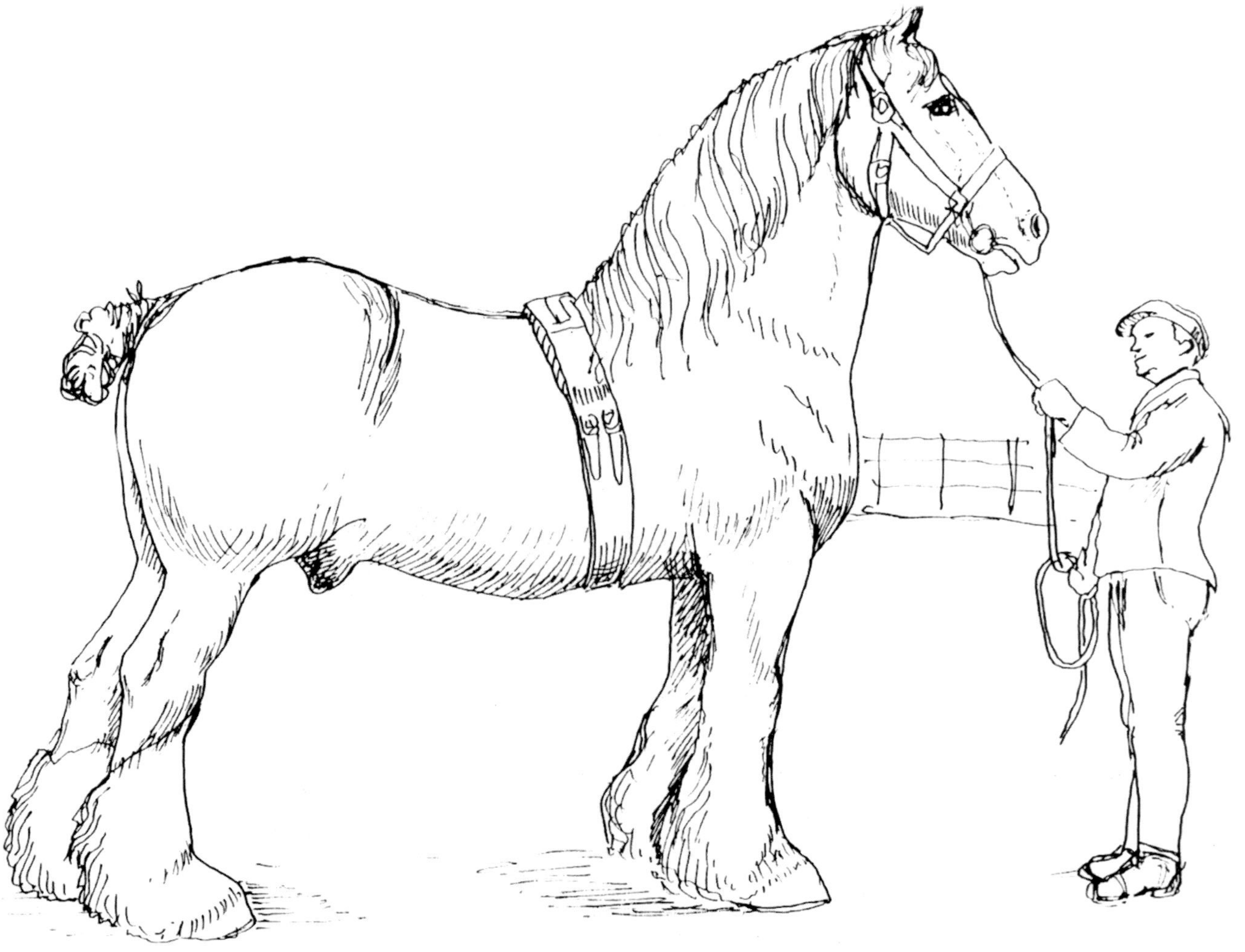

Old type of Shire stallion

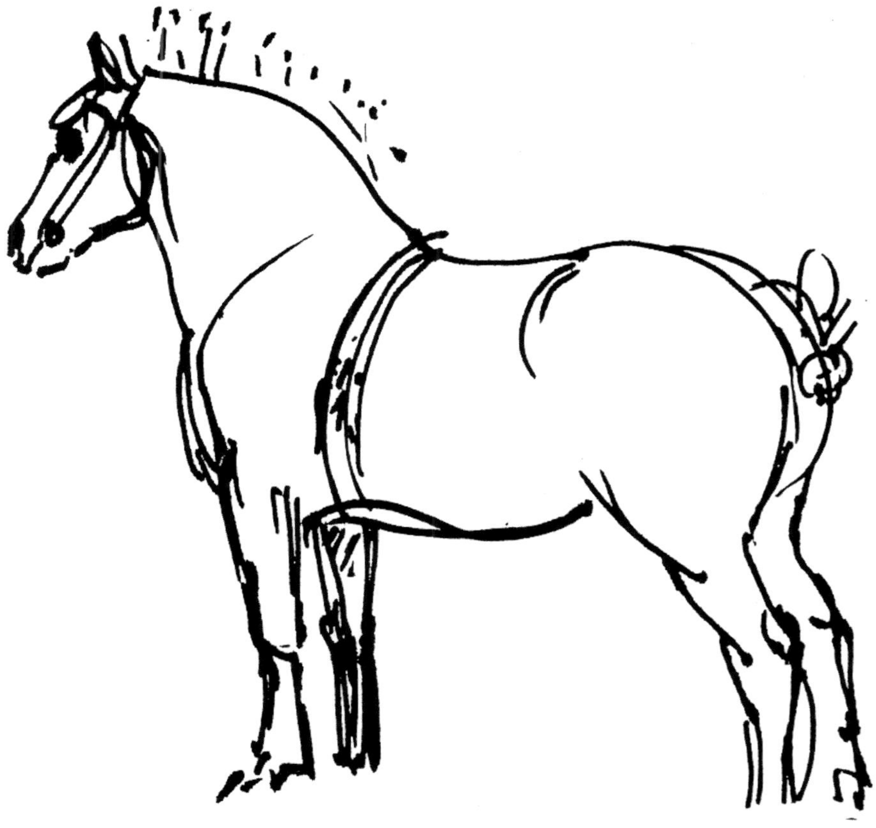

Percheron Stallion

The stallion wore a wide leather belt to which the handler could attach his sleeping rug and other items of luggage. As many of the overnight stops would have been public houses with stabling, the groom, having been deprived of human company after hours alone on the road and the comforts of wife and home, might easily fall for the temptations provided by these hostelries!

The Suffolk Horse Society far-sightedly encouraged small farmers to breed better horses by putting pedigree mares on farms which were subsidised to those who otherwise could not have afforded them. They then helped to place the foals with other careful breeders.

An Arab Colt Foal born on our farm in 1980

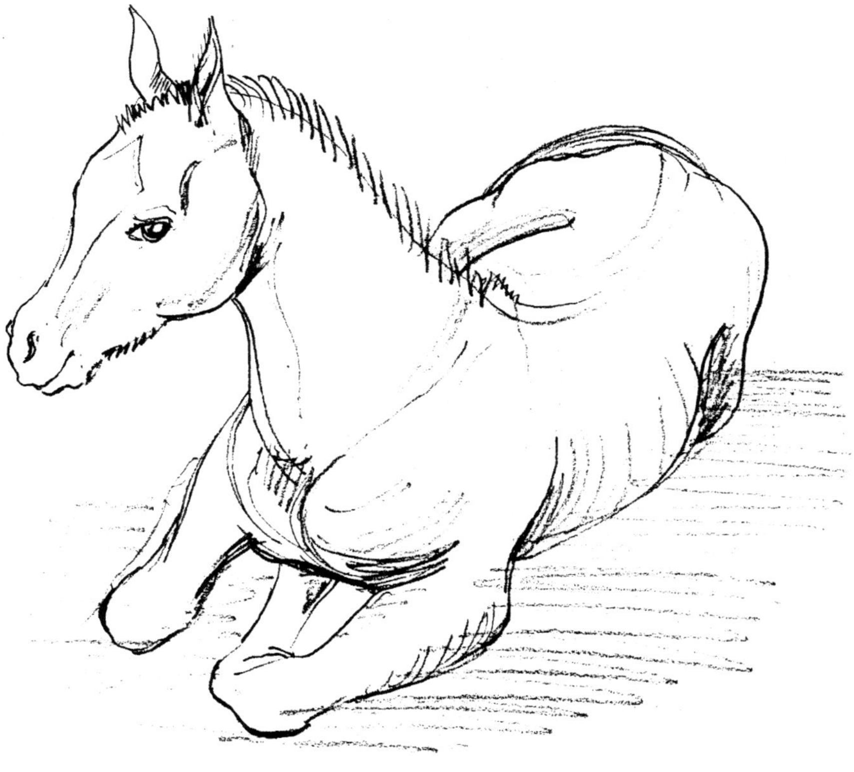

Chapter THREE

Cattle

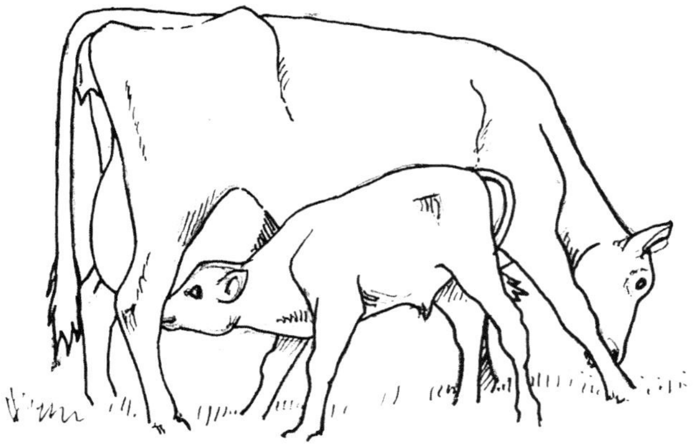

The Miracle of Birth

The miracle of birth is manifest around us constantly on a stock-farm. One might adopt a coldly mercenary attitude to nature's plan for reproduction but personally, I never failed to feel humble and grateful, as if witnessing and partaking in some mystical event beyond human understanding.

The majority of births seem to take place during the hours of darkness, and if given the chance, the animal will temporarily reject her gregarious nature and sally forth to the utmost secluded part of her compound, no doubt reasoning that she can get on with the labour undisturbed by prying eyes of human and animal companions. That way she can lick her new offspring clean and make a lasting bond with it as she encourages it to stagger to its feet and find its source of nourishment. If another female animal is close by, she may imagine that the newborn is her own and try to adopt it, with disastrous consequences, as she will forsake it when her own offspring arrives.

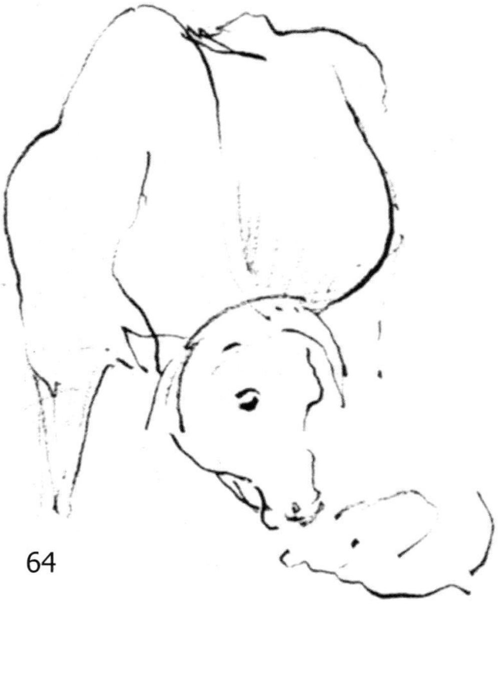

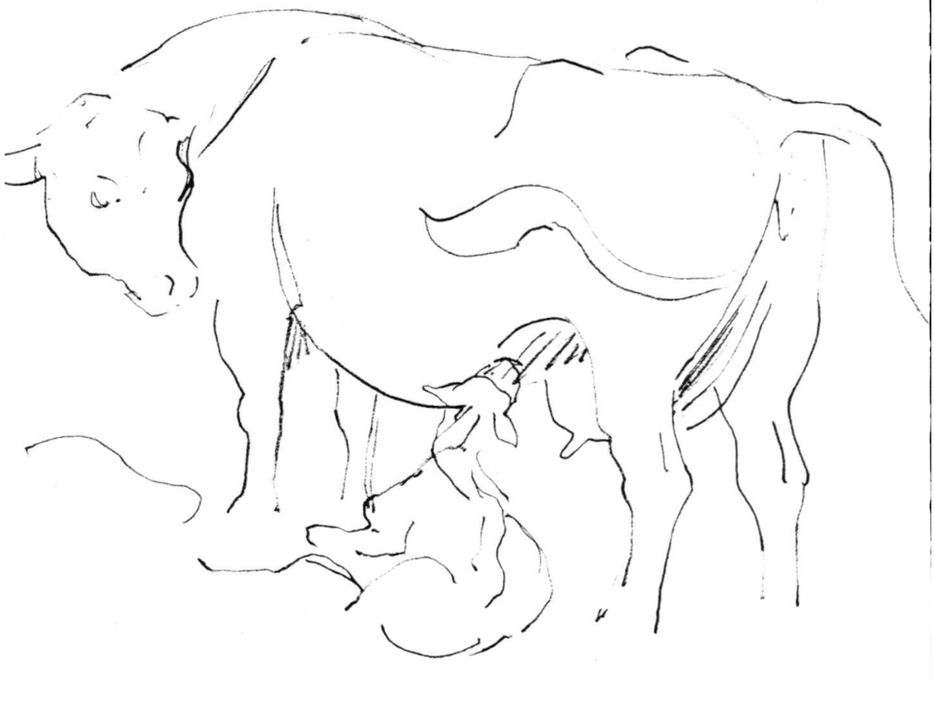

I know an exception to this rule - a female house cat when her time was near used to conscript her friend to join her for company, like a midwife, at the scene of her confinement! Understanding these considerations would somewhat mitigate my exasperation as I searched in the darkness and driving rain in order to bring back a newly-calved heifer to the warm, dry bedding of a safe pen.

Dairy Farmer is the Poor Relation

As the tenant farmer was always regarded as the poor relation of the much rarer owner-occupier, so was the dairy farmer regarded towards the cattle-grazing beef farmer, who was often known as a 'beef and barley baron'. The dairy farmer spent much of his time as a lavatory attendant in the winter months when his cows spent most of the day chained up in stalls. The grazier, by contrast, had a much easier life in the grass-growing season, as all he had to do was count his cattle once a day, check for lameness and ensure a constant water supply. Even in the winter it is much easier to feed fattening cattle in yards than to take on the twice-a-day tyranny of the milking routine, which is, of course, inherent in caring for the dairy cow. In addition, there are her calving problems and various ailments which must not be neglected.

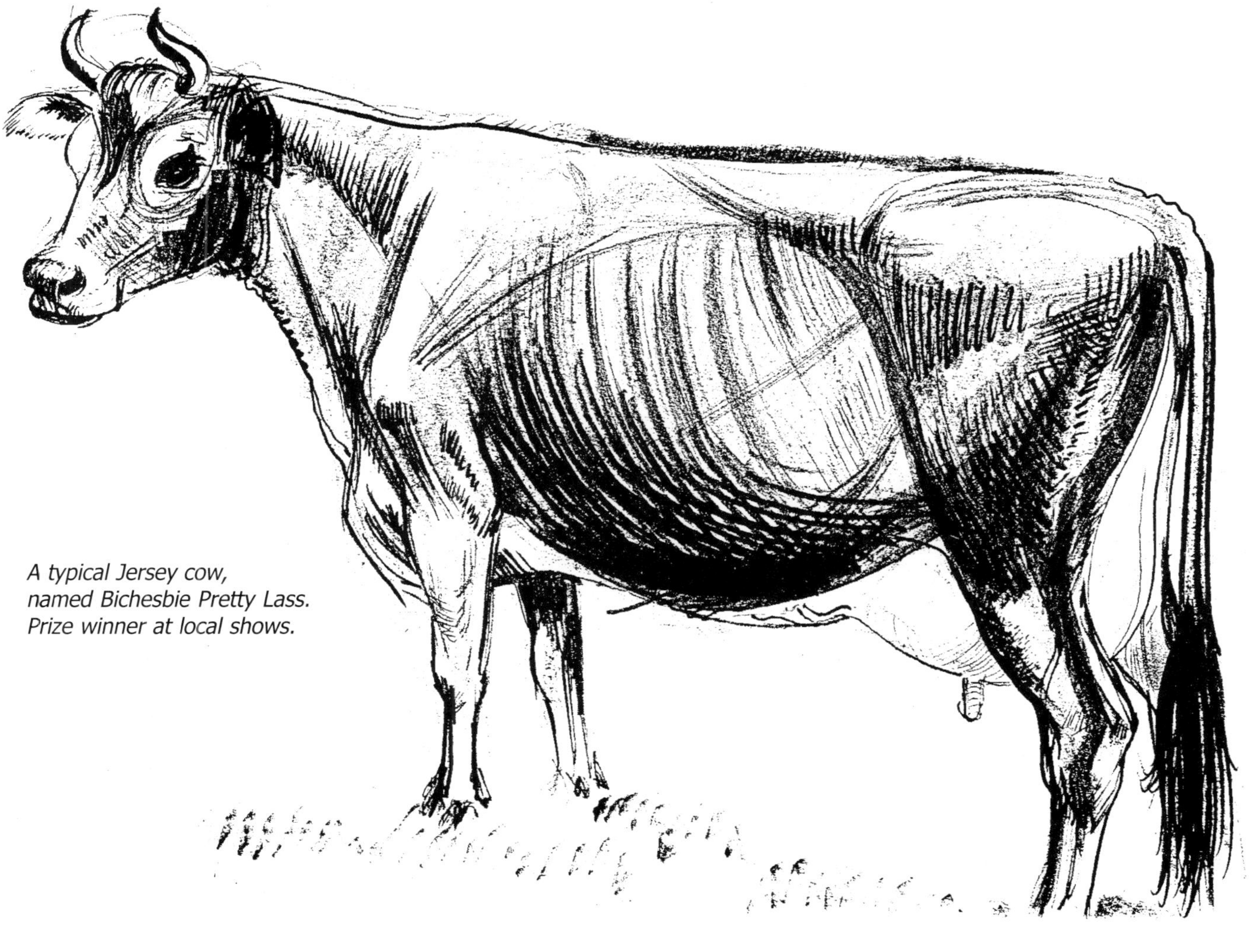

A typical Jersey cow, named Bichesbie Pretty Lass. Prize winner at local shows.

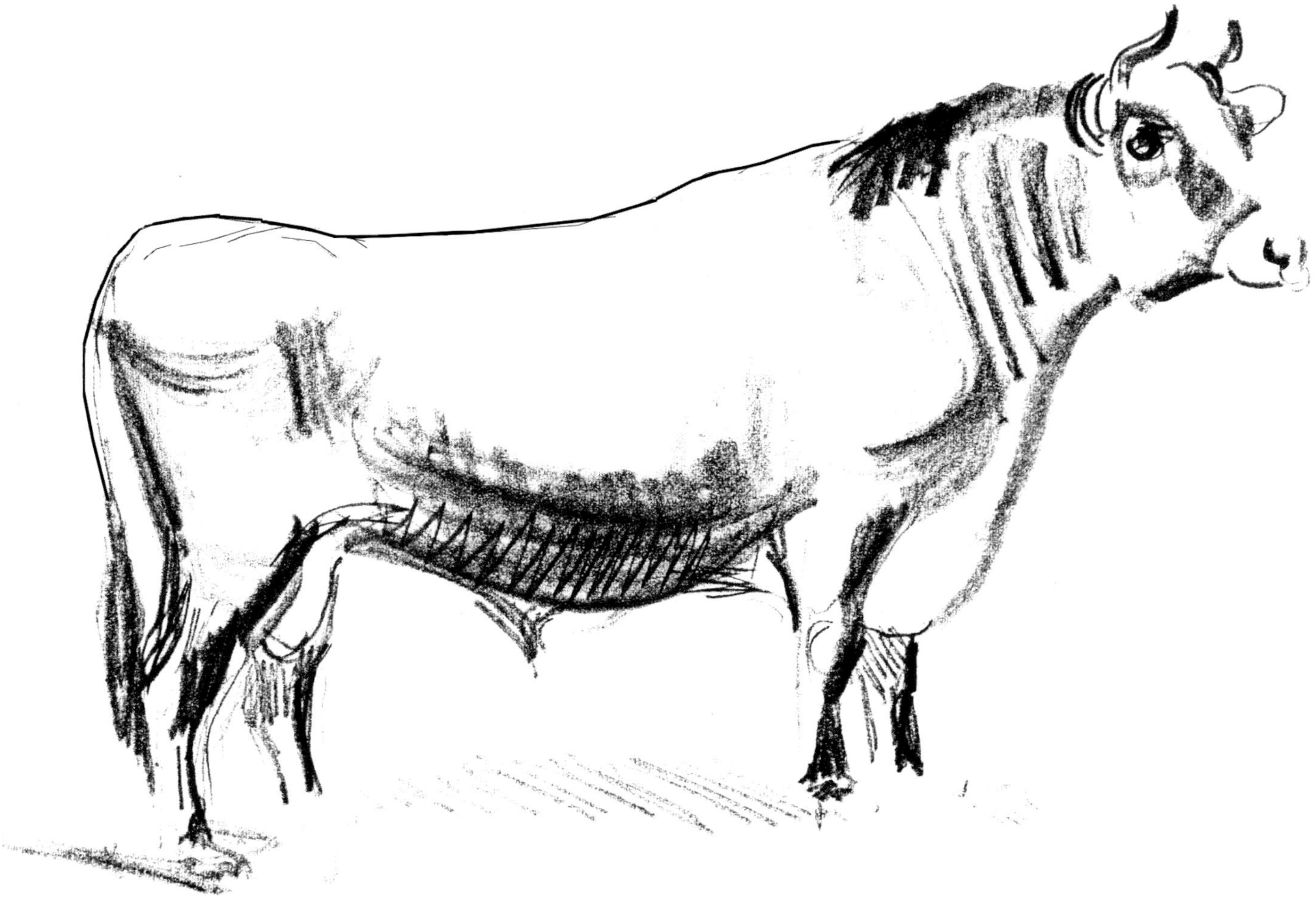

A Jersey bull,
Irton Emperor's Lad

In simplified terms, one could sum up by saying that beef cattlemen despised dairy cattle keepers and both sorts of cattlemen disliked sheep breeders, and *all three detest horses!* This could be partly because of grazing habits. Cattle need prior access to the best and longest grass to thrive. If sheep get into the same pasture in large numbers, they spoil it for the cattle as they can graze much more closely. Horses graze the closest of all but are very selective and never stop eating, or so it seems. They also aggressively chase away other stock from the food put out for them. They are apt to canter about for no good reason, ruining the turf with their pounding hooves. As someone remarked, they have five mouths!

When a farmer is struggling to establish his business, dairying is a great temptation as there is quick cashflow. You can buy a freshly-calved cow or heifer today and sell her milk tomorrow, whereas beef production is a much slower return on the capital invested, as it may take three years to fatten a beast from a calf.

The Joys of Hand Milking

The cow's calf was weaned onto bucket feeding as soon as it had received the all- important colostrum from its mother. This contains the antibodies that ward off disease. The cow then quickly forgot her calf and became accustomed to standing and lying in a bedded stall with a water bowl and manger into which was put suitable quantities of hay, roots and concentrated feed. Most cows were so interested in their food that they would not object too strongly to a person sidling up to them with a three-legged stool and a stainless steel milking bucket into which he or she would direct the milk by vigorous manipulation of the four teats. This required considerable skill and well-developed muscles of the fingers and forearms. The bucket was gripped tightly between the knees and the head thrust firmly into the cow's side. In summer when the flies were about, one's head and neck would be constantly flailed by the swishing, dung-covered tail.

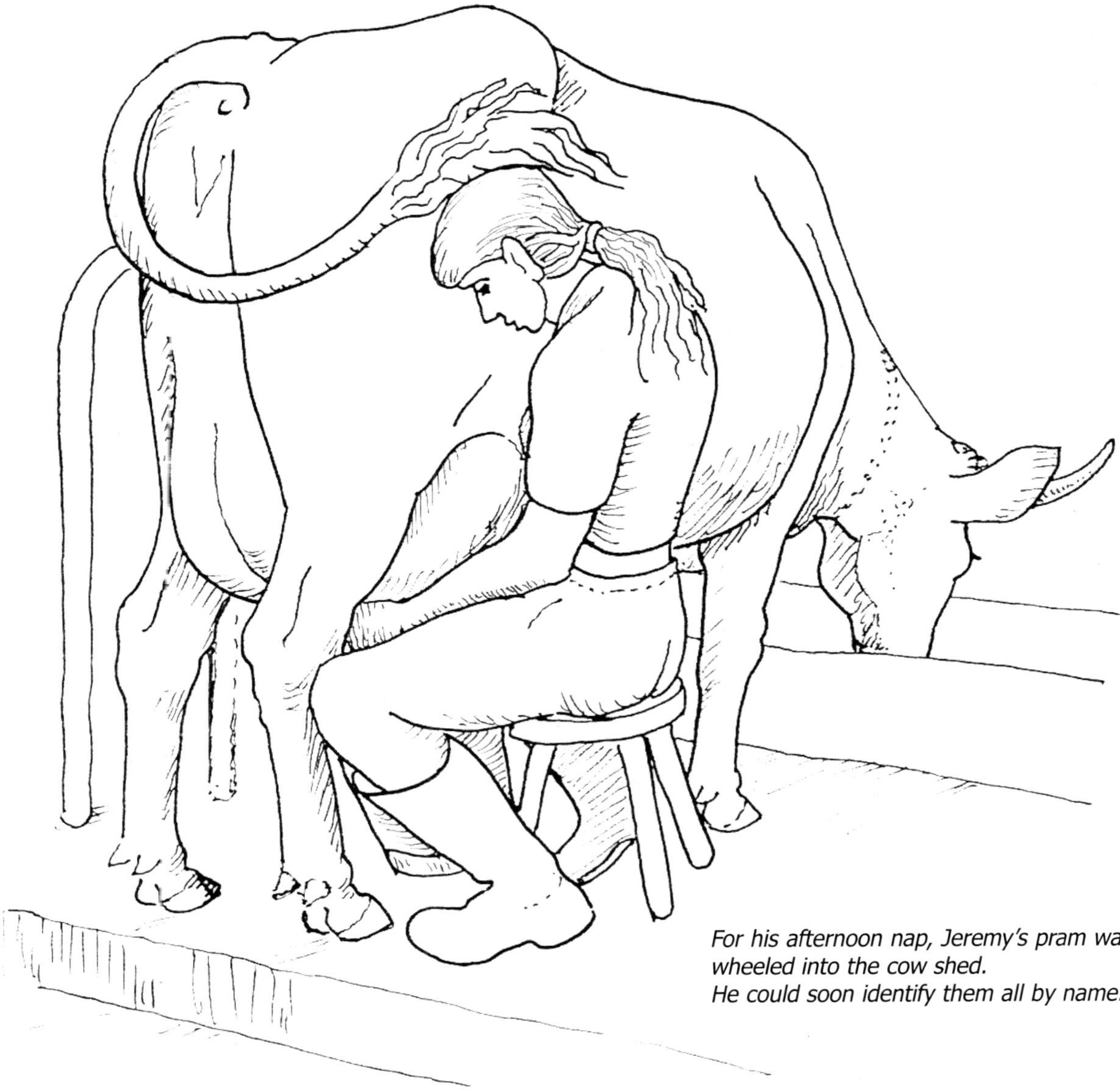

For his afternoon nap, Jeremy's pram was wheeled into the cow shed.
He could soon identify them all by name.

Some individual cows would cunningly wait until the bucket was nearly full and then, with one swift movement of the leg, send it and its contents flying. Such cows might have their hocks strapped together with kicking straps, or ropes attached to rings on the wall at ankle height. Of course, the ropes were just right for tripping those walking behind in the dark. I have seen a kitten being retrieved from a bucket of milk into which it had fallen. It was always better not to inspect the filters too closely!

Signs of Heat

The dairy cow's gestation period is nine months, and having calved and joined the herd, she concentrates on giving milk for a lactation of about 300 days. Then she has a short 'dry' period before calving again at approximately the same time each year. The calving interval is an important factor in dairy management and it demands that the cow should be inseminated about three months after calving. The cow is in season for only two days each month, and since no bull runs with a herd these days, it follows that the cowman must be alert to signs of heat (ovulation), so that the cow can be penned and the AI man (artificial inseminator) can be called without delay.

Fortunately, in every herd of cows, there are some individuals that point out the animals on heat by behaving like rampant lesbians, mounting on the backs of those ready to be served. The mind boggles at the thought of what would happen if humans behaved this way once a month!

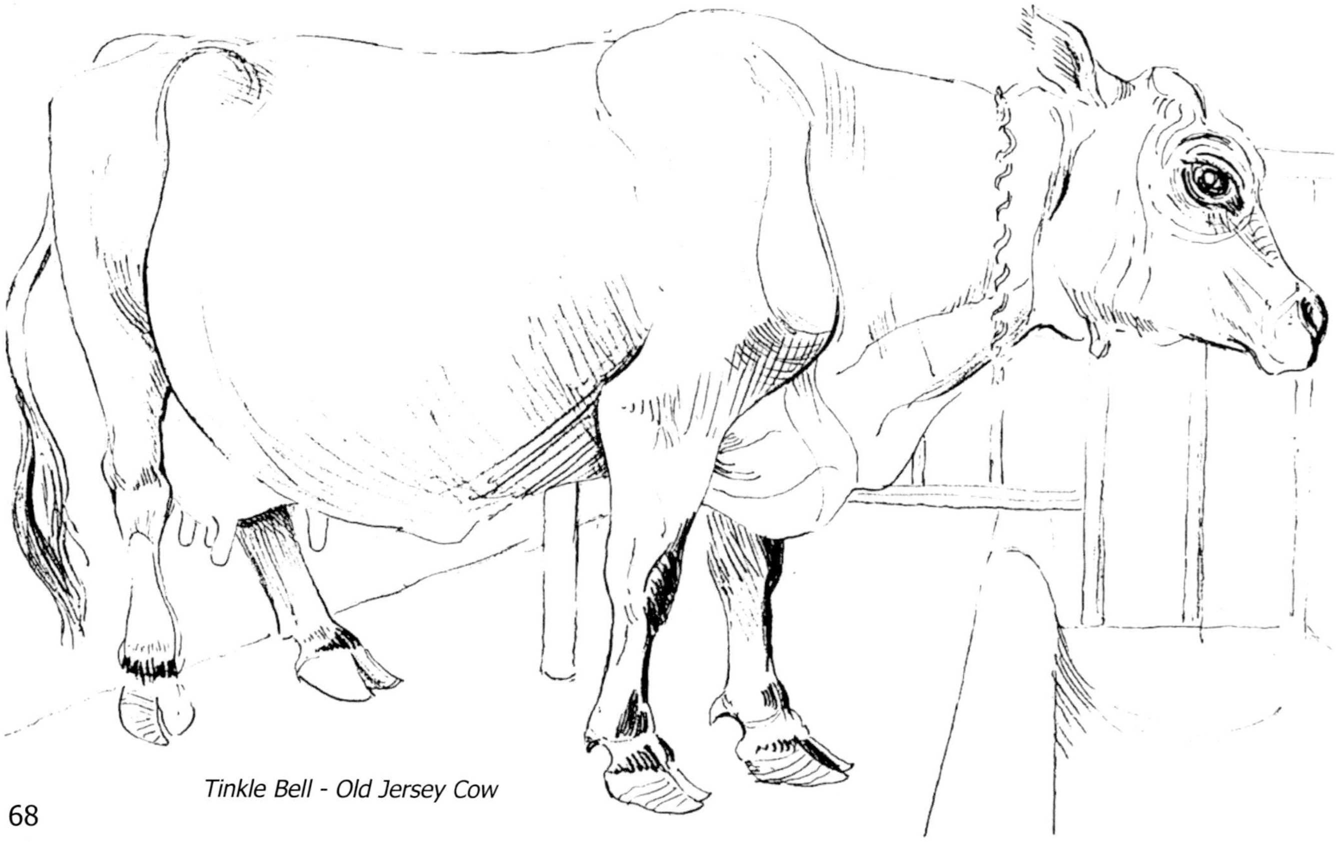

Tinkle Bell - Old Jersey Cow

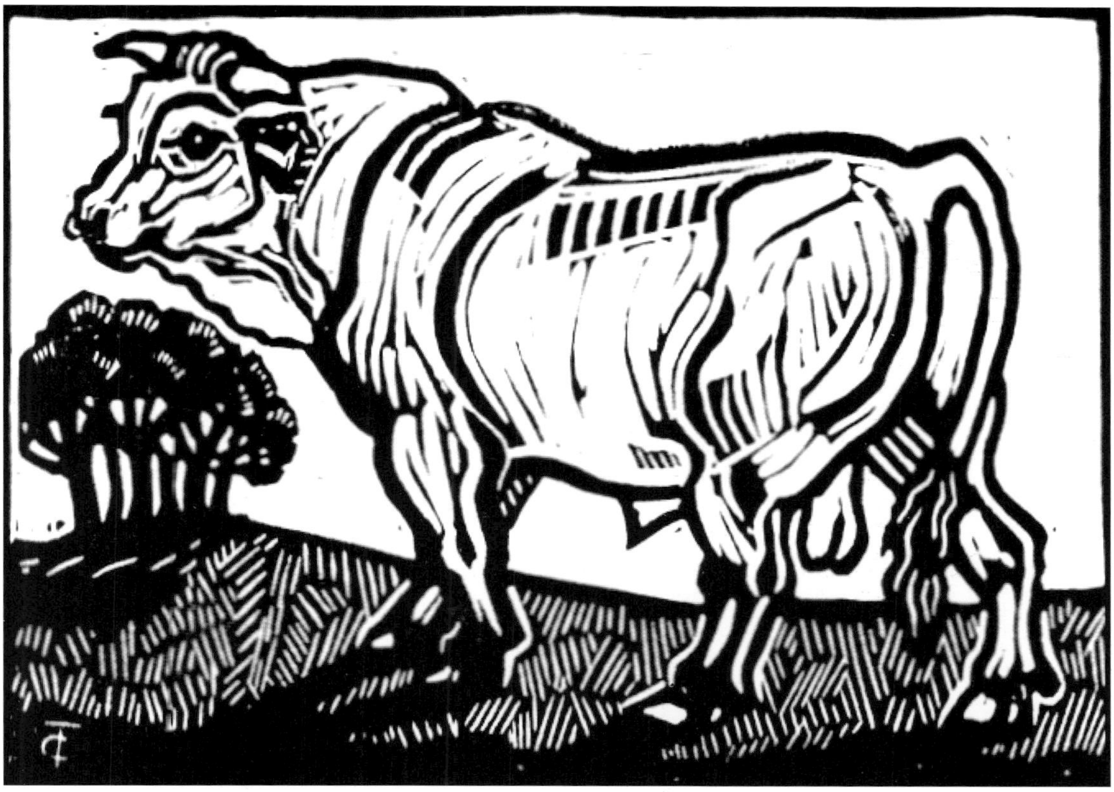

Short Horn Bull
Linocut

Establishing a Pecking Order

In a herd of cows, as in any group of animals or even people, there is a quite evident pecking order. A hierarchy occurs as some creatures establish their dominance over others. This will be seen as they have to pass through a gate or approach a drinking place. Those with inferior status will stand deferentially to one side while the leaders proceed.

When, in the interest of efficiency, cattle were housed loose in yards as opposed to being chained in individual stalls, it was found that there was an unacceptable amount of bullying. Spitefully dominant individuals would corner a victim and inflict serious injury, even death, to it. As this was usually caused by horns, a policy of dehorning was introduced. It is illegal to load or pen horned and dehorned cattle together. Some of the old show ring herdsmen protested mightily as they used to train, smooth and polish these pretty but useless appurtenances.

Some breeds, such as the Poll Angus and the Red Poll, are naturally hornless (polled) so it may be possible to breed the horns away. Nowadays, the vast majority of calves are treated at a tender age so that, as the blood supply is cut off, the horn buds do not grow.

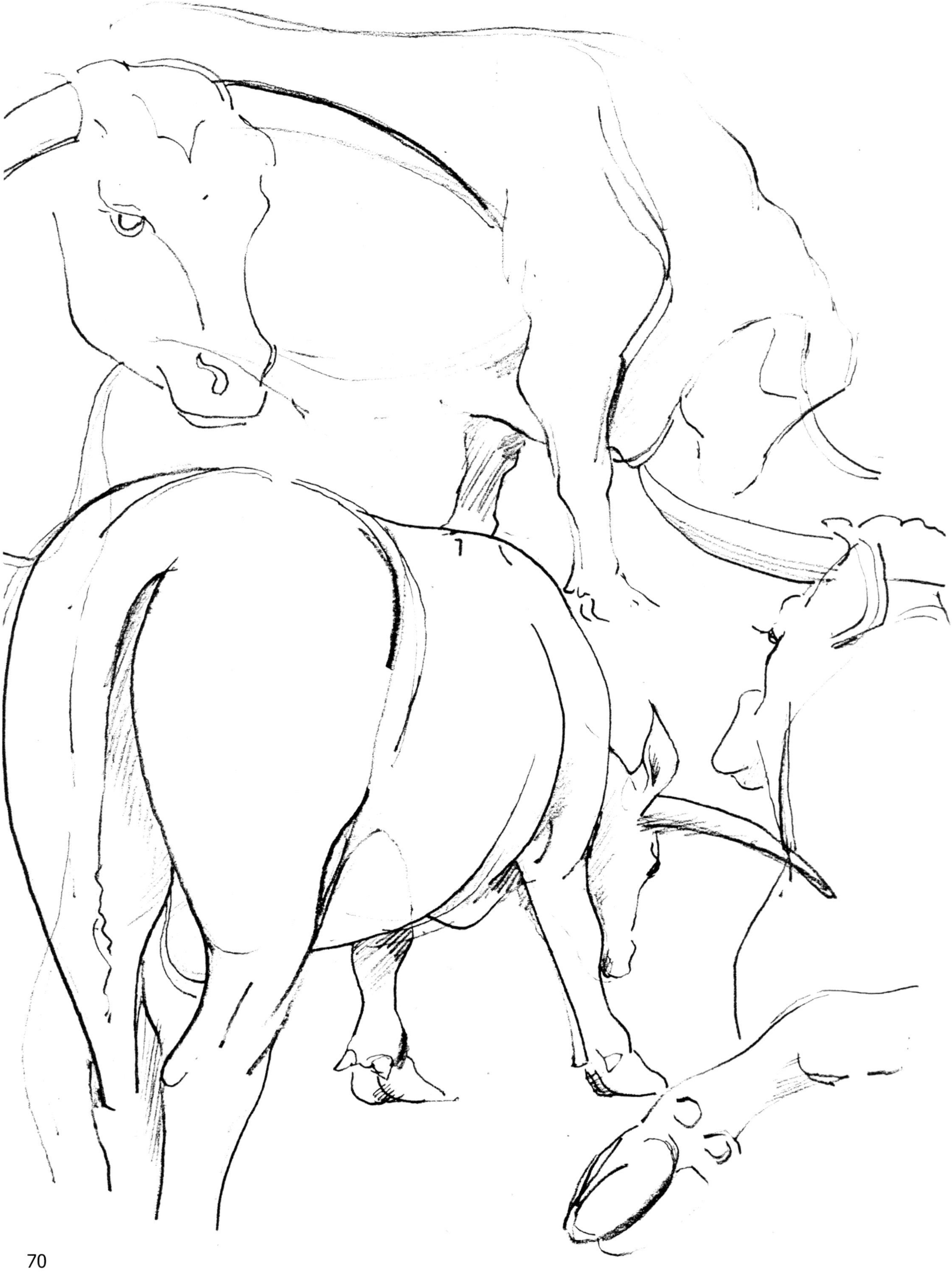

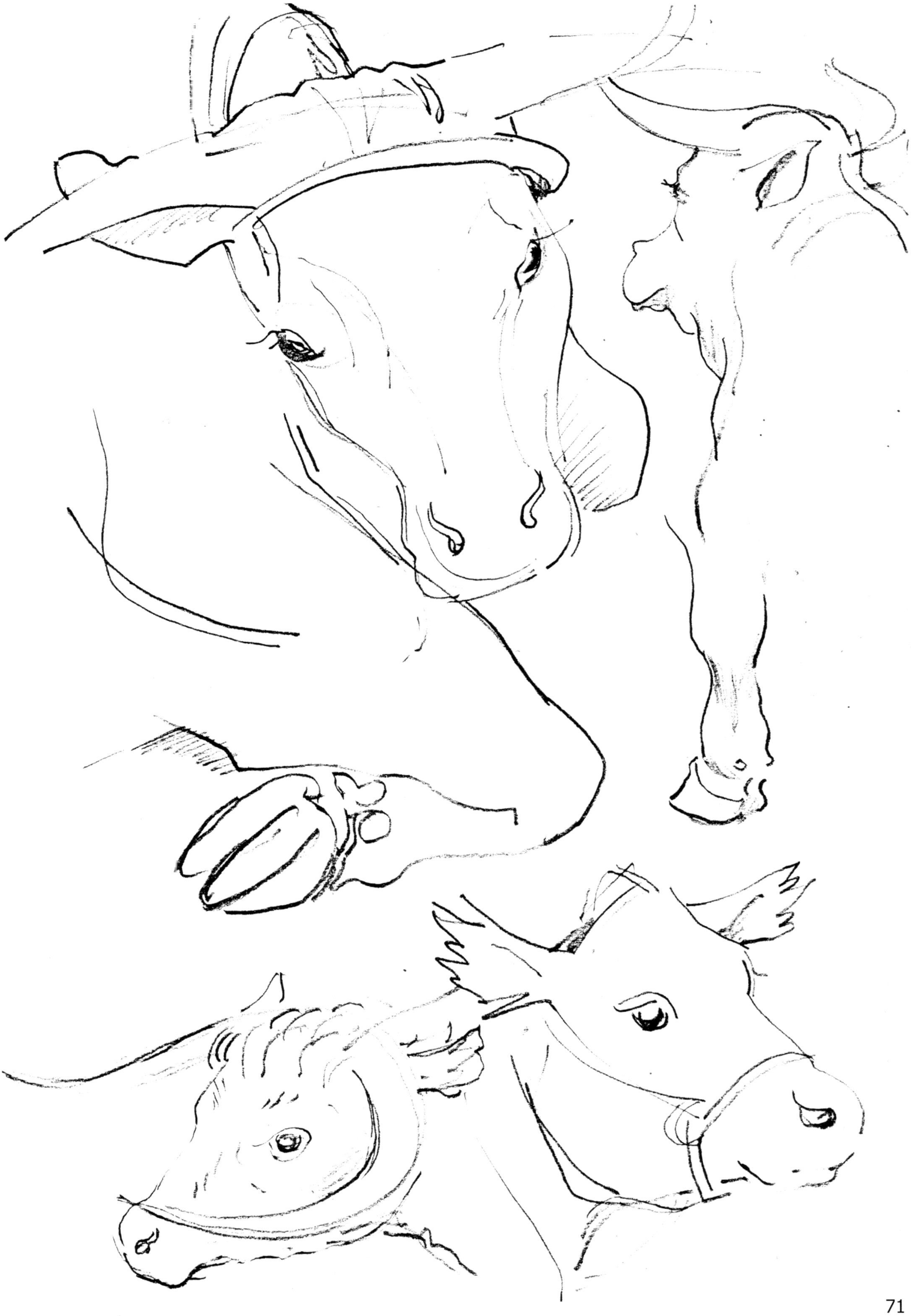

Stock lines at an agricultural show

Menace of the Gadfly

The countryman was heard to say, "The wife's gone gadding off to town today so we'll have to get us our own dinner". When the weather was hot and thundery, grazing cattle could be observed to stop cropping the grass or ruminating and become highly agitated. Then they would start *gadding*. As they stampeded, calling out in terror, they would hold their tails vertically or even curled over their backs as a signal or protection against the bites of the gadfly. To get some relief, they would usually rush for the nearest cool, shady pond or drinking place, and then splash in up to their bellies to submerge their legs. In this mad stampede they would be virtually unstoppable, breaking through hedges and fences in their panic as if the barriers did not exist, like a heifer on heat.

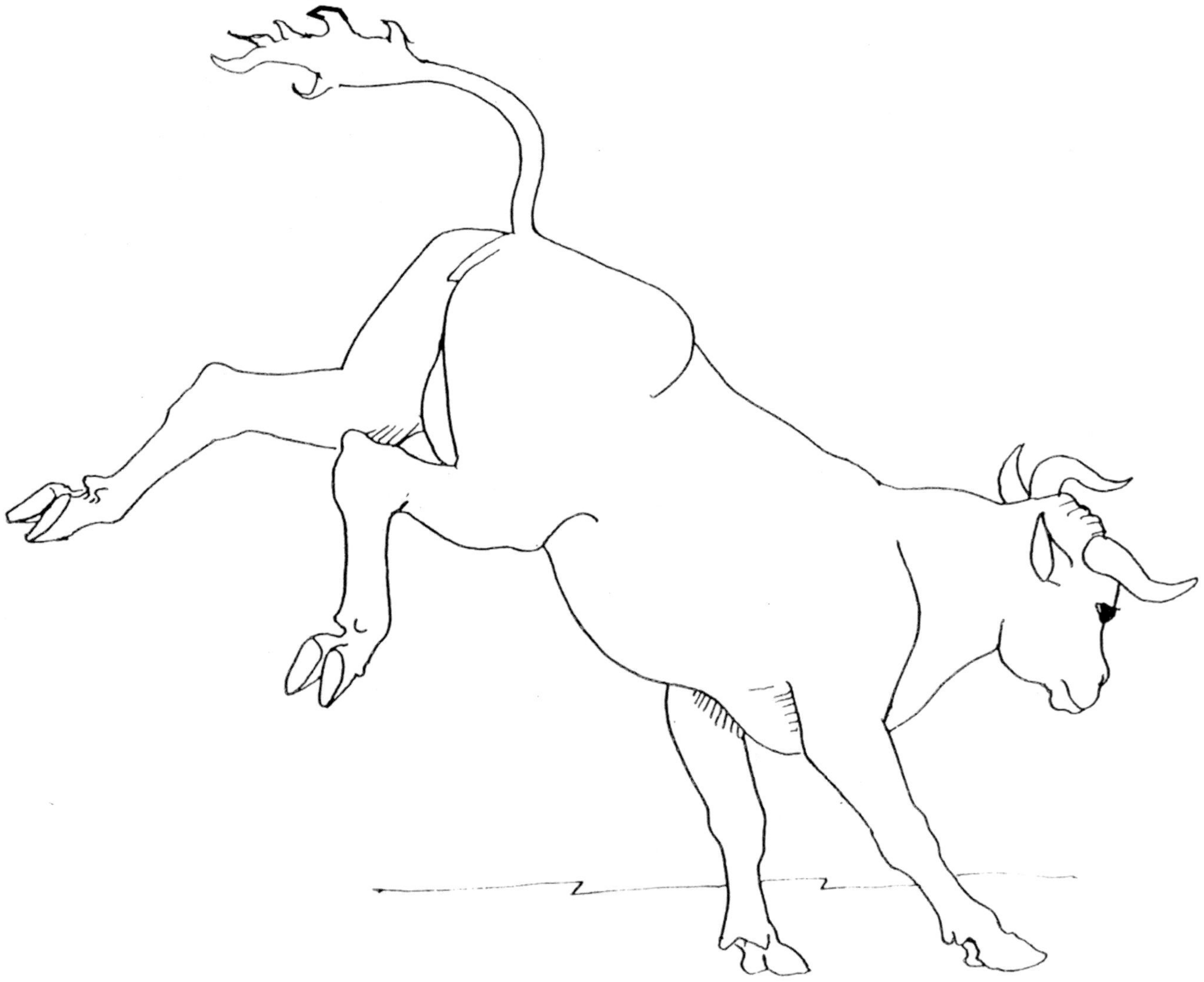

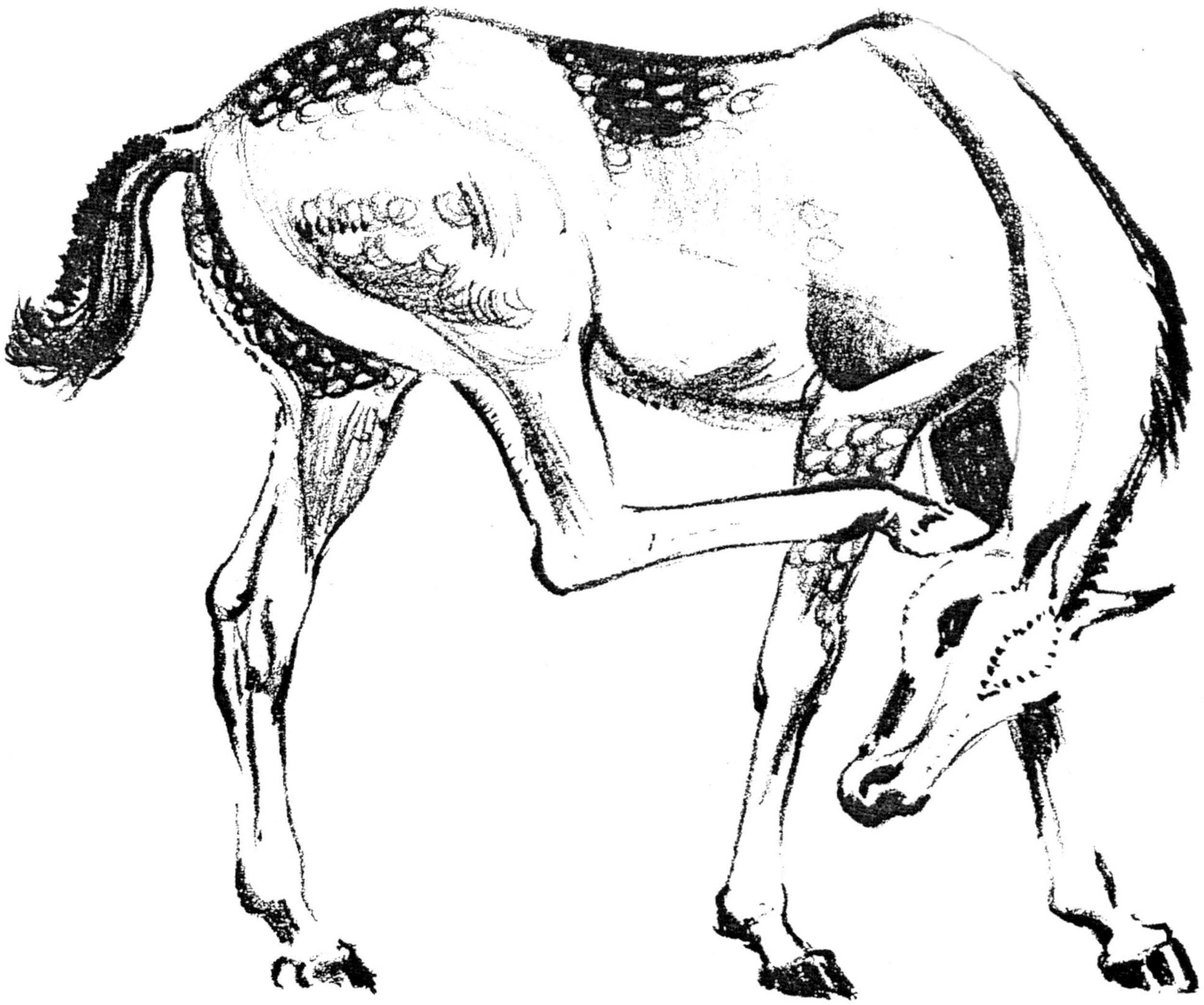

The warble-fly, which has no mouth, is about the size of a bumblebee and lays its eggs on the legs of cattle. The animals become unwilling hosts to the grubs of this fly, which migrate painfully through its tissues. The grubs emerge the following summer by piercing holes in the hide along the back, spoiling the hide for leather purposes. In recent years, owing to nationwide compulsory treatment, this pest has been virtually eliminated. The decline in the use of oxen as draught animals for tilling fields was partly due to their unpredictable behaviour if the gadfly was about. Horses are much less afraid of it and rarely get warbled, though it is not unknown. They have to contend with the botfly which lays its eggs on their forelegs. These are licked off and the maggots burrow under the tongue and then find their way into the stomach, where they remain for about nine to ten months. They pass out in the dung, the fly hatches out, and the cycle starts again.

Ploughing with Oxen

In early times, oxen were almost universally used for ploughing. Heavy horses, ancestors of our Shires, Clydesdales and Suffolks, were much fewer and kept as chargers for the knights and noblemen. When lighter ploughs were designed that could be pulled by two horses, the old teams of six and eight oxen were generally abandoned. When they were used for drawing carts on the road by means of the yoke on the shoulders, it might be necessary to have oxen shod. The cloven hooves were fitted with two plates. Beef cattle being sent long distances by road from Scotland or Wales to London would be accompanied by a smith, who would mend and replace shoes which had been broken or lost on the journey. A journey of 300 miles could be completed in about three weeks.

Oxen are slower, more placid and cheaper to feed than horses. Their natural grease causes the leather harness to remain supple with use rather than becoming brittle as it does with horses. I am told that the ox-ploughman had only three or four songs which he sang continually over and over again; when the singing ceased, the oxen stood still in their tracks until it recommenced. In spite of what I have said about animals being specially reared for prime beef, it was quite common to have what were known as *dual purpose* cattle such as the Shorthorn, which were good milkers and whose male progeny made good beef. With draught animals, as oxen used for fieldwork, you get the possibility of *triple purpose* breeds where you finally eat the tough old meat of the beast that tilled your land!

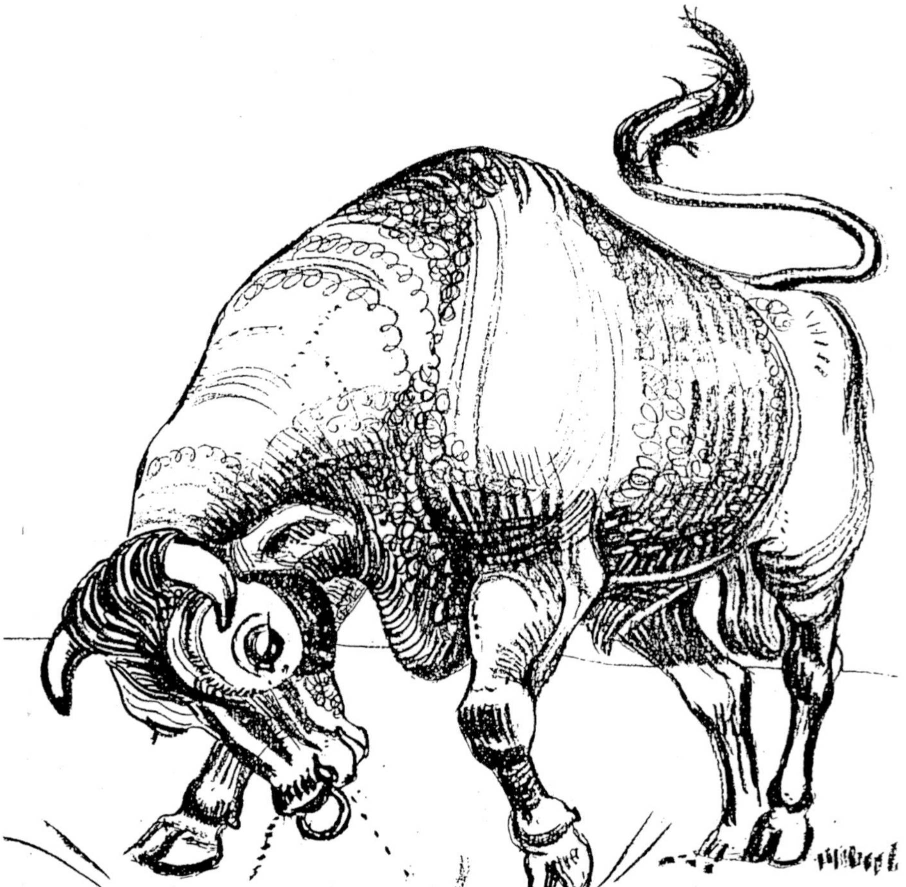

Short Horn Bull - lithograph 1963

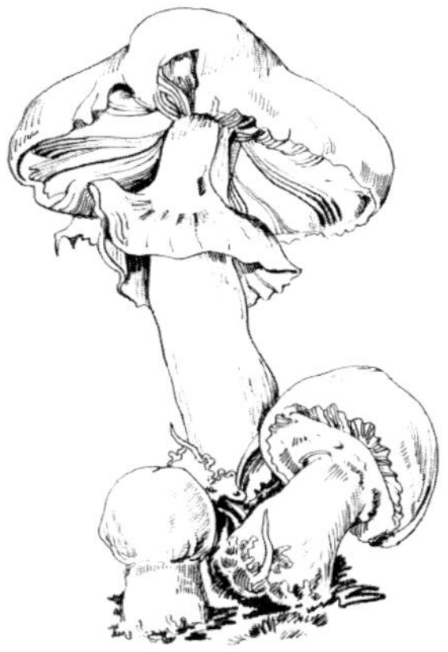

Small Farmers Diversified to Survive

Many of my neighbours in Leicestershire were small farmers who found it necessary to augment their incomes by sidelines, diversification and part-time jobs. Some might work in the local livestock markets, penning sheep and calves and recording the weights of cattle for the auctioneers. Others, with a flair for machinery, would become agricultural contractors who would carry out cultivations and harvesting, hedge cutting, fencing and ditching for the other farmers in their neighbourhood.

One of my neighbours became a potato merchant and another had a cattle lorry for hire. One farmer set up his daughter with a garden centre and another took in garden mowing machines to sharpen and repair. A man who lived in the village used his horse and tumbril to collect 'night soil' to spread about his fields, which grew excellent tomatoes as a result! Another man's horse and cart would be used by the local authority for him to patch the roads and trim the verges. One of my friends found work for a man and his two sons with JCB digger-loaders and excavators.

One retired farmer worked for the Milk Marketing Board, visiting farms each week to record the amount of milk and taking samples from each cow. Another used to inspect calves for the Ministry of Agriculture. In our district, many of the lanes had extraordinarily wide verges upon which our children loved to race their ponies. In summer, it was quite common to see these verges grazed by a herd of eight to twelve dairy cows in charge of a farmer's wife. She might be busily knitting as she ambled along using the free roadside paddocks, so that her husband the farmer could take hay from one of their small-holding meadows. This occupation was known locally as *tenting* which I suppose is a corruption of *tending* (the cattle).

As it was in the industrial revolution of early Victorian times, so in the silent agricultural revolution that has taken place in my lifetime; its progress seems quite ruthless regardless of the sensibilities of man or beast. Rather as a mighty fire creates its own draught, so is its progress seemingly inevitable and irreversible.

Once the sewing machine was invented, no-one would think of making a suit by hand and, if so, who could pay for it?

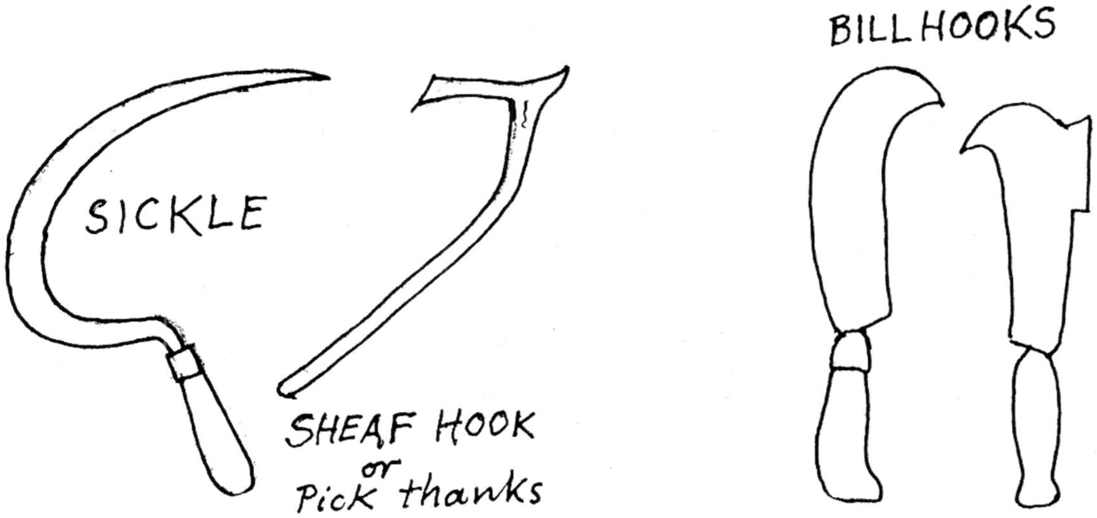

The Menace of Foot and Mouth Disease

On one occasion, when foot and mouth disease came to a farm three miles away, our spirits sank to an all time low point at the prospect of compulsory slaughter of all our lovely pedigree pure-bred cloven-hoofed stock. KEEP OUT notices were posted at our gates and all vehicles had to pass through strong disinfectant. Movement of livestock off the farm was prohibited so that cash flow was restricted, and expenses soared as bacon pigs went well beyond their sell-by weight and became heavy hogs worth much less per pound of meat! It was like throwing good money after bad. The more feed one provided, the less the animals would be worth, and one could not let them starve.

A similar situation exists at the time of lifting early potatoes because, as the crop is growing and increasing in bulk at the same time, the price is rapidly dropping. For instance, one might have to decide to lift five tonnes at £300 per tonne against ten tonnes at £150 per tonne six weeks later. In the second case, you handle twice as much produce for the same return of £1,500. Livestock are subject to many infections and contagious notifiable diseases such as tuberculosis, swine fever, scrapie and contagious abortion. As some of these may be spread by human contact, it may well account for a farmer's instinctive reluctance to have all and sundry tramping over his land.

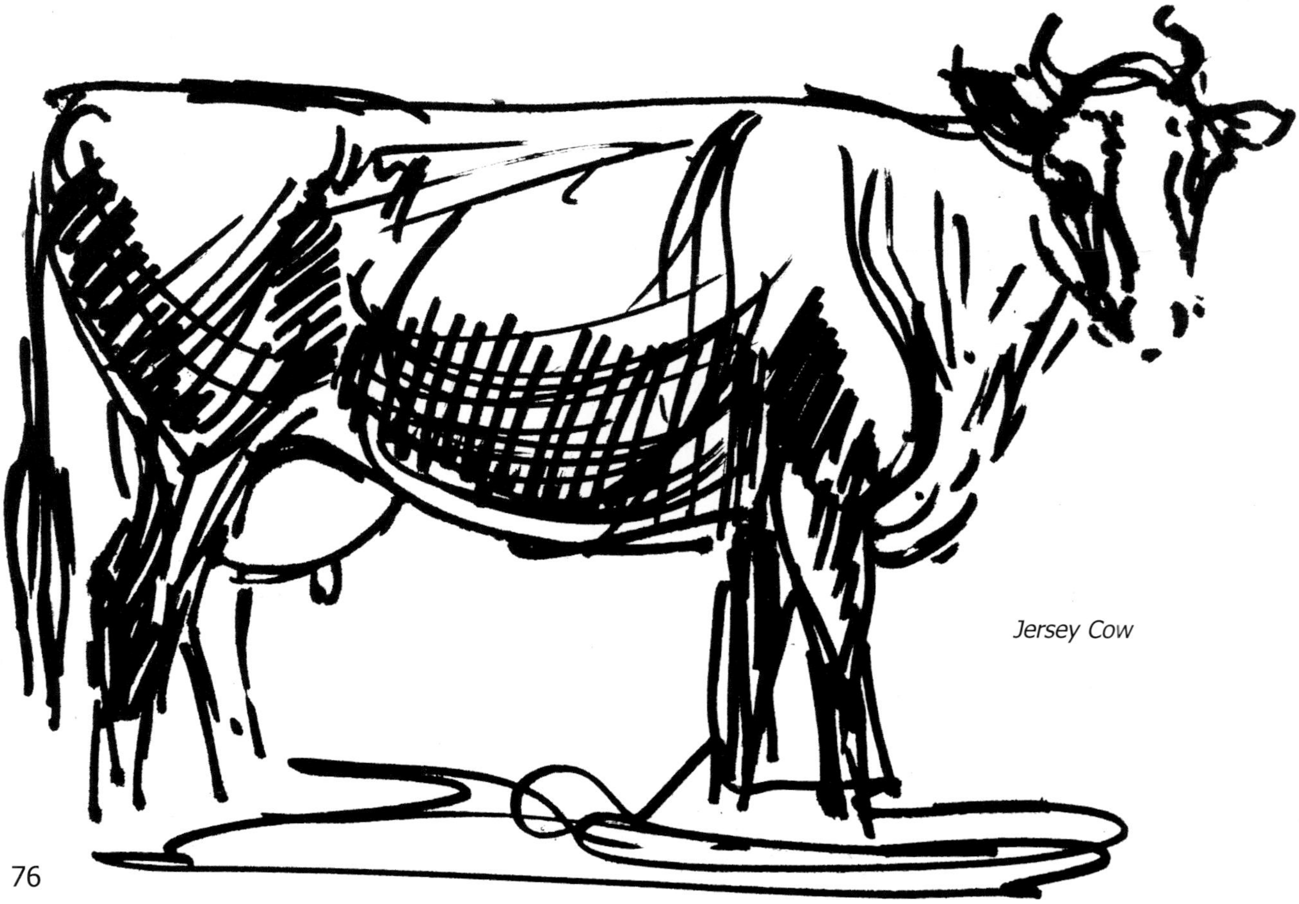

Jersey Cow

Trochar and Cannula for Bloat

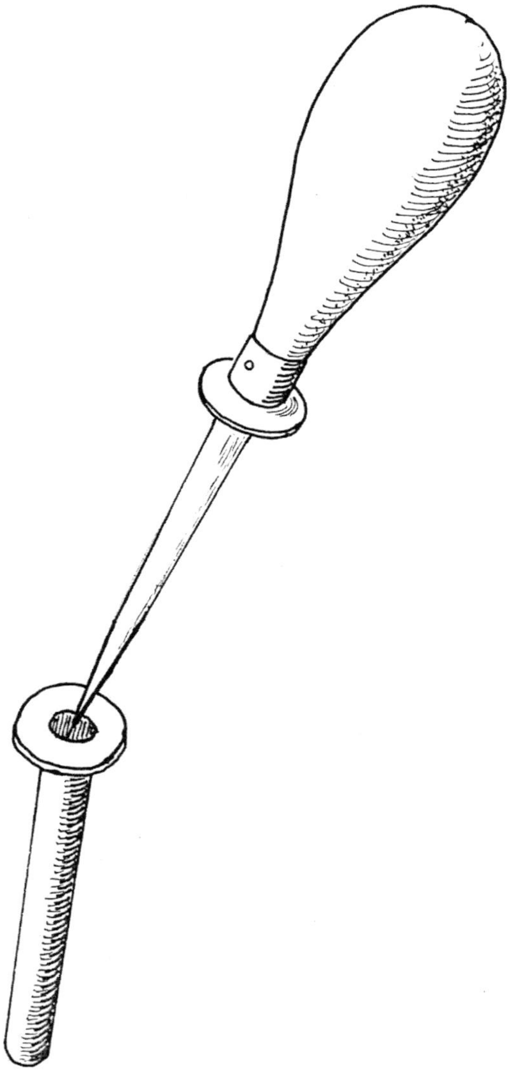

Necessity is the mother of invention, and also intervention.

In the days when clover leys featured in our crop rotation, it was quite common for sheep and cattle to suffer from hoven, or bloat, caused by the methane gas produced by prolonged grazing of this rich feed. The stomach becomes distended to an alarming degree and, if the gas is not released, death follows swiftly. Cows could be relieved sometimes by giving a drink (known as a drench) of linseed oil and turpentine to make them burp. However, the turpentine would immediately taint the milk, rendering it useless for a couple of days. As there would be no time to wait for the arrival of a vet, provident farmers and shepherds would provide themselves with a trochar and cannula - a circular pointed spear similar to the butcher's sharpening steel surrounded by a close fitting tube somewhat like a large pea-shooter. The two together would be plunged with great force into the appropriate place and when the spear was withdrawn the gas made its way out through the tube.

It was as well to warn any smokers around, as the presence of a naked flame in the vicinity could cause an unpleasant explosion! A farmer is always supposed to carry a knife, a piece of string and a sixpence (£1 coin now). I have been known to release the gas from a sheep using a penknife and a goose quill inserted in the hole. A cow's drench would induce it to cough, but these creatures have perfected the art of coughing simultaneously at both ends with deadly accuracy, so one soon learned to stand well clear!

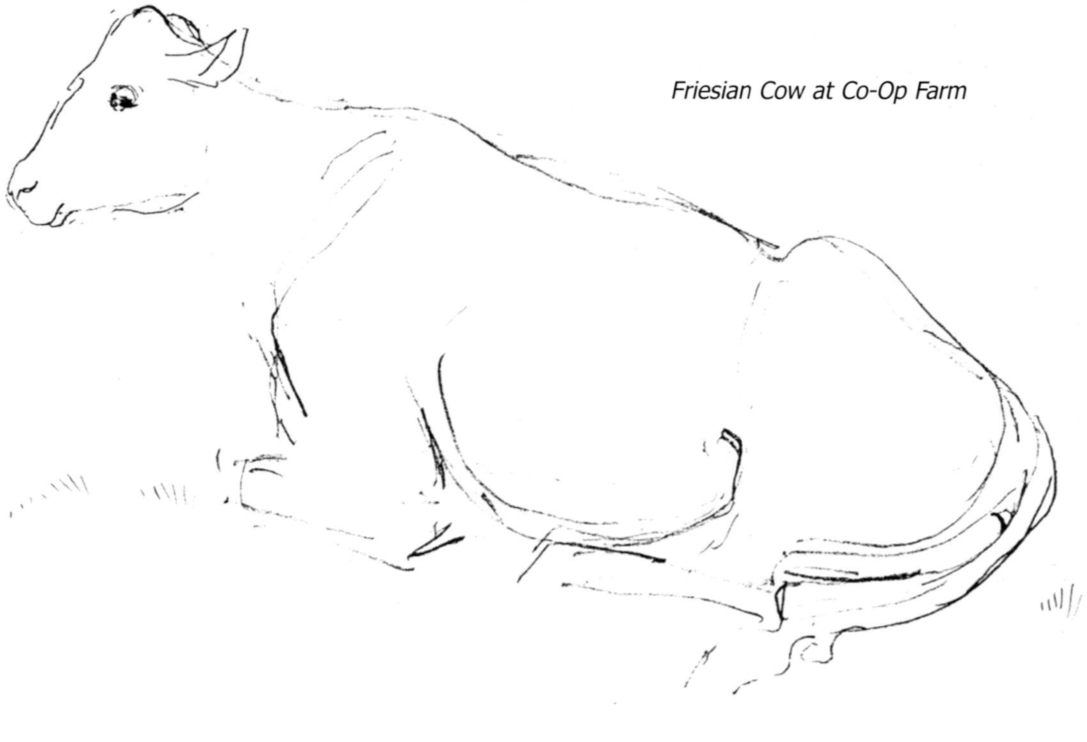

Friesian Cow at Co-Op Farm

Calcium Boroglucinate for Milk Fever

This land, this dusting of fertility seeded with life from the loins of the seas. This crust, this loam, this land, this clay; our cradle and our larder; this good earth, our blanket when we sleep at last. This is the surface and the substance of all we know of Life.

In accordance with good husbandry practice, it is advisable to have the soil on a farm tested at regular intervals. One of the top dressings a contractor will spread for you is lime, resulting in clouds of white dust which can be seen from miles away. The continuous selling off of meat and bone and thousands of gallons of milk is a constant drain on the resources of lime in the soil. A cow or heifer, in full flush of milk shortly after calving, is apt to go down with milk fever, caused by the sudden depletion of calcium in her system. She will lie on her side in a comatose state such that the observer might be forgiven for assuming that her end is nigh. However, do not despair, for armed with the knowledge of modern veterinary science, the farmer will select from his medicine chest a dark bottle containing calcium boroglucinate. This he administers either subcutaneously or intravenously through a flutter-valve held high in the air so that gravity causes the flow.

On coming back after as little as thirty minutes, one invariably would find the spectacular cure had worked and the stricken beast would be on her feet munching her cud. A smaller dose would effect the same cure for heavy milking ewes in a like condition. In pre-war years, I once saw a farmer with a bicycle pump inflating the udder of a cow and tying off the teats with bandages to keep the air in. When I had recovered from my astonishment it was revealed that he was in fear of milk fever and was therefore sending a message to the cow through the distended udder telling her not to deplete her calcium store further by secreting more milk!

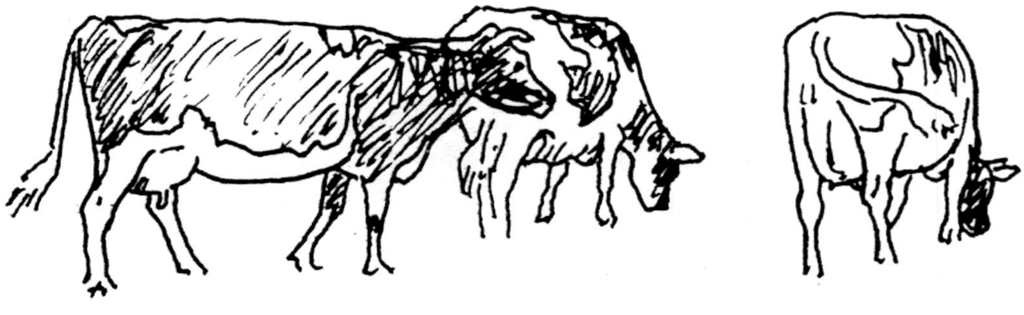

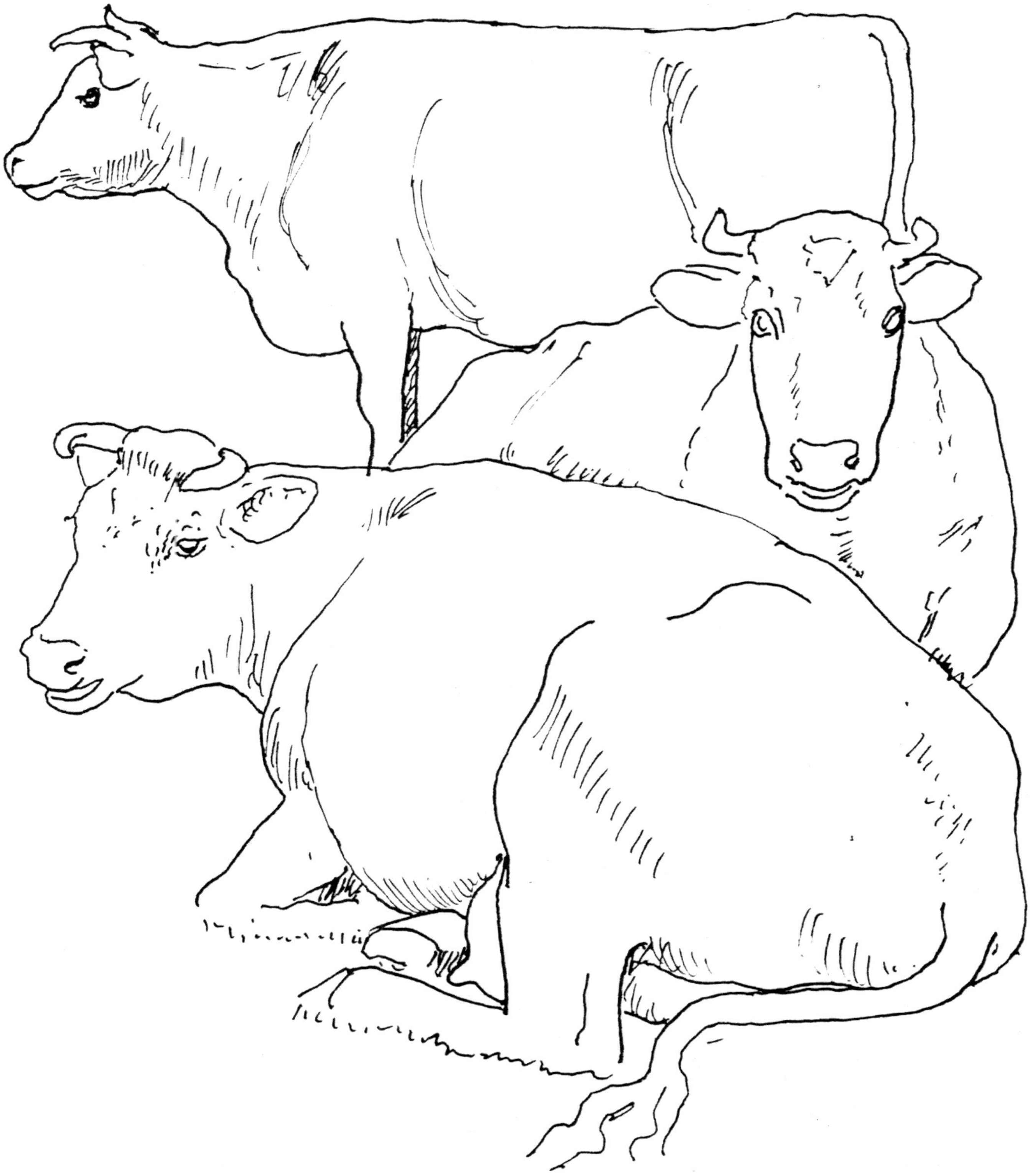

Shorthorn cattle chewing their cuds

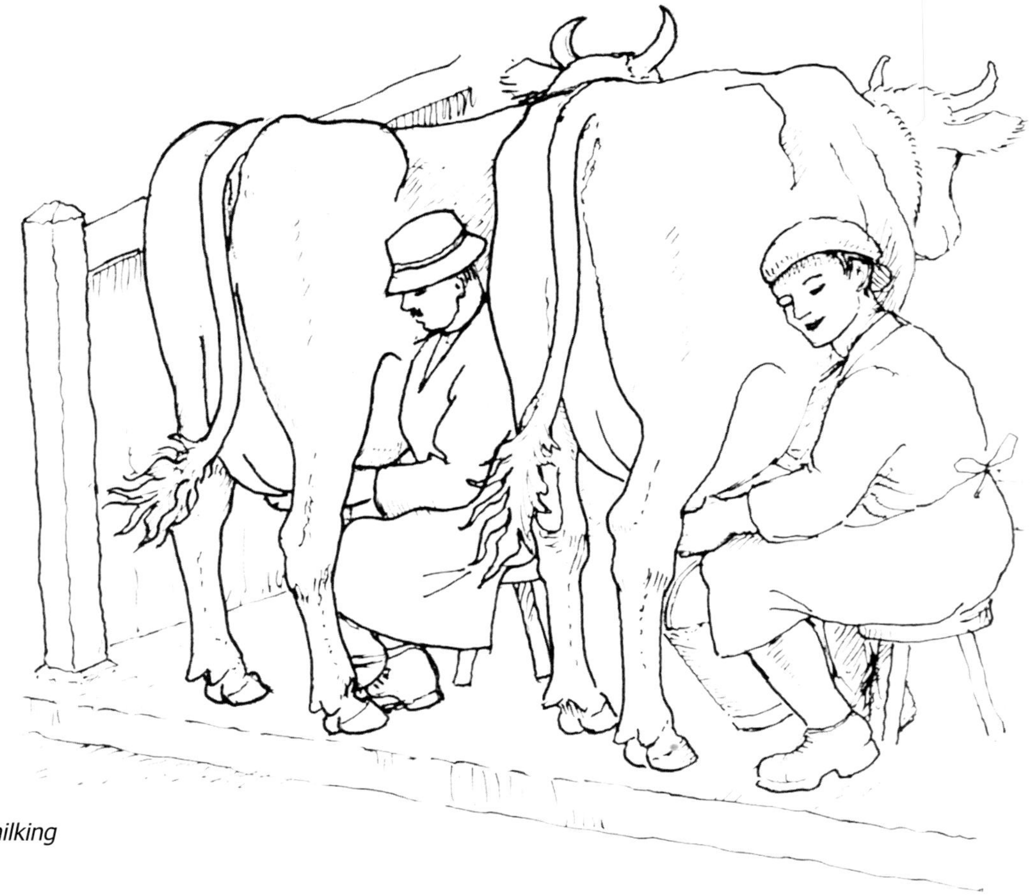

Hand milking

Four Stages in Mechanising Milking

Let us take the business of milking cows: I have lived to see it go through at least four discernible stages.

1. A man would be exhausted after milking ten cows by hand which would take about two hours, night and morning.

2. Then an electric vacuum pump was introduced and with portable sealed buckets he could milk thirty in the same time. The hand milker's days were numbered because his milk cost three times as much to produce.

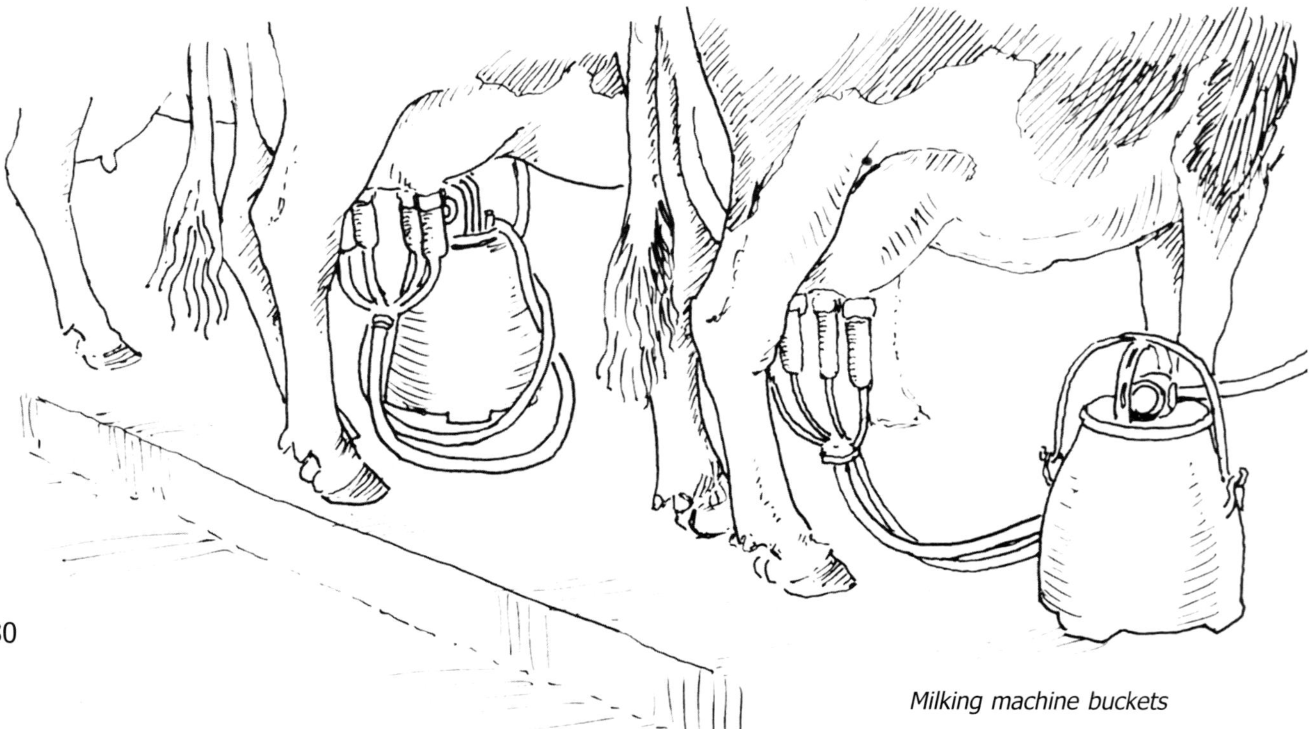

Milking machine buckets

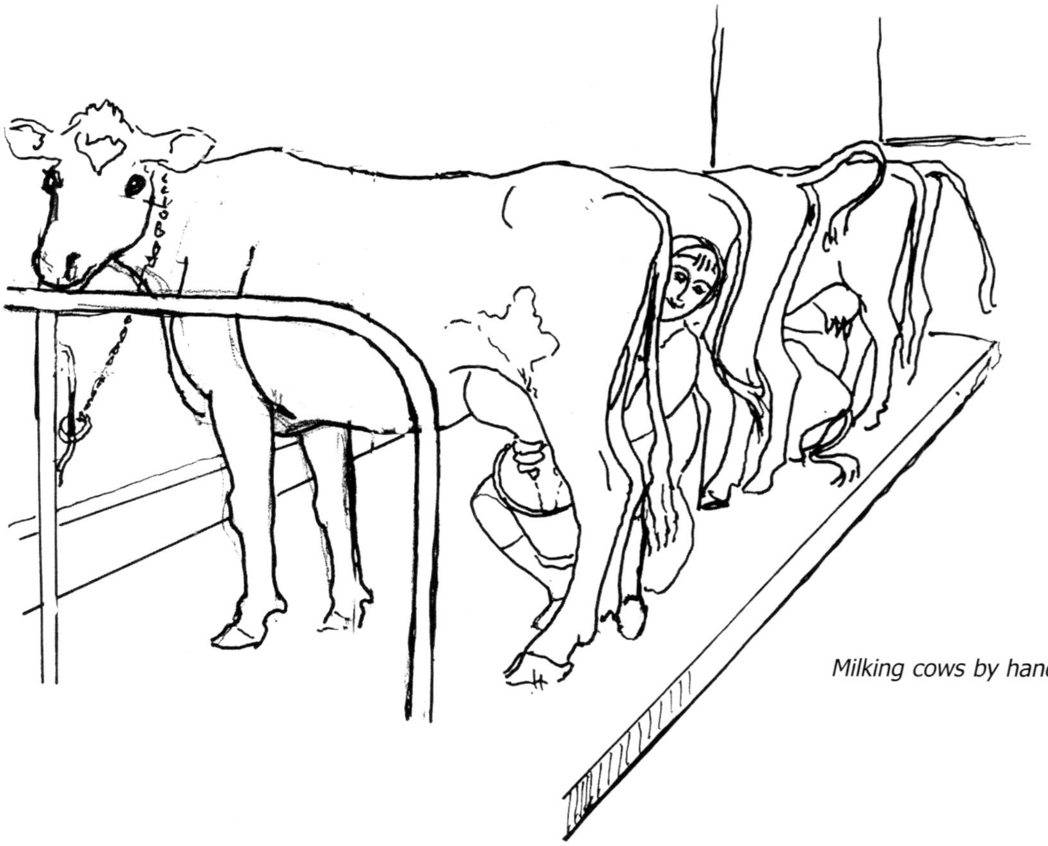

Milking cows by hand

3. Then a milking parlour was invented and instead of the operator walking between their stalls, the cows came to him and stood on concrete platforms to save him having to walk about and bend his back. This way a man might be expected to cope with sixty cows. The sealed bucket man's days were numbered. The price of milk and wages were geared to one man milking sixty cows twice a day, not thirty as before.

4. Finally, a herring-bone type milking machine was invented whereby the operator works in a pit with the cows coming in 16 or 20 at a time and standing with their udders at his eye level. This enables him to milk 120 cows a day or more.

When one method supersedes another, men are laid off and the unit cost is lower so that the milk can be sold more cheaply to the consumer. No way would anyone pay ten times as much for the doubtful privilege of having it milked by hand into an open pail!

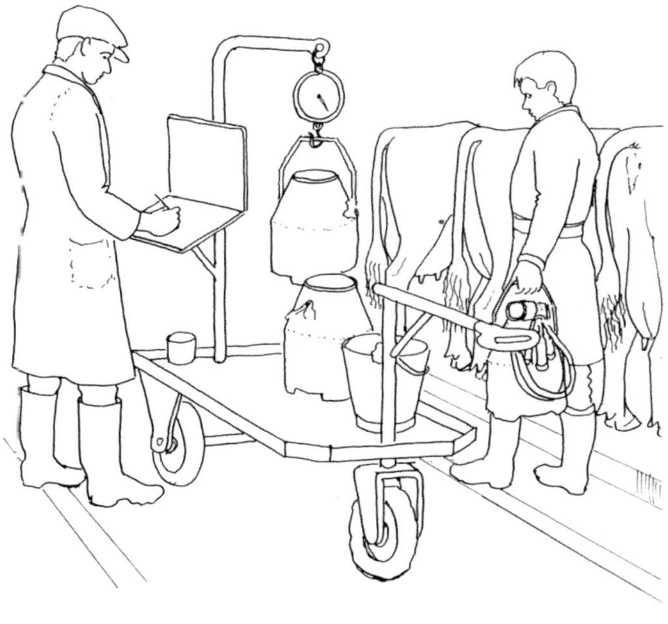

Dick Walker, the herdsman, and Bruce, the apprentice

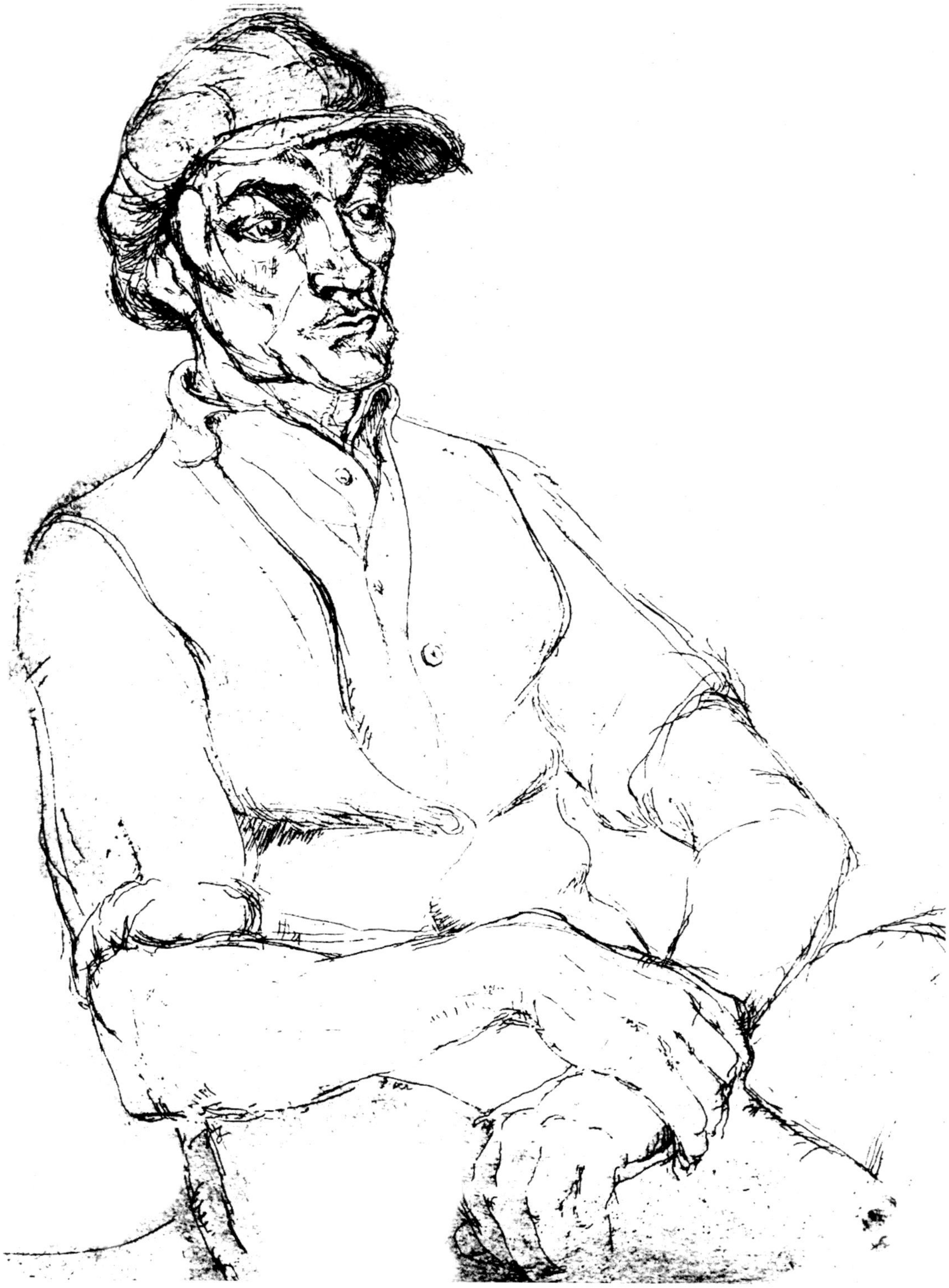

Horace, the herdsman, who thought that the Aurora Borealis was the Germans practicing their searchlights

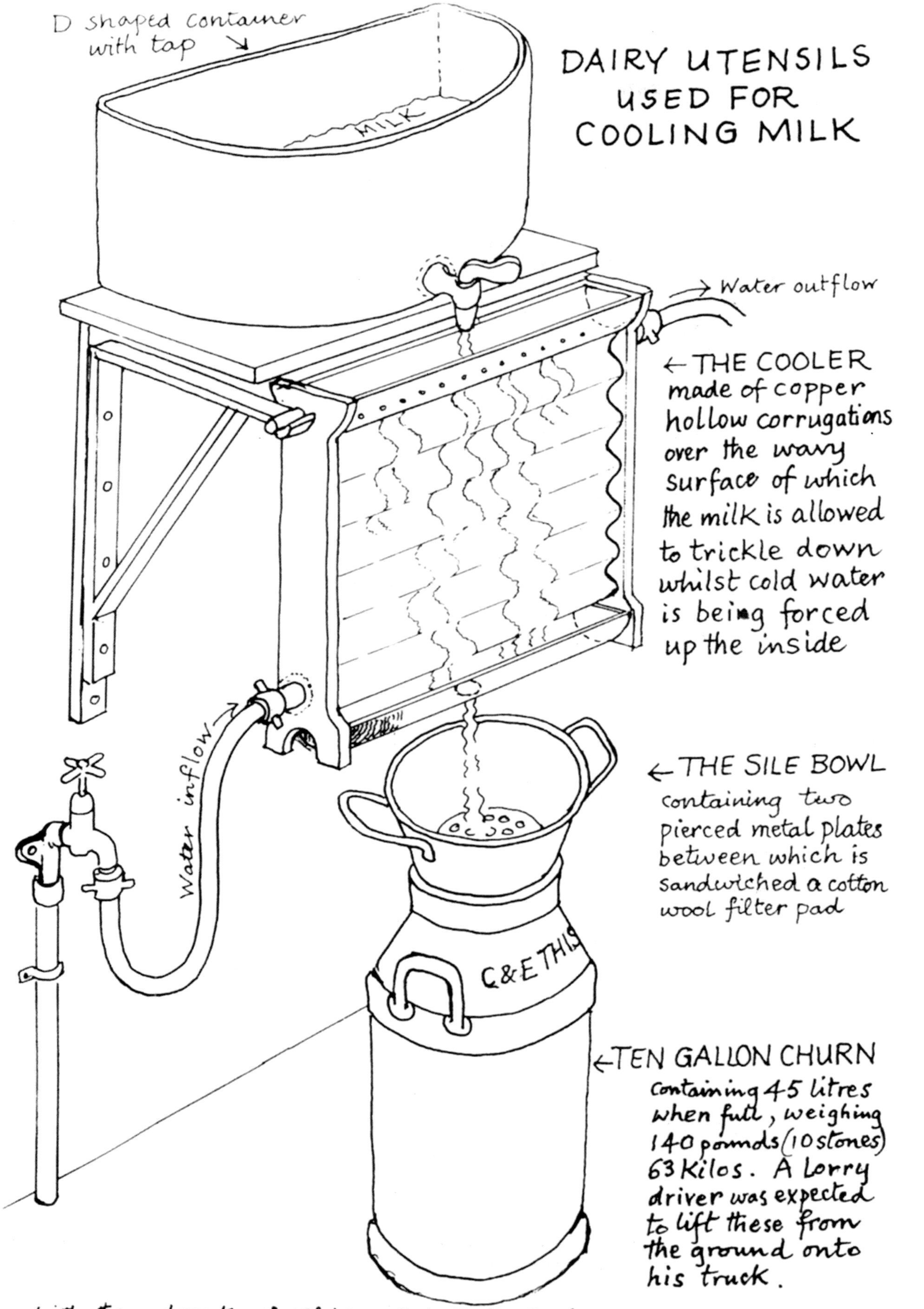

With the advent of refrigerated Bulk Tanks, a million milk churns have all but disappeared from the farming scene. In the days of my youth there was a platform milk churn stand on the road side at each dairy farm gate throughout the land & they were never vandalised!

Bulls

When the pedigree bull was about ten months old, a young man was instructed on how to groom him and lead him about each day, holding a rope attached to his headstall (halter) to prepare him for the show ring.

The show bull is indulged with a gourmet menu and becomes accustomed to rich living. As he rapidly becomes too big for his boots, he prances about on the end of his tether and refuses to be led along the path of righteousness. Then is the time when he must be ringed.

There is a hand tool, somewhat like an immense ticket hole-puncher, which neatly punches a round hole in the gristle between the nostrils. This is followed immediately by fixing a copper ring, ½" thick and 2½" diameter, through the hole. The ring is hinged on one side and after being inserted, it is held closed by a very small grub screw on the other. Like many things in life, the instructions are easily given, but in reality the execution is quite different! The creature's massive head must be restrained and its horns can be quite lethal. Having his nose pierced does not exactly put in him a good mood! To approach this frightened, bellowing animal a second time with the ring requires valour beyond the call of duty... so naturally the farmer himself must do it, or lose face. This minute grub screw has to be inserted and made fast with a screwdriver.

I quickly learned to have someone hold my cap to catch the screw as my trembling hands caused it to fall frequently from the tossing, snorting nose. Then someone had a brilliant idea - the screw and screwdriver were made in one piece, the handle breaking off when tightened!

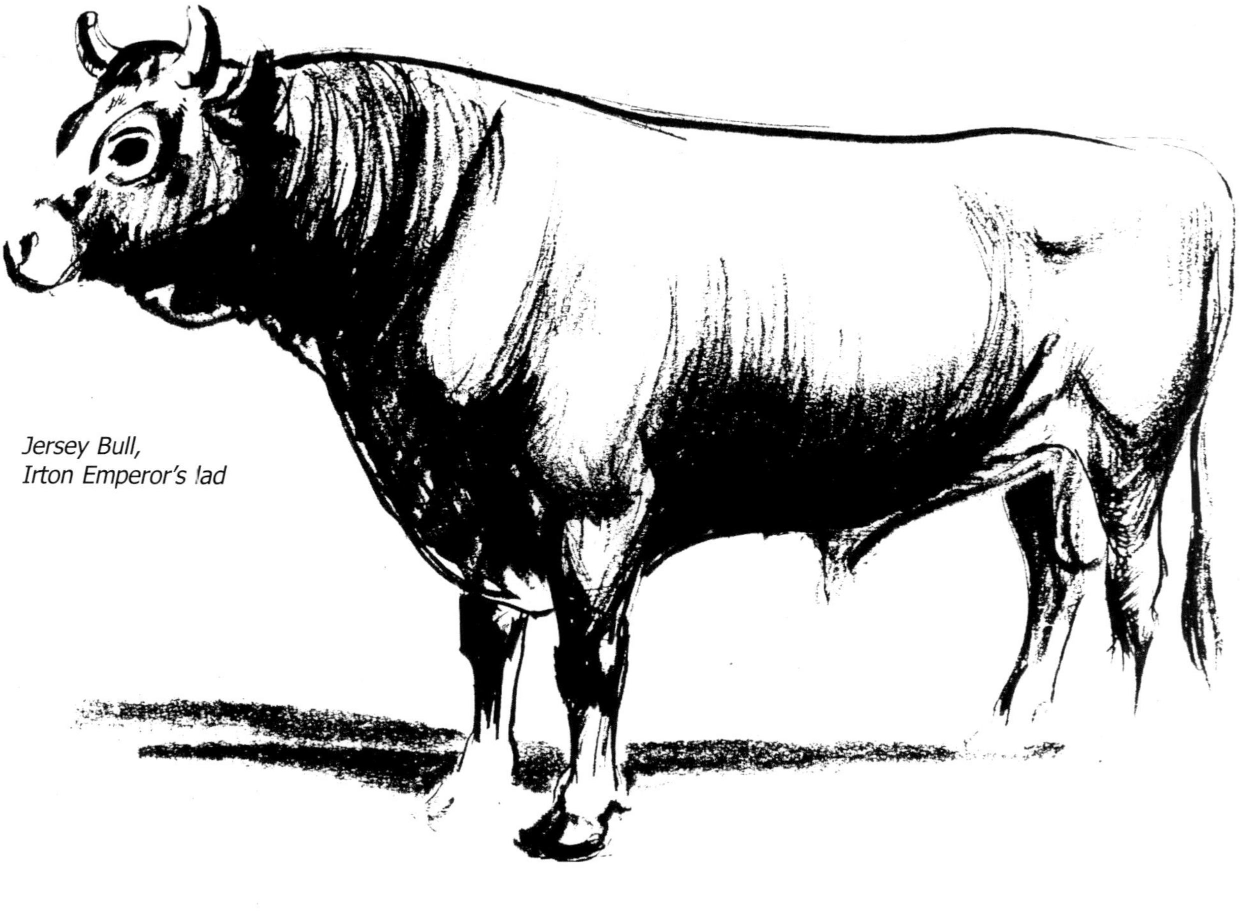

Jersey Bull,
Irton Emperor's lad

Entires are Liable to be Aggressive all the Time

It may not be generally realised that sires of the herds and flocks to be seen on farms are, by definition, uncastrated males, sometimes known as ENtires with the accent on the EN. Over many generations, these have been selected by breeders looking for qualities which include masculinity and a large well-proportioned frame.

Because in the wild he had to protect his herd by fighting off predators and repulsing the attentions of other marauding males, he had to be physically large, active and aggressive at all times, but especially at breeding times. Females can be almost as aggressive in defence of their young, but bulls, stallions, rams and cockerels must be treated with great respect as they are aggressive all the time.

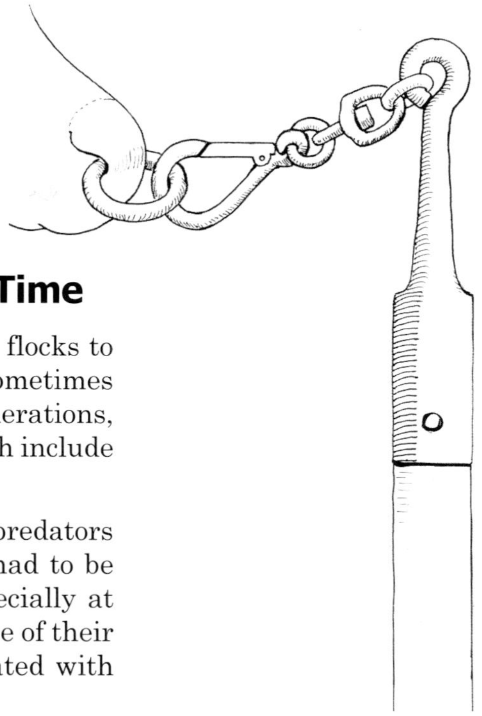

Bull Pole with a swivel link and spring clip to go through the nose ring.

In general, the bulls from beef breeds such as Herefords are more placid than those of the dairy breeds such as Friesians. Because of advances in artificial insemination, it is unusual for a dairy farmer to keep his own bull nowadays. In the immediate post-war years, however, each dairy farmer had at least one bull and most likely two - an old one for the cows and a younger, unrelated one for his home-bred heifers.

These were usually kept in special pens or chained at one end of the cowshed. As they were only released for a short time to serve a cow, it was a bit like having an unexploded bomb in one's midst. Quite often, after a brief moment in the open with a nubile willing partner, a bull would quite naturally show his resentment at being returned to confinement in his dark stall. This was a time of great danger if things went wrong.

One should always be prepared to learn from the tragic mistakes of others. The father of a friend of mine was killed by his own bull as he tried, single-handed, to return him to his pen after serving a cow. The doctors said at the post-mortem that his chest was crushed like an egg-shell by the creature's mighty head and horns. This farmer, who was only fifty-six at the time of his death, had served in the yeomanry and survived the horrors of the battles of the First World War, only to have his life taken by a moment's indiscretion in his own farmyard! As my friend was only just nineteen years of age, he was considered to be too young and inexperienced to assume the responsibility of running the farm, so he joined the police force and the farm was sold up.

A bull can be led by means of a bull pole attached to his nose-ring by a stout spring clip. There was also usually a chain around the horns and down the centre of his nose and fixed to the ring. The handler must always be careful to walk at his side and not pass in front of his head. A grazing bull was sometimes fitted with a mask contrived so that he could see only downwards to graze and not directly forward. There is also a device to which a bull can be securely tethered, enabling him to graze in a circle and to be moved to a fresh plot each day. Water would have to be taken to him in buckets.

A dairy cow needs twenty gallons of water each day - quite a lot to carry in buckets if the water bowls freeze up!

People would be well advised not to walk in a field containing a bull, a stallion, or a ram, and certainly not with a loose dog. When the dog goes near the grazing animal or otherwise attracts attention, likely resulting in its being attacked, the dog will run for its master, bringing the attacker with it. There are also animals known as 'rigs' which behave like entires because of their being imperfectly castrated. They should be avoided in like manner, as they can be equally dangerous.

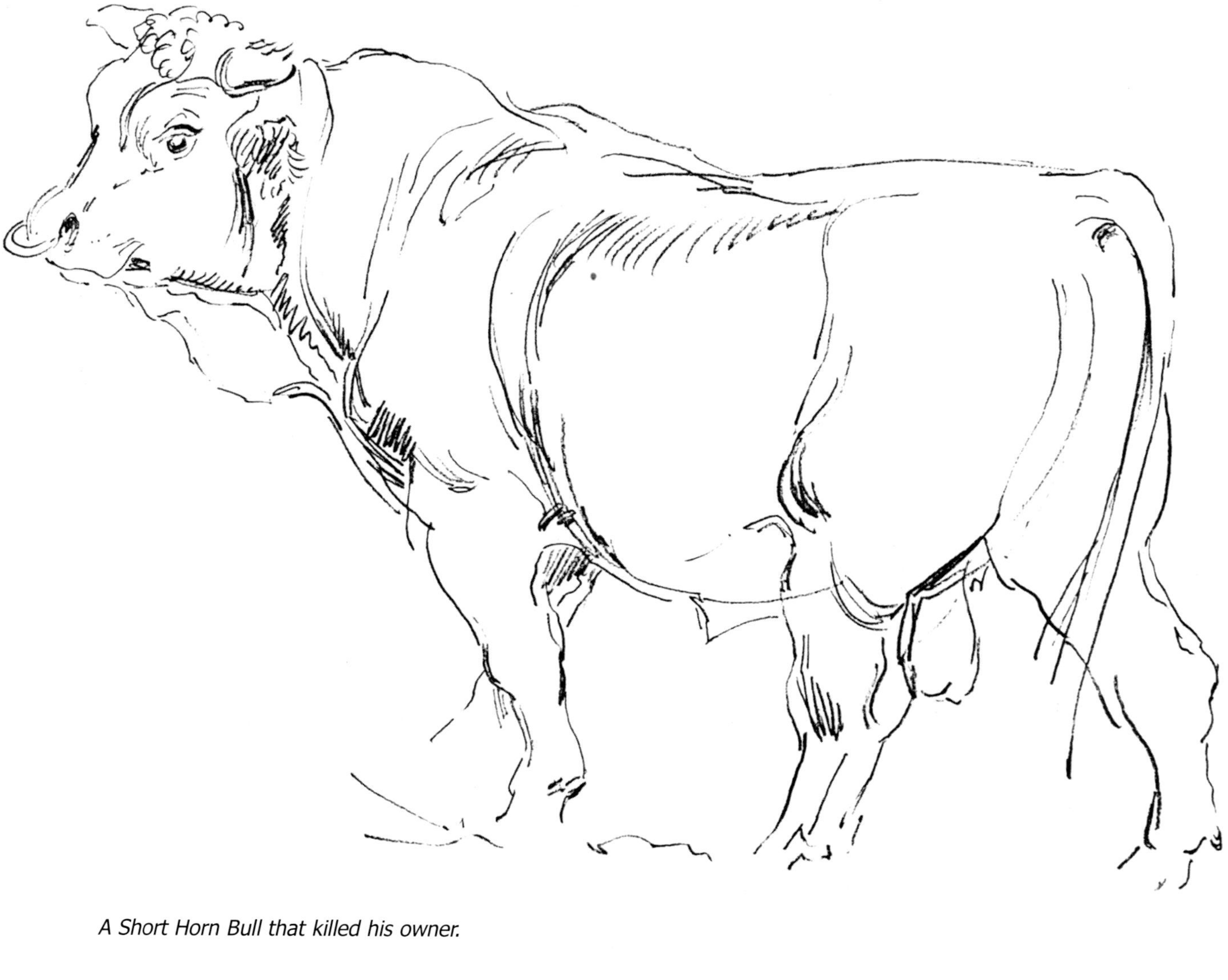

A Short Horn Bull that killed his owner.

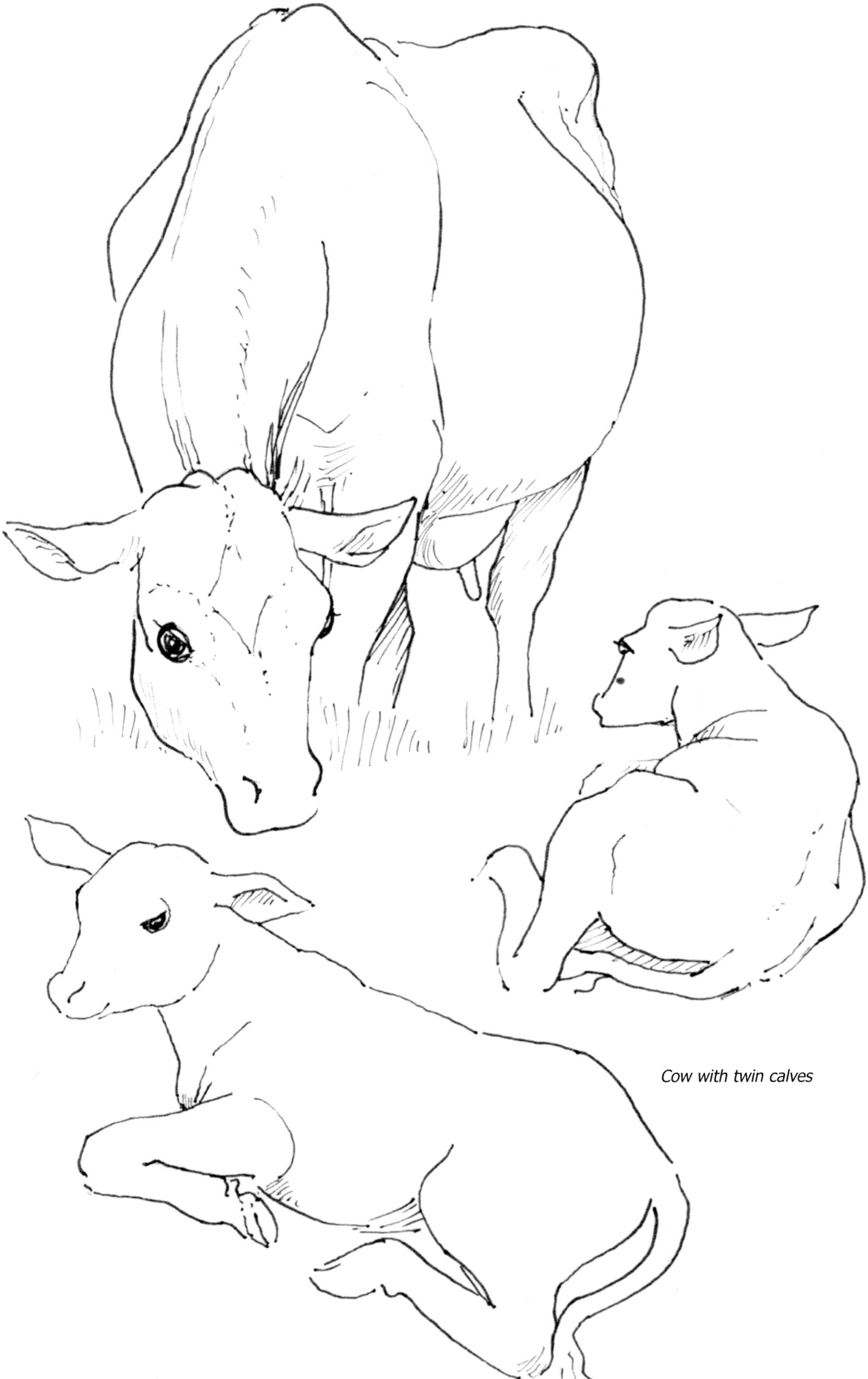

Cow with twin calves

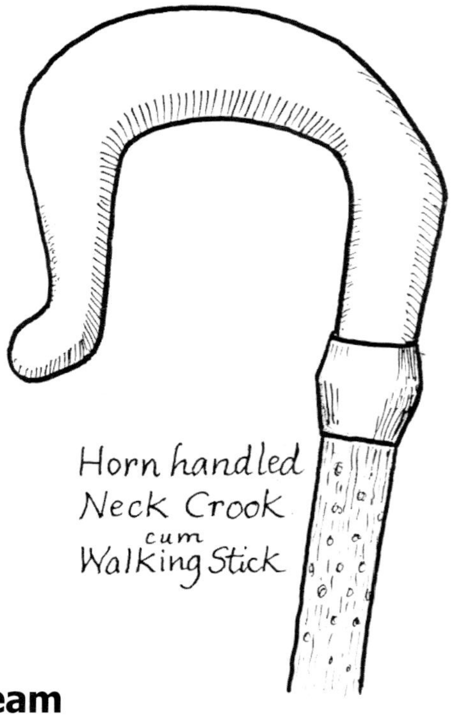

My Impossible Dream

During the many hours I spent milking dairy cows, I would sometimes dream about getting a chance to redesign nature's handiwork. This would be approached from three considerations: *position, let down,* and *composition,* borrowing ideas from three other animals.

1. A forward *position* for the cow's udder, like that of the elephant's, would be more conveniently away from the lashing tail and sloppy emissions at the animal's rear.

2. The cow's *let down* usually lasts about ten minutes to produce five gallons. A whale suckling its calf at sea can squirt out twenty gallons in ten seconds.

3. The *composition* of the milk could be more like the seal's 20% butterfat. The seal's calf doubles its weight in six weeks, whereas the cow's calf, receiving only 5% butterfat, takes six months to do the same.

This animal might be called an ELEWHASEAL, and its appearance would be mind-boggling!

The cow placidly chewing the cud looks a picture of idle contentment whereas, in reality, she is the hardest worked animal on the farm. It takes approximately one hundred gallons of blood pumped through the heart to make one gallon of milk. Some cows become so distended that they require pre-milking *before* they have had the calf! Her normal output would be two hundred gallons per lactation of 300 days - the amount required by one calf, but by selection, we have bred cows to give ten times that amount.

We look for a straight back on a cow, whereas draught animals such as horses have a hollow one and camels have a humped back to carry their load. Which is most efficient?

When rising from rest, a cow lifts her back legs first, while a horse rises onto its forelegs first. I wonder what the reason may be?

Elizabeth as Goatherd on Woking Common

In 1940 Elizabeth spent the summer as a goatherd, being responsible for overseeing 30 of these wayward animals as they grazed and browsed on Woking Common. It may not be generally known that goats usually prefer to browse on small shrubs and bushes, even to the extent of climbing onto the low branches of trees rather than grazing the grass as sheep do. Because of their enthusiasm for eating everything in sight, including the washing off the clothesline, these intelligent animals have been accused of helping to create the deserts of Africa. When the vet was called to one goat in obvious distress, it was found to have the elastic from a pair of pants caught under its tongue!

In order to facilitate milking, they are encouraged to jump onto a low table. The operator works from behind, being careful to avoid the little black pellets that may come from time to time as the nanny eats from a bucket.

When the milk had been made into cheeses, Elizabeth would deliver them to a retail shop on her bicycle. The milk was considered to be safe from TB, and suited some who were allergic to cow's milk. Goats were to be seen on many smallholdings, and at Bitteswell one could usually be seen tethered on the village green.

We had occasional visits from a goat owned by a friend from Coventry. It always contrived to nearly strangle itself on its tethering chain.

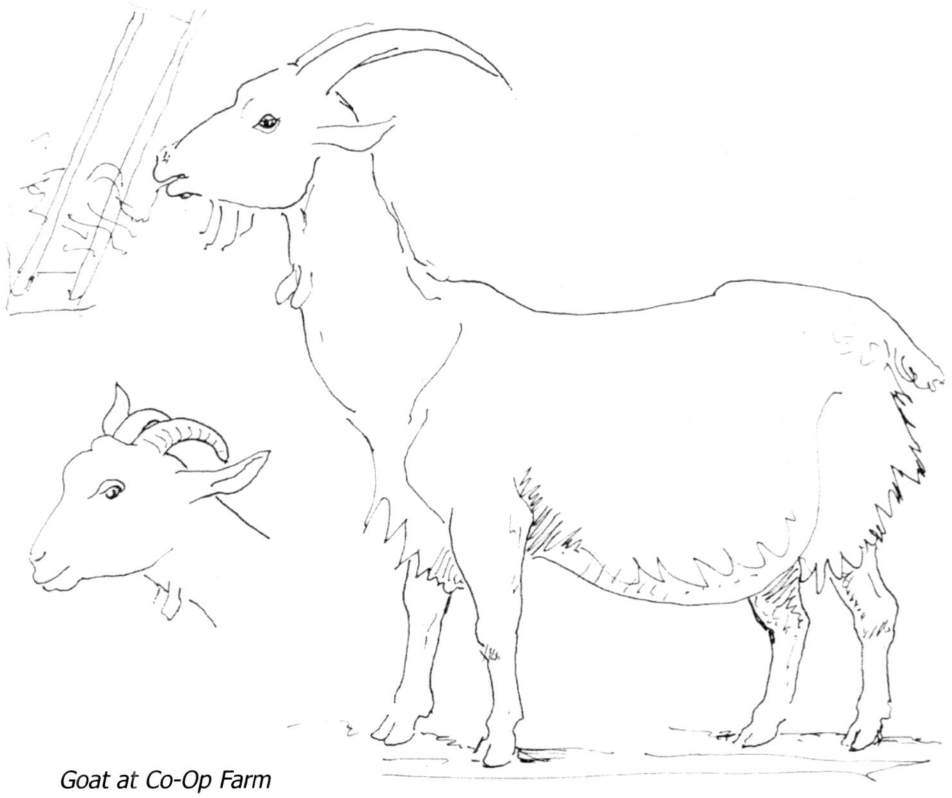

Goat at Co-Op Farm

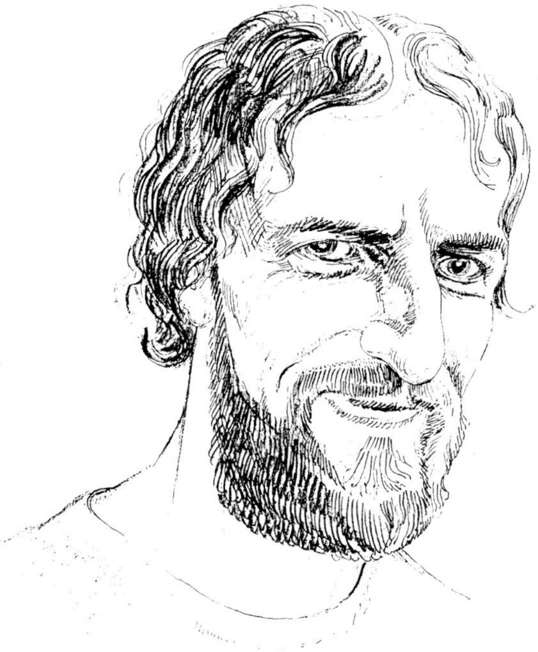

Colin Grieves, a Scotsman from Clackmannanshire

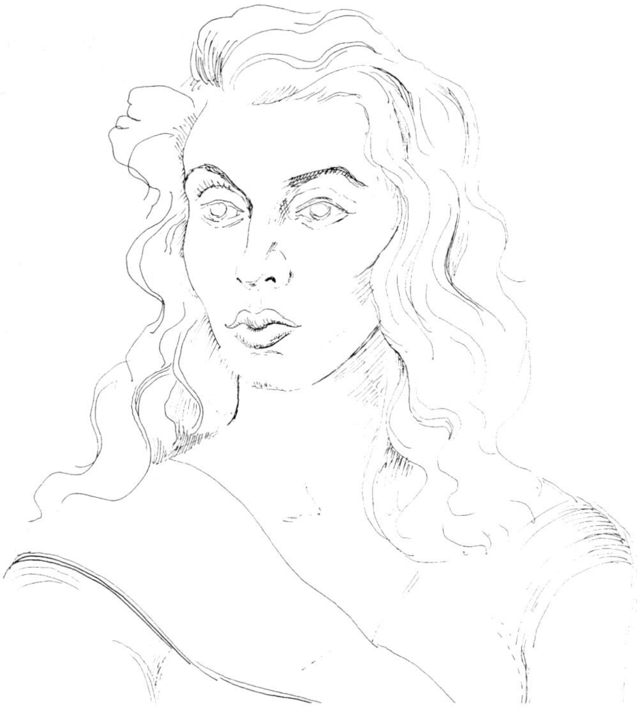

Zilla Mae Mawby (See page 189)

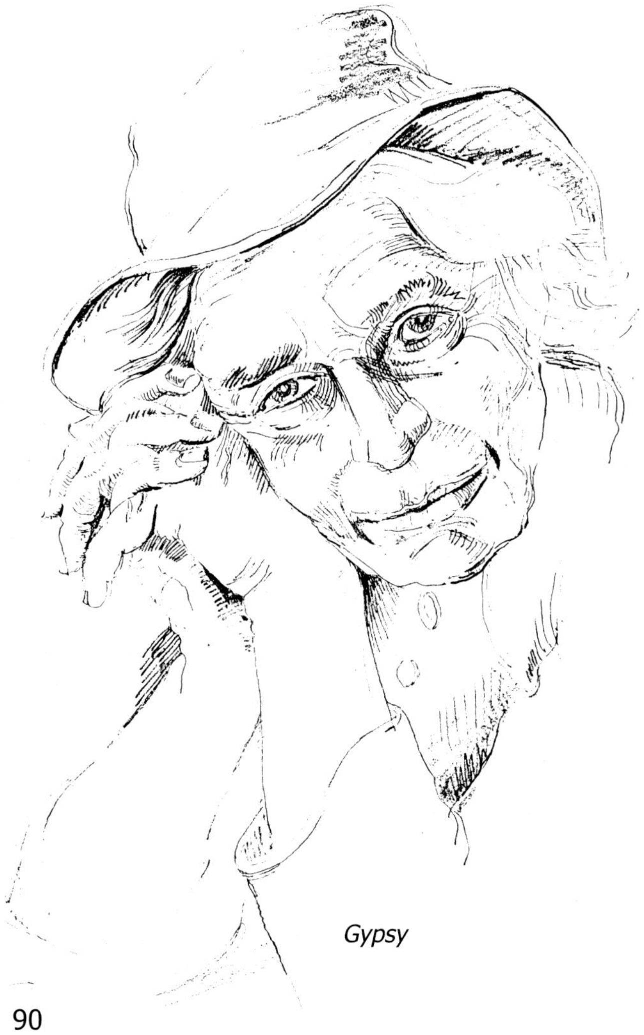

Gypsy

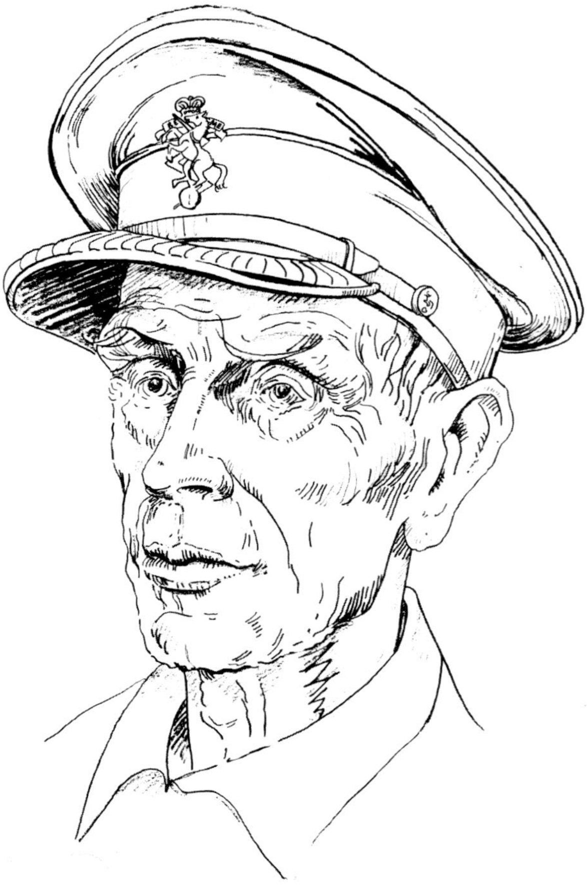

Jack Watson

Some of the farm helpers, part of an excellent team of workers.

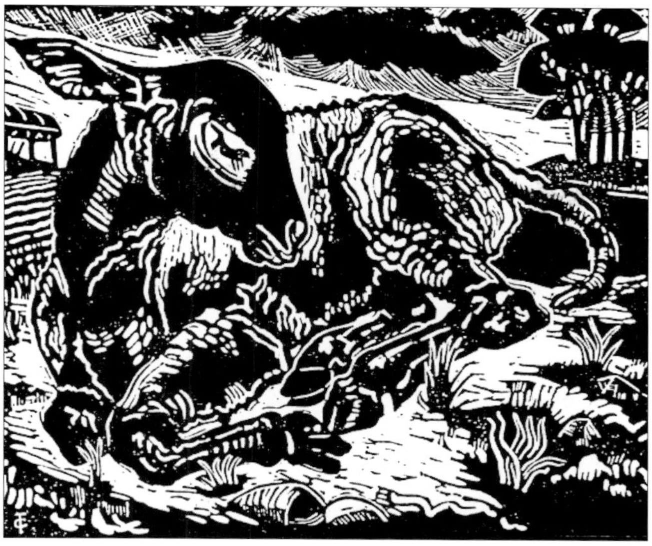

The Cade Lamb
Linocut

Chapter FOUR

Sheep and the Shepherd's Year

'The Lambs are Coming Early this Year'

In general, I have found that townsfolk are blissfully unaware of the efforts farmers make to supply the butchers' meat they eat from cattle, sheep, pigs and poultry. Food animals are *unmated females and castrated males*, known as *clean* animals. You might think of them as enforced, unwilling celebates! On the other hand, there are the cows and bulls, ewes and rams, sows and boars, etc. These sexually mature and active animals are eventually sold for less than half the price for manufacturing purposes, an ignominious end after a riotous life of continuous breeding! To the townsman all cattle are 'cows', even those destined for prime beef, which should be called steers or heifers. Cattle and sheep to be used for breeding are known as *store stock*..

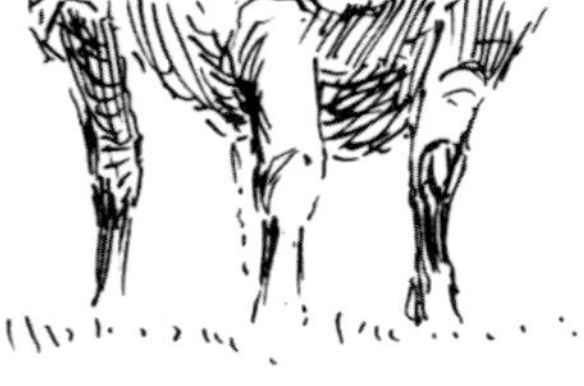

In order to give an idea of the complexity of some farming projects, I will attempt to give a description of the management of a lowland breeding flock for fat (prime) lamb production. Contrary to popular belief, wool is a minor by-product in this country - hardly worth the cost of shearing. Knitting wool in the shops can cost much more per pound than the farmer often receives for a whole fleece.

The annual cycle for the ewe may be thought of as follows: tupping (mating), conception, gestation, parturition, birth and bonding, lactation, shearing, dipping, weaning, culling, and flushing before tupping again.

In addition to this, all sheep need routine dosing against worms, vaccination against diseases, paring of feet and running through a chemical bath against foot-rot. They need expert supervision to notice if they have been attacked by the blowfly, whose maggots, when hatched, will eat the sheep alive, usually starting round the tail. This area must be kept clean by frequent 'dagging' (the unpleasant job of cutting away soiled wool from around the tail).

If a fly is attracted to lay its eggs in a rotten front hoof and the sheep lies down, the maggots can migrate upwards over the shoulder where they are more difficult to notice until much damage is done. Ewes are frequently inspected for mastitis (inflammation of the udder) and loss of teeth caused by advancing years. (Like cattle, they have incisors only on the lower jaw.) Shortcomings in these respects will mean the animals are culled and drafted to weekly markets or to special sheep sales, where younger replacements may be purchased. Well-grown home-bred female lambs (theaves) are sometimes selected for future breeding.

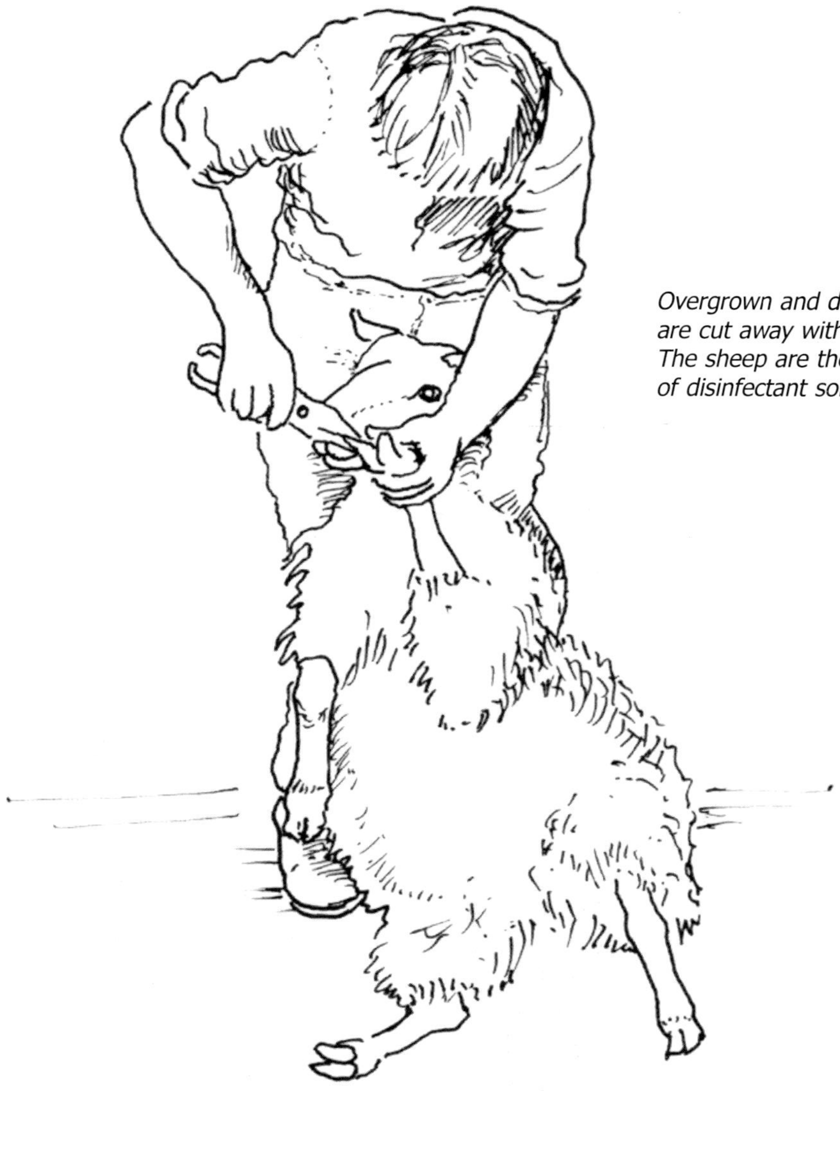

Overgrown and diseased parts of the hooves are cut away with knives and clippers. The sheep are then walked through a footbath of disinfectant solution.

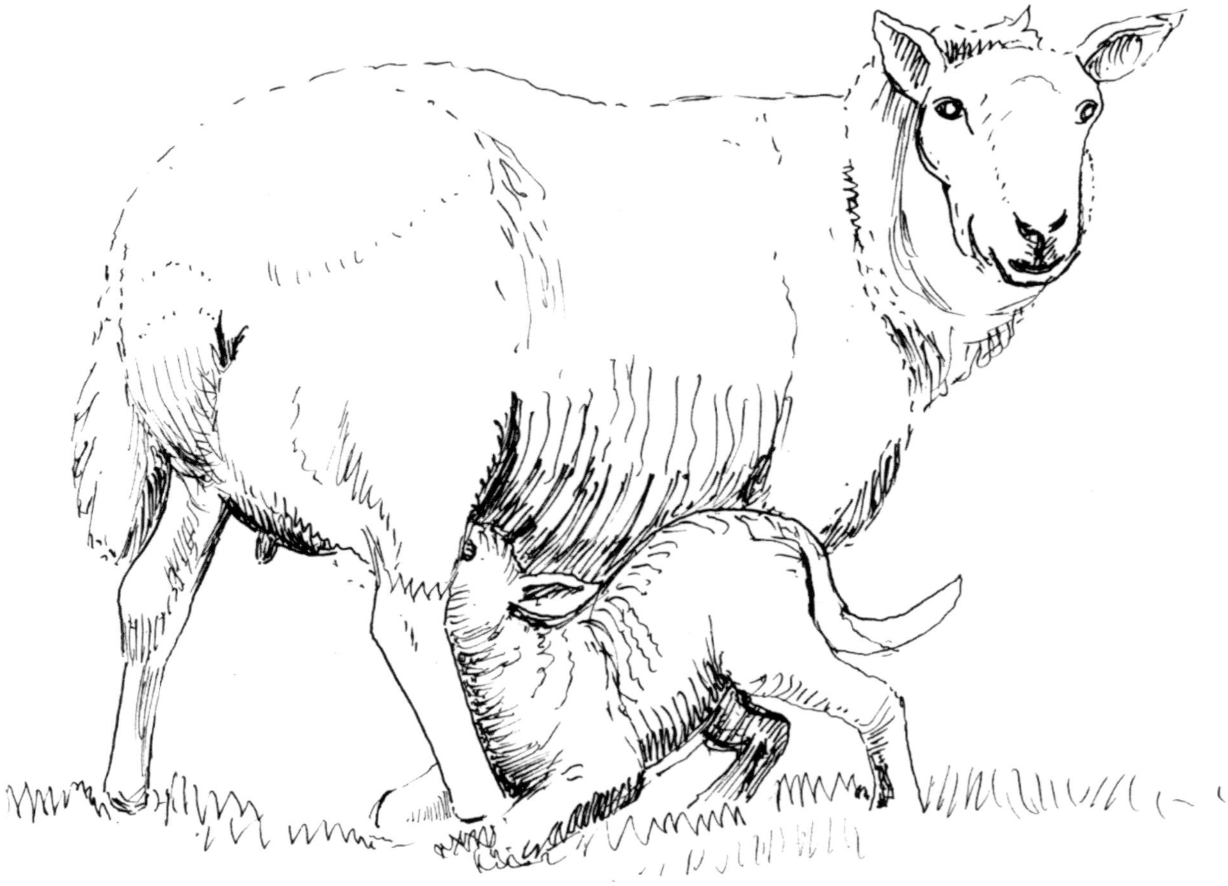

After weaning, the other lambs are segregated onto fresh pastures so that they will put on weight quickly. At weaning, there is great tribulation for two or three days as ewes and lambs call for each other, and it is most important that they do not get back together until the ewe's milk has dried up.

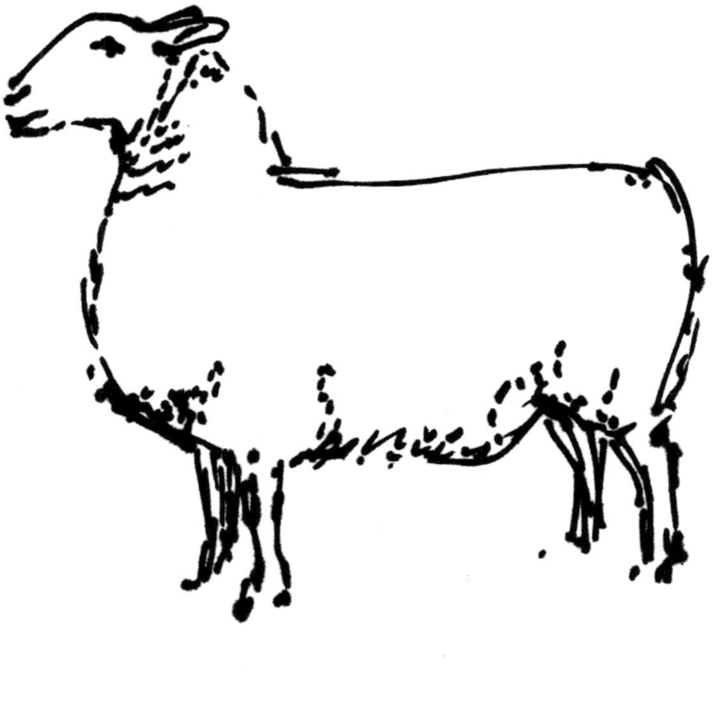

Home-bred Border Leicester female lamb (Theave)

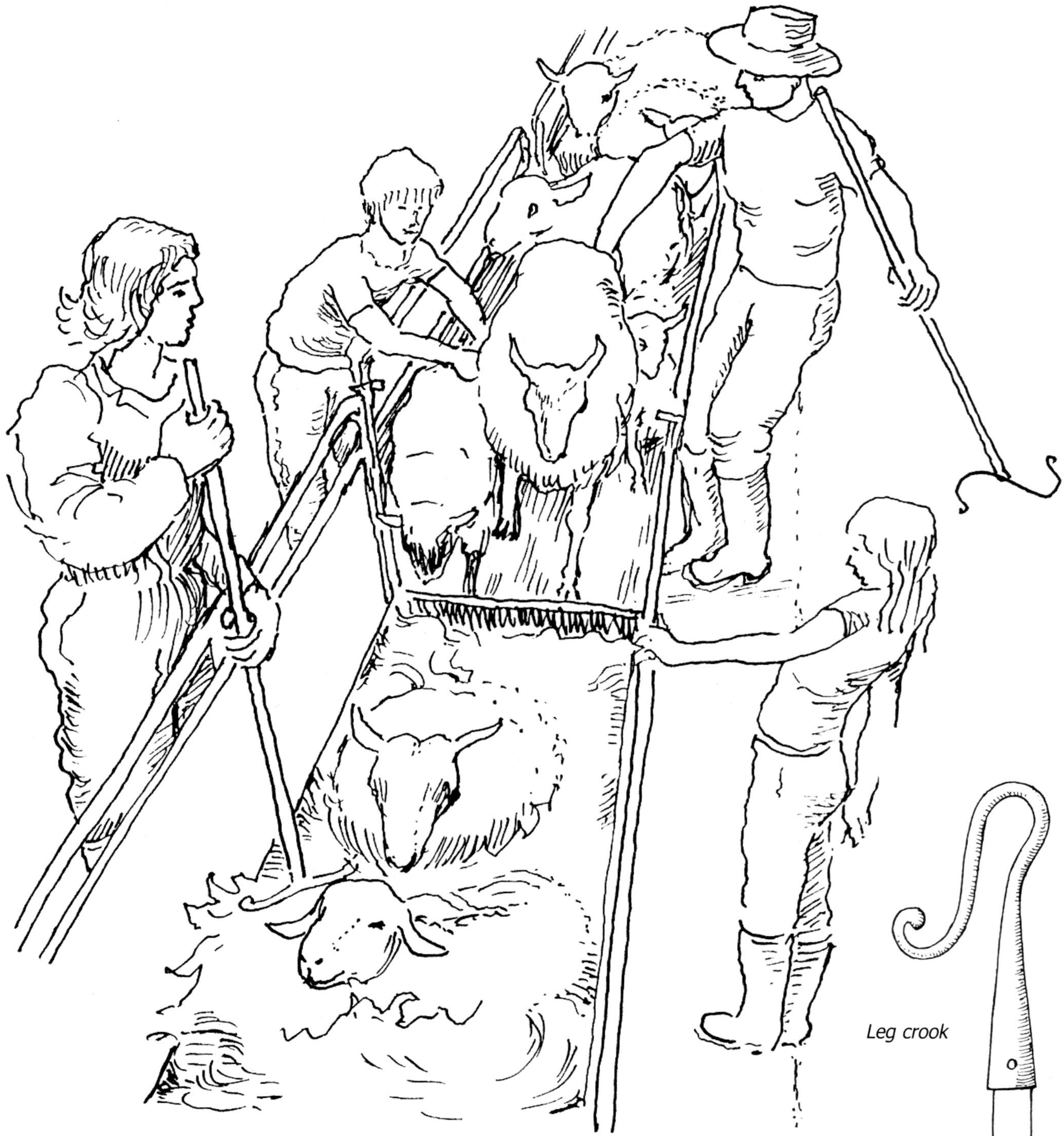

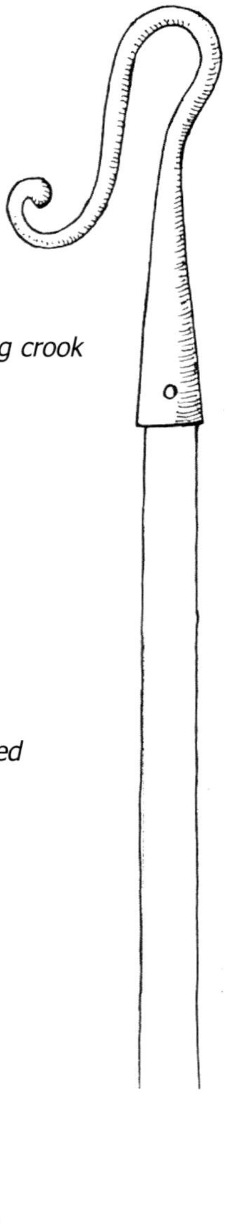

Leg crook

Sheep had to be dipped twice in the Summer months. The dip was a concrete pit with a sloping ramp at one end, filled with water to which a strong disinfectant was added to protect the sheep against fly strike and sheep scab caused by a tiny mite which burrows into its skin. Plenty of people were needed to chivvy the line of reluctant sheep which were dunked as they swam by a person wielding a special dipping crook.

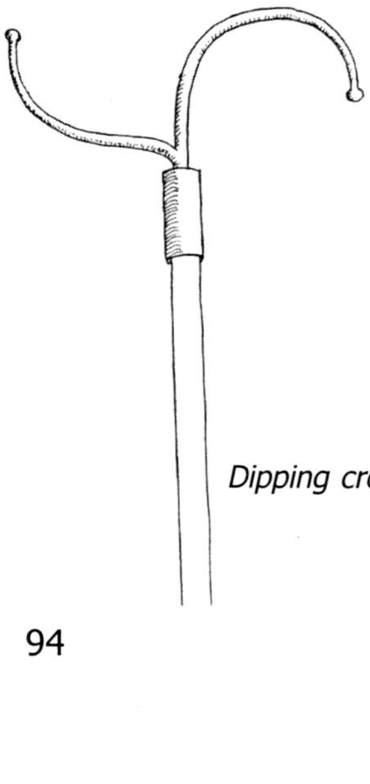

Dipping crook

Prime Lambs Selected for Meat Market

Those lambs destined for meat will be brought into pens to be drawn (selected) for market. They are channelled down a narrow passage with a guillotine type gate at one end and a drafting (two way) gate at the other. Here they will be 'touched' across the loins and tail (or dock) to ascertain their condition. This ability to touch and judge is a highly skilled business, the aptitude being acquired only after many years' experience. It must be remembered that a lamb may be rejected by the government grader for being too fat as well as being too thin! As rejection means loss of subsidy, those lambs rejected would have to be taken back to the farm until such time as their condition has been remedied.

I have found that, in general, people are flattered if their help and expertise are sought. Two retired farmers who lived nearby were really pleased to help us with selection, and were therefore on hand to help with penning and loading. These friendly bachelor brothers used to spend too much of their time, as they told me, watching the wireless. They really looked forward to market day when they felt wanted and important instead of lonely and useless. We all enjoyed some earthy banter and reminiscences of former years, when we were footloose and fancy free.

At the drafting gate the lambs would be weighed, and as the estimated dressed carcass is roughly half the live weight, we would be looking for those of about 90lbs (40.8kg) live, which would yield 45lbs of meat, or whatever weight was currently in favour with the supermarket buyers. Those selected are marked on the head or neck with a paint spray or crayon and turned out into a paddock to await transport early the next morning.

At market, when they have been officially weighed and checked for rejects by the Ministry of Food grader, he puts a mark of paint on the head. Then they are drawn into matching pens of ten or twelve to await the auctioneer, who calls out the weights as he sells them. When they are sold, a punch hole is made in the ear to prevent them from receiving the subsidy twice.

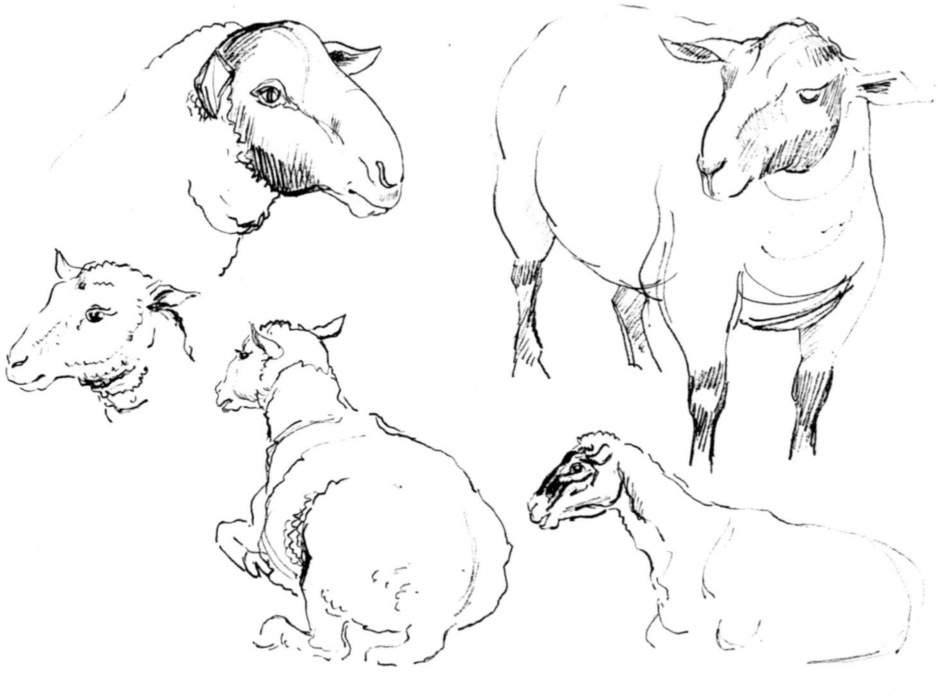

Early Lambs Command a Better Price

In the autumn months of September, October and November, the markets are glutted with lambs born in the late spring. This is natural timing, as the ewes and lambs can best utilise the rapid growth of nutritious spring grass. This super glut naturally depresses the market, bringing prices down. Therefore, if management can cope, it is considered better to go for early lambs which are scarce and therefore command a better price.

Because the weather in February and March is usually unsuitable for outdoor lambing, large buildings are needed if heavy losses are to be avoided. Grain or potato stores can be used if that produce can be sold off in time. Parts of these buildings are then usually divided into individual pens for a ewe and her lambs.

As the gestation period is about five months, lambs born in February are the result of mating in September. Many times in spring, I have heard townsfolk remark that "the lambs are coming early this year", rather in the way that they may refer to the emergence of snowdrops and crocuses! They seem to be naively unable to connect the births with the mating and conception, carefully planned and organised by the farmer last autumn - five months ago!

This is how it happens: the shortening days of autumn bring the ewes into season. They prefer to mate with rams of their own breed, but they are usually disappointed in the Midlands, where Suffolk rams are the favoured breed for crossing purposes. The ewes, which are put on poor pasture after weaning from their lambs in August to dry up the milk, are moved to a better plane of nutrition, so that they are being *flushed* into rapidly improving condition. This increases the numbers of lambs conceived at the time the rams are introduced. Farmers on poor hill pastures prefer single lambs, but on rich lowland pastures, we always aim at 200%, usually settling for 175% or an average of one and three-quarter lambs per ewe! There is a place in New York called Flushing Meadow which, no doubt, has some historical connection; perhaps it is now used for flushing out the gangsters and their molls!

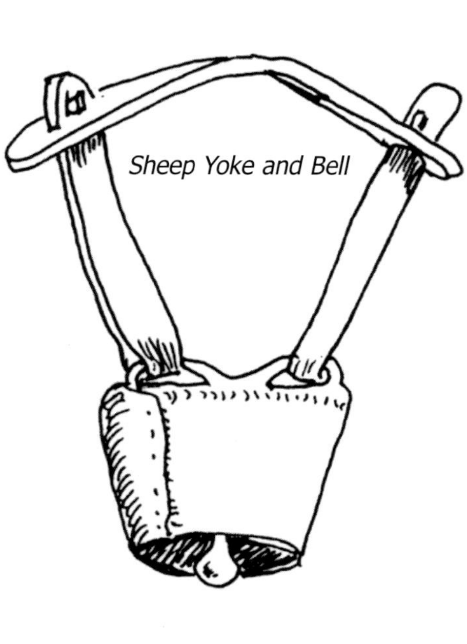

Sheep Yoke and Bell

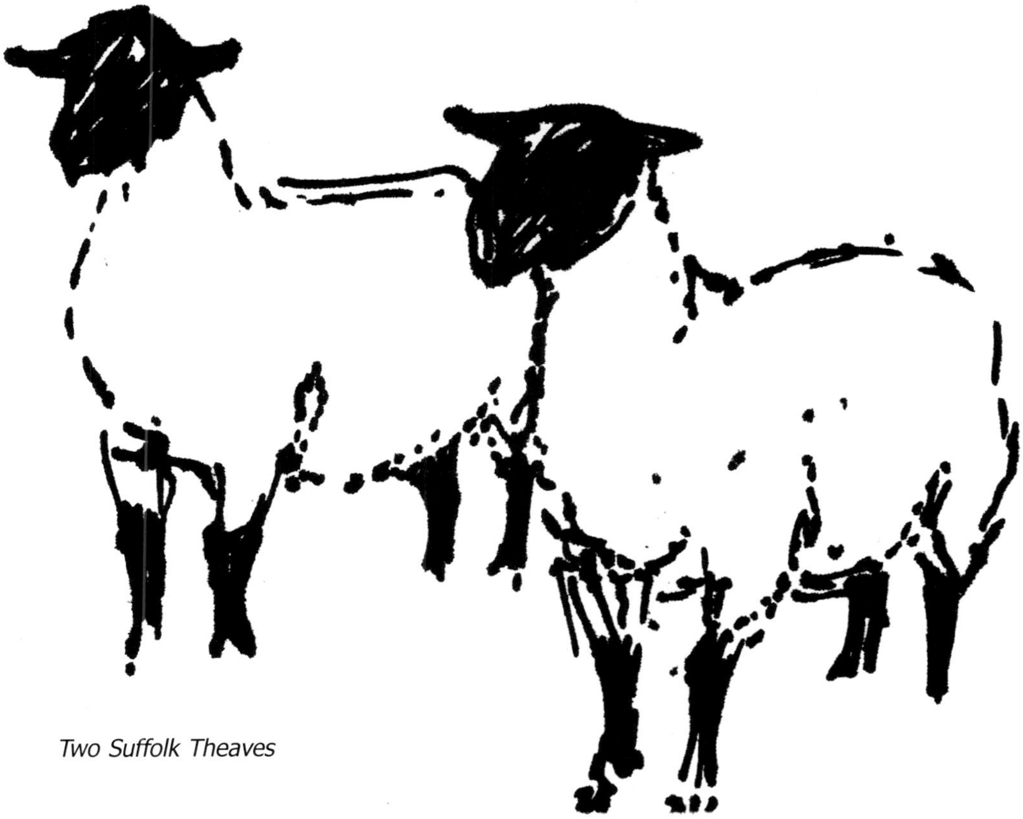

Two Suffolk Theaves

Firstly, the ewes are 'dagged' to remove soiled locks and the wool is clipped from around their tails to facilitate mating. The tups are fitted with a harness to which is attached a coloured crayon, cunningly sited between the two front legs, which leaves a tell-tale mark upon the ewe's back when mating. When fitting the crayons, ribald remarks are made by those present, such as "Be careful not to get any on you!" The colours are changed at intervals so that the flock can be divided into three equal time zones for expecting lamb dates. The ewes may also be scanned later to see the number of foetuses so that those expecting multiple births (triplets or quads) can receive extra nutrition.

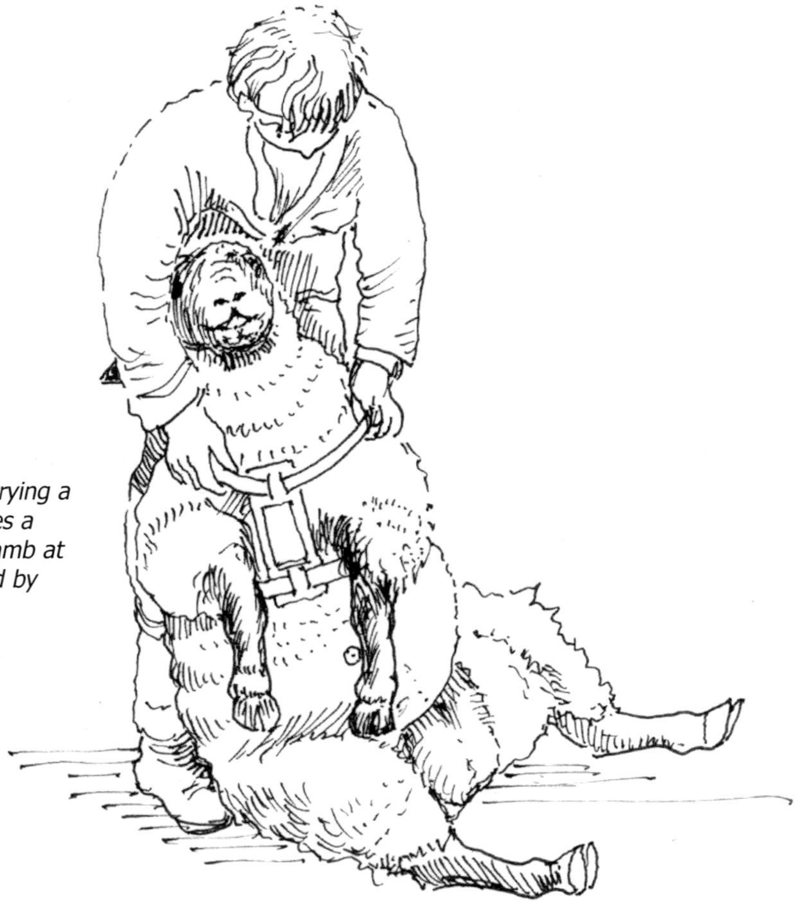

At tupping time the ram is fitted with a harness carrying a crayon so that when he mates with a ewe, he leaves a coloured mark in her rump. Blue for those due to lamb at the end of February. Then the red lot lamb followed by green for those which will lamb in April.

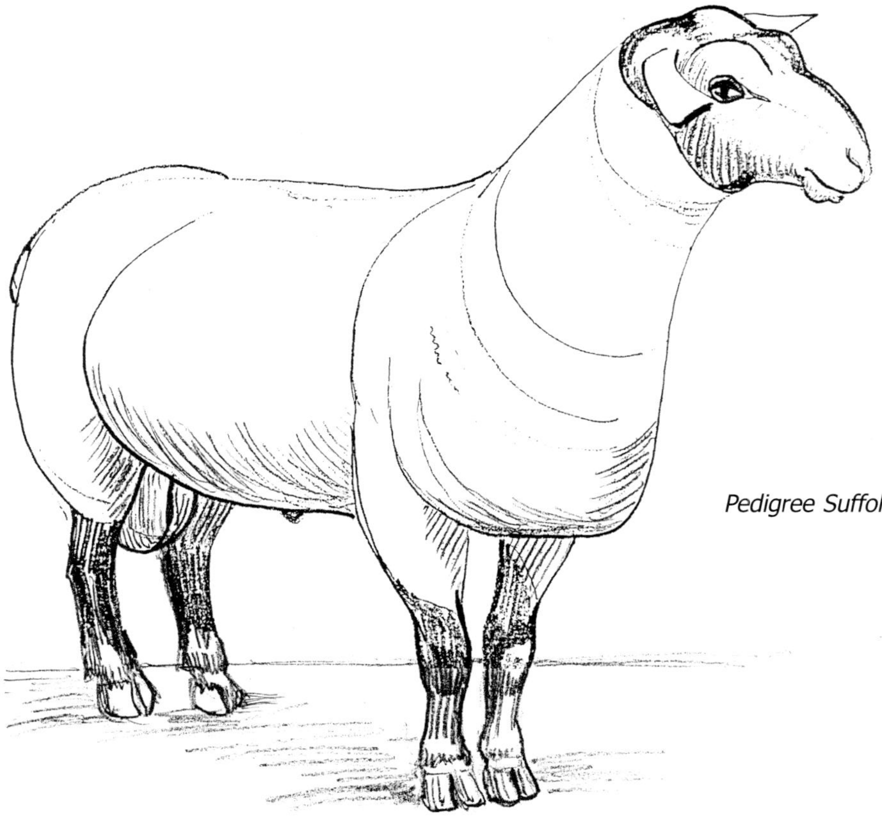

Pedigree Suffolk Ram

Good Rams are Costly to Buy

Rams are usually bred by specialist pedigree breeders and cost many hundreds of guineas. They must be very well grown and of excellent conformation, having very good feet, especially the back ones, on which they must spend a disproportionate time! They have lots of work to do in a short time, each satisfying 25 to 35 ewes. They should get on agreeably together or they will waste time fighting. Rams are quite capable of killing each other by charging head down from a long distance and the clashing of heads can be heard a long way off. They can break a man's leg if they take him by surprise from the rear.

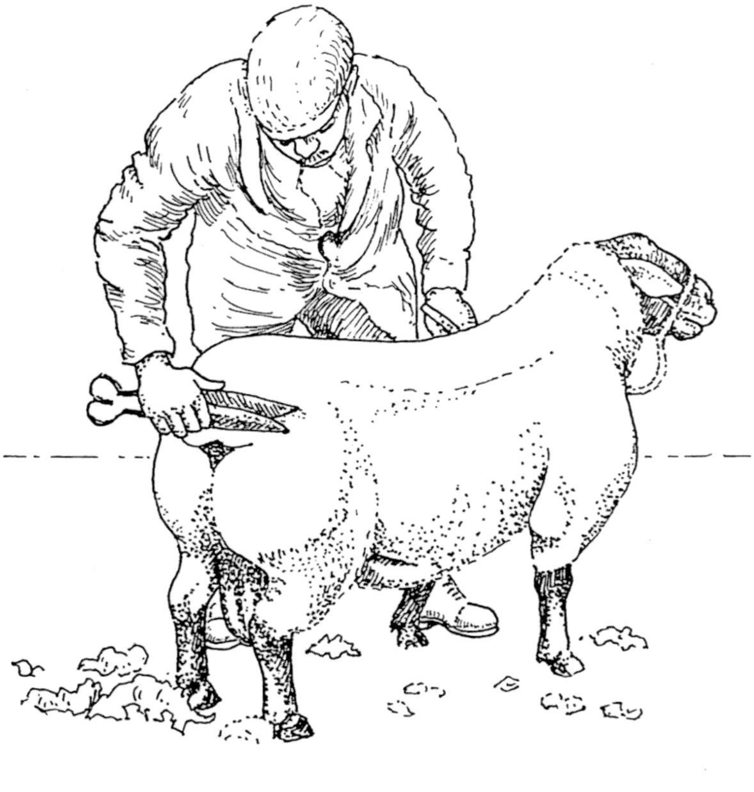

In preparation for the Autumn fairs, ram breeders wash and clip their rams' fleeces. This is very skilful work, like that of a sculptor or topiarist. It is intended to emphasise the rams' deep chests and broad backs. The result may be thought of as an optical illusion.

Tying two fighters close together by the neck for a few days usually does the trick. Normally the rams will have grazed together for a couple of months so they will be accustomed to one another long enough to have established a pecking order. An older 'two-shear' ram will not attack a shearing as the latter will submit at once, and everyone knows there is no fun to be had from fighting a pacifist who will turn the other cheek!

Six weeks prior to lambing, ewes are fed in troughs on an increasing ration - up to 4lbs each of concentrated feed, mostly cereal, containing protein, oil and fibre. There will also be minerals and trace elements available to provide heat and energy for growth; calcium for bones and milk, and copper, cobalt and magnesium in small quantities.

Creep feeding is made possible by a device set into a line of hurdles or wire netting that allows growing lambs access to feed denied to their mothers. The more portly matrons cannot squeeze between the adjustable rollers set into the frame of a hurdle, while the lambs go in and out at will.

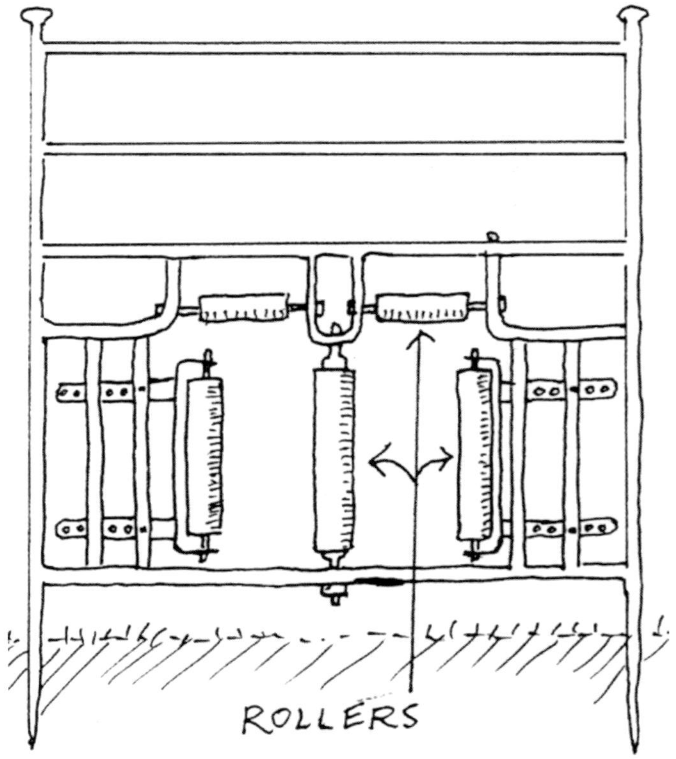

Hay, which is dried grass, is fed in mobile hay racks. Silage, which is pickled grass, may be offered ad lib. Barley and oat straw is sometimes palatable, but too much bulky roughage obviously may cause prolapses. Wheat straw is normally used for bedding as the stems are more woody. It is very important that ewes have access to good clean water at all times, especially when lactating. Lambs are likely to jump into water troughs and drown while at play, while ewes can get bogged down at the muddy edges of natural watering places when they are heavily pregnant.

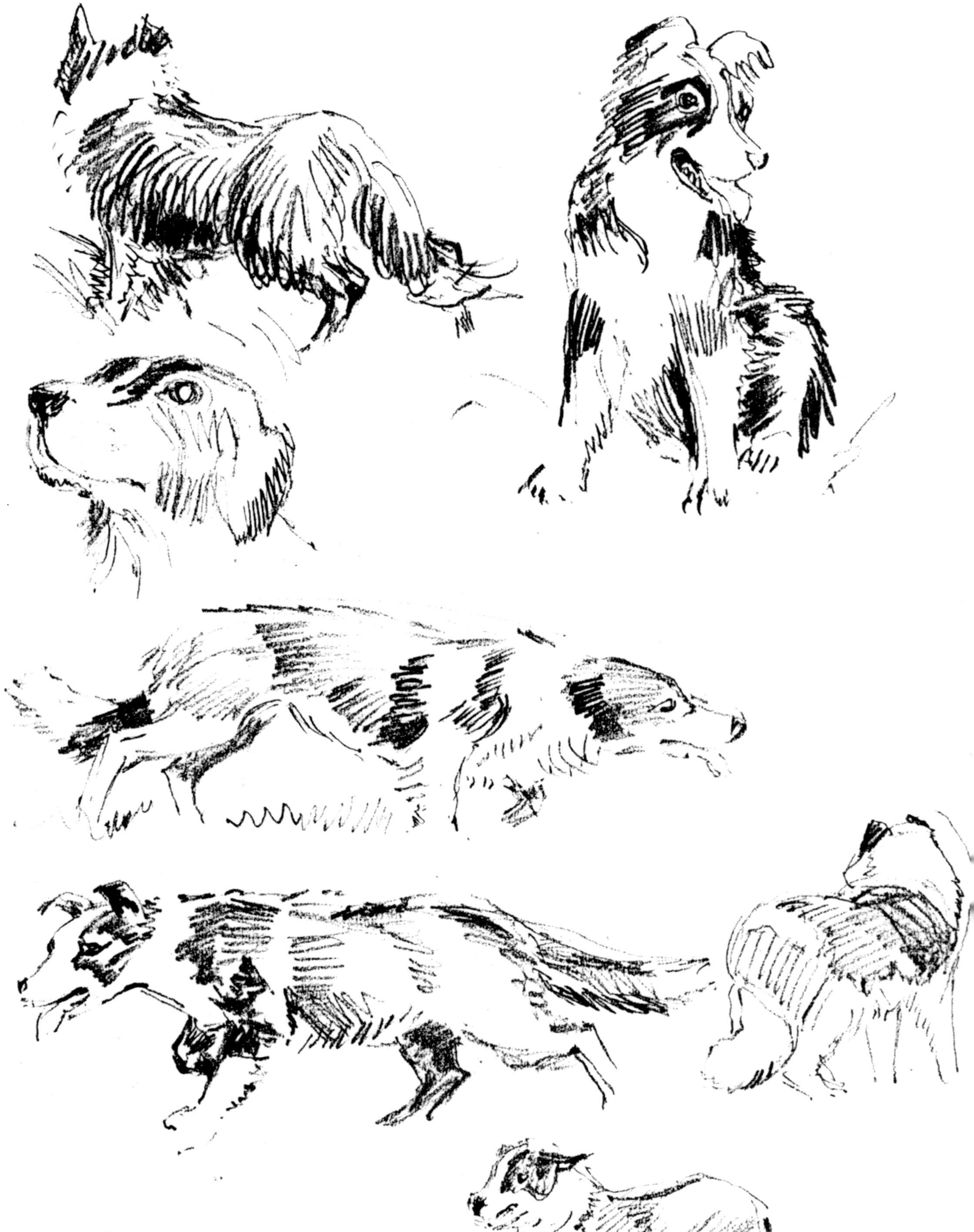
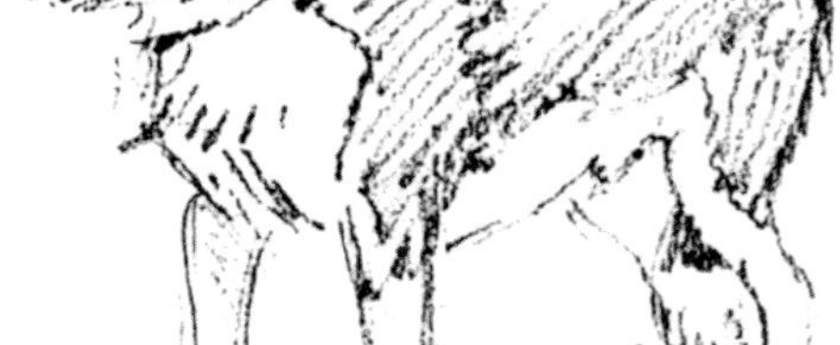

Our sheep dogs

The Menace of Sheep-Worrying Dogs

At this time, one has to watch for unexpected premature births, sometimes as a result of stolen matings with a neighbouring ram which has made a quick extra-curricular visit. Abortions can be caused by sheep-worrying dogs left to wander in packs by irresponsible owners who couldn't care less what their pets get up to when they go out all day. A farmer is well within his rights to shoot a dog he catches among his sheep.

A neighbour's Alsatian and a mongrel bitch once decimated our vulnerable pedigree flock. It was not a pretty sight to find limbless dead and dying animals scattered all over the parish, where they had fled in abject terror from their bloodthirsty tormentors. Like the expression, "the troubles" in Northern Ireland, our terminology is at fault, through massive understatement - a 'worried sheep' does not sit down and scratch its furrowed brow! It runs for its life with great distress when heavily pregnant.

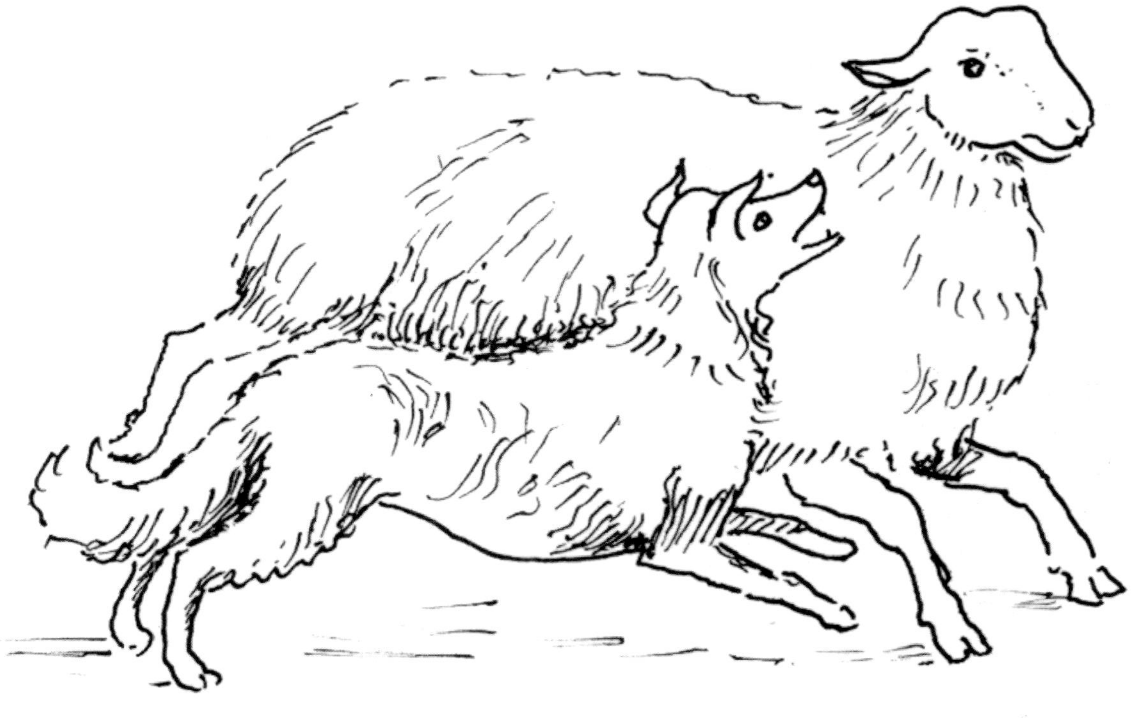

A worrying dog causes panic among the sheep, leaping and snapping it singles out one ewe and chases it relentlessly up and down the field until it is completely exhausted.

Four Stages of Lambing

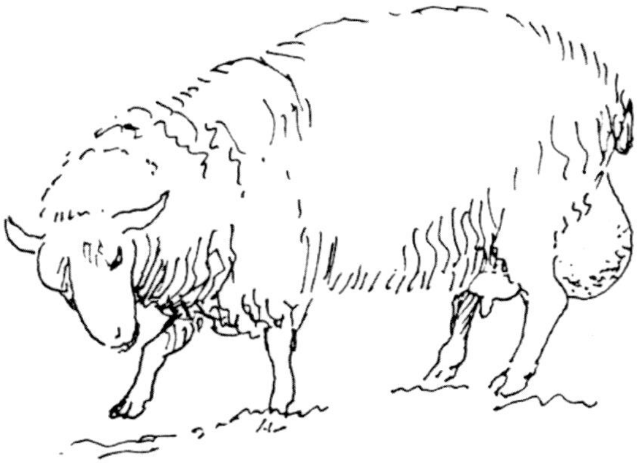

A sign of lambing, she goes to a corner on her own, begins to paw the ground glancing at hor hindquarters making soft bleating noises. Then the water bag appears hanging like a yellow globe

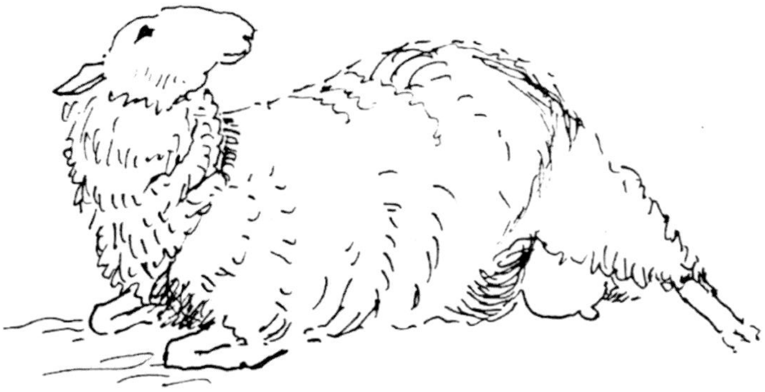

The ewe strains with head high and leg extended, calling out with exertion.

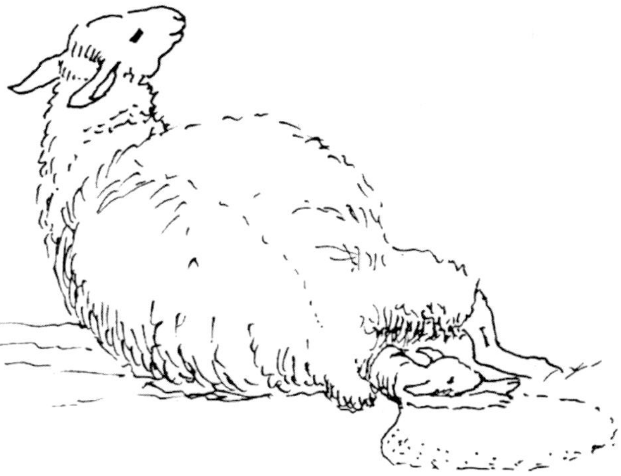

The water bag bursts and the lamb appears in the diving positcon

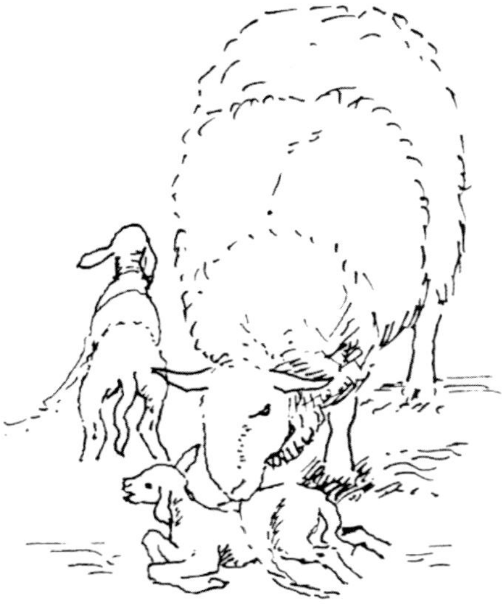

The ewe licks the membrane and fluid away and nudges the lambs gently to their feet to take their first wobbly steps to seek her udder for milk.

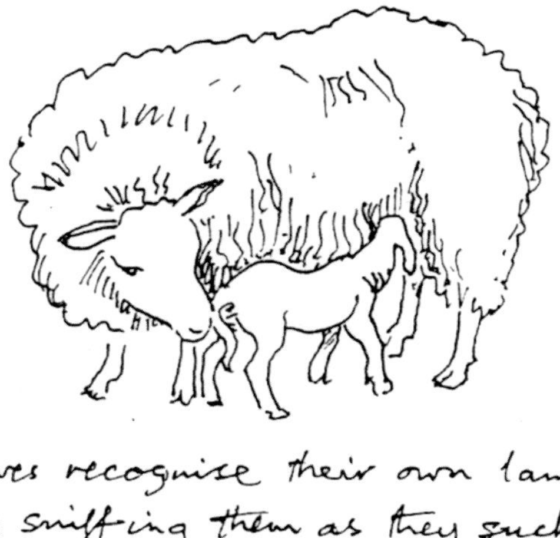

Ewes recognise their own lambs by sniffing them as they suckle. They would butt strange lambs away.

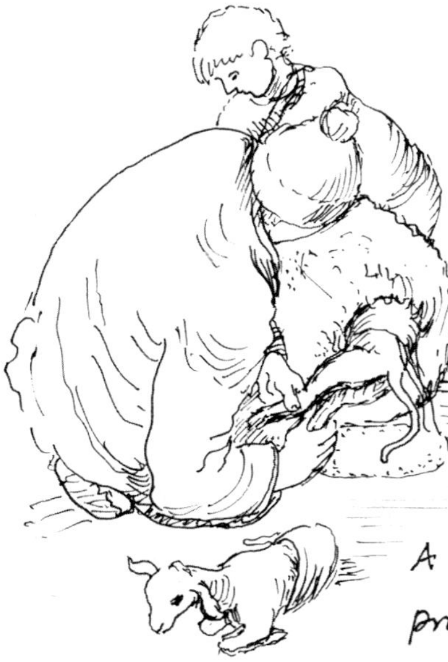

A breech presentation

Several days before lambing, the udder of the ewe becomes distended. Later she will be seen to seek a quiet spot where she will make a nest, scraping the ground and turning around in circles. Then she will lie with her head in the air and back leg outstretched, calling out with the contractions and exertions of labour.

Then the waterbag appears and the amniotic fluid is discharged, followed normally by the lamb's forelegs, with nose between, in a diving position. There are many variants on this position. If things go well, the ewe will soon stand up and lick the lamb clean from its 'cling film' covering, making encouraging conversation not heard at other times. In a few minutes the lamb will struggle to its feet and suckle, unless the ewe is busy presenting another lamb. This is a dangerous time, as another ewe, which is soon to lamb may kidnap the new baby, only to reject it when her own appears.

As the ewe normally has only two functional teats, it is ideal for each ewe in the flock to rear two lambs, and this can be achieved by careful switching of surplus lambs from triplets and quadruplets or buying in 'cade' lambs, orphans from other farmers. The National Farmers Union branch offices sometimes run lamb banks, putting farmers in touch over the telephone when they need extra lambs.

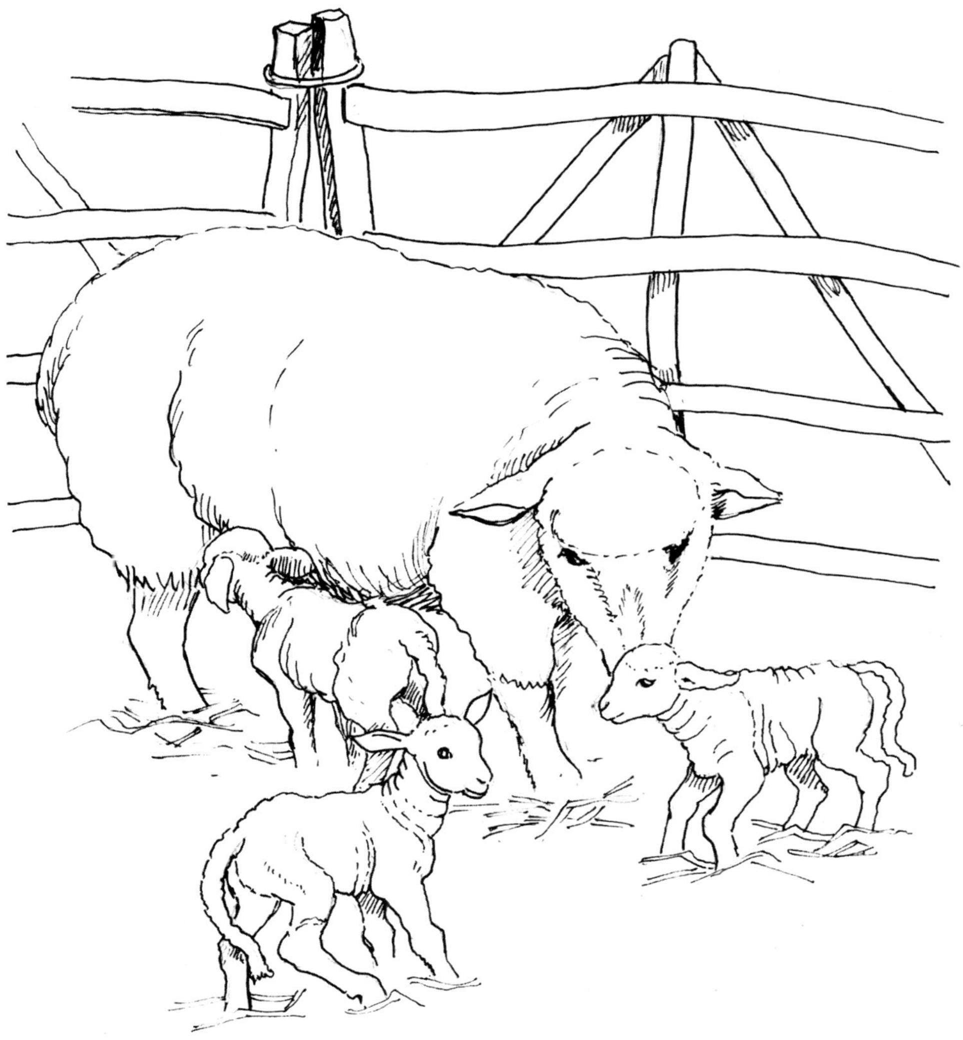

Ewe with triplets

Subterfuges to aid Fostering

A ewe does not readily take to a strange lamb, so there are various subterfuges used to coerce her. The most commonly known is that the foster lamb is dressed in a coat made of the skin of the mother's dead lamb; or it may be soaked in her amniotic fluid so she can lick it dry.

The presence of a sheep dog may so arouse a ewe's protective instinct that she will let a strange lamb suck. There is also a useful device known as a fostering crate which holds the ewe in a neck yoke so that she cannot see which lambs are feeding. Once the mother's milk has passed through the lamb it begins to acquire her scent and she will adopt it readily. Sickly lambs and those waiting for adoption are bottle-fed and kept under a warm lamp in the sick bay.

As for the midwifery, there are many kinds of malpresentation leading to death if the shepherd is not on hand with timely intervention. Only much experience will guide one as to when to investigate manually and how to rectify the position, working in the dark by sense of touch in the very confined space of the uterus. Using slip gel for lubrication, limbs and heads often have to be pushed back against the powerful expelling muscles. Sometimes two lambs try to come at once or a breech presentation may try to emerge tail first. A still-born lamb is always troublesome, as it lacks its natural lubricant and does not struggle to help itself. It is rare and costly to resort to the vet and caesarean section.

As the ewes in a large group begin to drop their lambs, they are swiftly moved into individual small pens. A ewe will usually follow a shepherd holding the lamb suspended at his side. Once inside her own pen with food, water and bedding she has plenty of opportunity to become bonded to her lambs before going out a few days later to join a larger group.

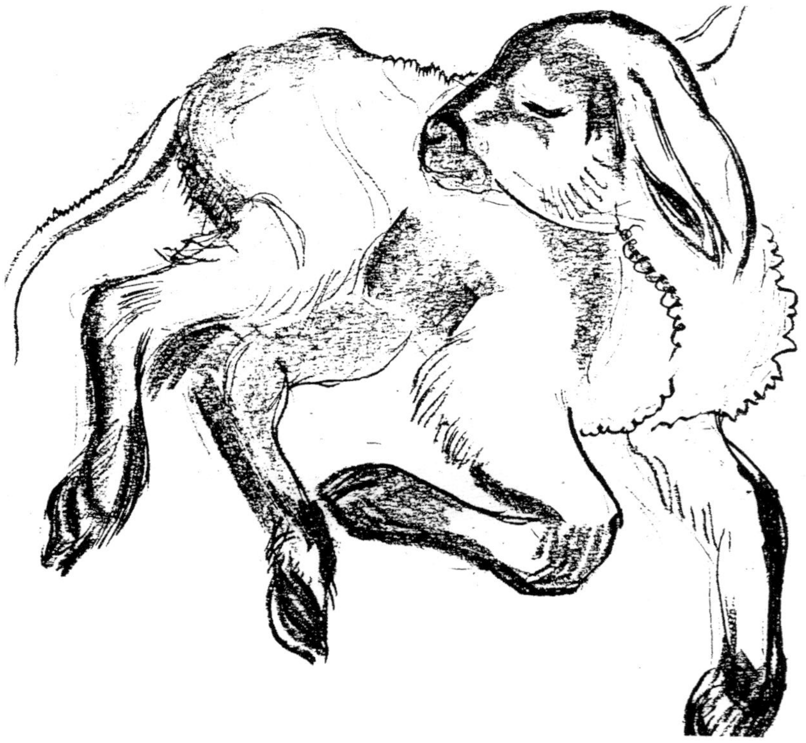

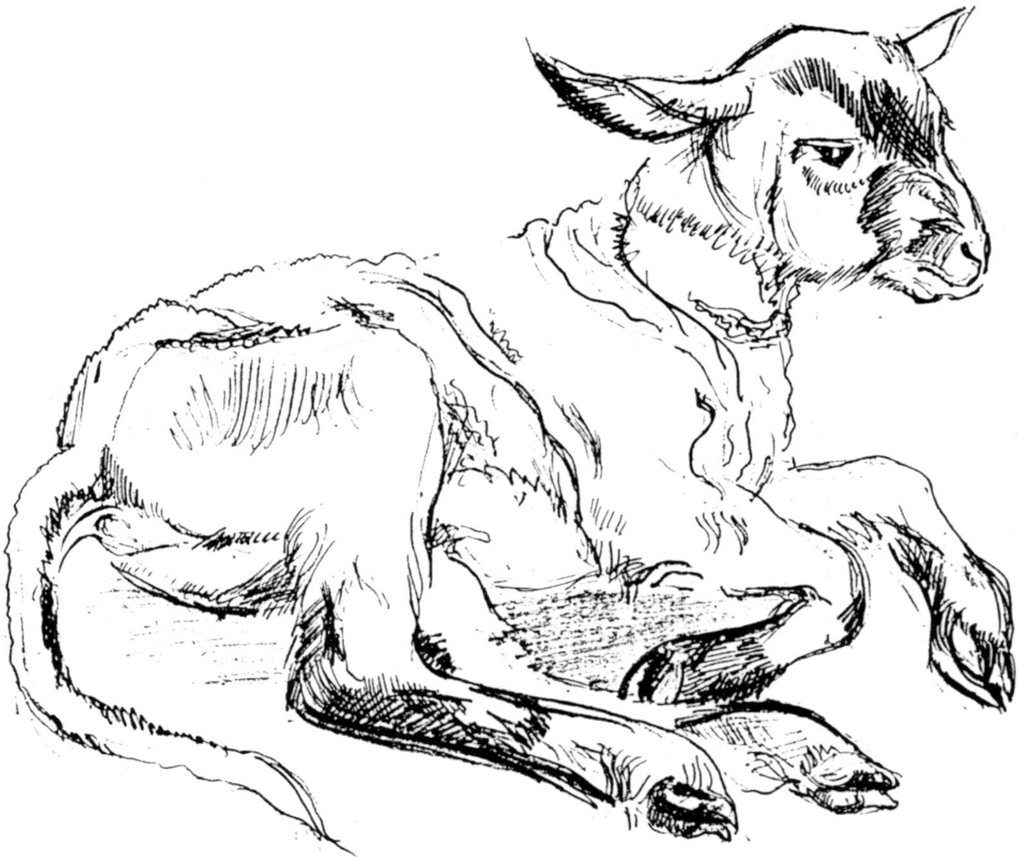

Processing of New Lambs

Now begins the 'processing'. The little lambs' navels are dressed with iodine to prevent infection. The afterbirth is removed. The same serial number is sprayed on to the ewe and her lambs so that if later they become separated from each other they can easily be reunited. The ewe's udder is checked to see that it functions properly and is clear of wool and dirt. Ewes and lambs (and shepherds) may need reviving drinks. Eartag numbers may be recorded. Lambs must be checked for abnormalities. If they are not seen to be drinking they may need to be held onto the teat for their first drink. When strong enough, the lambs are fitted with rubber rings around the tail and the unlucky males get two rings, the second around the 'purse' for castration purposes. This is completely painless after about one hour, and being starved of blood they both drop off in a few weeks. The ram lambs are said to be two stone lighter!

The tails are taken off lowland sheep, as on rich pastures they become heavily soiled by 'daggings' into which the ubiquitous blowfly lays her eggs. Mountain sheep on poor pasture produce dung in the form of hard, rabbit-like pellets which does not soil the wool. Also, as mountain sheep walk on stones and rocks, they suffer less from foot-rot and over-grown hooves.

Since a high proportion of lambs are born in the night and all the processing has to be done each day, it is an extremely busy time for the shepherd and his assistants, who have to snatch opportunities to sleep and eat when they can. Some prefer to live with the sheep on the site in an old caravan, which probably suits the womenfolk as there is not much time or opportunity to wash and change (or even undress) for days at a time! The Biblical Shepherd is surrounded by an aura of holiness. One might say the unwashed modern shepherd is often just surrounded by an aura, or should we say aroma!

In the Midlands, shearing is usually done at the end of May or in early June. Hot, dry weather makes the wool 'rise' and the natural lubricant called lanolin flows. The job is often done piecework by gangs of itinerant specialists who bring their own shearing clippers and the motors to drive them. It is then the farmer's job to keep a steady flow of sheep ready for the husky handlers, and to take away, roll up and pack the fleeces in enormous wool sacks or 'sheets'. Lambs are not shorn and when all the flock are put together again the lambs often fail to recognise their new-look mothers!

At the wool depot, these enormous wool sacks are handled with ease by men with little trolleys who are equipped like Captain Hook. The grader is supposed to be able to recognise instantly any one of about 350 grades, and having weighed the sacks he proceeds to throw the fleeces into the appropriate containers surrounding the weighing machine.

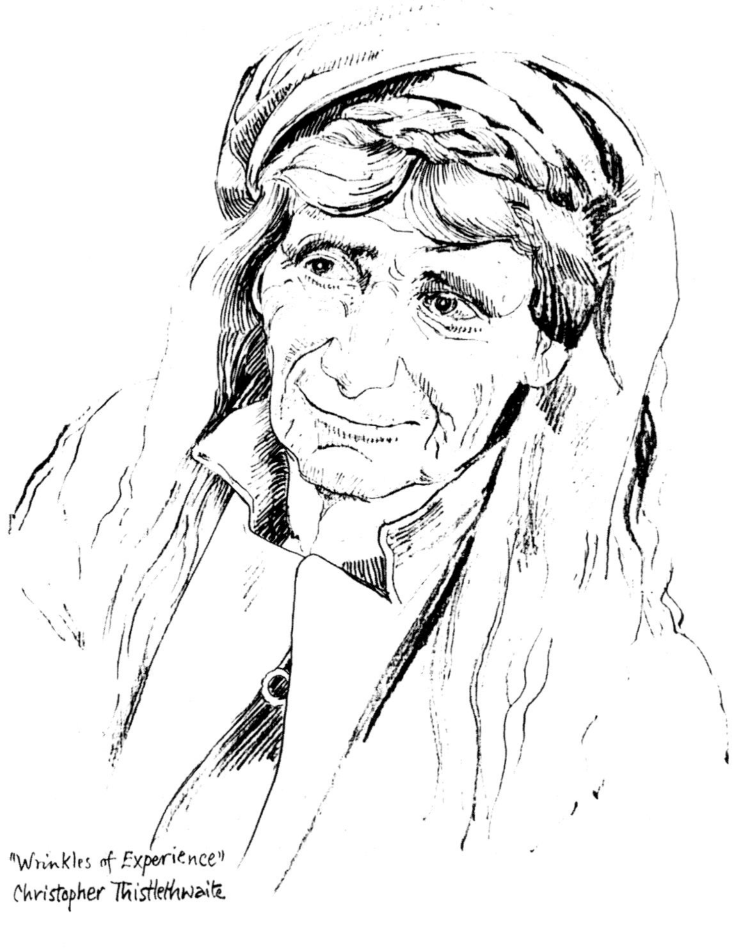

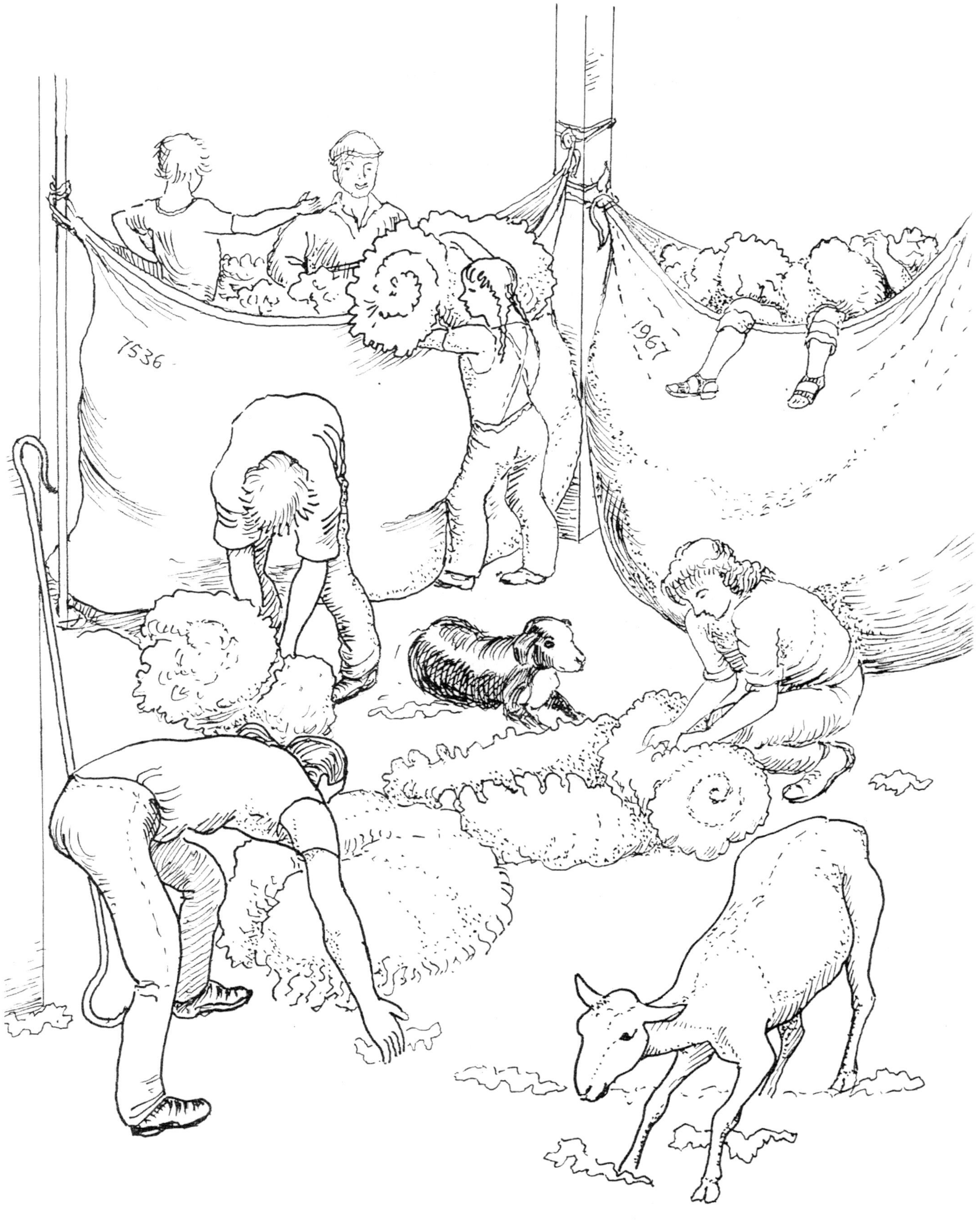

A whole fleece is laid on the tarpaulin outside uppermost. Then the long edges are folded inwards to the middle and the fleece rolled up firmly. Wool from the neck end is twisted into a rope which is wound tightly round the bundle and tucked under itself.

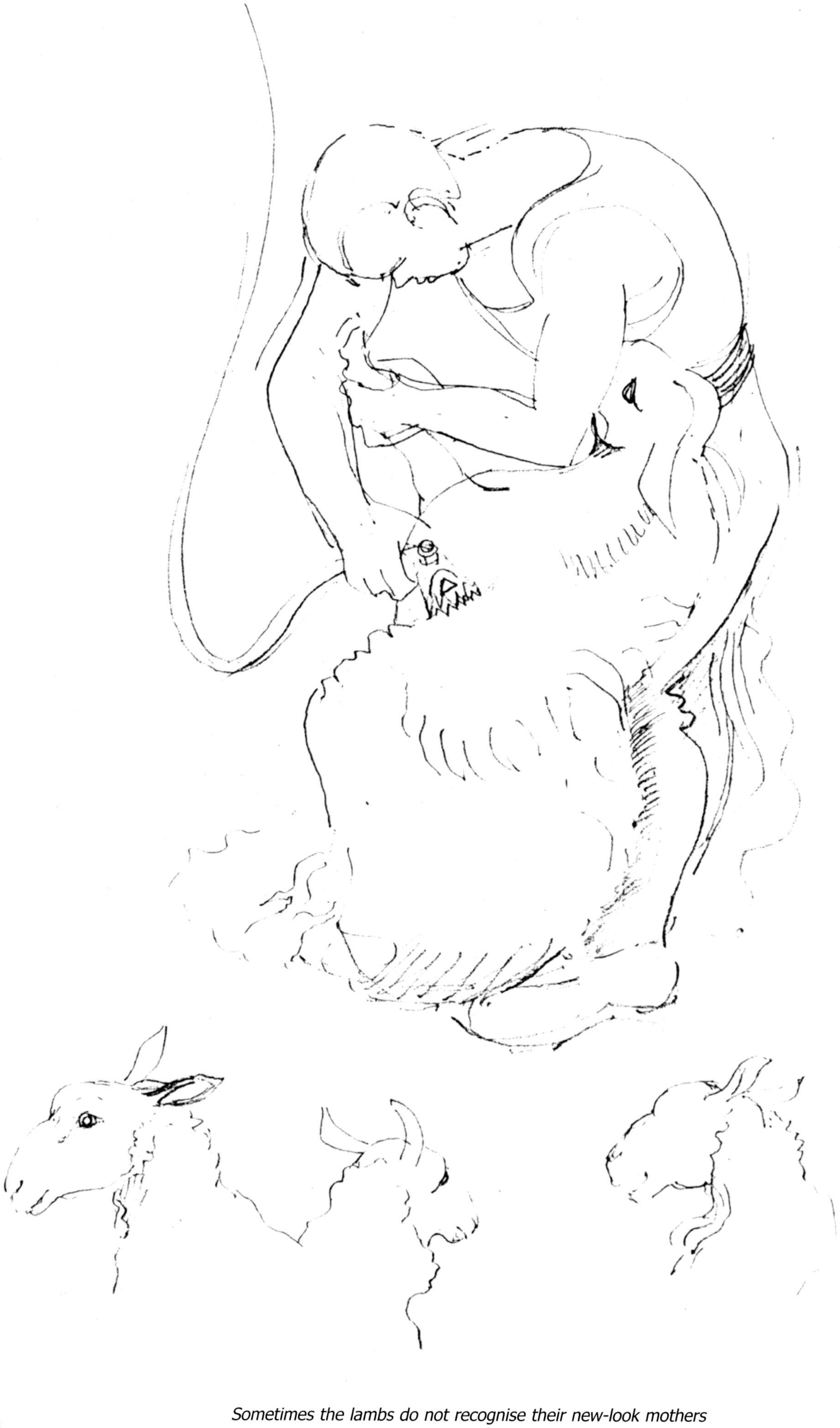

Sometimes the lambs do not recognise their new-look mothers

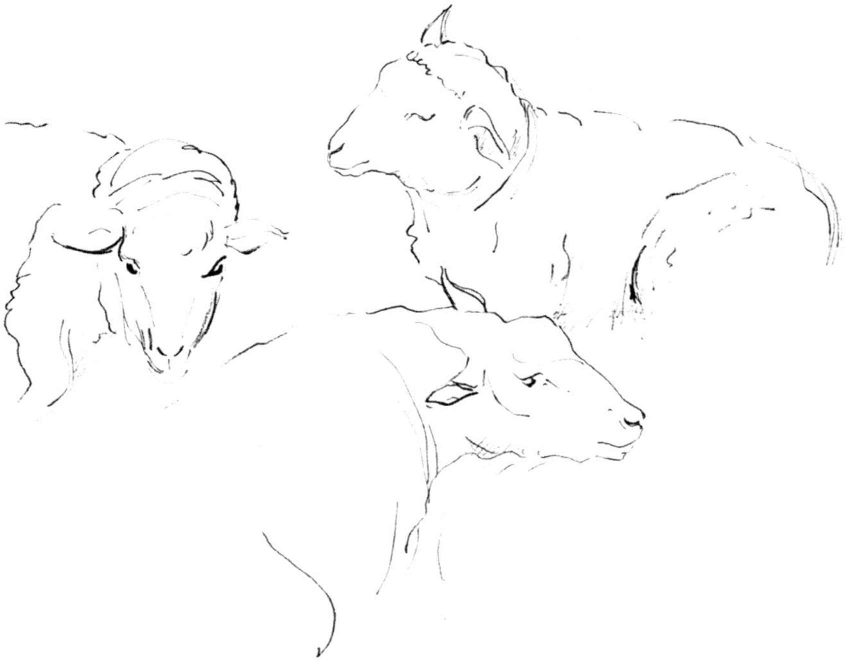

Shearer using electric clippers

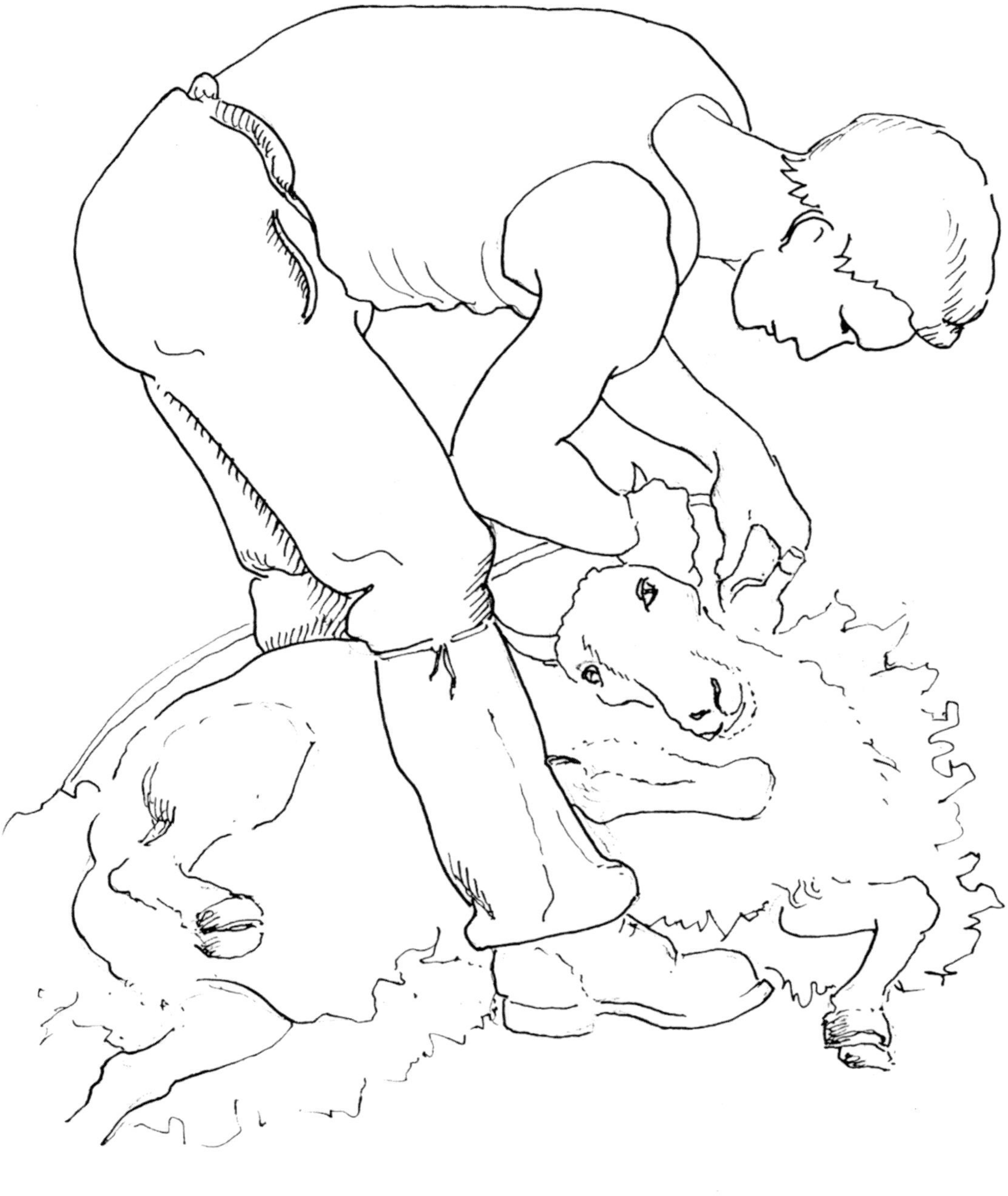

Under the Watchful Eye of the Law

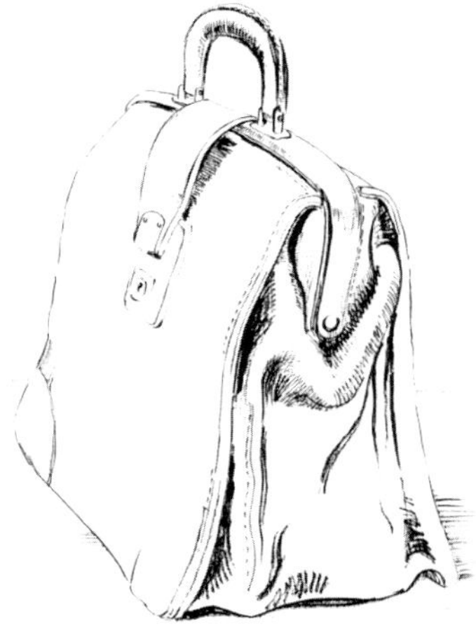

A few weeks after shearing, when they have had time to grow some more wool, sheep are dipped in a disinfectant bath by order of the ministry. This is partly against the attentions of blowflies and partly against parasites known as ticks and keds and one that causes scab. This hides in the *suborbital fossa,* a groove beneath the eye, so that even the head must be submerged. In years gone by, the police had to be informed of intent to dip at a certain time and an officer might turn up with a watch to ensure that each animal soaked for a full minute. As it was a filthy, splashy, unrewarding job he did not need much persuading to retire to the house for a cup of tea while we proceeded at our own pace!

Farmers often go to some lengths to keep a 'closed' flock or herd, buying in only the occasional male animal to improve the strain and rearing their own female replacements. Thus they avoid the possibility of importing disease from the market. There was an occasion when I felt the need to buy forty ewes to increase our flock and selected a likely lot recommended by one of our friends who was a show judge. They were duly bid for and purchased, the auctioneer giving me a handsome premium to encourage me to patronise his sale yard again.

A few days after they had been delivered, I was showing them to a friend and one broke away from the group and looked distressed. On examination, we found that she and several others were blind. The vet diagnosed New Forest Disease and we had to catch all of them every day for several weeks to dress their eyes with ointment. When I approached the vendor for some recompense for all our trouble, he replied that they must have become infected in the market or the transporter, as he had no sign of New Forest Disease on his farm.

Having bought sixty theaves (young ones) from market on the Welsh Border, a few days later I was informed by the Ministry of Agriculture Veterinary Department that they, and all the rest of my sheep, would have to be dipped again in their presence, as a Welsh farmer had sent a consignment of ewes infected by scab to the market that same day. This made it obligatory for all the thousands of sheep present to be traced and dipped. For us, it was an expensive exercise at an inconvenient time of the farming year, and no recompense was forthcoming from the ministry or from the auctioneers at the sale yard.

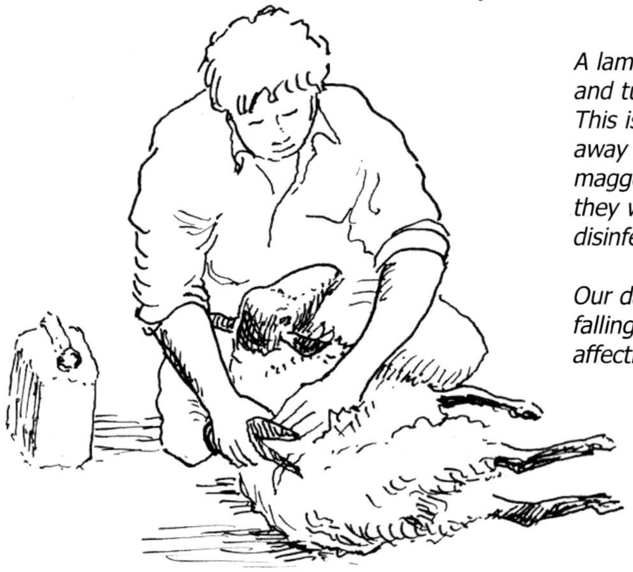

A lamb or ewe may be seen to wag and shake its tail very swiftly and turn its head to bite at its back end.
This is called 'fly strike'. It must be caught and all the dirty wool cut away with hand clippers revealing a mass of yellow, wriggling maggots burrowing into its skin. They would eat the animal alive if they were not noticed. The maggots are killed by splashing some disinfectant dip solution over them.

Our daughter, Julia, when only three years old, saw the maggots falling from the sheep onto the ground. She showed her misplaced affection by saying, "Aren't they sweet little things, Daddy?"

The Good Shepherd Gives His Life For His Sheep

The concept of the Good Shepherd from biblical times really does persist today. I am told that there is a graveyard in Scotland where three shepherds were buried in one week. They had literally given their lives for their sheep in blizzard conditions. The shepherd knows his sheep and they know him and follow him. Although they may look all the same to other people, he will know many ewes and lambs as individuals - the circumstances of their births and the highlights of their lives while they have been in his care.

The shepherd's dogs, working closely with him day by day, form an almost telepathic bond with him and have been known to work most intelligently with little or no guidance, relying upon their instinct and experience in times of danger or unusual stress.

The drawing of the dog's hindquarters is from a sketchbook taken on a trip to the Grasmere Sports in 1938. The hounds were made to follow a gruelling trail laid by a runner dragging a bag of aniseed over the rocky hillsides.

Which reminds me of a peculiar survival in Westmorland, a remnant of an old Celtic language which is, or was lately, used for counting sheep. In Borrowdale the numerals one to twenty are as follows:

1 - 5: Yan, tyan, tethera, methera, pimp.

6 - 10: Sethera, lethera, hovera, dovera, dick.

11 - 15: Yan-a-dick, tyan-a-dick, tethera-dick, methera-dick, bumfit.

16 - 20: Yan-a-bumfit, tyan-a-bumfit, tethera-bumfit, methera-bumfit, giggot.

In Wasdale, the form was:

1 - 5: Yan, tian, tudder, anudder, mimph, etc.

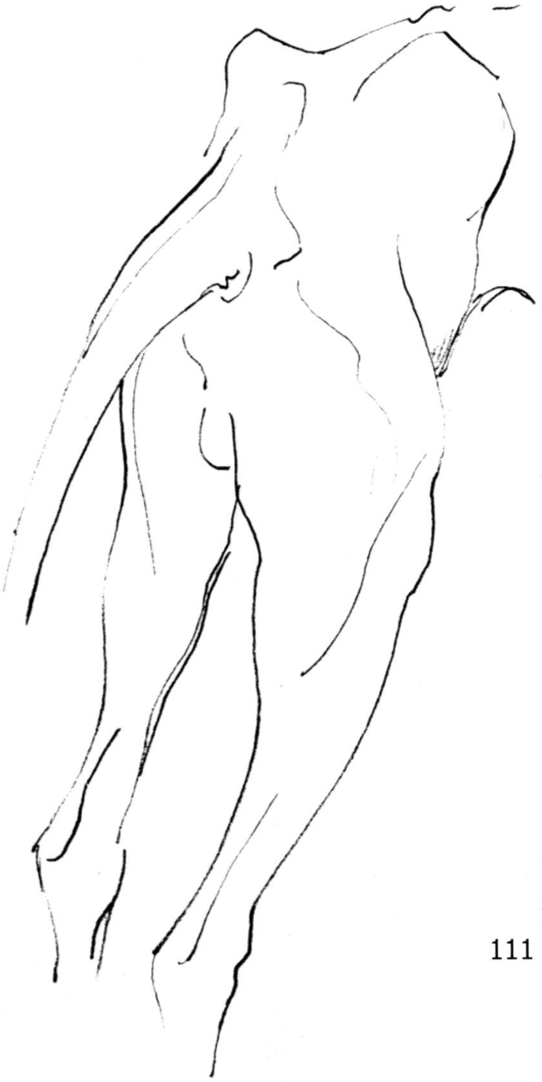

Hind quarters of a hound trail dog

Sheep dogs love their work but they need constant practice. On our small intensive farm there was not enough work for a sheep dog, so we used to keep yellow Labrador retrievers. Their kindly nature and equable temperament is such that they would never harm our small children, or indeed, anyone else, no matter what the provocation. We obtained them from a gamekeeper who had an illustrious stud of well-trained gun dogs. The first was a dog named Rusty. He gave us great pleasure and lived for fourteen years.

The second was a bitch named Russet, who, having matured into a well-grown, good-looking charmer, was introduced to a likely suitor who belonged to a farmer in a neighbouring village. (In those days, the stud fee of £10 was about the same as the price of a fat lamb.) In the course of nature she produced an excellent litter of eleven, and we allowed her to rear eight. Her second litter was eight, and she reared all of them. There was little difficulty in selling the pups for between £15 and £30 each.

Russet was secured at night in a kennel surrounded by a six foot high iron fence, but one morning she was found *inflagrante delicto* with her former lover. He had travelled a quarter of a mile during the night and surmounted this palisade to have his way with her. My wife, Elizabeth, being of a truly upright nature, felt it her duty to confess this stolen service to the dog's owner. He told her he would be satisfied with half the stud fee, and later she duly paid the £5!

We all found the pups most attractive, with their oversized, wrinkled skins and winning ways, so I thought I would make a visual record. When sketching these little creatures asleep in a mass, one creeps up stealthily and expects them to remain still for a few minutes at least, but they are on the move all the time, constantly changing position with one another.

Adult Labradors are extremely soft-mouthed, for carrying downed game birds back to their masters. Rusty would collect eggs from a nest in the hedge bottom without breaking them. Russet, when she got bored in the long summer days, would appear in the yard to present us with a completely undamaged laying hen. Of course, the bird had to be returned to our neighbours' house ¼ of a mile away with profuse apologies!

Russet
The Labrador bitch

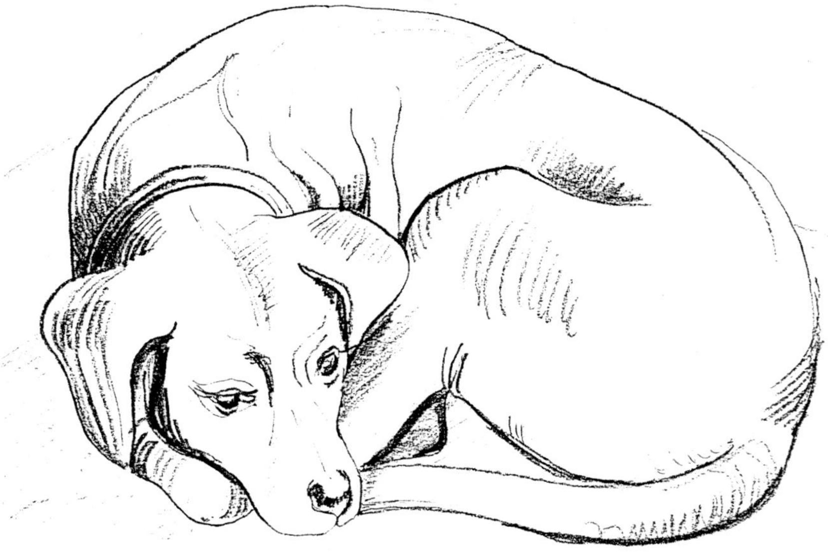

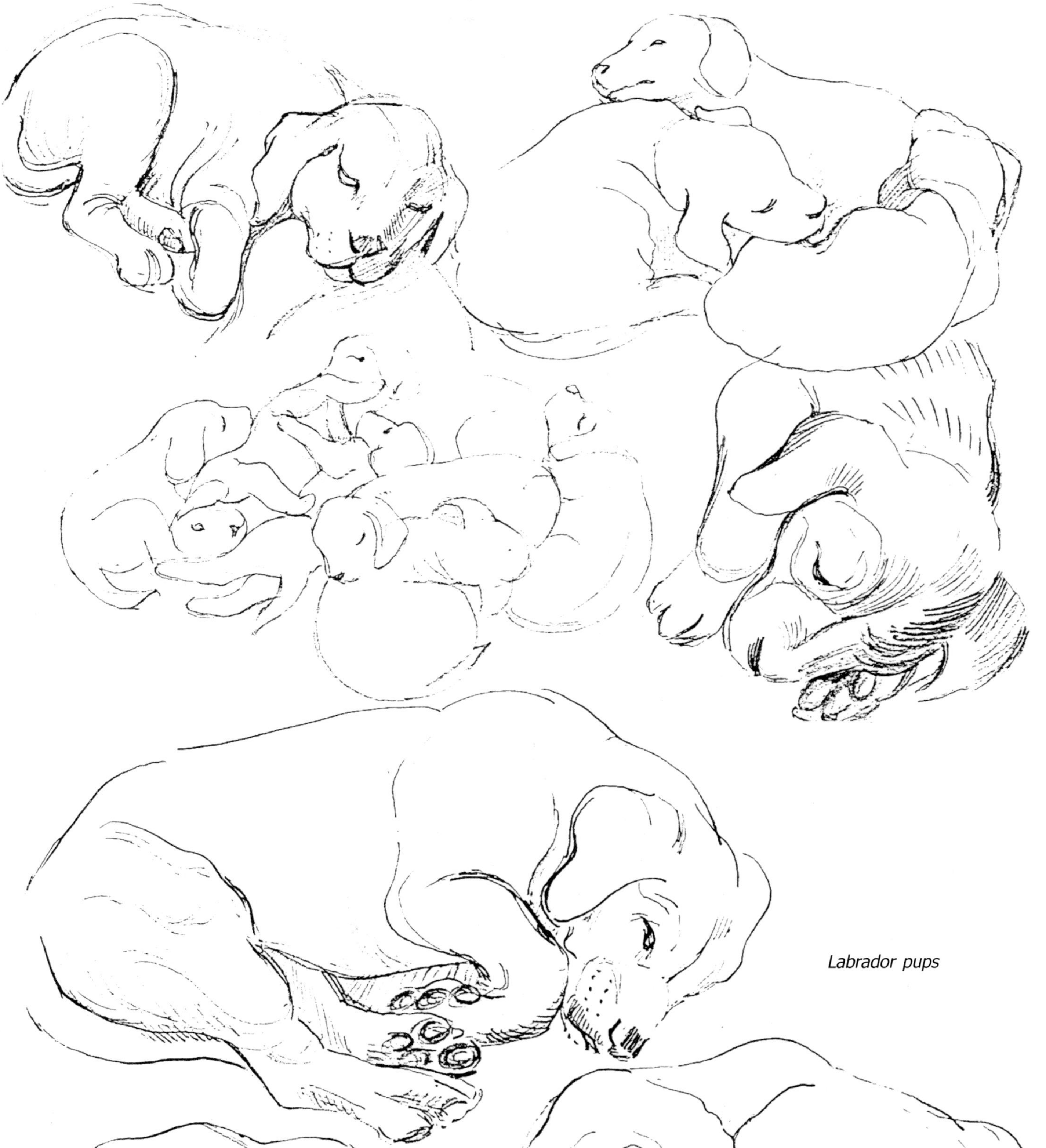

Labrador pups

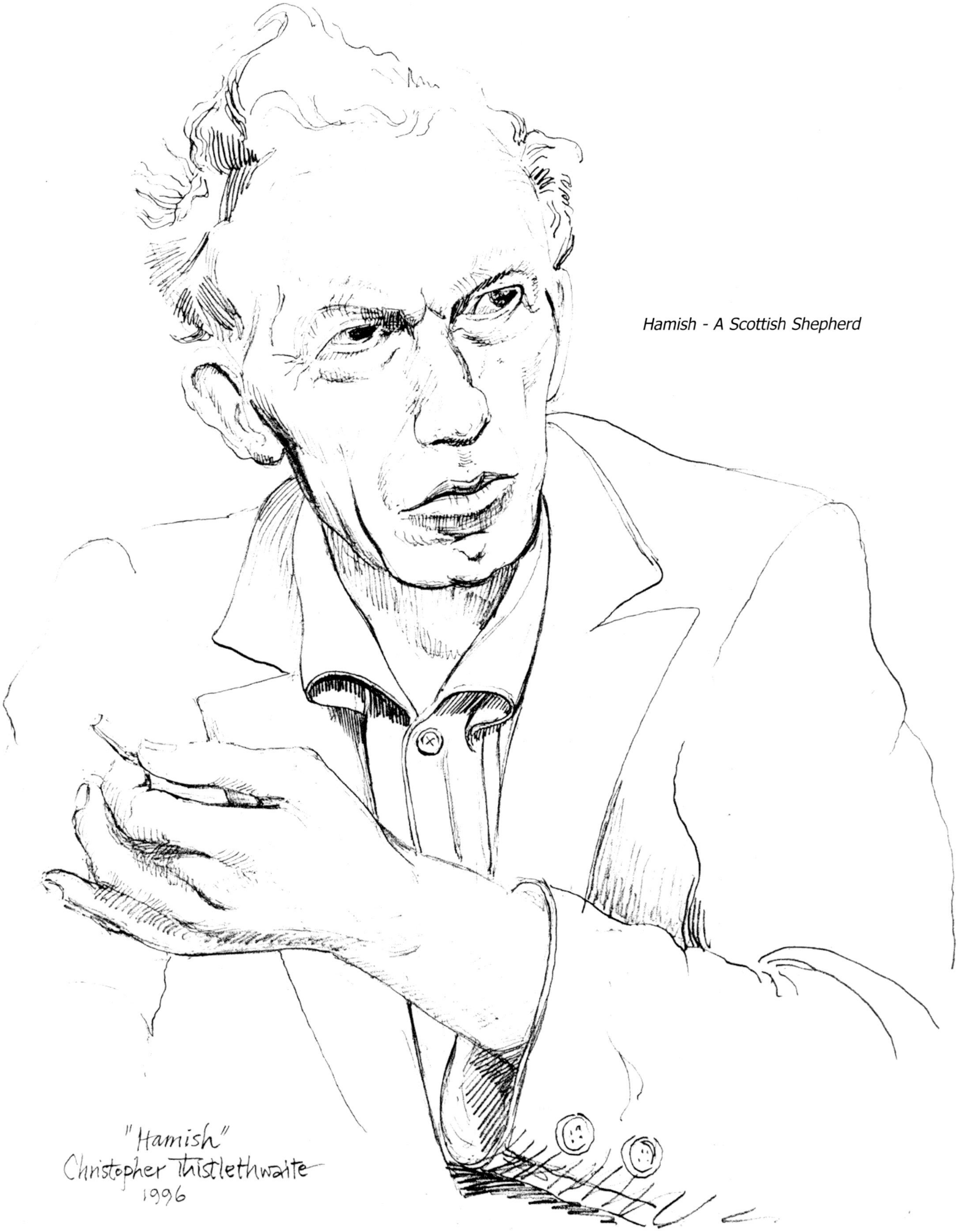

Hamish - A Scottish Shepherd

He that observeth the wind shall not sow, and he that regardeth the clouds shall not reap

When planning the day's work with the men, alternatives must be given to allow for sudden changes in the weather and one must be aware that the rain that spoils the hay helps the potato crop to increase in weight. In like manner, the wind that blows the girls' skirts at the same time blows dust in the eyes of the boys!

I have found that those engaged in outdoor work on the land, while they become expert at reading the weather signs, do not grumble, accepting what comes in a fatalistic way without complaining. Sometimes I have come across superstition, such as the case of the cowman who blamed bad luck with the calves on a malevolent Deity getting his revenge for our bringing in the hay on a Sunday!

One cannot but be impressed by the more spectacular manifestations of nature. I have several times witnessed, in the thundery heat of the hayfield, a twister whirlwind progress across the ground, lifting half an acre of dry crop high into the air and depositing it yards away all over a hedge and the branches of a tall tree.

Another time, when hauling bales, I was sheltering under the wagon when a bolt of lightning shook the ground beneath - a nearby elm tree was riven the length of its trunk. On another occasion, I was on the way to a barn dance when I noticed smoke coming from the trunk of a dead tree on the boundary fence. Thinking of Moses and the burning bush, but hearing no voice from the cloud, I returned to call the fire brigade. The lightning had ignited the tinder dry material in the hollow trunk!

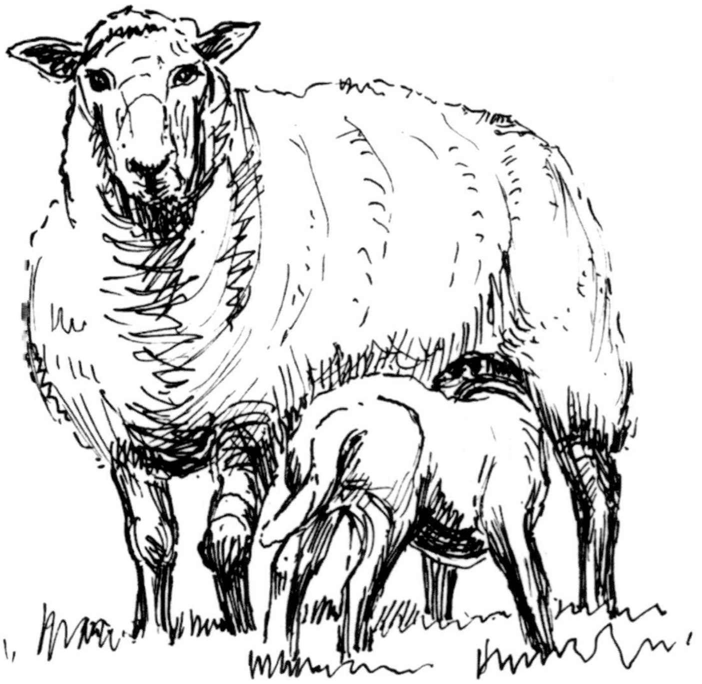

Anthropomorphism

People often, and quite wrongly, attribute to animals human thoughts, sentiments and powers of reasoning. This is often called anthropomorphism. Animals are motivated purely according to instincts, and men have learned to use them to their advantage. Two examples that come to mind are sheepdogs at work and homing pigeons. Someone said to me, "Why do the silly sheep prefer to lie on the hard stony granite road rather than the soft warm grass field alongside? We have to blow the horn to move them as we drive along to visit you."

This is the way a human thinks: "If I had to lie in a sleeping bag on a groundsheet the grass and earth would feel softer to my bony hips and elbows than the two inch granite stones on the roadway." The sheep's instincts on the other hand tell them that their natural home is on the stony ground of the mountain slopes. It suits their feet better and they don't mind their bony legs grinding on the stones; they had a million years to get used to it before men interfered and brought them down to the soft ground where they get footrot!

Thus it is clear that sheep and humans think and react quite differently in the same circumstances.

In wintry conditions, it would seem to me that free range poultry would much prefer to be inside a warm shed instead of cowering out of the wind in six inches of snow with a frozen water trough. Their ancestors, the jungle fowl, lived in the warm climate of the Far East, unlike ducks and geese that have enough downy feathers to keep themselves warm.

One day as we were coming to the end of the shearing occupation, a friend, who is a noted calligrapher, announced his intention of making a visit to see the operation. One of the team who was a university lecturer dryly remarked that as he was a lettering expert he could be responsible for stamping the letter 'T' in red paint on the flanks of the sheep before they were released from the shearer's grasp.

Another day, as we were engaged in dipping sheep, his valuable spectacles were knocked off into the evil smelling soup. Luckily, there was a tank handy into which we ladled all the dip while looking in the four foot deep bath for the precious object.

Easter was early and our nine year old son caused some puzzlement by working on his winter sledge, fitting an open topped box. From a vantage point high on the hay bales in the Dutch barn he would watch the remaining 'in lamb' ewes for signs of labour. At the appropriate time he would importantly trundle his little sledge to fetch the lambs back in the box, the proud ewe walking along behind and both feeling very pleased with what had been accomplished.

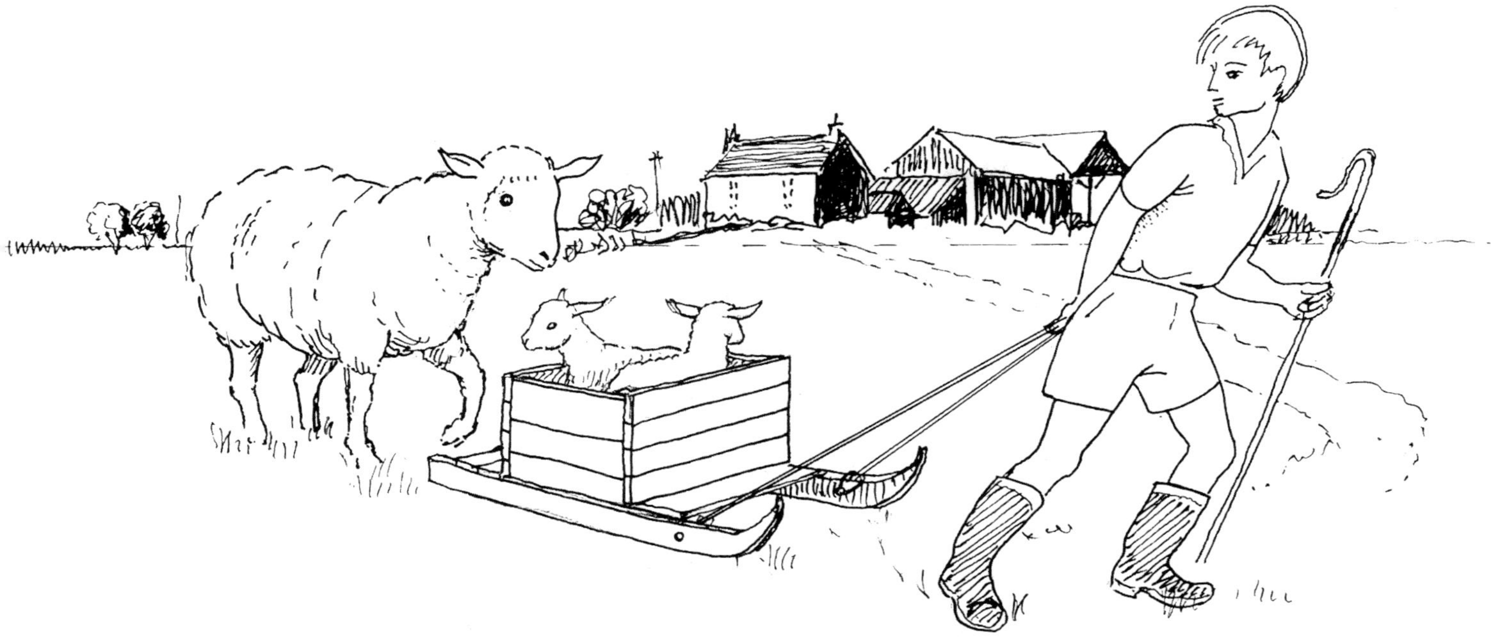

Anthony bringing home twin lambs in a home-made sledge

It was quite common for children to have useful jobs on a farm such as feeding calves or collecting eggs. Rounding up the sheep on ponies was a job I used to enjoy as a child. In the inter-war years, when farms were totally neglected, good pasture land was often covered with self-sown hawthorn bushes and briars, making little thickets in which the ubiquitous rabbit would thrive. Their burrows and warrens would spread across the fields in all directions, causing pitfalls for the trotting ponies and a dearth of good grazing for sheep and cattle. In addition, there would be stumbling blocks in the form of ant-hills, heaps a foot high at three yard intervals, further impeding one's progress. Along with seeding weeds and overgrown hedges, to a conscientious farmer or worker who knew how it should be, it was a scene of great and wicked desolation. I remember one such old man turning to me and saying with great vehemence, "Surely to God if old Hitler were to come over here and see all this neglect, he would change his mind about invading our country".

Shortage of Shepherds and Dangers of Sheep Scab

On the moors and fells of the North of England and Scotland there is a dearth of young men being trained to be shepherds. The heavy boots and shepherd's pony have given way to the quadricycle, an all-terrain vehicle, thought by some to be the biggest advance in sheep farming since the collie dog.

Some men, often ones who had taken undue risks by careless use of organo-phosphorus sheep dips, have suffered very unpleasant side-effects. Consequently, the government have relaxed the rule on compulsory dipping, and this will likely have dire results for the national flock. There are always a few sheep grazing near the summits of mountain ridges that will fail to be gathered for the annual dipping by flock-masters from one side of the ridge or the other, and these few harbour the disease-causing mites of sheep scab. This debilitating disease will quickly become endemic, wasting the years of meticulous hard work which had virtually eliminated it.

Homing Instinct in Animals and Birds

Sheep born and reared on a certain area of mountainside get a strong attachment to it. They know where to shelter in a storm and where the choicest grazing is. They are said to be 'heft' to that area, and traditionally must be sold with the farm if it changes hands. If you were to transport them many miles away they would find their own way back. This homing instinct is well known in birds to most people, but farm animals have it too.

I remember as a young man taking three dozen young cattle, steers and heifers, to some summer grazing situated ten miles away from the farm where they had been reared. Six months later we were bringing them back, but for some reason took a different route completely unknown to these animals. At first they had to be constantly urged along as they tried to graze the roadside verges. Then about three miles from home they began to sniff the air and quicken their pace, calling out with anticipation. The last two miles were covered at a quick trot as they turned unerringly into the farm yard. You could almost hear them saying, "How nice to be home at last".

'Don't Go in There Again!'

One day in the spring, I was called out from my meal to assist with a ewe that had been straining in labour for some time, to no avail. Getting my assistant to hold the animal by the neck, I rolled up my right sleeve and applied slip-gel to my hand and forearm and proceeded to investigate. As I had suspected, it was a quite common mal-presentation known as 'a breech'. The tail and rump appear with the lamb's thick hocks and rear legs lying forward under its belly, making it too bulky to pass through the birth canal.

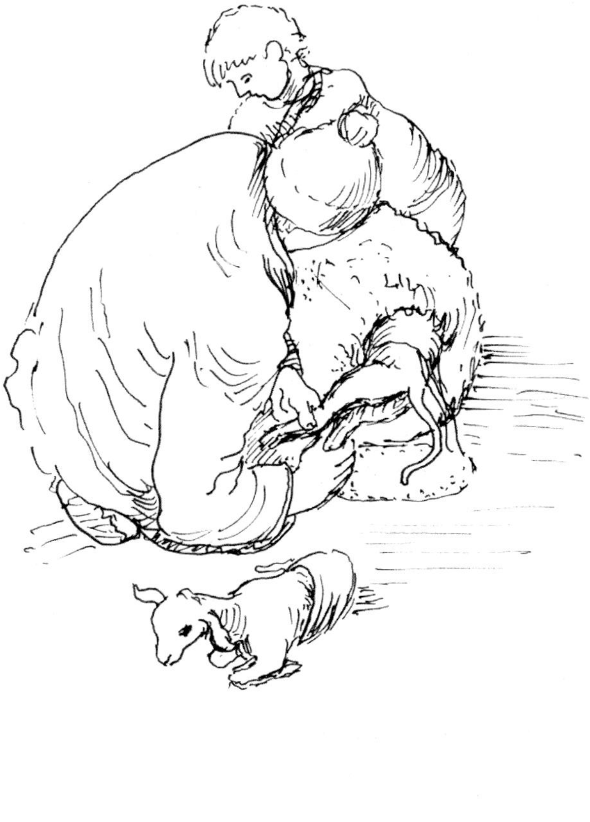

I pushed the rear of the lamb back into the uterus, gently found each rear leg, and pulling the legs by the fetlock, straightened out the hocks so that the feet and legs could come first. These were quickly followed by the body, head and forelegs and, as the ten pound ram-lamb appeared somewhat listless after his birth trauma, I cleared its airways with a straw and gave it a good slap on the ribs to start it breathing so that it let out a faint bleat. A little town boy who had been closely observing these proceedings was heard to say, "You daft wee thing, that will teach you not to go in there again!"

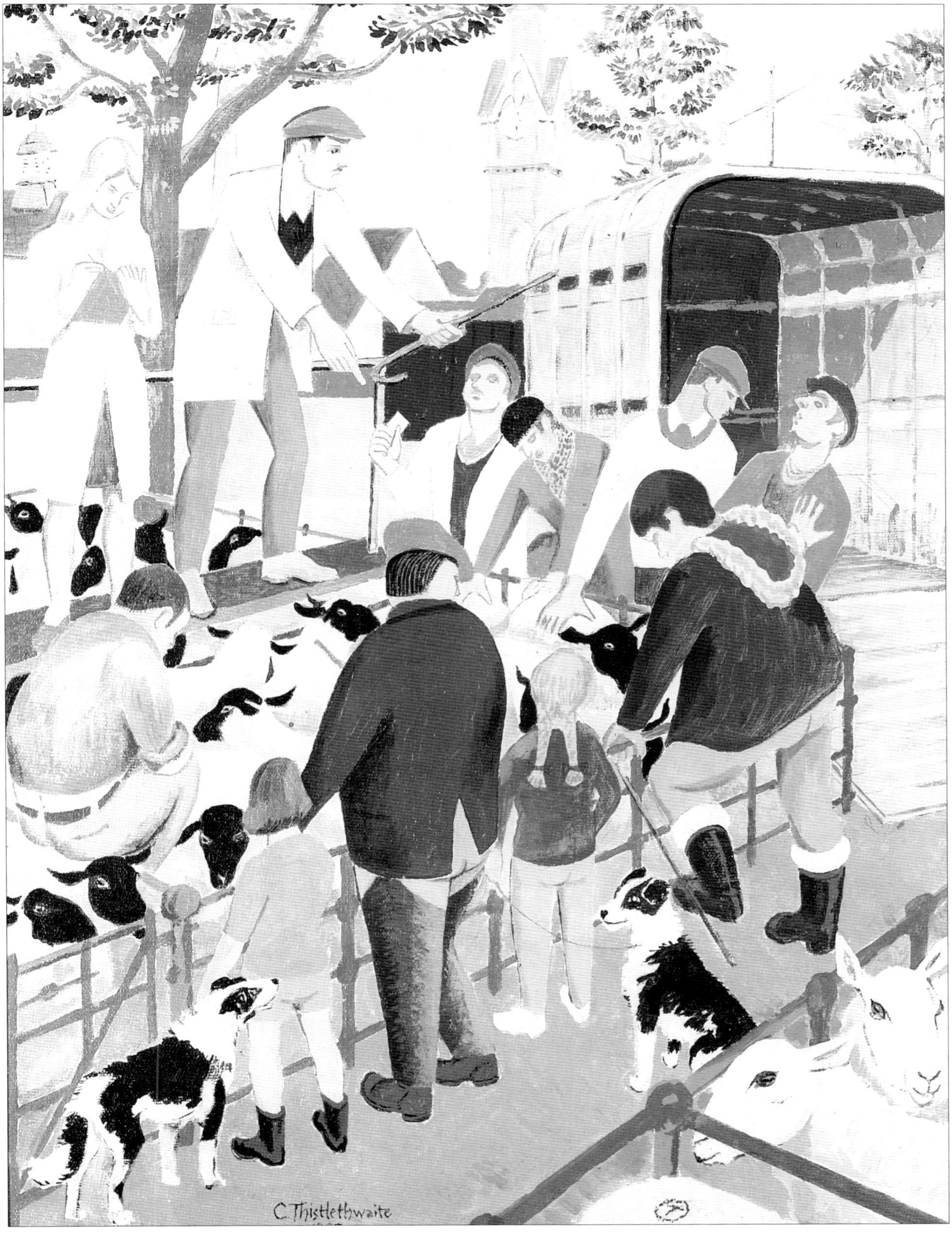

Sheep being sold at Leicester City Cattle Market (now closed but the landmark clock remains)

Chapter FIVE

Pigs

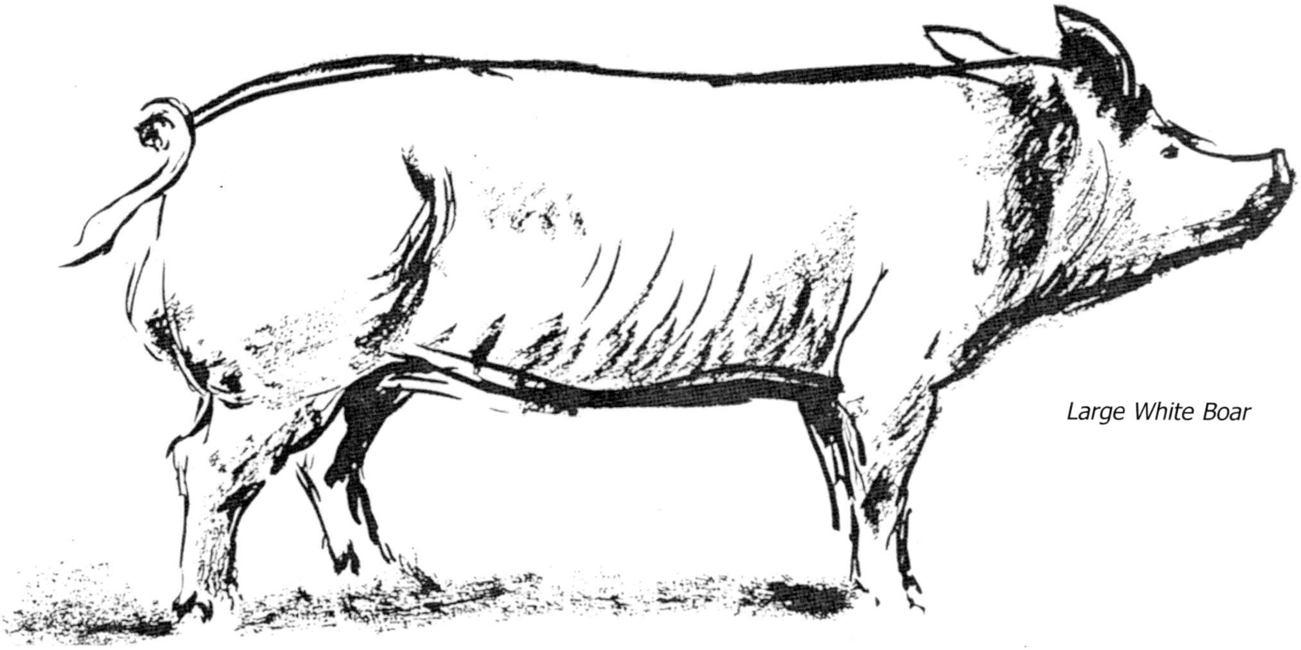

Large White Boar

The Wayward Boar

One of our large white boars grew to be quite enormous, the size of a donkey, and was totally wayward. He could lift a heavy oak five-barred gate off its hinges in order to wander about the farm at will. It was evident that he could not be contained, so his days were numbered. When the time came to load him for market, he became suspicious and would not be tempted into the trailer by food. Upon the principle that "if food does not motivate an animal - try sex", we first loaded a nubile gilt to be his distracting playmate and to occupy his mind during the journey to the mart.

A mature boar, when confronted by a strange boar, will perform a terrifying threat display, pawing and scraping at the ground to make clouds of dust, while champing his jaws to create a mass of frothy foam through which his wicked tusks protrude. It can be even more spectacular and dangerous than an angry bull. You can imagine what it is like to have several of them confined in adjoining pens at the market.

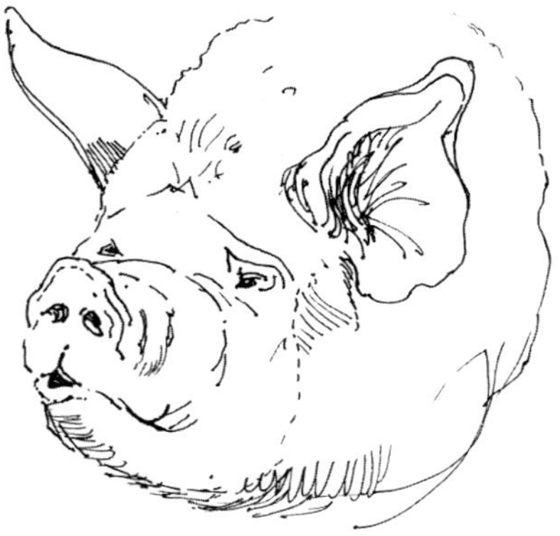

Fitting Rings on Pigs

An unringed grazing pig will soon cause a grassy pasture to resemble a ploughed field by its inquisitive snout and immensely strong neck. Therefore, in outdoor systems of management, fitting rings in the top of the fleshy part of the nose is an ongoing activity to reduce rooting. So that the animal can be restrained by making it fast to a ring on a post, a noose is dropped over the top jaw behind the tusks. The animal makes a great deal of fuss and penetrating squeals out of all proportion to the hurt being done, while the intrepid operator, with a special pair of pliers, clips a series of rings into the snout.

At the onset of labour pains, a sow will become hyperactive in the preparation of her bed for the confinement. In the chosen place, she scrapes a shallow depression of appropriate dimensions in the soil. Then she rushes about, feverishly collecting suitable dry vegetation, which she masticates into short lengths to make a warm nest. Because they are not well endowed with a hairy coat, small pigs require artificial heat if they are to survive in cold weather. An inexperienced worker coming to feed the pigs at 7am may find an unexpected litter born in the night, half of which are 'dead'. He removes several inert little bodies, placing them on the manure heap outside the pen door. He then cleans out the pens, piling the manure and bedding on top of the heap. When the farmer comes on his mid-morning inspection, he is surprised to hear grunts and squeaks coming from piglets revived by the heat given off from the muck-heap! My wife would revive unpromising piglets by bathing them in warm water and placing them on the stove in a cardboard box lined with hay.

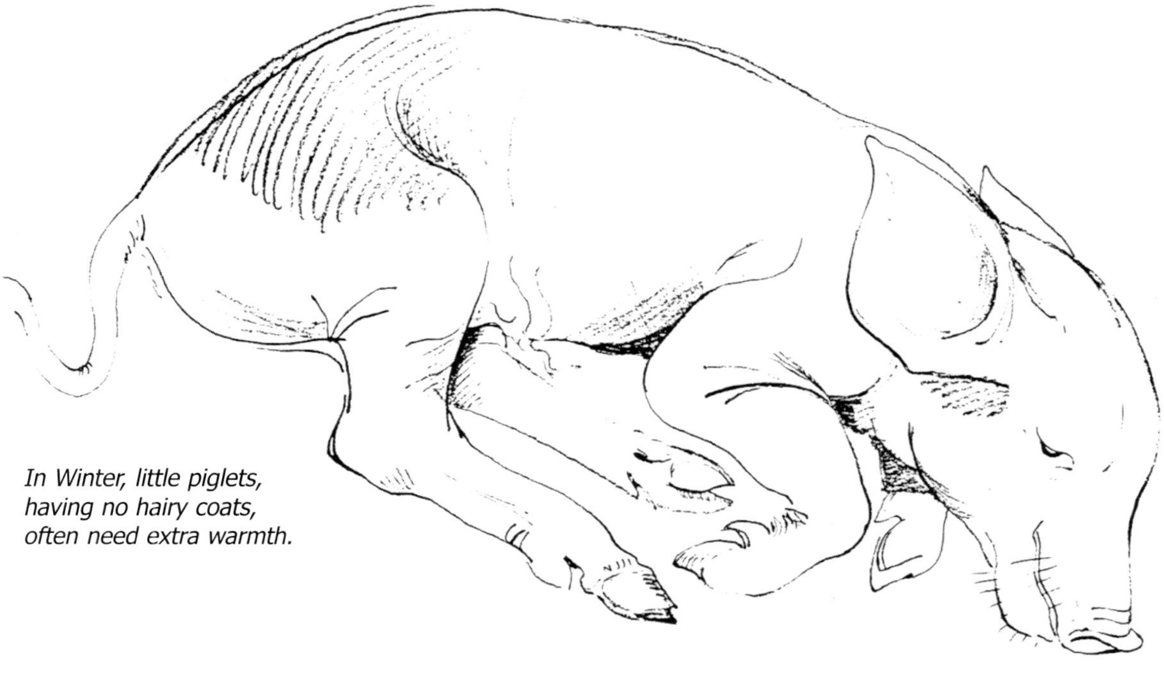

In Winter, little piglets, having no hairy coats, often need extra warmth.

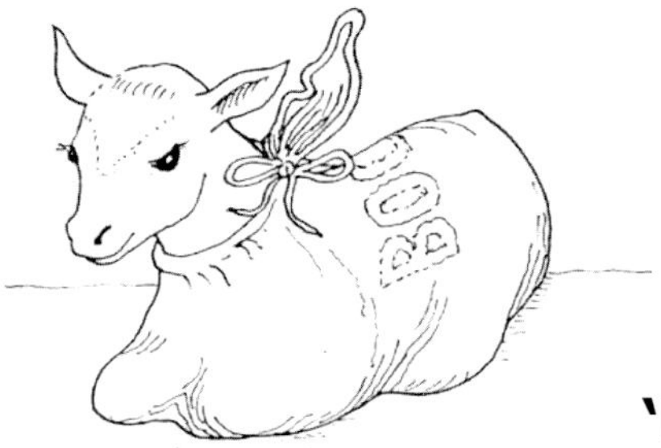

Calf transported in a feed bag tied behind its neck, like a child in a sack race on sports day.

'Pig in a Poke'

There is a multitude of names for the smallest pig in the litter. *Runt, wreckling or dillun* are three that come to mind. Small calves and weaner pigs, eight weeks old, would often be transported in hessian sacks through which they could easily breathe. Whereas the calf's head would protrude, the sack being tied tightly round its neck, little pigs would be totally enclosed. Hence the expression, "never buy a pig in a poke". When litters of small pigs are being handled for injection, castration, etc., they protest shrilly and the maternal fury knows no bounds. Sows, on hearing the lamentations of their dear ones, will rush from afar, jaws gnashing, and surround the luckless operators with threatening savagery, draining the valour of even the stoutest hearts.

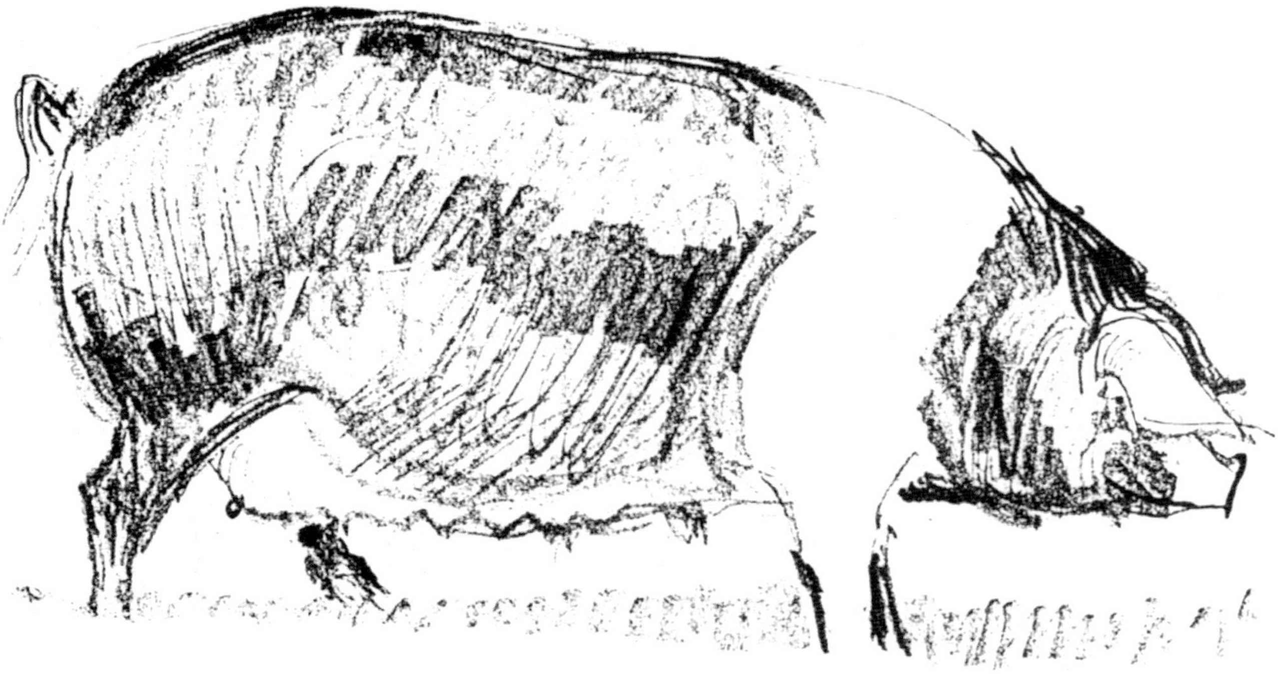

Wessex Saddleback Sow

Pigs reared together from infancy will not normally fall out; cross-suckling even occurs, some piglets availing themselves of any milk-bar proffered! Later, however, if a strange pig is introduced, possibly by mistake, it will suffer great persecution or even death from the rest of the group. Likewise, twenty new ewes introduced to a flock of eighty will be seen to be grazing a little apart even four weeks later. I mentioned earlier that ewes, like most animals, if given a choice of spouse, prefer to mate with rams that resemble themselves or their mothers. Unfortunately, they are usually disappointed as commercial lamb production demands hybrid vigour, so they are crossed with tups of a different breed.

Housed Animals are Totally Dependent

If animals are housed in buildings so that they can't forage and fend for themselves as are pigs, poultry, and to some extent cattle and sheep, all their needs must be attended to at least twice a day, 365 days a year. This is the very heavy responsibility undertaken by livestock farmers. Townsfolk usually lavish a great deal of care on the domestic pets which often seem to rule their lives. Compare this with a farmer who may have hundreds or thousands of lives in his care. A farmer may be seen at farm sales, shows and point-to-point races, but let us always remember he has usually done two or three hours work before and must do two or three hours on his return.

Feeding and watering, cleaning out and bedding down is an ongoing chore for the stockman. It follows that the location of food trolleys, fodder stores, and water bowls or taps is of vital importance so that the operator can work with maximum efficiency and is not constantly retracing his steps or walking about empty-handed 'with one arm as long as the other', as it has been described. For instance, the bucket of grain taken to the poultry in the afternoon comes back full of eggs. The cart taking out manure could come back laden with kale.

In the cold wintry weather, I always found that providing drinking water was a much greater problem than the feed for outlying stock, as normal plumbing takes little account of hard frosts. A great deal of time was spent thawing pipes and water troughs by lighting straw fires, boiling kettles, or using a blow-lamp to break up twelve-inch-thick blocks of solid ice, while thirsty animals stood by complaining noisily. I have often been soaked to the skin twice in one day during blizzard conditions when snow was up to the horse's belly and the hubs of the five foot diameter cartwheels.

That reminds me of when our second son was about due. It was in early January and in Arctic conditions. As our farm was a quarter of a mile from the public road, I would clear a track through the snow drifts at nightfall with a home-made snow-plough, against the possibility of a midnight dash to the cottage hospital's labour ward.

SHOULDER YOKES for carrying buckets

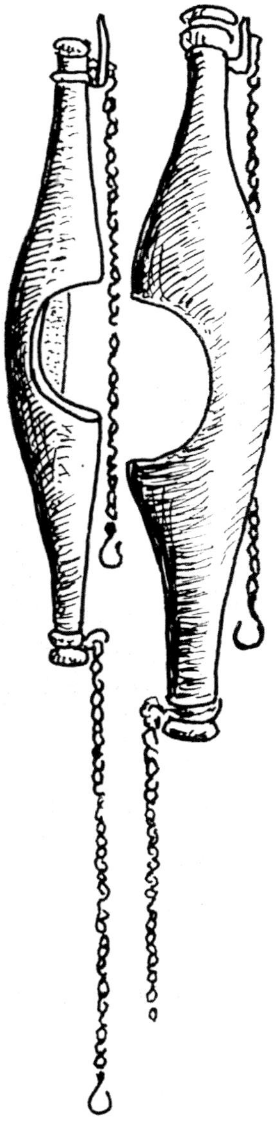

The Sausage's Endless Cycle!

Pigs and poultry, being mainly grain fed indoors, must have well-controlled living conditions and good housing to be cost effective. A pig may consume 3½lbs (1.6 kg) of grain to gain one pound (0.45 kg) of meat. When it is killed, it will produce less wastage than, say, a lamb where only 50% of live weight results in meat - a 90lb live lamb giving 45lbs of meat. If a hen is given 100lbs of grain a year and lays no eggs, it is a total waste of resources which could have sustained life in a starving person for many weeks. Faced with the choice, a hungry person will eat the 3½lbs of grain rather than wait for it to turn into one pound of pork or poultry meat!

I have seen a child given a sausage at school dinner put it, untouched, into the pig-swill bin. It is interesting to conjecture how many times the sausage completes the circle before someone finally decides to eat it.

No farmer or stockman worthy of the name will neglect or ill-treat his animals; rather he takes pride in his charges. Their welfare must come before his own comfort and convenience. The ploughman returning from the field or the huntsman from the chase, each must see to his horses' needs before his own. If he neglects his animals they will not serve him well the next day. The cow that is beaten and afraid will not 'let down' her milk. Nature has a way of getting her own back.

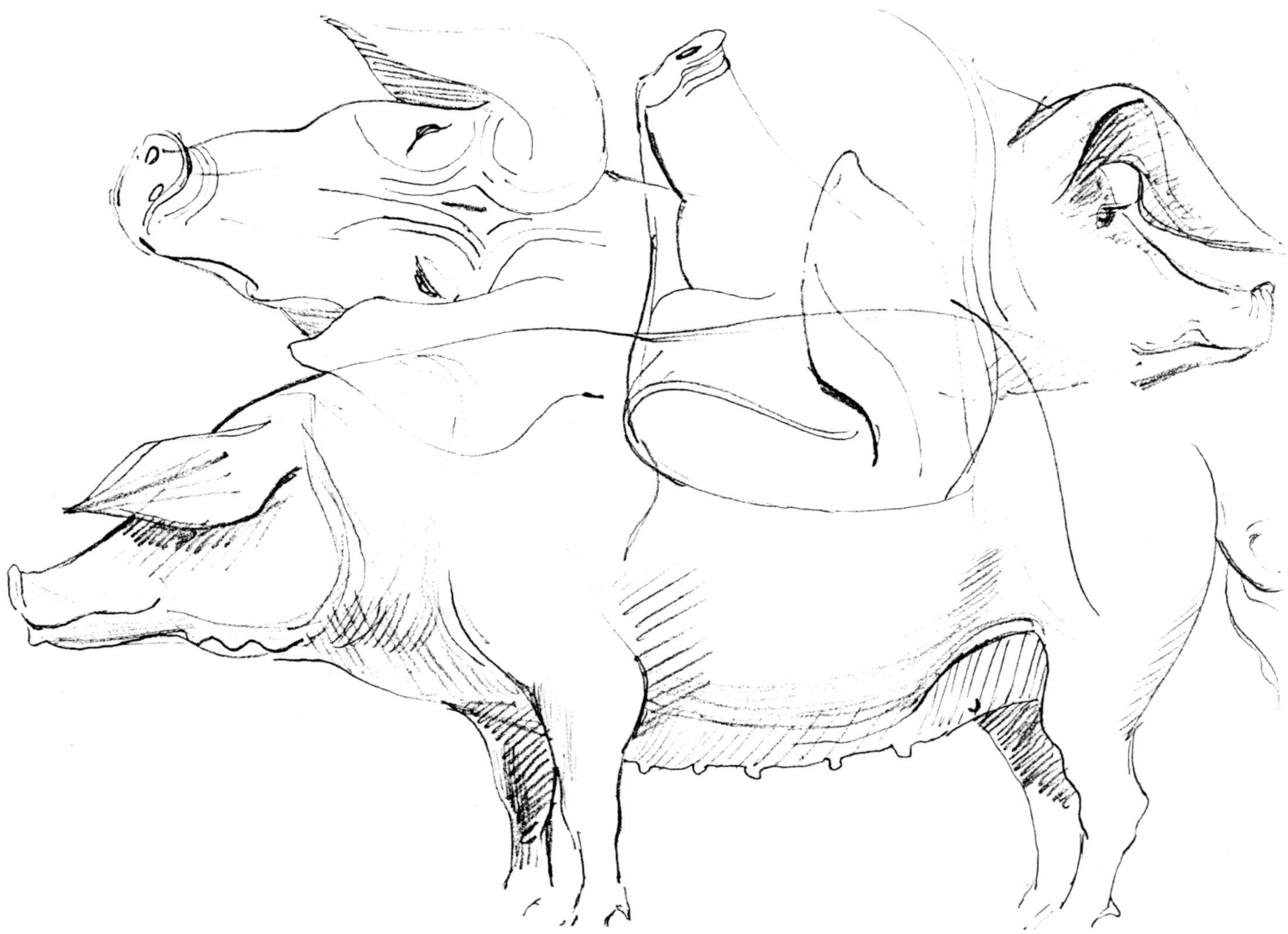

Two of Leicestershire's most famous delicacies, Pork Pies and Stilton Cheese, grew alongside one another as pigs thrived upon whey, the chief by-product of cheese making.

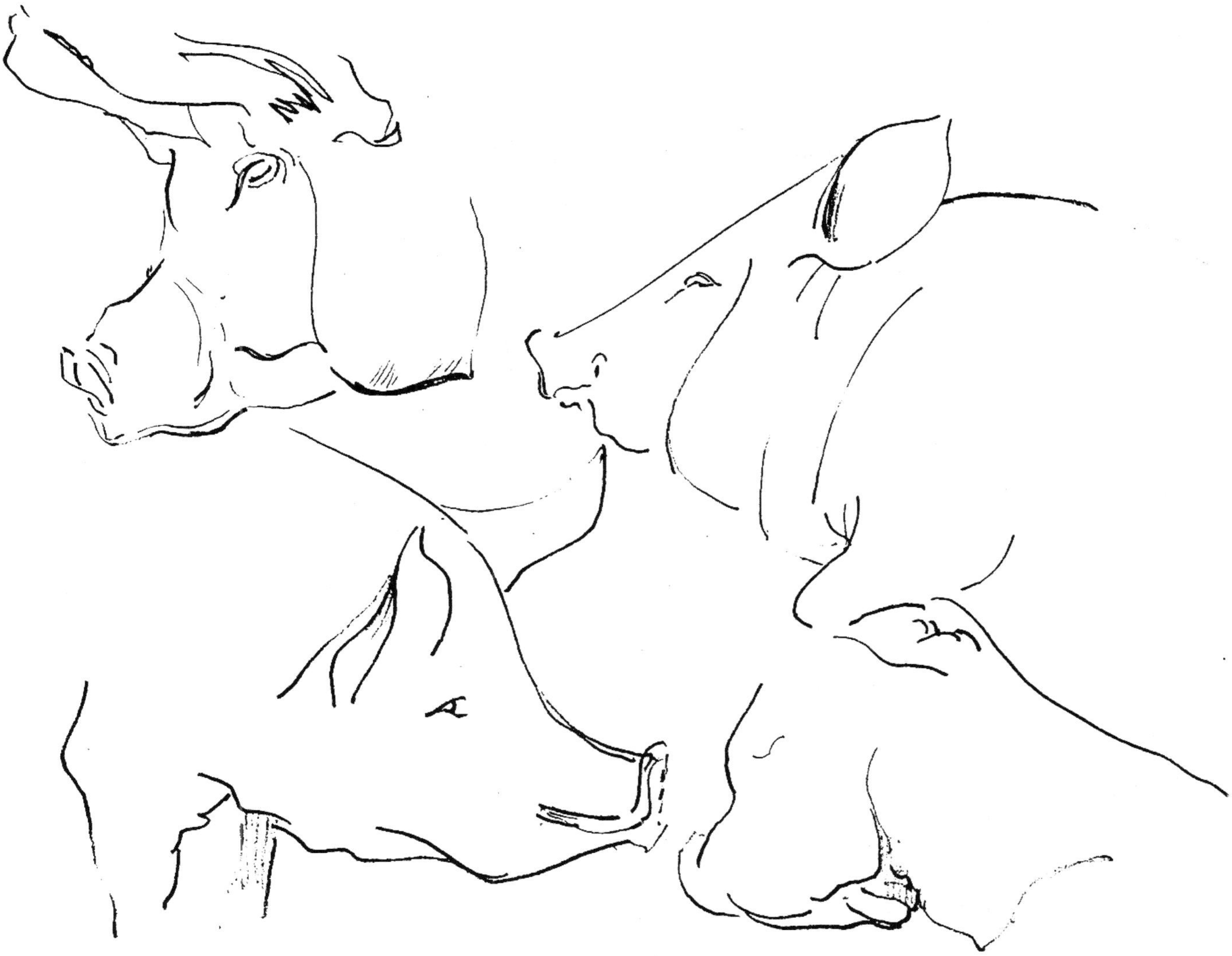

Imagine how a waitress in a transport café feels when confronted by a coach-load of ravenous young farmers. They call out their orders with an insistent ferocity, each wanting to be first with his snout in the trough. Just so when feeding pigs, it pays to approach with stealth.

Those who decry pigs being confined on concrete will nevertheless complain if they see a field of small arks or Nissen huts sheltering those pigs which have been emancipated to outdoor living, confined only by electric fencing. The corrugated iron is too shiny when new, soon to become ugly, rusty and battered with age. As pigs are notably lacking in hair, when they are raised in outdoor systems, costly feed which could sustain starving human populations is often wasted in maintaining their body heat in British winter conditions.

Under good management a sow might be expected to produce two litters in a year: four months in-pig (pregnant) followed by two months suckling, and within a week of weaning she will become pregnant again. I have known members of my 35-sow herd to farrow their third litter on the exact date of their first, a year earlier. From a herd of this size we used to sell about 650 pigs annually, many of them for bacon.

Selling Pigs at Different Stages

The weight of pigs was usually calculated in scores (20's) of pounds, thus a baconer of 10½ score would weigh 210 pounds (95.3kg). Pigs could be sold at different stages for these different purposes:

1. A sow could be sold with her litter, and I have even seen a litter born, or farrowed, in the market place.
2. A litter can be sold as 'weaners' from eight to twelve weeks old for someone else to fatten.
3. Older pigs can be sold for pork as 'cutters'.
4. 'Baconers' are heavier still, and used to be consigned straight to a bacon factory.
5. Once they are beyond a top bacon weight they are known as 'heavy hogs' and go for manufacturing.

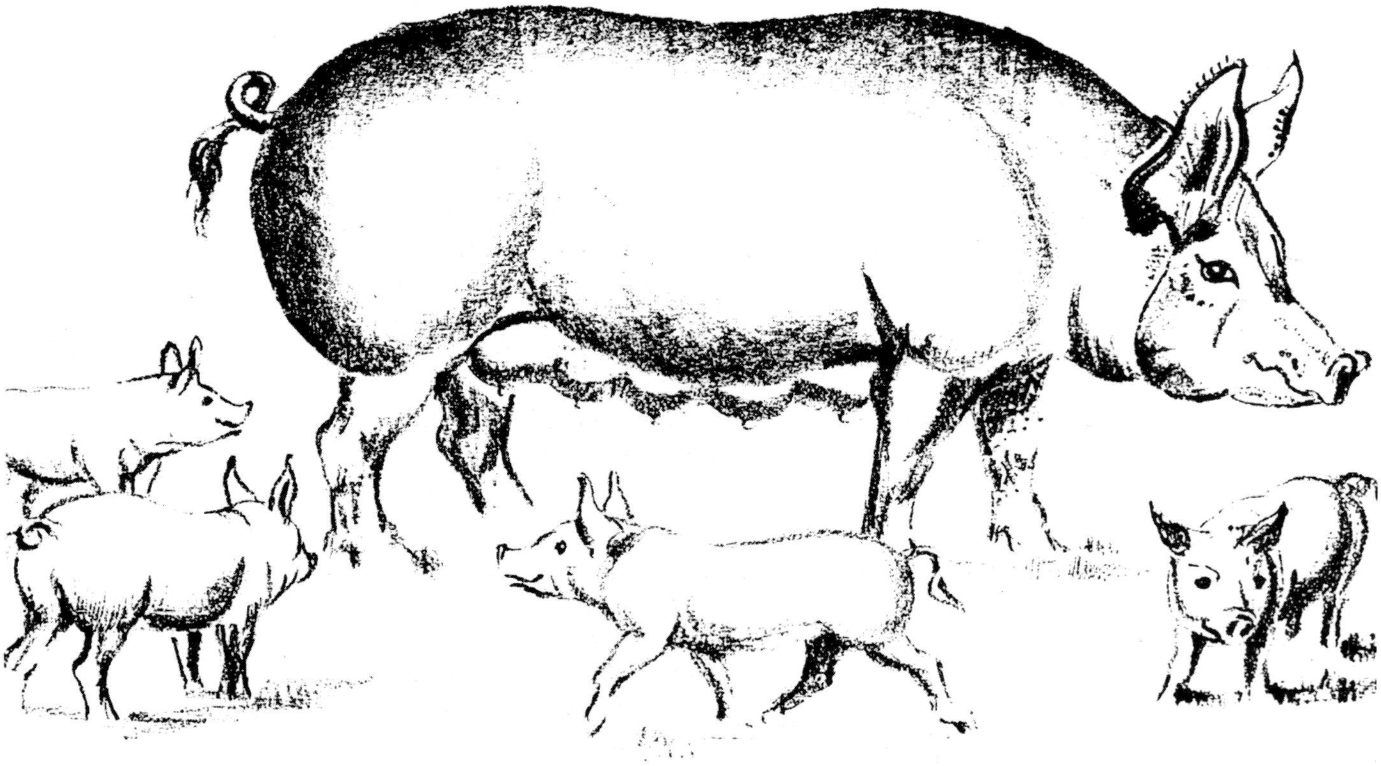

Large White Sow and litter
Lithograph - 1962

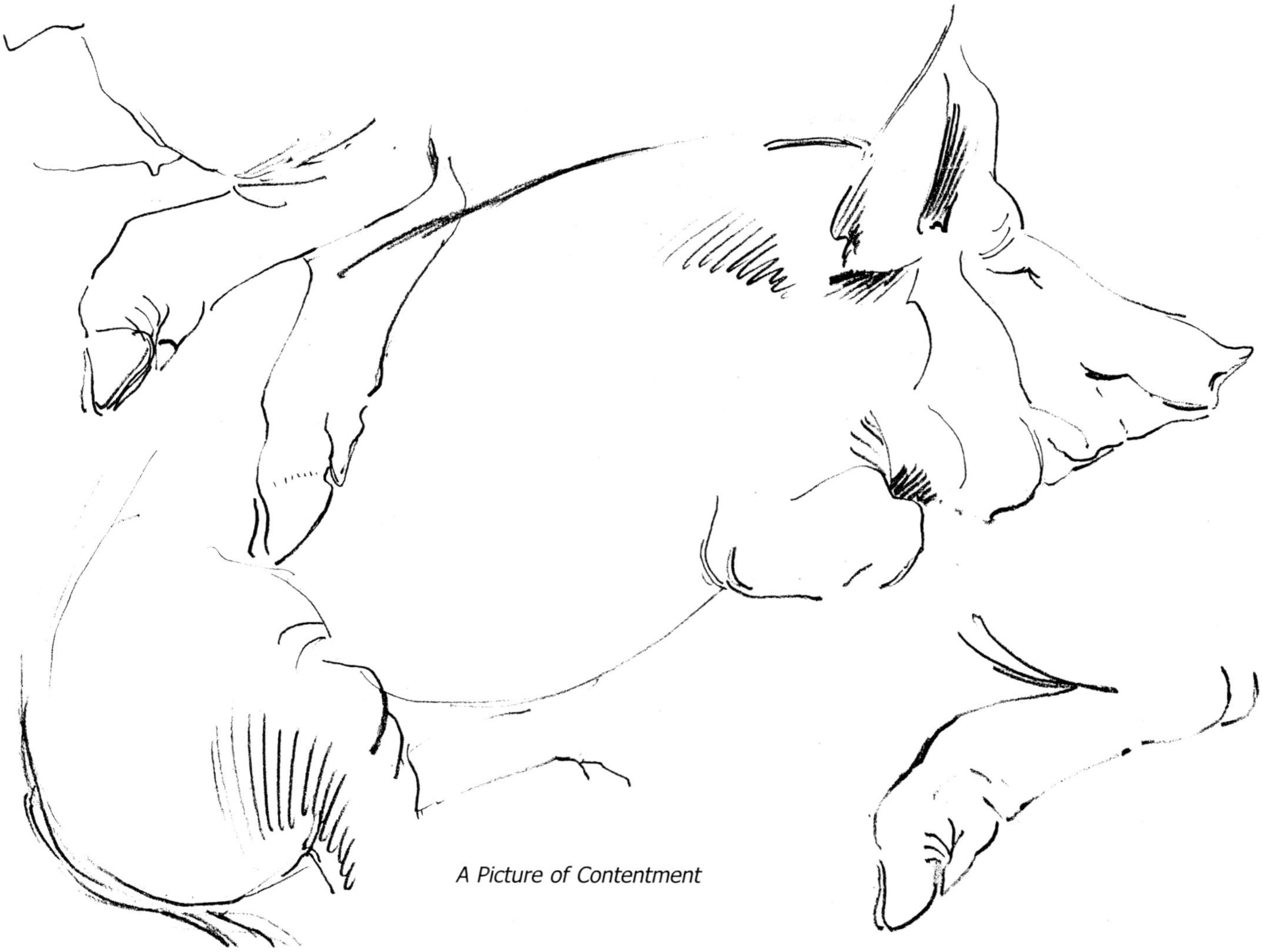

A Picture of Contentment

The Boar Takes His Time

Whereas a bull, a ram and a stallion make short work of their coupling (30 seconds), the mating of a boar may last ten to fifteen minutes, possibly because a sow can conceive 20 piglets. To most people's astonishment, his member emerges in the form of a corkscrew which is no doubt the origin of a common vulgar euphemism! There was a story about a small-holder who took a young gilt pig to a boar in the next village. As he had no trailer, he contrived to wheel her there in a barrow to be mated. The next morning when he came into the yard after breakfast, he was amazed to see her sitting in the barrow waiting to go again!

Penis bones are known in many mammals: whales and dolphins, walrus and seals, dogs and cats, rats, mice, squirrels and hedgehogs, monkeys and apes. It is to be assumed that man has lost his because of his bipedal gait. Many a man must have cause to regret that through the evolutionary process this bone has been lost, although on reflection, it might have presented an unacceptable fracture hazard!

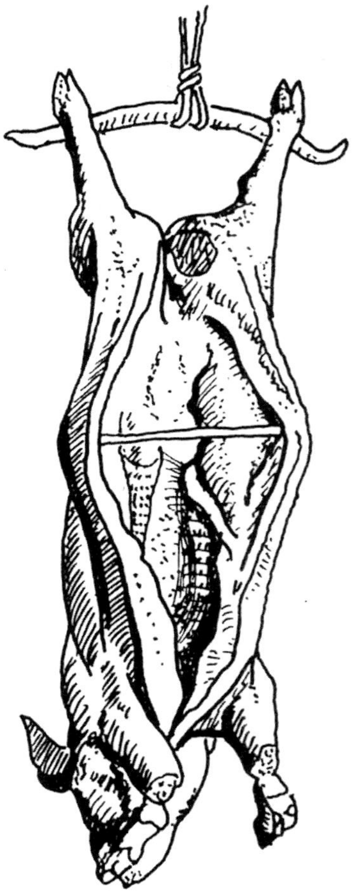

PIG'S CARCASS

Killing a Pig

Killing a pig was usually arranged for a cold period, sometime in the autumn, perhaps October or November, and there would be a lot of bustling around in the farmhouse kitchen for several days before and after the event. At the appropriate time, the selected pig would be brought out to the slaughterman, struggling and protesting very loudly. One strong man would hold the noose over its snout, two more would have to grasp an ear apiece and a fourth would twist the tail and push the unwilling creature towards the cratch, which is something like a wooden stretcher on short legs, alongside which a pile of straw was provided for the pig to fall upon when despatched.

Pigs being smooth and plump are noticeably lacking in built-in handles, unlike cattle, sheep and goats, some of which the thoughtful Creator considerately provided with horns to be grasped and pulled to coerce a reluctant creature to go whither he would much rather not!

The straw was set on fire and people would work in groups of three to singe off the wiry bristles that cover the porcine carcass. After that, copious amounts of scalding water, scrubbing brushes and scrapers were used to shave the remaining stubble. When this had been achieved, the pig was lifted bodily onto the cratch to be carried stretcher-fashion to a suitable roof beam up to which it was hoisted by a kind of coat-hanger stretched between its Achilles tendons. After the entrails and pluck (heart, liver and lungs) were removed, the carcass hung for a day before the butcher came to do the skilled work of cutting, sawing and jointing.

The women in the kitchen were kept very busy at this time making pork pies, sausages, faggots and brawn. They spoke darkly of chitterlings, scratchings and bathchaps. There were trotters and collars, slippers and butts. As several households were involved in this feverish activity, it was natural that the produce would be shared by mutual consent. We, in our turn, would be given similar amounts when our neighbours killed their pigs.

It was left to the men, directed by the butcher, to carry the hams, shoulders and sides of bacon down into the cool cellar where they were placed in shallow containers that were set upon the tiled thrall. The bacon and hams were then treated with salt and saltpetre and brine spooned over them until they were judged to be ready for hanging, wrapped in linen bags, on large hooks screwed into the kitchen ceiling beams.

I well remember in Somerset being instructed to cut off some ham as guests were arriving. On opening the bag, I found only a hambone picked clean by the perfidious rats, which had run along the beam and entered unnoticed through the loose neck of the bag!

The Naked Flesh-Coloured Pig

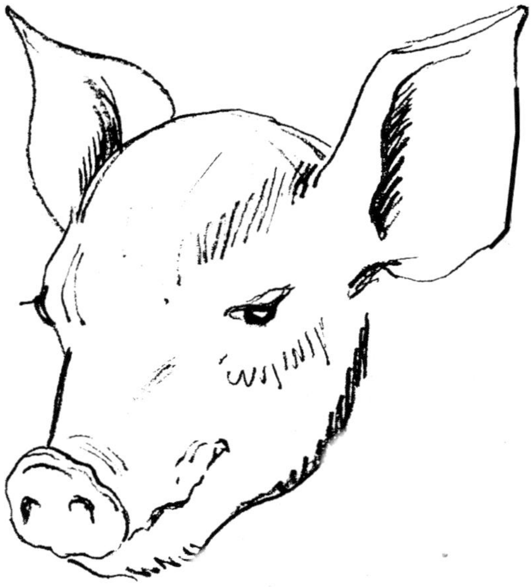

The telephone rang and when I lifted the receiver I was addressed by a person from London who was renting a thatched lodge cottage nearby. He was in a state of great consternation and thought I might be able to help. He and his wife had been looking through their windows into the field adjoining his cottage garden and had noticed a large flesh-coloured pig walking about naked in the sunshine; could it possibly be mine? Having admitted the possibility, I enquired politely how I could be of assistance. "Well," said he, "from time to time this large animal sees fit to relive himself onto the pasture close to my house, and my wife and I would be horrified to think that a fly might go and walk on that and then come in through the window and walk on my cakes and jam tarts when I am having my tea."

I readily agreed with him that this was a strong possibility and suggested a few more choice objects in the vicinity over which the fly might have walked his tiny feet, and then I asked him whether he thought I should employ people to follow each of our several hundred animals around with gigantic poop scoops day and night throughout the year!

Eventually he conceded, albeit grudgingly, that that would be impossible and he would step up his war against the flies or move elsewhere. The amazing thing to me was that these people had obviously lived such a sheltered existence that they seemed blissfully unaware that farm animals (unlike people in novels and movies) have to visit the lavatory from time to time in the way of all flesh, the resultant fertiliser being the source of production of all this *organic food* so highly prized by discerning people!

It occurs to me that most townspeople, if given the choice, would much prefer to grow their crops on nice clean white granules of artificial fertiliser rather than the rich, smelling, oozy offerings of the farmyard manure heap!

Townspeople are often swift to complain if a naturally-caused agricultural smell should offend their delicate nostrils. It may come from farmyard manure or from hay or silage curing, the natural products of organic farming. I have always told them that if they don't like the country smells, why come and live in the country and then complain? Far better to remain in the town, taking deep nourishing gulps of diesel fumes and cigar smoke!

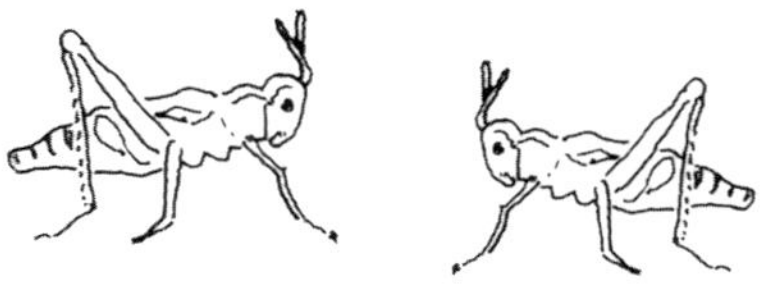

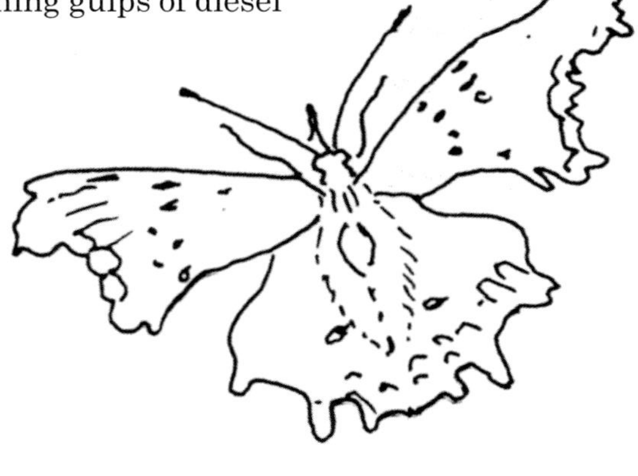

Chapter SIX

Poultry

Trapped in the Chicken Brooding House

The postman not only delivered letters, he would collect them, too. A telegram arriving at a village post office for an outlying farm would be given to the next available person going in that direction. An elderly lady on her bicycle was bringing us a telegram when she heard cries for help, and after some searching, she found them coming from a small wooden portable chicken brooding house. My wife, Elizabeth, had gone in to see to the paraffin heaters when the door had blown to and trapped her. As I was away at market, she had resigned herself to having to spend many hours crouched in the stifling heat until my return. The rescuer was so convulsed with laughter as to be scarcely able to release Elizabeth from her predicament.

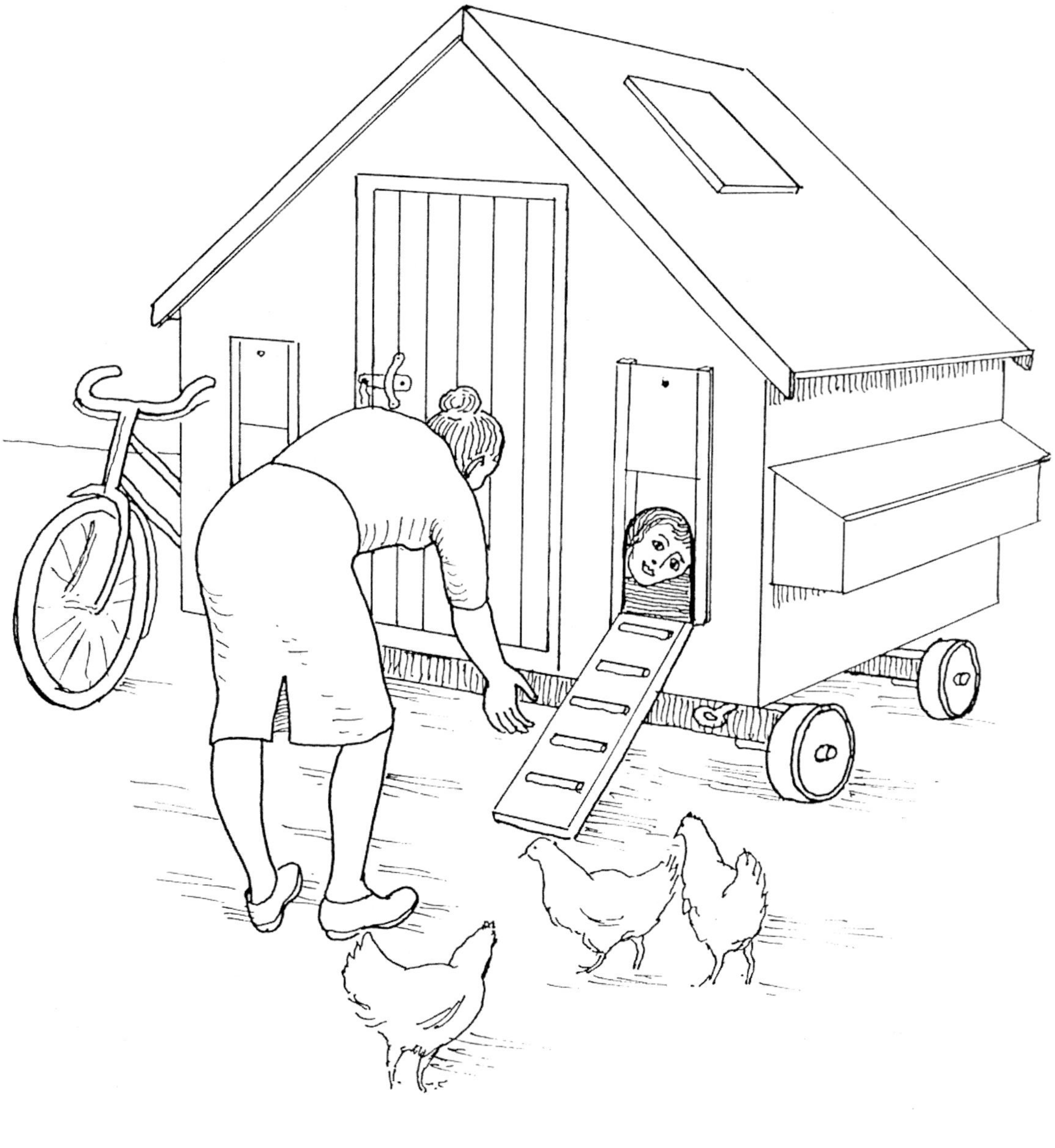

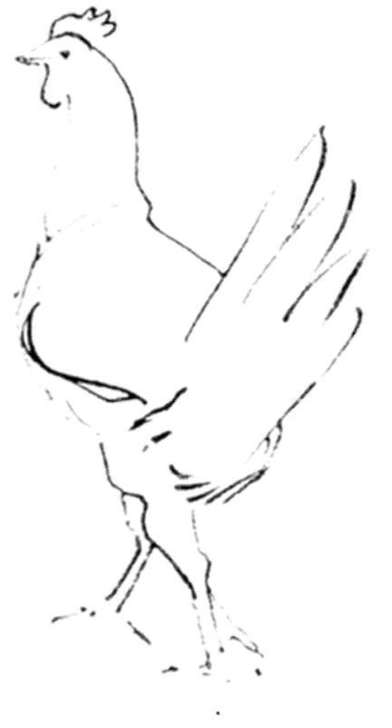

On small mixed farms, the poultry enterprises were traditionally in the care of the farmer's wife. A few bags of poultry mash would come with the cattle cake order, and she would also use the shrivelled, substandard 'tail' corn from the barn. Income from the sale of eggs would be considered her personal pin-money.

Free-range poultry used to live in sectional eight-foot by six-foot wooden houses on small iron wheels so that they could be moved by a horse. If large horned animals also used the same grass field, there would have to be a barbed wire fence a few yards away from the huts or they would suffer being rubbed and poked by horns. The houses might typically be 50 to 100 yards apart, placed near the perimeter of a grass field.

Town dwellers don't realise that such free-range hens had to be visited three times a day: at first light to let them out and open nest boxes; mid-afternoon to feed and water and collect the eggs, and close the nest boxes; they then had to be shut up when they had gone to roost at night or the fox would get them. Shutting up time could vary from 4:30 in midwinter to midnight in midsummer, and you could see what an unpopular, antisocial job it was! Hence, without taking sides in any moral argument, it must be an incontrovertible fact that the vast majority of eggs today are produced by battery hens in spite of what it may say on the box. I maintain that free-range eggs are virtually non-existent, as anyone can see that they would cost far too much if produced under the conditions described above.

The tyranny of shutting the fowl houses was apt to ruin any evening activity for young and old; imagine, when enjoying a dance or a dinner date, the constant glancing at the setting sun and the wristwatch. As one passed the poultry field on the way home, torches would be produced and immaculate trousers stuffed into dirty gumboots as the rain started turning the surroundings of each hut into a sea of mud. One also had to run the gauntlet of the barbed-wire fence, which contrived to rip the clothing in unspeakable places.

Timing was all-important. Arrive five minutes early and half a dozen stragglers, like naughty children, would be pecking around. These would take a seemingly interminable time walking up the slatted ramp to the little pop hole. On the other hand, arrive thirty minutes late and old Reynard would have reduced sixty laying pullets to a bunch of squawking feathers.

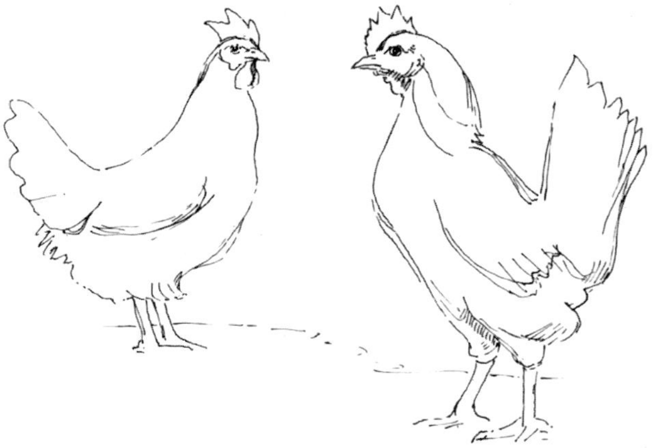

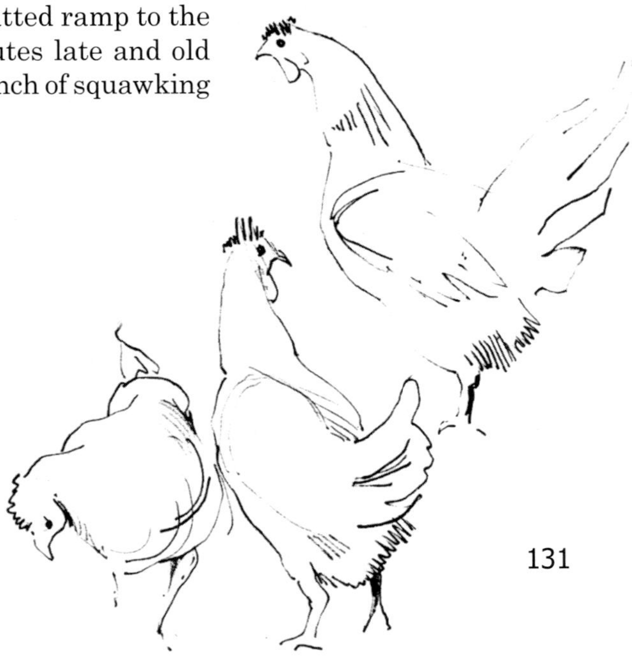

A Paraffin-Heated Chicken Brooder

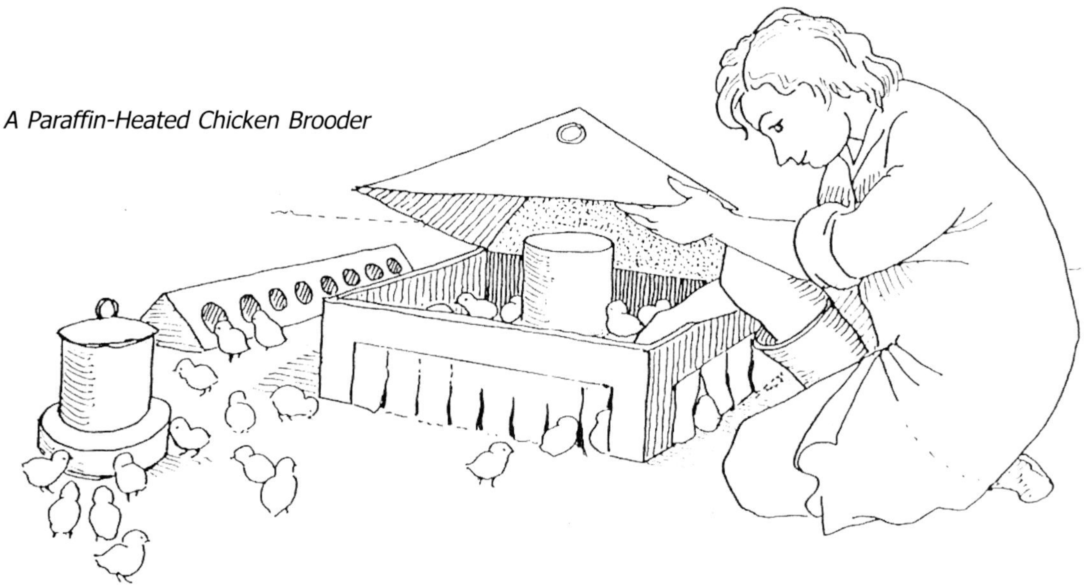

Free Range Eggs Are Dirty

Another point to consider is that, particularly in winter, a fair proportion of free-range eggs are dirty eggs. Mud and droppings are brought in from the fields on the hen's feet and deposited in the nest box and on top of the eggs. Further contamination is caused by broken and soft-shelled eggs coming into contact with unbroken eggs in the same nesting area. Battery eggs are clean because they roll clear of the birds as soon as they are laid. As dirty, free-range eggs have to be washed, this adds further to their cost and could force harmful bacteria through their porous shells. "Where ignorance is bliss 'tis folly to be wise". If soft-hearted people like to believe they are buying free-range eggs, who am I to disillusion them? It all depends what you mean by 'free-range'. I maintain that if your eggs are not dirty or washed they are not 'free-range'.

Our own home-produced eggs were sold to a local hatchery for a premium. The white-speckled Light Sussex hens when mated with a Rhode Island Red cock produced sex-linked chicks. That is, the male chicks were white and the females were red. Ordinarily, hatcheries had to employ highly-paid, highly-skilled, and often oriental sexers, who very swiftly handled each chick under a bright light to determine its sex. Of course, the females were much more valuable than the males. The chicks were put 25 at a time into special cardboard boxes and dispatched all over the United Kingdom by rail.

Our Rhode Island Red cocks were bought from the renowned flock of Mr. Golden at Leire at the cost of five guineas each, the price of a fat lamb or a ton of potatoes in those days. They were 'dubbed', which meant that their fine head wattles were removed to avoid damage to them when fighting!

In the post-war years, the eggs we took on the milk round were imported from Australia and Canada by sea, so they must have been several weeks old when they were eaten. Packing-station eggs were all stamped, the English ones carrying the image of a lion passant guardant. I once caught a man scrubbing the little lions off with Vim as you could get a little more for unmarked ex-farm eggs!

Ratty's Warm Larder and Nest Egg

At slack times it might be decided that the fowl huts be cleaned out and moved to fresh ground. It had to be remembered that they would have to be relocated not more than a few yards away, or at nightfall the disoriented birds would squat in a disorderly heap on the previous site of their home, offering themselves as a prime target for Charlie Fox and his family. If the hut had been in one place for several weeks, on moving it forward one would find the dry ground beneath had become the home of numerous vermin. There were little warm nests of hay from the nest boxes connected by underground passages to little larders packed with grain, thoughtfully scattered each day for the pampered birds, and brought in grain by grain and stored against hard times by Mr. and Mrs. Rat and their extended family.

When threshing corn stacks, towards the end of the day there would be much excitement as the rats left their diminishing home. Small mesh wire was unrolled and men and terriers did their best to exterminate the pests. This activity was accompanied by shouts and blows. On one such occasion, I observed a large male rat proceeding with an unusual gait, hopping like a kangaroo. A closer look revealed that he was holding a large hen's egg trapped between his front legs and his chin. Though death was imminent, all the commotion could not persuade him to leave his nest egg!

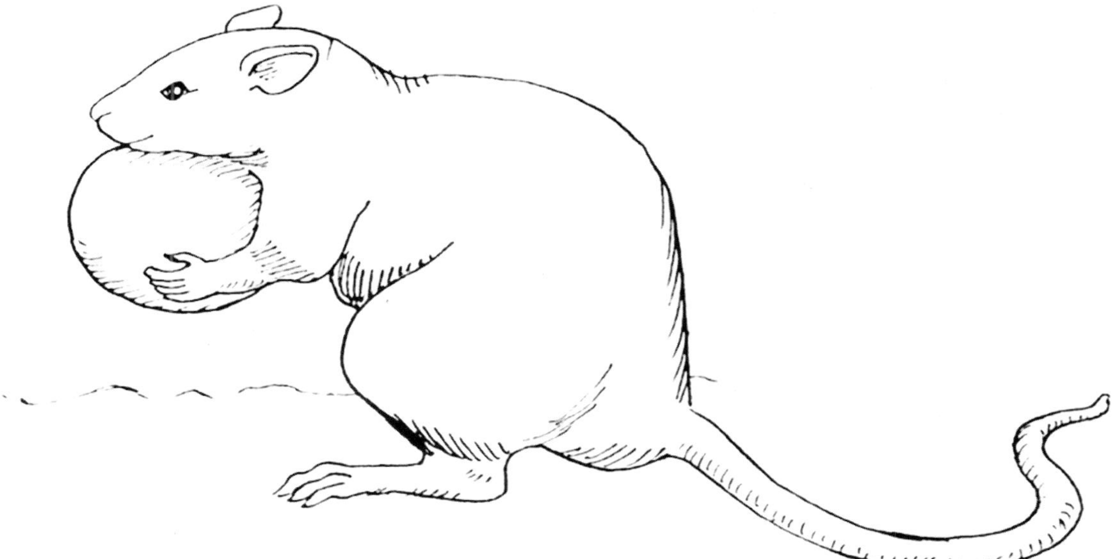

Rat with his hen's egg

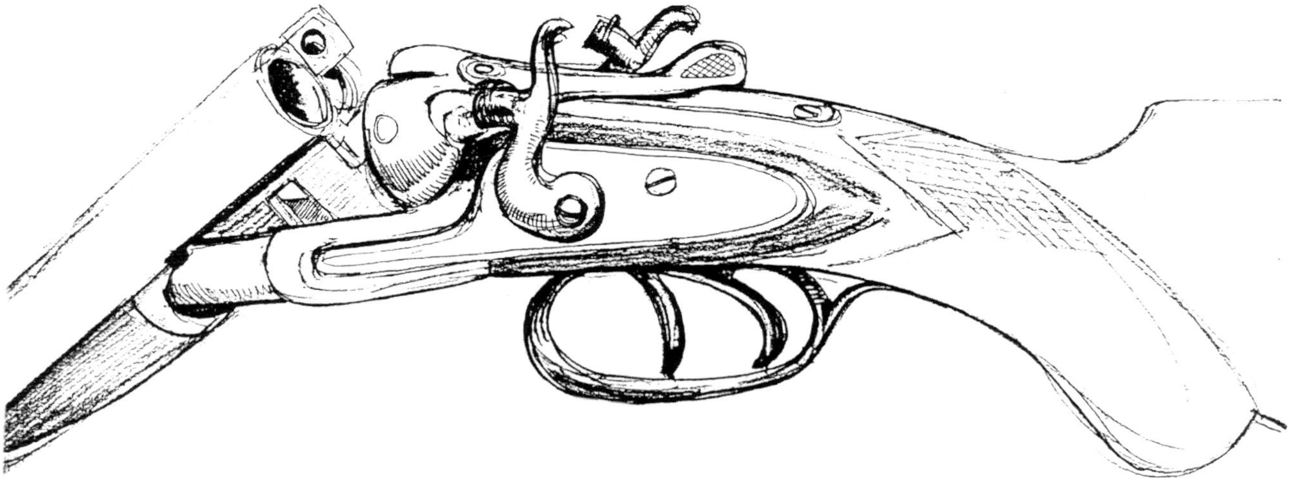

'Daddy, Where are the Indians?'

My wife complained several times that the wood-pigeons were playing havoc with the crops in her newly-sown garden. Eventually, I went indoors and came out with the ancient, double-barrelled 12-bore shotgun. My little son, aged three and a half, had not previously seen his father so equipped to do battle, and looking anxiously up and down the farm road, enquired with due solemnity, "Daddy, where are the Indians?" Such is the persuasive power of the television western that the little lad really expected to see a war party of Apache braves come whooping from the spinney, while his fearless old dad would drop on one knee and mow them down with his Winchester! In fact, father redeemed the day by raising the gun in an instant and blew the head clean off one of the offending birds, much to his son's approval and to his own astonishment.

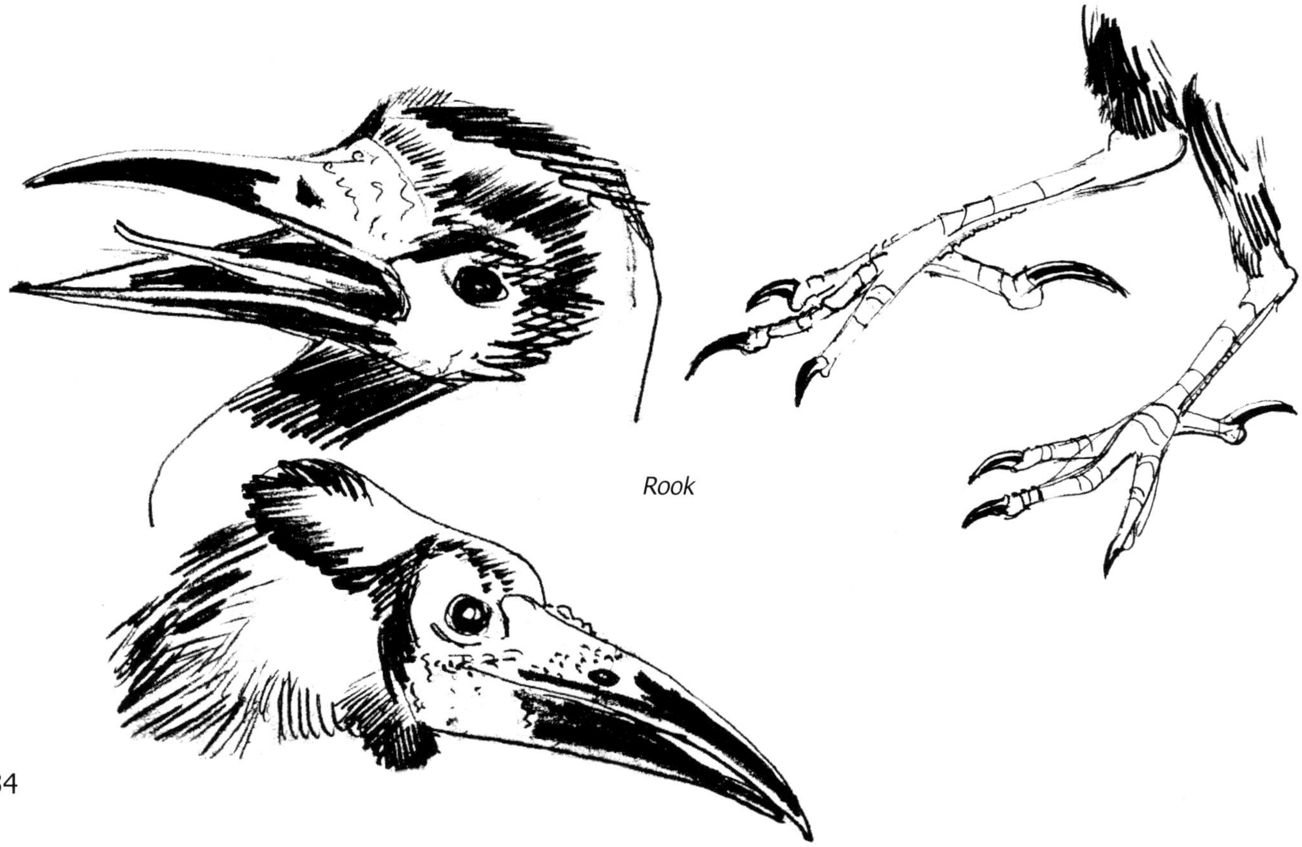

Rook

Motherly Vengeance of Broody Hens

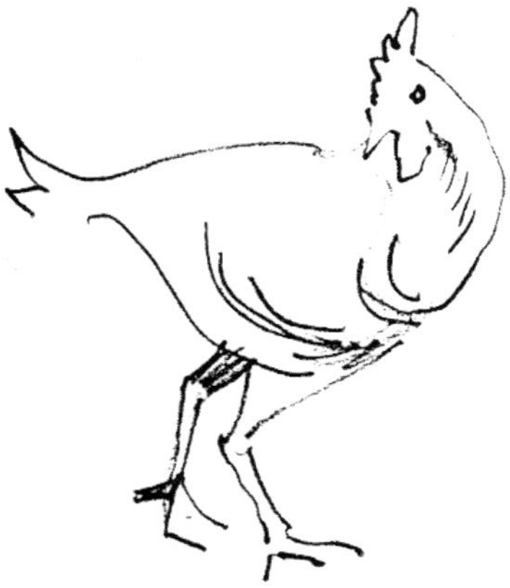

On a subsequent occasion, six mother hens were confined by a wire-netting enclosure with about seventy baby chicks. These were being harassed by the predations of a pair of carrion-crows. Again, the old sharpshooter raised his gun, and the dead but still fluttering crow fell out of the sky into the pen below. Seldom have I seen such fury as that of the six broody hens rushing at the carcass to wreak their motherly vengeance on the space invader! Mother love, or the protective instinct, endows normally placid animals with a capacity for great ferocity in defence of their young offspring. I have seen a ewe send a fox from a weakly lamb by stamping and butting.

Visitors who walk quickly through a field of cows would normally not be of interest to them, unless it were near feeding time, but let them take a dog, even on a lead, and cows will gather round to investigate, thinking that it is a calf from afar or, on closer examination, a threat to their calves lying at home or soon to be born. But a small, quiet dog could be carried close to the body and it might not be noticed.

Animals Destroy the Evidence of Birth

A shepherd carrying home a pair of new born lambs holds them by their front legs away from his body so that the ewe will see and follow them. If held close, they would not be seen by the ewe, who would think them lost and constantly return to the spot where they were born. This nest is made by the ewe turning in a circle and scraping the ground as if to make it safe from snakes and scorpions. It takes on her distinctive scent from the amniotic fluid and the afterbirth. Animals often eat this, as it would betray to a predator the proximity of an exhausted mother and new-born, weakly off-spring.

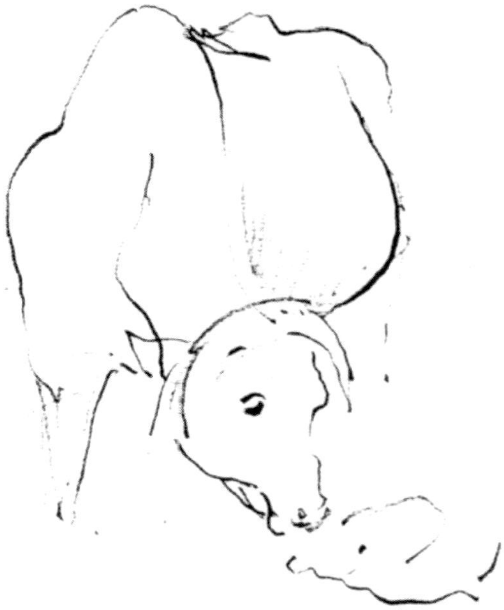

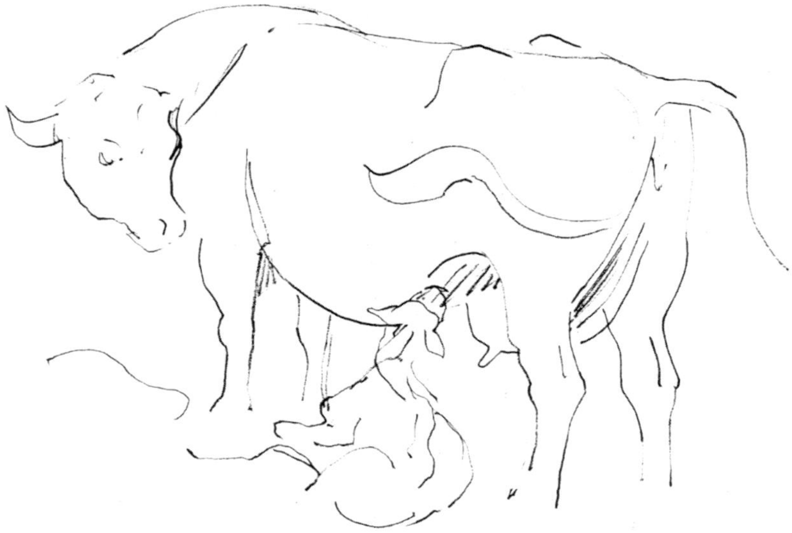

Newly born calf

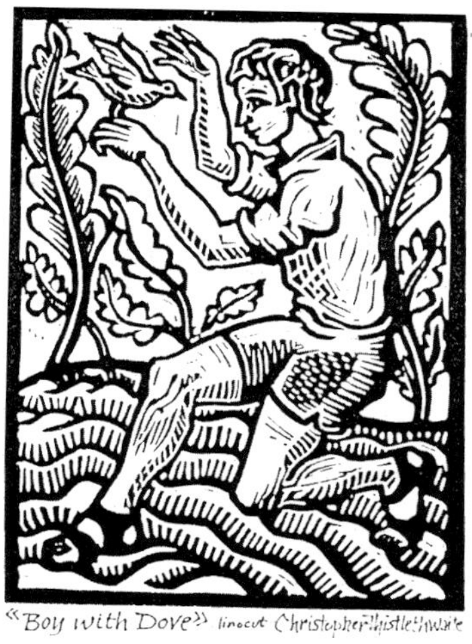

«Boy with Dove» linocut Christopher Thistlethwaite

Martin Finds an Instance of Sex-Reversal

An enlightened, dedicated teacher from a nearby town's junior school organised a farmyard in the playground and we supplied hens, cockerel, and geese and gander for the children to care for. These birds were rather like school boarders, as they returned to us during the school holidays! One teenage boy named Martin was encouraged to keep poultry at home. He reared the chicks, constructed the accommodation, sold the eggs to his mother, kept accounts and now runs his own business. He was astonished to find something quite common with fowl, an instance of sex-reversal! A hen which had hitherto happily been laying eggs, started to grow wattles and to crow in the morning and behave like a cockerel! Martin had lost one of his egg providers and the neighbours objected to the early morning disturbance in quiet suburbia!

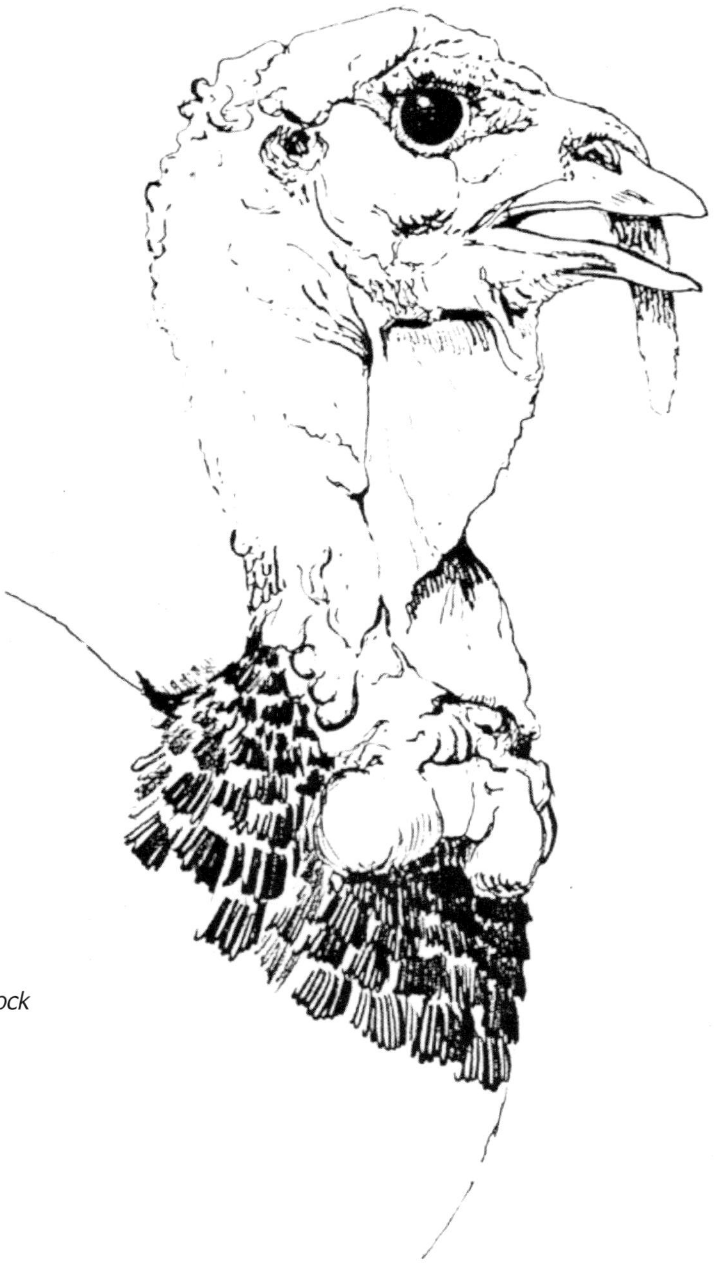

Bronze Turkey Cock (Gobbler)

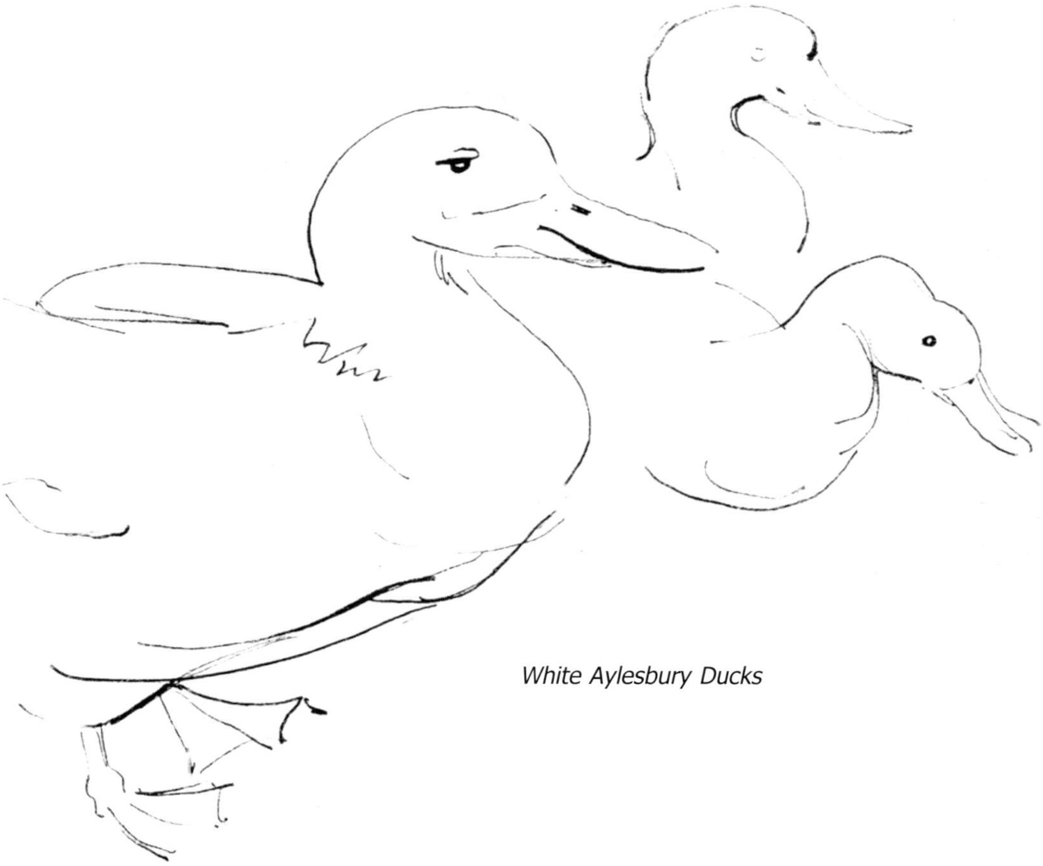

White Aylesbury Ducks

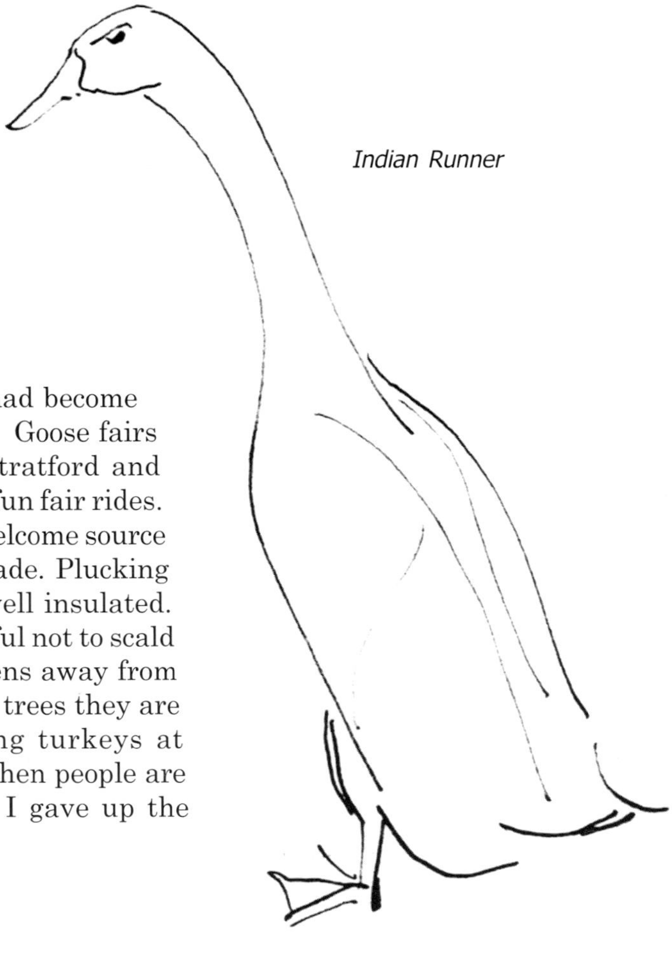

Indian Runner

Goose Fairs

The law locks up the man or woman
That steals the goose from off the Common
But lets the greater felon loose
That steals the Common from the goose.

At Michaelmas, the end of September, geese had become fat on gleaning the corn left on the stubbles. Goose fairs were held in market towns such as Warwick, Stratford and Nottingham. The main streets were taken over by fun fair rides. Ducks and geese, turkeys and guinea fowl were a welcome source of income, many orders coming from the hotel trade. Plucking the waterbirds is a great labour as they are so well insulated. Therefore, we used a hot water method, being careful not to scald them. Guinea fowl are quite fierce, driving the hens away from their food with piercing screams. As they roost up trees they are very difficult to catch. Plucking and delivering turkeys at Christmas can become an awful chore at a time when people are already over-stressed. After two or three years I gave up the unequal battle!

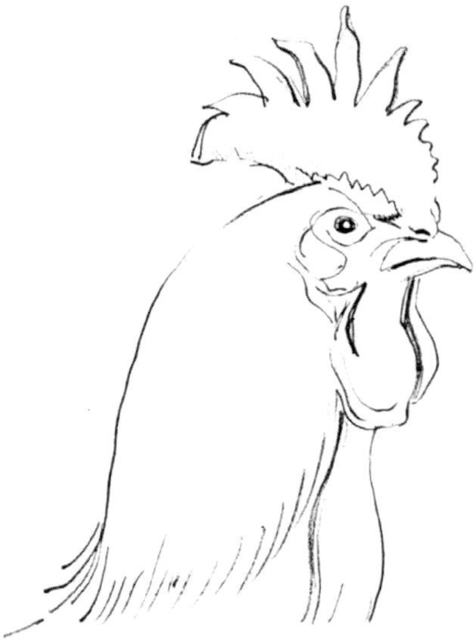

Unwanted Headgear Left by Poultry-Maid

At a masked ball, people amuse themselves and others by becoming 'incognito' and assuming different personalities. They do, however, take the precaution of having holes pierced in the masks to coincide with their eyes so that they may see their whereabouts and enjoy the effect their appearance conveys to those around them.

I remember an incident where things were slightly different. Someone had taken a small galvanised bucket filled with chicken feed pellets into a field where, in addition to poultry, there were ewes grazing the pasture. Being diverted by some distraction, the poultry-maid had taken a different route home and left the bucket behind, where it was the subject of hopeful investigation by a ewe grazing nearby. Finding a few handfuls of feed remaining in the bottom, she regarded it as her legitimate windfall. She proceeded to help herself rather vigorously, nuzzling into the bucket and lifting her head at the same time. By some remote quirk of fate, the handle flew upwards over the crown of her head and settled neatly behind her ears.

When the ewe realised she was well and truly trapped, panic set in as she careered blindly about the paddock in all directions, her anguished cries of distress being amplified and distorted from the depth of the clanging galvanised pail. The other members of the flock, not recognising their former flock mate, who was now changed beyond belief into an ovine ogress about to devour them, took to their heels and stampeded through a weak spot in the hedge, reasoning that discretion was the better part of valour!

It was providential that someone was on hand, and alerted by all the unusual commotion, summoned help to run down and uncover the poor demented ewe from her unwanted head gear!

Several times I have observed cats to be caught in a similar predicament, though not with such spectacular results. Wild animals that live near rubbish tips often suffer painfully as a result of going after a tantalising tit-bit left at the base of a tin or bottle. Which reminds me. Quite apart from creating visual untidiness, abandoned glass bottles can start fires, and along with tin cans and other metal objects can be a source of serious injury to animals' feet. Many times I have had to spend valuable time and energy on the unpleasant job of removing litter louts' rubbish from our hedge bottoms, ditches and spinneys.

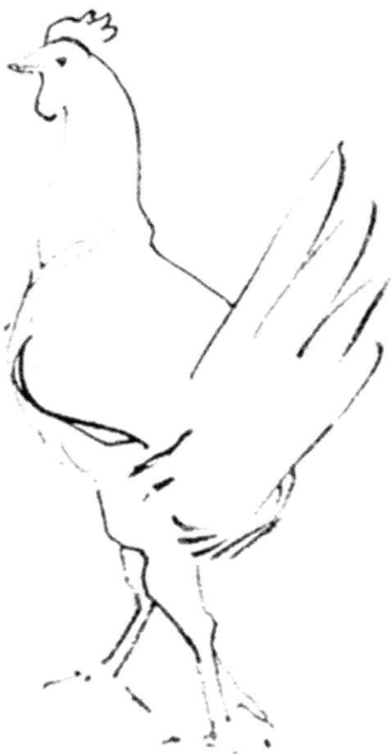

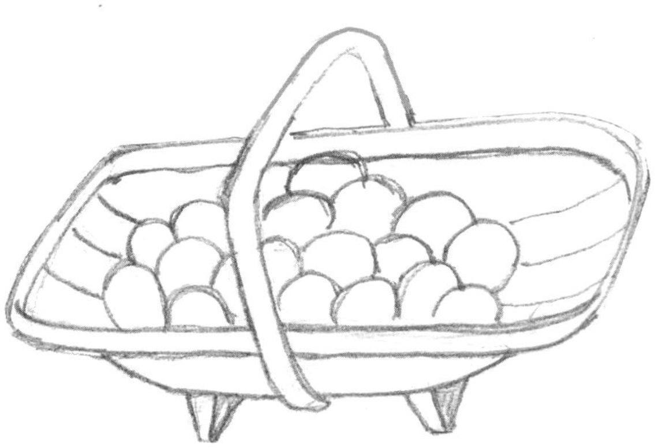

Poultry Guano Fiasco

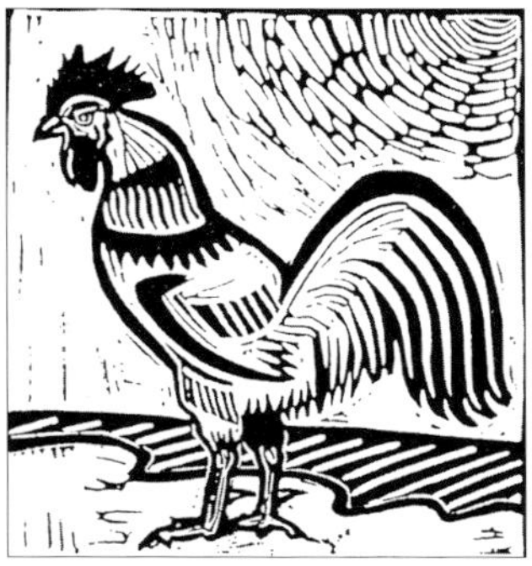

Chanticleer Cockerel
Linocut

The growth that follows taking off a crop of hay or clover is called the aftermath or lattermath, and is known in Leicestershire as *eddish*. In a dry summer this can be slow to grow away and remains an unappetising yellowish green. In order to restore the soil's nutrient depletion caused by removal of a heavy crop of hay, I contracted with a friendly egg producer to empty the battery cage effluent from his slurry pit using his vacuum tanker to suck it up and blow it out onto the bare pasture, as the machine was pulled by my tractor across the field.

Things were going well until the outlet became choked by feathers. I stopped the tractor but left the powerful pump in gear as I went to the back of the machine to investigate. As I was manipulating the levers, the obstruction cleared itself and suddenly I was completely enveloped in a deluge of evil-smelling, slurpy slurry! For a horrible moment, I thought I was blind and deaf, but mercifully I was able to feel my way to the tractor where I found some cloth to wipe my eyes, ears, nose and mouth.

This horrifying experience necessitated an unseemly dash to the farmstead to strip off my useless clothes and hose myself down. Clad only in my birthday suit, I was making my way upstairs for a proper bath and had nothing at all to cover my confusion when Elizabeth came round a corner giving a conducted tour to some rather prim town visitors! As you may guess, I was frequently to be reminded of this fiasco by all who heard of it and also by the pungent aroma, which persisted for days!

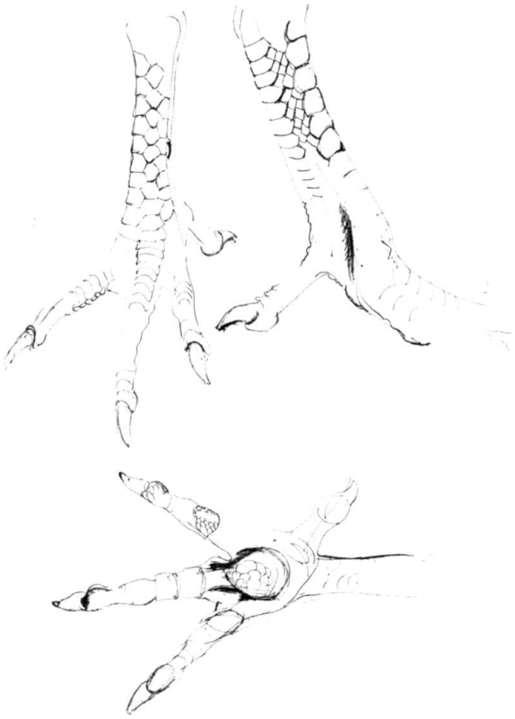

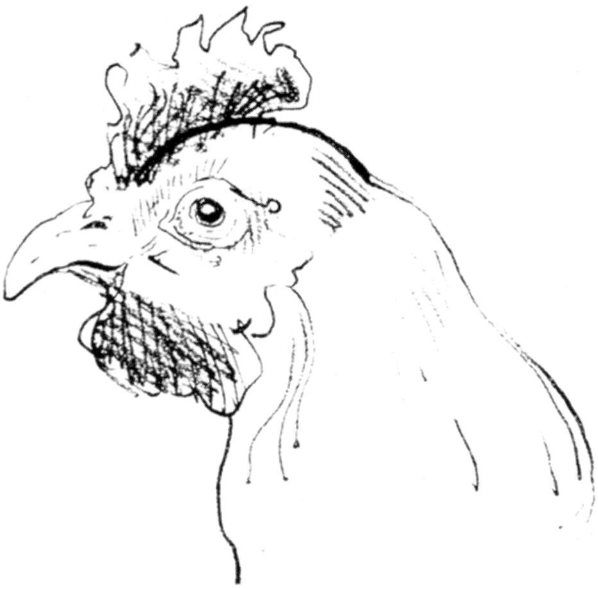

Pullet feet - note the large pad underneath

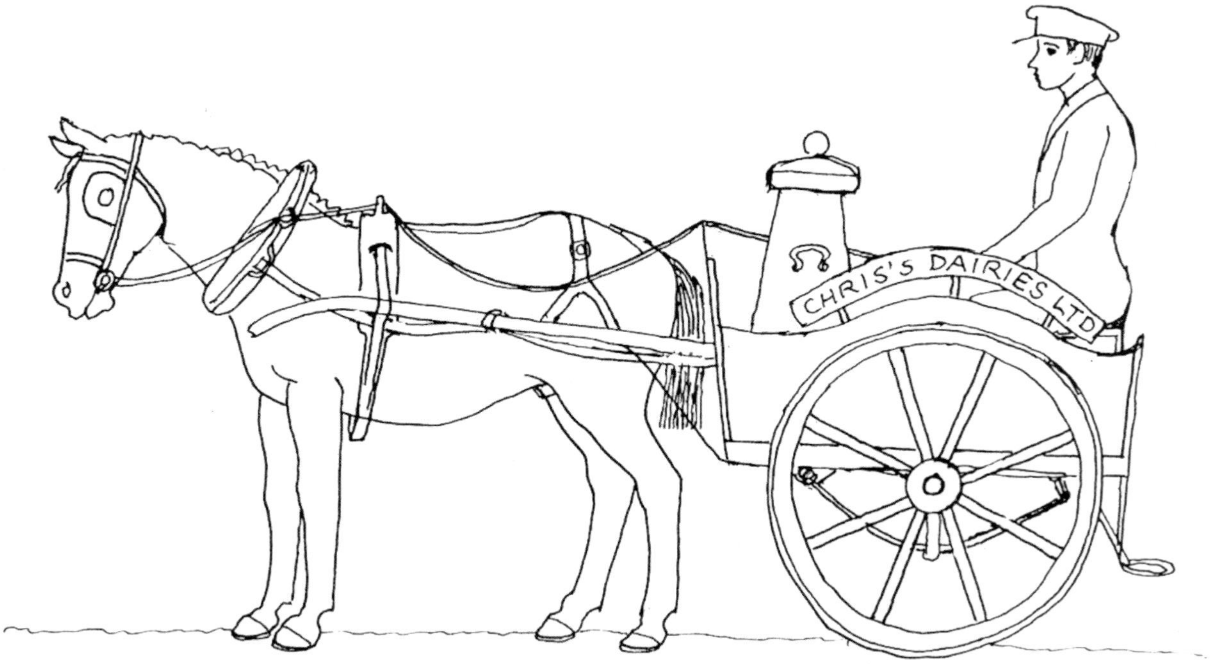

Chapter SEVEN

Producer Retailing, Marketing and Trophies

Having established a milking herd of Jersey cattle, we decided that extra profit and satisfaction could be gained by direct marketing to the customer on her doorstep 365 days of the year! Such was the confidence and enthusiasm of youth that when the goodwill of a local milkround came on offer it was snapped up at £10 per gallon! Bottling, filling and washing equipment, sterilising and refrigeration plant was purchased along with a large electric battery-powered vehicle.

At that time, in small villages, it was customary for milk to be ladled from a churn into the customer's jug, although some non-tuberculin-tested milk was delivered in bottles with cardboard tops. In the village of Ullesthorpe a farmer's daughter pedalled round her customers with a milk can mounted on a side car attached to her bicycle.

The days of these small, non-tuberculin-tested milk rounds were numbered, and as they came on the market, their goodwill was added to our round, along with a lot of outmoded, useless equipment.

The Roundsmen's Personal Enterprises

The roundsmen that delivered the milk for our business were rugged individualists, and many turned out to be as much concerned with the profitability of their own enterprises, using my customers as their clients. This complicated the accounting of receipts as their money could easily become mixed with mine. The first was a bookie's runner and phoned in all the bets he had taken from his last customer's house! One ran a catalogue sales service which would no doubt enhance his wages.

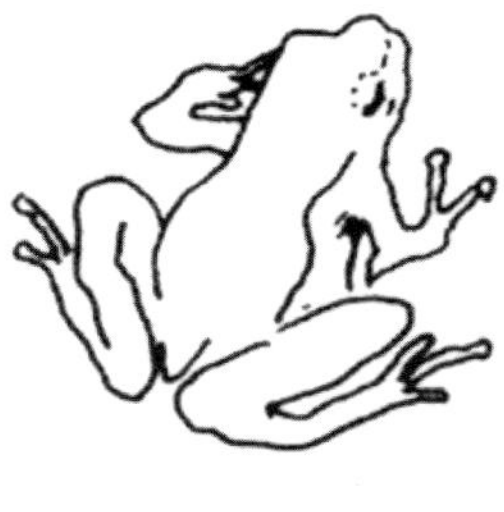

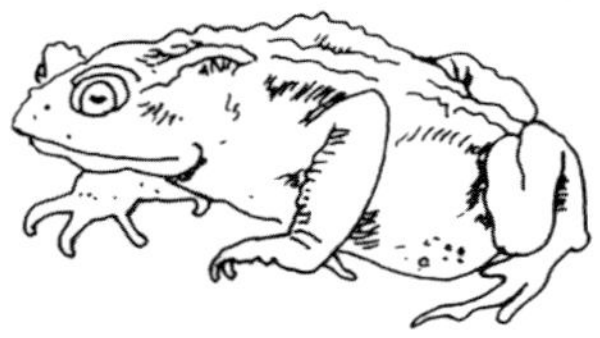

One, a small-holder, would put vegetables from his market garden amongst the milk bottles. Another came very early in the morning and was to be seen syphoning petrol from my vehicle into his own car, with which he did a taxi service in the afternoons. I certainly breathed a large sigh of relief on the day when we sold to a larger concern nearby and I could once again give my undivided attention to the real business of farming.

'In Another Person's Shoes'

When you are in contention with another person or have to cope with exasperating behaviour, I have found that it makes sense to try to put oneself in the other person's shoes. Imagine what difficulties and stresses the other fellow may have to endure, and the tension should go from the situation.

I once knew a baker's roundsman who would carry his heavy basket of bread and confectionery up flights of stairs to a fourth floor flat, arriving at the top gasping for breath. He swore that the occupant looked into his basket and deliberately asked for something other than what she could see so that he would have to make the journey again!

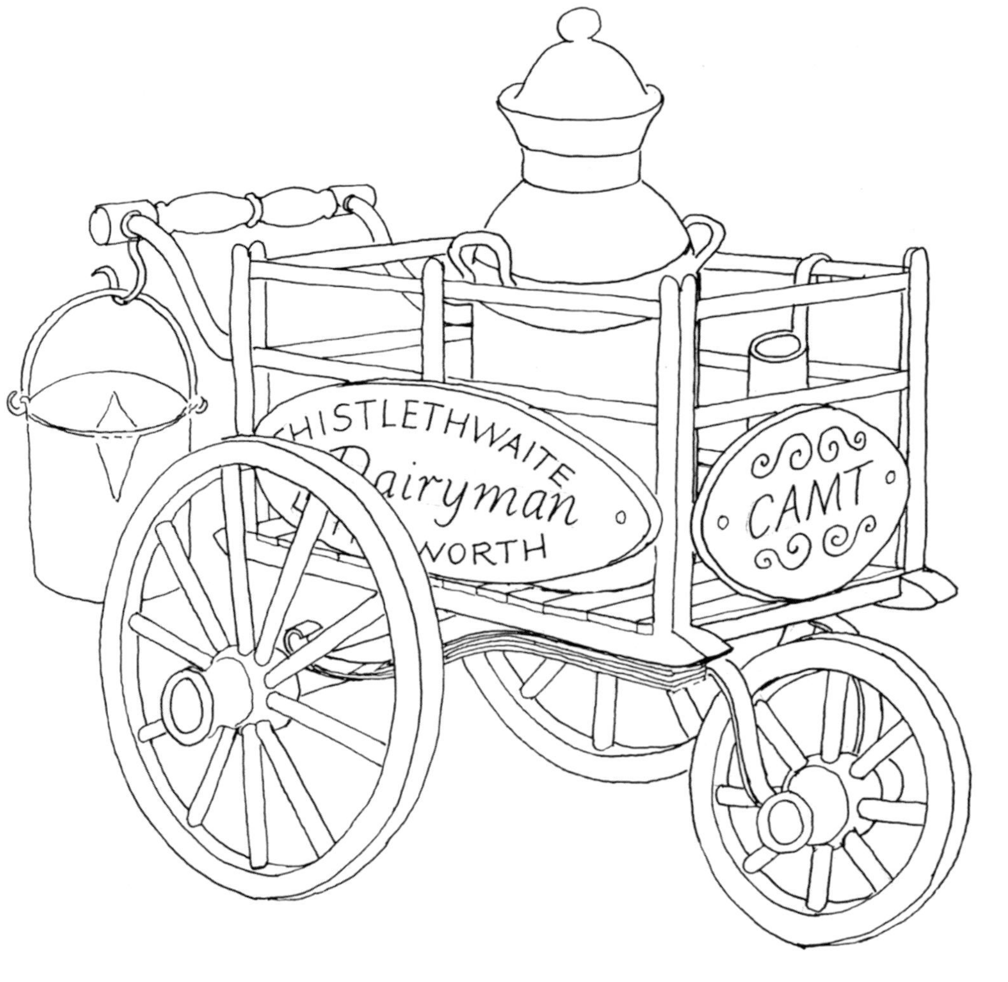

Having a milk round gave me a first-hand knowledge of that kind of inconsiderate behaviour to tradespeople from those who would be charming if you met them socially. I used to have to help out on Saturdays collecting money or when the roundsman had a well-deserved holiday. The delightful, bejewelled partner I held in my arms for a fox-trot at the expensive hunt ball the previous night presented a very different side of her character as she stood on the doorstep in her pink plastic curlers to contest a few pennies on her milk bill.

Ribald jokes are made about milkmen and I must admit to having fantasies about regular stops where I would be seduced in for a drink and 'a look at my photos' by a young woman dressed in housecoat, perfume and evidently little else. In reality, it was much more likely to be a warm-hearted, middle-aged matronly lady whose tea was stewed and whose cups were chipped all round and coloured with lipstick. Such people I thought of as the salt of the earth, and a great source of earthy local gossip.

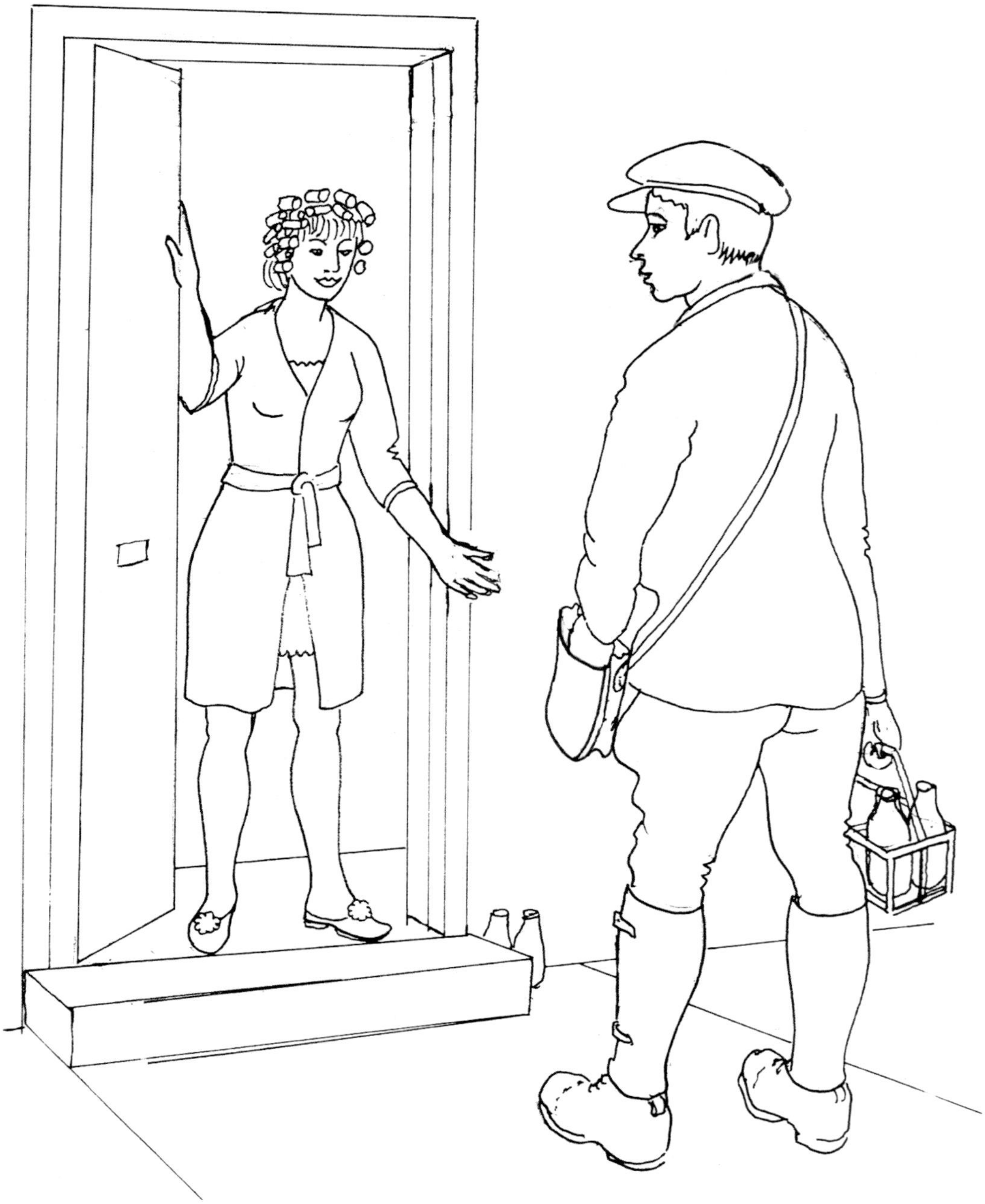

Collecting cash for milk

The Feckless Few

Truth is often stranger than fiction. There was one particularly feckless family who in 1955 won £100,000 on the football pools. This was a great deal of money by today's standards. The news attracted a large number of new 'friends' and, although they continued to live in a council house, the fortune was dissipated in a couple of years, leaving them in their former penniless condition. I am told that in their affluent days, they would hire a taxi and go to the nearest town for fish and chips. It reminds me of the man that stole a million pounds who, when asked by the judge where it had all gone, replied, "Wine, women and gambling of course - I didn't waste a penny!"

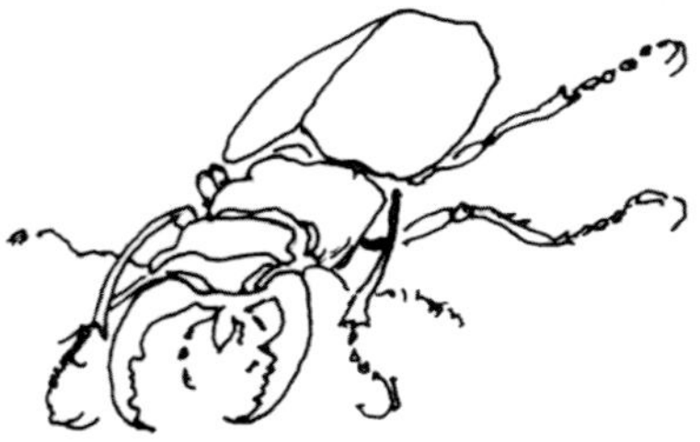

It is said that conscience makes cowards of us all, but some seem noticeably lacking in that respect. There was one lady customer who owed the equivalent of £50 when we took her on, and still owed £50 when we gave up ten years later! Some people paid every day, while others ran up a large bill and then made an excuse to change to the opposition, leaving us with an undischarged debt.

Our chief competitor, a wily dairyman from Lutterworth, once told me that he took a holiday in an Eastbourne boarding house. On leaving the establishment in the morning he glanced down at the doorstep only to see one of our milk bottles there! You can imagine how he said to his wife, "I can't even get away from the blighter by going 200 miles away on holiday!"

Misuse of Milk Bottles

Milk bottles usually cost more than the value of the milk in them and they make, on average, very few journeys before going missing. I had occasion to walk round to someone's back door and noticed that his garden path was neatly edged with a pattern comprised of hundreds of our milk bottles! In another man's garage workshop, our bottles were used to store nuts and bolts, screws and nails, and others contained oil, turpentine and meths.

In a well-to-do area, one could trudge up a long drive laden with bottles to find a 'no milk today' sign when the occupant could easily have told us the previous day. By contrast, our best drops were among the clusters of tenement yard cottages sharing a dripping tap and an outdoor earth closet. The appalling conditions of damp and deprivation seemed to encourage their fertility as they were all getting free and cheap milk for expectant and nursing mothers! A crate of 20 pints could be unloaded to good effect while taking only a few paces; the doors were close to each other and the bill for the milk paid by the ever-benevolent taxpayer!

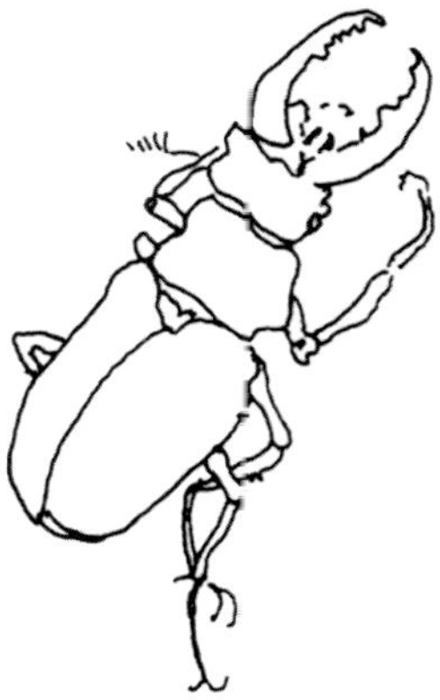

The Jolly Farmer

Having served the general public as a producer-retailer of milk and potatoes, I gained a valuable insight into human conditions and behaviour and a certain, almost familiar repartee which seems to be expected from 'the jolly farmer'. This charade was difficult to maintain when greeted by "You're late today" when you have had to cope with a flat battery or tyre and two-foot snow drifts along the way. To add to the irony of the situation, these caustic comments were usually uttered at 9:30am by pyjama-clad sluggards whose beds were still warm, while I had been up since five!

One Sunday lunchtime, when I was preparing to carve the joint, the phone rang. "He's forgotten to leave my cream," a plaintive voice whined from five miles away, the torrent of verbal abuse making it clear that someone was expected to bring it NOW.

The Inadequate Mother

We delivered milk to a house where the back yard was littered with rubbish and vermin and a constantly running water tap. Getting no reply at the door, I peered through the filthy windows to see a room devoid of furniture and other objects, where two small, nearly naked children, under three years old, were playing with sticks on a carpet of newspapers! Then I remembered that I had just seen the feckless mother perched on a bar stool drinking gin in a pub two hundred yards away! As her husband was a bricklayer, they should not have been short of money. She must have felt inadequate and unable to face up to life's responsibilities, so she easily succumbed to the warmth and friendliness of the local hostelry where she could spend her days in an alcoholic wonderland, while her children suffered in squalor, deprived of mother's love and mental stimulation.

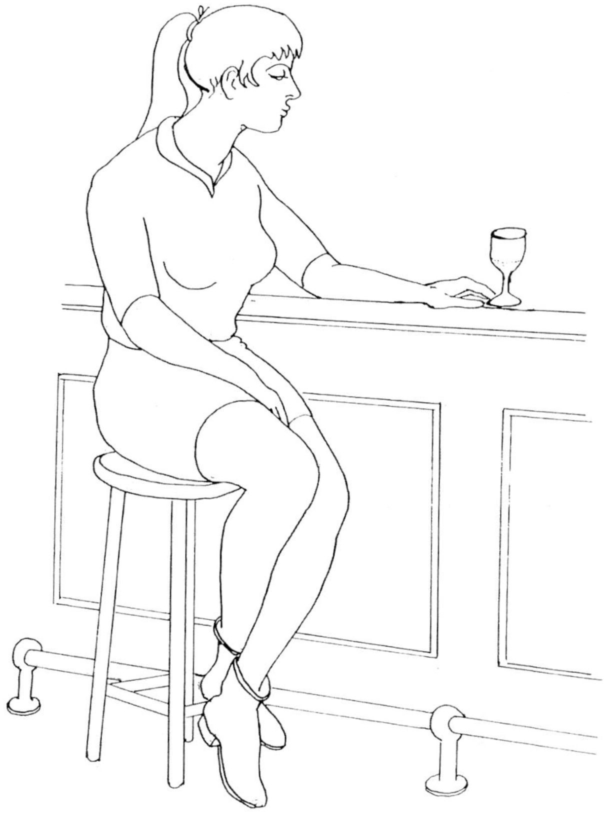

The Inadequate Mother

The Almshouse Ladies

One village was graced by a beautiful quadrangle of a dozen almshouses with a chapel at one end. It was home to charming old ladies, lonely and living on memories in their declining years. There was a demand from these for half-pint bottles and we kept some specially for their use. The snag was the quite disproportionate time it took to deliver them. You could tiptoe along and set the bottles down without a clink on the door steps, but some watchful eye would be sure to see your shadow; a door would open and you would be sucked in to see a picture, read a postcard or hear the budgie. Several old dears were almost blind and money had to be taken from a purse on trust. To demand the money that they *really* owed seemed almost indecent, so it would be my pleasure to accept whatever was proffered, including foreign coins and metal buttons!

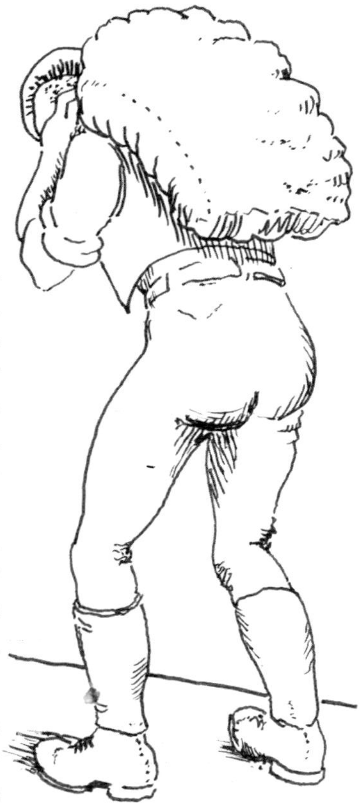

People who keep loose dogs that bite at the heels of tradesmen don't deserve to have goods delivered until they are prepared to control their dogs. Because they call every day, sharp-eyed, kindly milkmen are invaluable as social health visitors. Many a life has been saved by a timely word spoken in the right place concerning someone's non-appearance or change of habit with the milk bottles.

When delivering 1 cwt (eight stone, or 51kg) sacks of potatoes around the city, it was noticeable how many people who ordered lived in cul-de-sacs or unadopted unmade roads, so that a sack barrow was needed to wheel the potatoes to the door.

What the Eye Does Not See...

When halfway round my route, I would phone home from a call box to see if more orders had been made that day. If the location was near at hand, I could surprise a customer by delivering her potatoes within minutes of the call being made. There is often a great difference between reality and perception. I was often appalled by the vermin (rats and mice) and the filthy conditions obtaining at the back of fish and chip shops that might look quite presentable from the counter. "What the eye does not see, the heart does not grieve over!"

The composition of our Jersey milk was such that if diluted with equal parts of clean water, it approximated in composition to human mother's milk. Butter made from it was such a bright yellow colour that people thought we had used artificial colouring matter.

Best Yielding Herd

For several years I served on the Milk Producer-Retailer's Committee of the county National Farmers Union. The quarterly meetings in Leicester provided a good opportunity to meet and exchange views and news with some of the most progressive operators in this field.

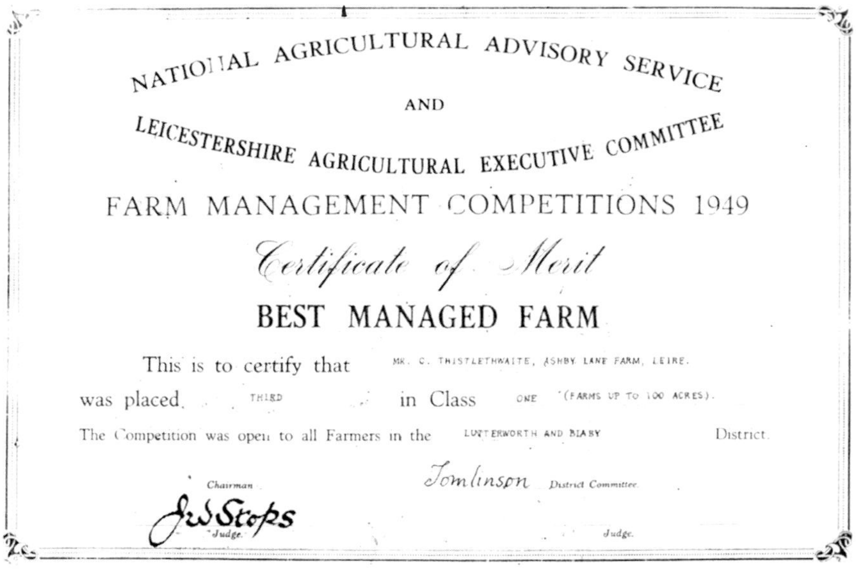

NATIONAL AGRICULTURAL ADVISORY SERVICE
AND
LEICESTERSHIRE AGRICULTURAL EXECUTIVE COMMITTEE
FARM MANAGEMENT COMPETITIONS 1949
Certificate of Merit
BEST MANAGED FARM
This is to certify that MR. C. THISTLETHWAITE, ASHBY LANE FARM, LEIRE.
was placed THIRD in Class ONE (FARMS UP TO 100 ACRES).
The Competition was open to all Farmers in the LUTTERWORTH AND BLABY District.
Chairman Tomlinson District Committee.
J.W. Stops Judge. Judge.

The Milk Marketing Board's Milk Recording Society weighed and tested the butterfat and recorded the yields of all our cows. It was a highlight of the year when I scrubbed my calloused hands and donned my best suit to be awarded the Challenge Cup for the Best Yielding Herd, presented in the Grand Hotel by the charming wife of a local dignitary. It is the hope of reward that sweetens labour but the genuine applause of one's peers is way beyond monetary value.

Best Managed Farm

The Agricultural Executive Committee, in conjunction with the local branch of the National Farmers Union, used to run a competition with classes for the best managed small, medium and large farms in the district. With an eye on publicity and thinking it would be good for morale, I used to enter in the appropriate section.

On a given date three or four elderly gentlemen, experienced farmers all, would walk every acre and inspect every animal and bird, asking searching questions as they walked. Nothing escaped their eagle eyes. All must be spotlessly groomed and polished. There must not be a wisp of hay or straw out of place. No weed must appear among the root crops. When the outdoors were well inspected, I would ask them into the farmhouse to see the books, recordings and trophies and rosettes.

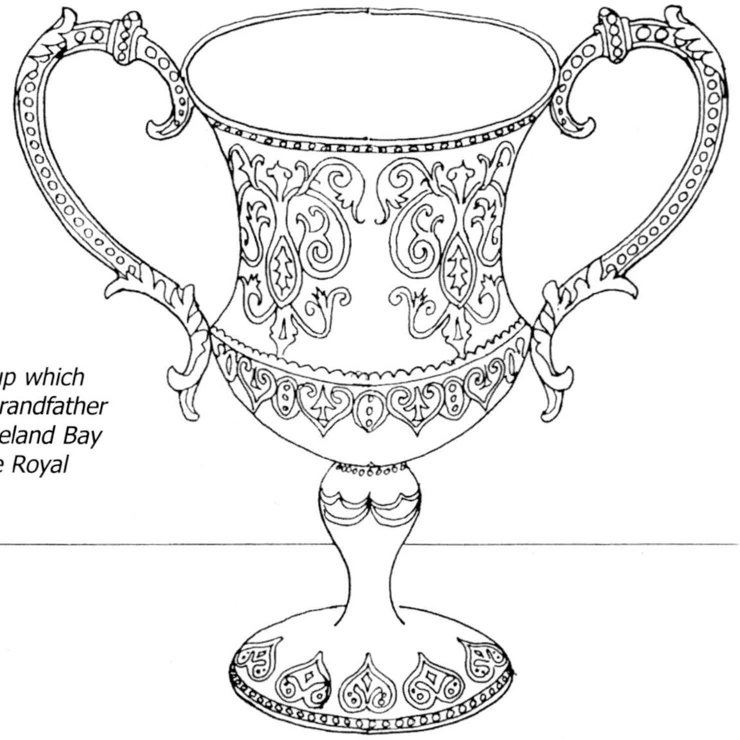

A finely-crafted silver cup which was won by my great-grandfather for a prize-winning Cleveland Bay like those which pull the Royal carriages

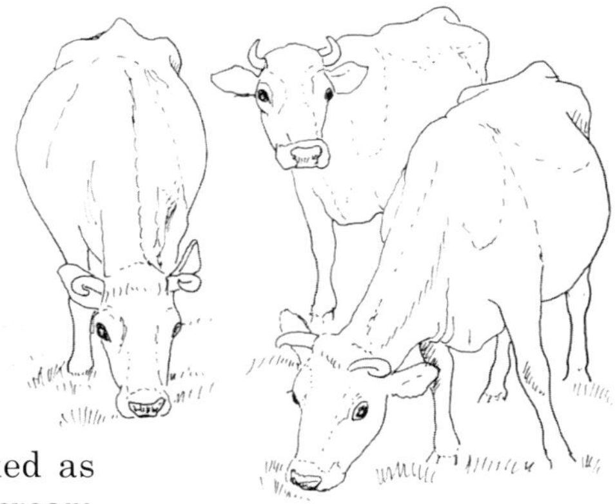

The Family's Uncomplaining Loyalty

This is when any shortcomings outside would be overlooked as Elizabeth, dressed in her most fetching attire, plied them with cream cakes and scones and other exotic victuals never to be forgotten. One was overheard to remark as he climbed into his car. "Still waters run deep; he certainly caught himself a winner there!"

Modestly, I can only conclude that others did not compete in great numbers as we used to feature amongst the winners most years. This was a great morale-booster to our worthy team of workers and to Elizabeth and the family, who would be hijacked and pressed into service at the drop of a hat when accidents and emergencies occurred. They always worked with uncomplaining loyalty and no thought of reward, knowing that I always had their long-term interests at heart.

The English Jersey Cattle Society

As we had pedigree cattle, we became members of the English Jersey Cattle Society and attended with much pleasure meetings and social functions of the East Midlands Branch. A more dramatically radical cross-section of society it would be hard to imagine, with noble Earls and their ladies hobnobbing cheek by jowl with bucolic herdsmen and muddy-booted farmers like myself! I remember one formal dinner when my neighbour at table caused some consternation. Having drunk from the finger-bowl, he proceeded to eat the bread roll on his right, thus causing the whole table to do likewise!

Cows of the Jersey breed, besides being truly beautiful to behold, give by far the richest milk. Therefore, they were most sought-after by the landed gentry to provide them with cream and butter from their home farms. Their deer-like appearance always enhances the view across parkland as they graze their tree-lined pastures. The society's herd book reads like Debrett or Burke's Peerage, and it is headed by several herds owned by Her Majesty such as those at Sandringham and Windsor.

Collective sales of pedigree Jersey cattle were regularly held in Reading sale yard and sometimes at Crewe, the chief auctioneers being Harry Hobson & Co. and John Thornton & Co. We were such regular visitors for buying and selling that we knew every inch of the way - Rugby, Southam, Banbury, Oxford, Reading - a two-and-a-half to three hour journey along twisting roads.

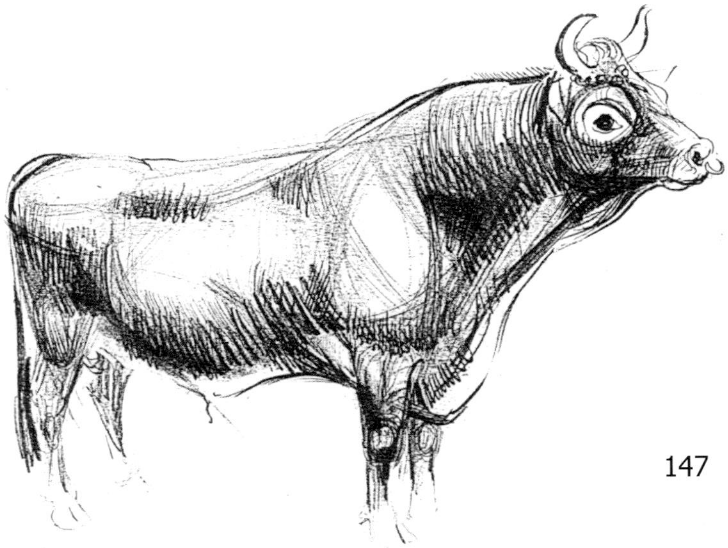

Jersey bulls can be very dangerous. They are light and nimble on their feet like those used for Bull Fighting.

Real Gentry are Kind and Considerate

We were always well-received and fairly treated in our dealings with the titled gentry. A noble Lord used to greet me warmly after church and discuss the harvest prospects or the lambing average. A local Earl sold us his pick-up van and when we arrived to take delivery we talked to his legs as he lay on the cobbled yard checking the brake cables! Later, when Elizabeth had a puncture in a horse-box trailer near his gate, he came out with his jack and graciously changed a wheel for her, no doubt admiring her legs as he did so!

Generalisations are usually dangerous to make, so I speak as I find. An old fellow said to me with a knowing look in his eye, "Beware of horsy people - hunting, show-jumping, racing and polo folk, they be an immoral lot, always having affairs with grooms and stable-girls who are no better than they should be! By contrast, look at your cow-keepers and dairy maids who be gentle, faithful and pure as driven snow." Certainly we met several Jersey breeders who were, in our opinion, gentle but eccentric cranks who were not above mixing magic potions to improve the performance of their doe-eyed, uncomplaining beasts!

In my dealings with rich and noble landed gentry, I have observed the genuine 'toff' to be kind and considerate while the nouveau riche tend to 'put on airs' and treat the hoi polloi with sickening condescension as they look down upon them from their elevated seats in the saddle. It was for that reason that Our Lord, who was born in one man's stable and buried in another man's tomb, chose in his moment of glory to make his triumphant entry into Jerusalem seated on a humble donkey. A war horse might have been seen to make him proud, this meekest and humblest of men!

The Market Place

Marketing usually meant a very early start. It was not unusual for the transporter to arrive at 5am to load stock carefully selected the previous day. The driver might have two other pick-up points and then two more similar loads into a local market that day. He would clean his truck, and after the sale he would be on the lookout for clients who would provide him with return loads.

Owing to traffic conditions, very little livestock is driven to market these days, so the farmers' horse-drawn float has been replaced by a stock trailer, often with an upper deck, pulled by a four-wheel-drive vehicle, an estate car or pick-up. This motley assortment of vehicles forms a slow moving queue waiting for cattle, sheep and pigs to be unloaded, weighed, graded and penned. When they used to accompany me towing a trailer laden with pigs or sheep, my children used to refer to the scene as the "Wacky Races" from a popular children's TV programme.

A great deal of goodwill and co-operation is needed for the activity to go smoothly. The auctioneers' men seem to have a telepathic ability to sense what action is required. One of the more bizarre scenes from behind is that of the drover penning sheep. To make himself appear wider and more threatening, he opens wide his smock or raincoat and flaps it energetically, thereby giving what I am told is a plausible imitation of an authentic 'flasher'. Anyway, it as surely frightens the sheep as humans have often been told that their sexual behaviour frightens the horses!

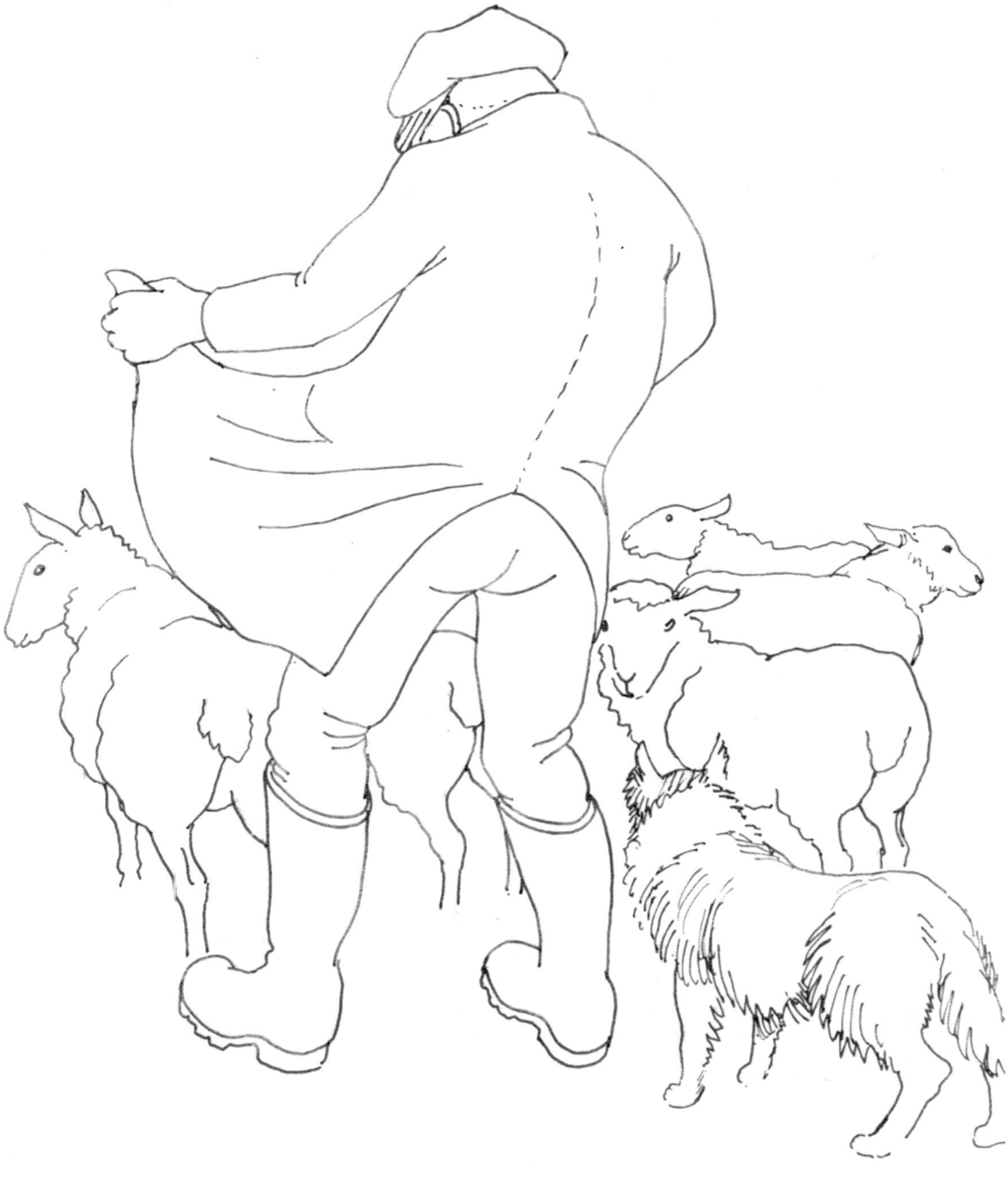

Dealers

A considerable percentage of fat stock is bought at the markets by a handful of shrewd buyers for the wholesale meat trade. Animals sold for rearing and breeding as opposed to immediate slaughter are known as *store* animals. Here again, many are bought by dealers who have no intention of keeping them for more than a few days, when they will be sorted and bunched into well-matched lots to be sold for a quick profit to other farmers who may lack the time or expertise to buy in auction market.

The large dealers and buyers, because of the sheer volume of trade they bring, command much respect and power. This can, of course, be abused by unscrupulous men who may illegally use underhand methods to operate 'rings' to interfere with the free market price. An auctioneer must be on the lookout for unfair practices and try to keep faith and good humour between buyer and seller, and this calls for great skill and understanding.

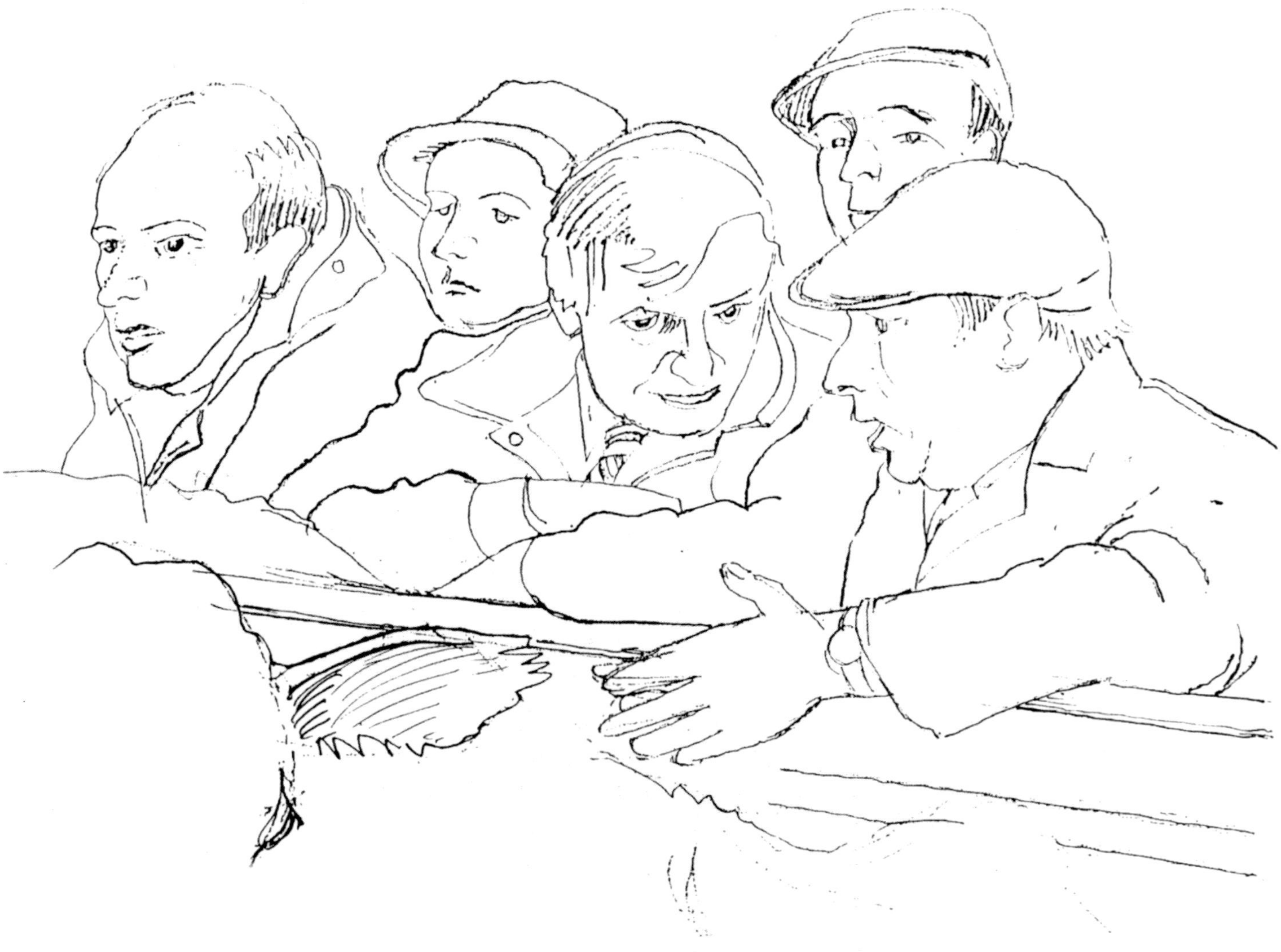

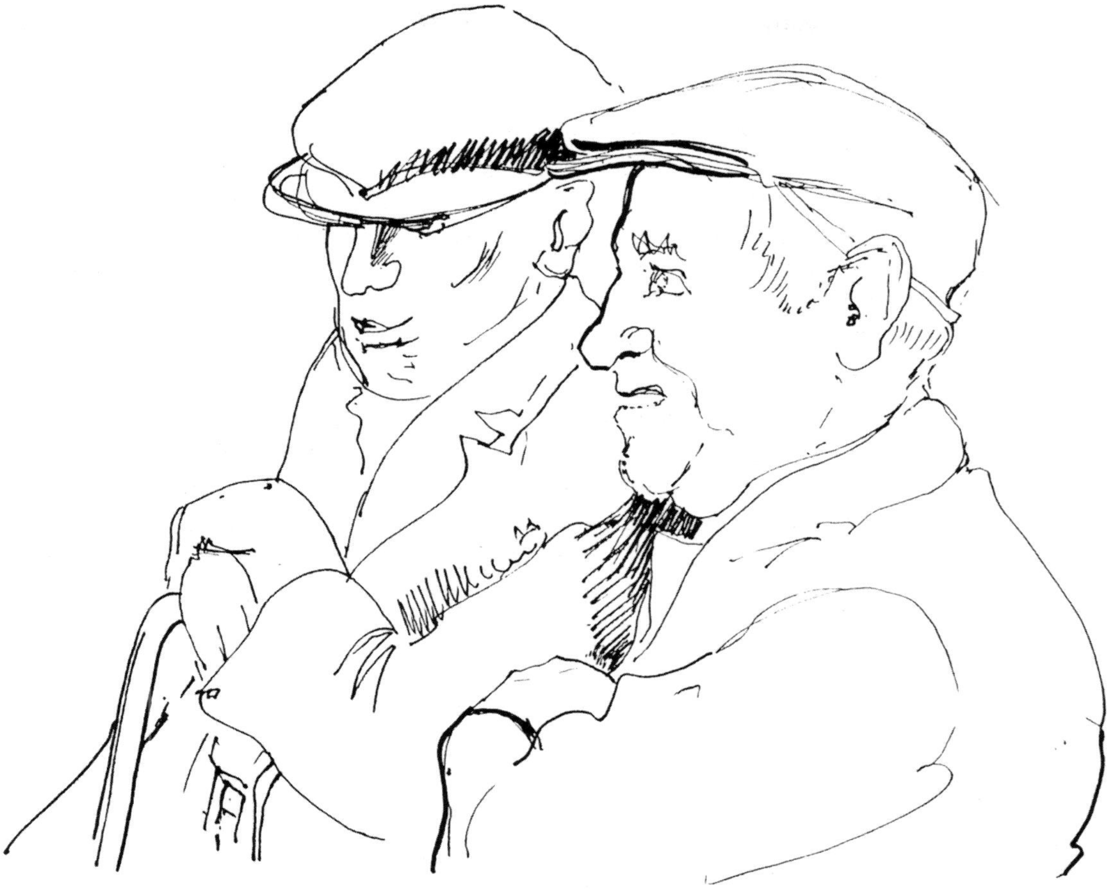

'Standing In'

Here I mention a custom known as 'standing in'. A friend, with a good eye for cattle and a shrewd gauge of the market values, would go early before the auction sale and approach a seller who had, say, ten store cattle. "What are you expecting to get for them in the ring?". "Five hundred apiece." the seller replies. "That's a bit optimistic," says my friend. "I tell you what I'll do - I'll stand in with you at £450." The seller agrees, knowing that my friend has put a bottom in the market by offering an upset price of £450. Anything the cattle fetch above that figure is shared equally. If the cattle do realise £500, the £50 is divided £25 each. So my friend goes home with £250 for his day's work!

Auction Ring

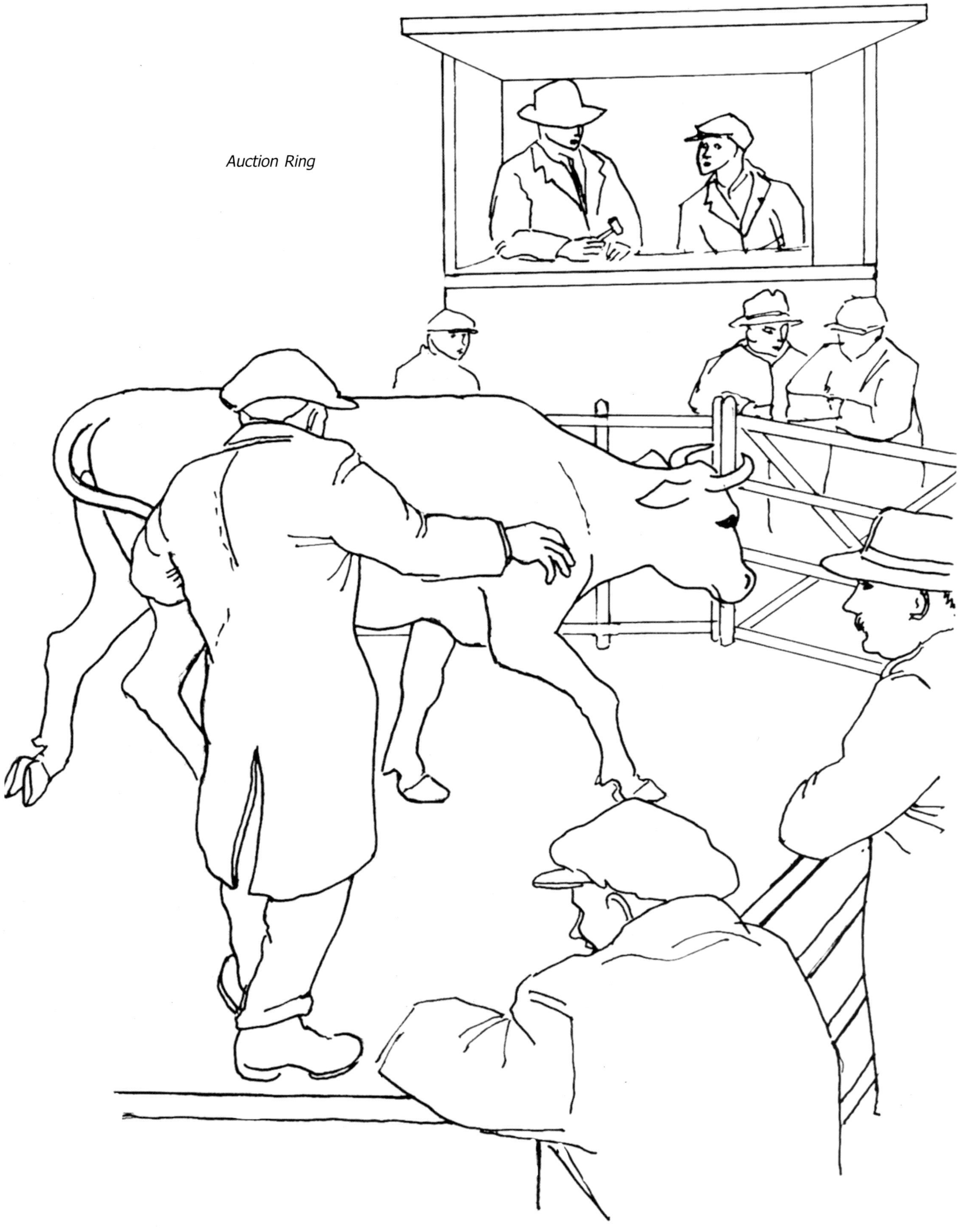

Flamboyant Characters

Market cafes do a roaring trade in bacon baps and strong tea, while the bars are propped up by portly patrons either celebrating their conquests or drowning their sorrows. Many are being 'treated' by agents and travellers who have nobbled their clients for cheques outstanding on feed, fertiliser and seeds accounts. Each man seems to be waiting to be caricatured, larger than life in clothing and features. Gnarled hands grasp crooks and thumbsticks. You find men with broken noses and crooked teeth, their heads surmounted with outlandish head gear - deerstalkers and stetsons, peaked caps and fedoras, berets and balaclavas.

Slaughter-men and drovers, truckers and tractor drivers; auctioneer's men in white coats; the odd farmer in a bowler hat and sporting a buttonhole or a corn dolly; breeches and leggings, bib and brace - all is fashionable with the casual flamboyance of the fields. Learned and ignorant jostle with toffs and tinkers. Surely the market-place is a great social leveller! While little deference was shown to the rich and powerful, a soft spot was always reserved for a female or a youthful seller whose stock could coax an additional bid or two from the most hard-bitten buyers. The owner was usually allowed into the ring with his or her animals to show them off and often would promote extra bids by waving a £10 note to go to the buyer as 'luck money'.

Farmers generally avoid direct compliments. After a long tale about a man who went courting in the dark without a lantern and found himself wedded to an ugly wife, the old farmer said to me "'Tis plain *you* didna' go courting without a lantern, like he did." Another, after a close inspection of my spouse in full flush of youth, said with admiration, "Bah gum, tha didst well for thissen!" And never a truer word was spoken, for she has supported me valiantly in every adversity along life's journey and shown selfless love and devotion to our four children, of whom we are justifiably proud.

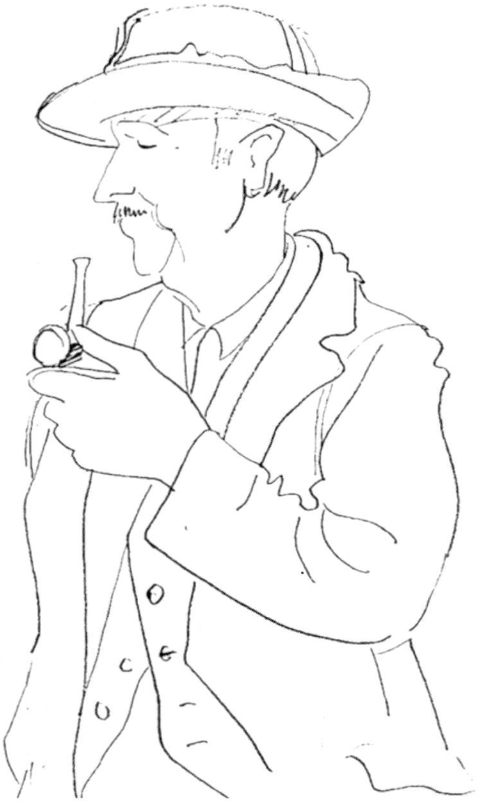

A highly-valued shepherd, 1950

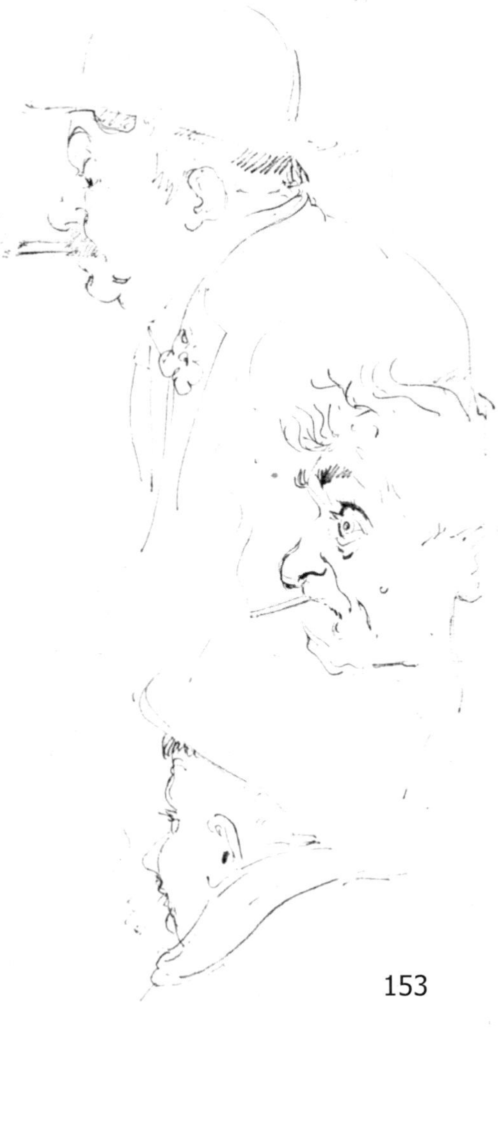

Creation of Wealth is No Crime

It is better to be silent than to speak of things about which you know nothing. Farmers always have to suffer jibes about feather-bedding and subsidies, usually from the chattering classes who have never produced anything in their lives of real worth. There are some, who should know better, who speak of wealth creation as a crime of which to be ashamed. If a farmer plants one potato to get back twenty, he has created wealth and fed his fellow men.

If a wheelwright makes a cart or wagon out of wood he has fashioned from a tree, he has created wealth and assisted the local farmers to bring in the crops they have grown. I have often been amazed at the abysmal ignorance of some academic wiseacres in their ivory towers and boardrooms. Many do not know the different between straw, hay and silage, let alone being able to recognise an ear of wheat, barley or oats. Yet they presume to patronise the sons of toil, peasants who labour mightily to put the food on their tables three times a day at a very reasonable price.

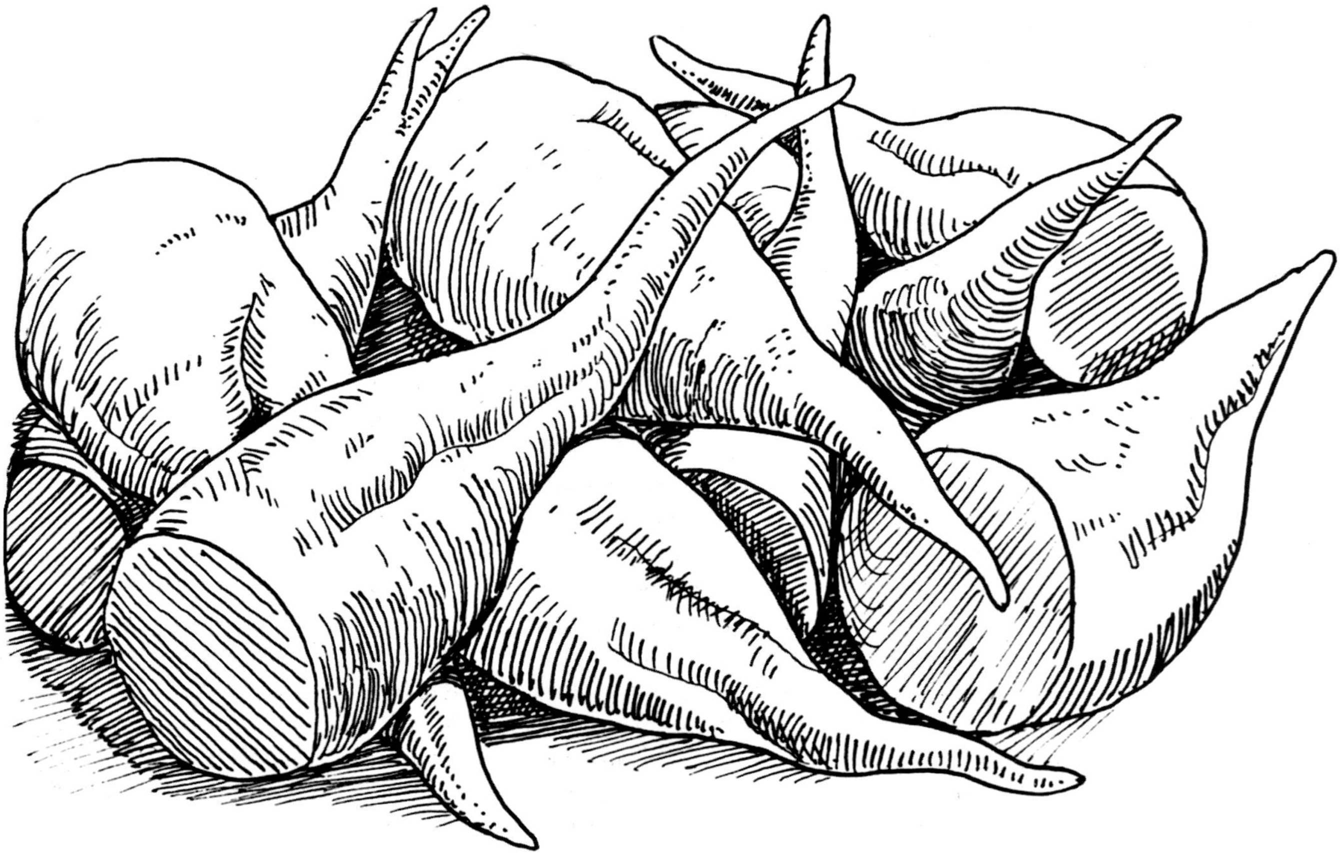

Sugar - beets are like gigantic parsnips. They are grown on contract to the local sugar-beet factory. A level of 18% is regarded as a good sugar content. Tops are useful stock feed as is the processed pulp which may be bought back by the grower.

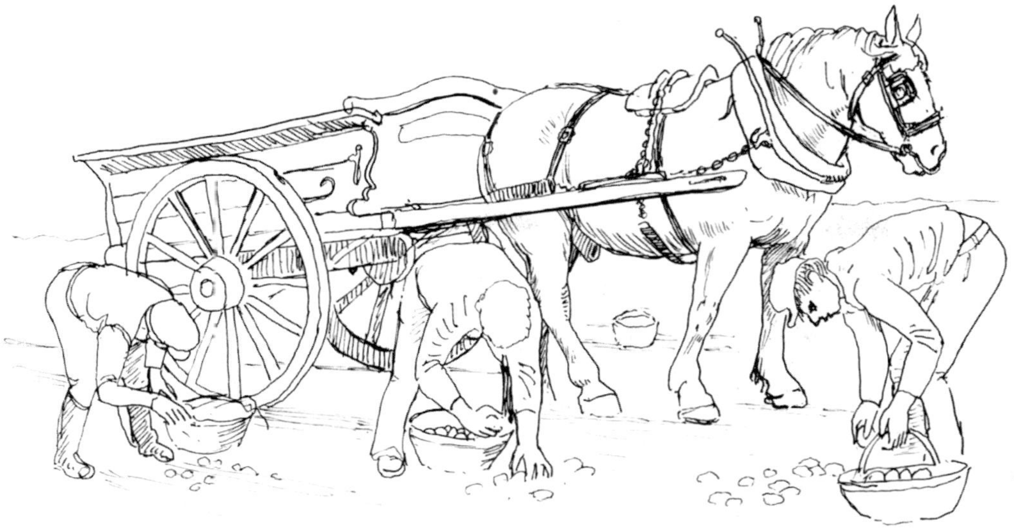

Harvesting the potato crop

Subsidy is a Bribe to Make Food Cheaper

Subsidies act against normal market forces and I have always thought of a subsidy as existing for the benefit of townsman-consumer to make food cheaper to him and her so that they don't demand bigger wages. A subsidy exists as an incentive or bribe to make the primary producer do something obviously unbusiness-like, such as selling below the cost of production. Let us assume that 40lbs of lamb meat costs me £25 to produce; I may need £30 from the market to make lamb production pay. However, I will be induced to take the unbusiness-like action of selling for £20 (ie. *less than cost*) in the certain promise that a further £10 will come along a month later as a subsidy. The buyer pays only £20 for something worth £30 in the fond hope that he will pass on that advantage to the consumer to make his food cheaper - but does he really pass it on?

Quotas for hops, potatoes and sugar-beet have been in existence a long time - restricting the amount allowed to be grown in the interests of orderly marketing; the difference between a shortage and a glut being quite marginal.

How the Real Price of Food has Dropped

Recently, however, this quota system has been applied also to milk production so that dairy farmers had to make a 10% cut in production and be penalised for any milk produced in excess of that amount. It would seem to me unreasonable to have to restrict production in this country when we are still busily importing liquid milk and dairy produce from abroad. In 1947, a person on average wage worked over eight minutes to buy a pint of milk. In 1973, it took four minutes and in 1992 it took only two minutes. Likewise with eggs, in 1955 it took an hour's work to buy a dozen eggs. Twenty years later in 1975 it took less than fifteen minutes. Now I guess it would take less than a minute to buy a barnyard egg to throw at a free-ranging politician! This story is true for practically everything we eat that is grown in this country, but we should remember those numbers work in reverse for the farmer, who can buy less and less of everyone else's time with the food he produces. A call-out charge for a plumber or an electrician is likely to be £35 before he does any work at all! (The price of a whole fat lamb - 40lbs of meat.)

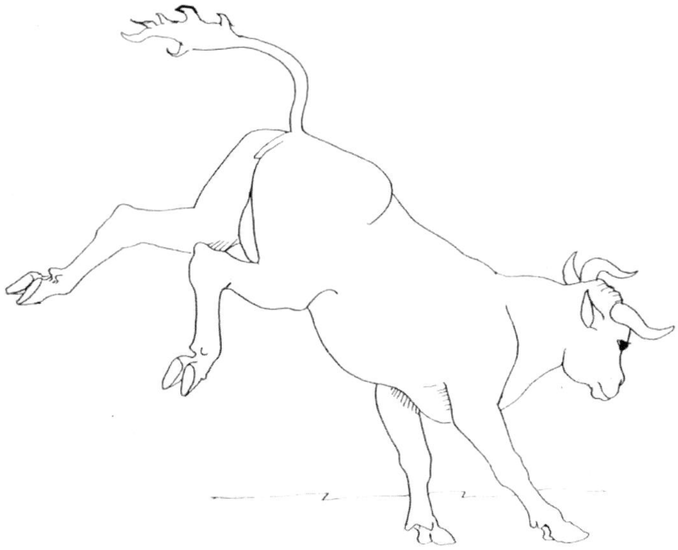

Chapter EIGHT

Veterinary Visits

Tuberculin Testing of Cattle

A dairy farmer would of necessity have dealings with his local veterinary surgeon, quite apart from having recourse to him at times when his animals might be sick or injured. At least once a year a letter would come from him serving notice that the Ministry of Agriculture had directed him to do a routine tuberculin test of all bovine animals on his holding.

This involved two visits with a day's interval between. On the agreed date, the cows would have to remain in their stalls after morning milking and the vet would bustle round putting two injections into the clipped folds of skin on their necks. The thickness of the skin was measured with callipers and the measurement called out to the assistant with the clipboard, who carried a list of all the animals together with their names and ear numbers. On the second visit, the skin was measured again to assess the extent of the animal's reaction to mild doses of bovine and avian tuberculosis.

The Hilarious Rodeo

The cows, being tied by neck chains in stalls, presented few problems; neither did the young calves confined in their individual pens. However, the outlying young stock presented more of a rodeo show as they would have to be rounded up into a suitable compound where they could be handled one by one. The sight of the vet and helpers clad in strange garments alerted the beasts that something unusual was about to happen, and generally they made sure that it did!

The stage was set for a burlesque of hilarious proportions as a small posse of ill-assorted assistants tried unsuccessfully to hustle three dozen wild, suspicious animals into a small shippon or hovel deep in manure. One heifer, more flighty than the rest, would be determined to avoid capture and slip past the gate to go romping round the field on her own, capering and cavorting with her heels in the air for all the world like the cow that jumped over the moon!

The scene of the chase might have to be re-enacted several times with many extravagant 'banana skin' variations before they were safely inside. Then intrepid men had to plunge bravely into the mêlée of trampling hooves to catch and wrestle with each creature, left arm around the horns and fingers and thumbs up the nostrils. The struggling beast had to be held still long enough for the vet to read and call out its earmark before injecting it with his two loaded syringes, which were slung round his neck along with the callipers.

In the gloom and confusion accidents could easily happen. Tempers became frayed and profanities abounded as each one relieved his feelings in his own way. Ear numbers could not be read and the vet would inject himself as he tripped and lost his gum boot in the suction of the quagmire! Toes were liable to be trampled in milling feet and horns were poked into eyes and other painful places. I, for one, was always most relieved and thankful when the rodeo was safely over. We could repair to the farmhouse for well-earned refreshments, and prepare from the clipboard the battle-stained foolscap lists with all their names, numbers and measurements for the vet to take with him for sending on to the ministry. At times like this you may be sure I lavished thoughts of great affection on the faceless men in Whitehall for ensuring the continuance of our annual rodeo show!

Handling cattle for injection and other treatments when they are located in outlying situations has become much easier with the advent of the tractor-mounted cattle crush. The cattle are funnelled into the device one at a time and secured by a yoke clamped round their necks. Sadly, a promising young relative of sixteen years met his death when a beast suddenly raised its head as he was endeavouring to read its ear mark in a cattle crush. Cattle are routinely treated against brucellosis (contagious abortion), husk worm, which attacks the lungs, and foul of foot, which sends them lame. Dairy cows are prone to mastitis, one type of which, known as summer mastitis, attacks dry cows and causes the loss of the affected quarter of the udder.

Specialist Equine Vet

Veterinary surgeons usually work in group practices and tend to follow a speciality. For instance, one might deal almost exclusively with cats, dogs and small animals, while another, who has gained the confidence of the hunting and riding fraternity, will deal with horses and ponies. As today there are few genuine work horses, these animals are mainly used in pursuit of foxes or show ring trophies. I can imagine a vet getting sucked into a social life of prestige and privilege, where he would have to know his place with his more illustrious clients and mind his P's and Q's with others.

Since the horse in this country has become a necessary adjunct among the hobbies of the affluent, I suppose it must be a good source of revenue for those veterinary surgeons who watch after the health of these pampered steeds.

Horses suffer from innumerable complaints with strange sounding names such as farcy and glanders. They get ring-bone, side-bone navicular and spavin. They are also subject to laminitis, or founder, which is an inflammation of the sensitive parts of the hoof. They get fistulas and colic and other ailments which keep the vets busy prescribing and rendering their accounts.

A horse's tongue is pulled forward as his teeth are rasped at regular intervals. For some other treatments, his top lip is twisted in a loop of string, called a twitch, to distract his attention and it really works like an anaesthetic!

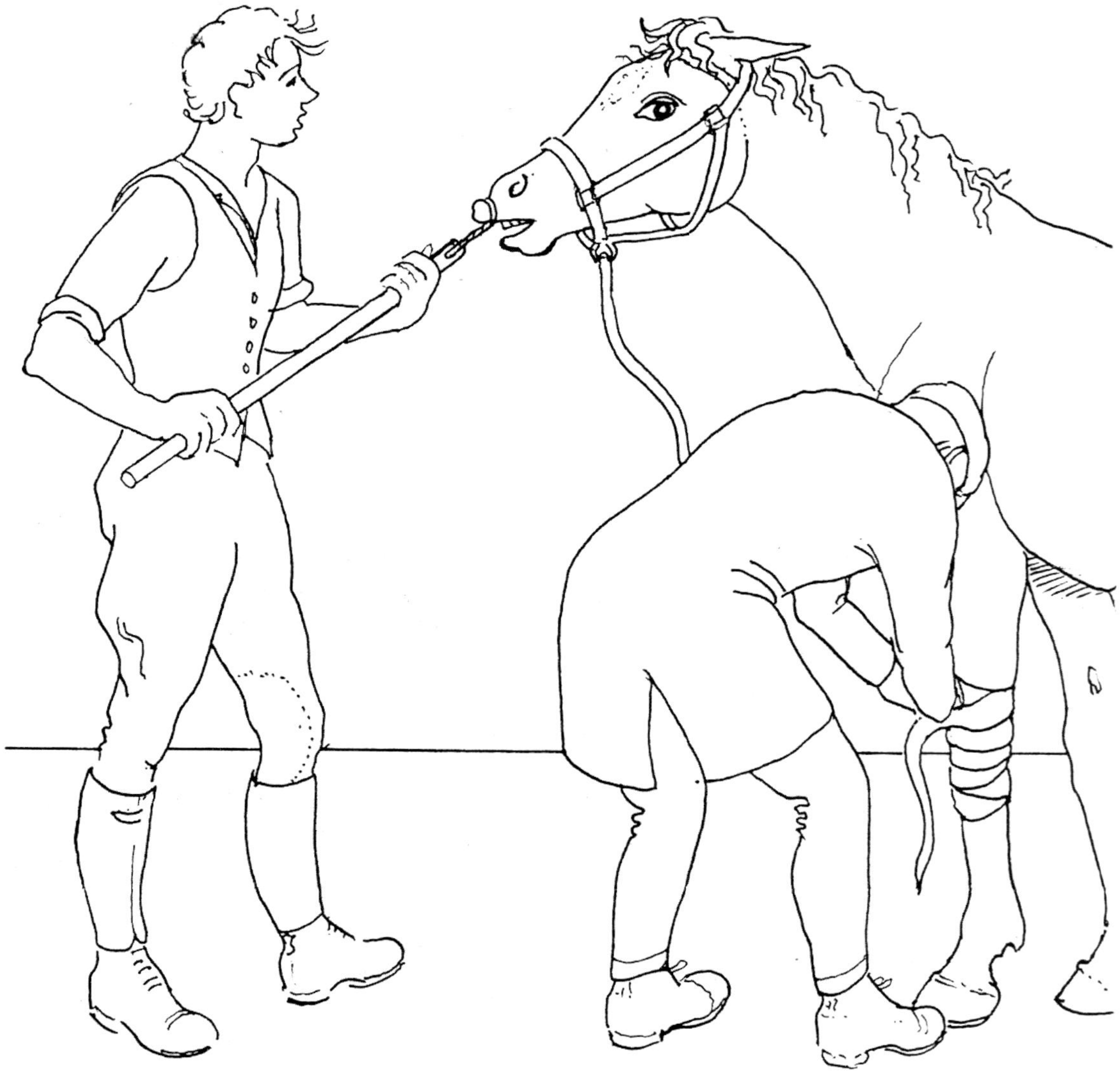

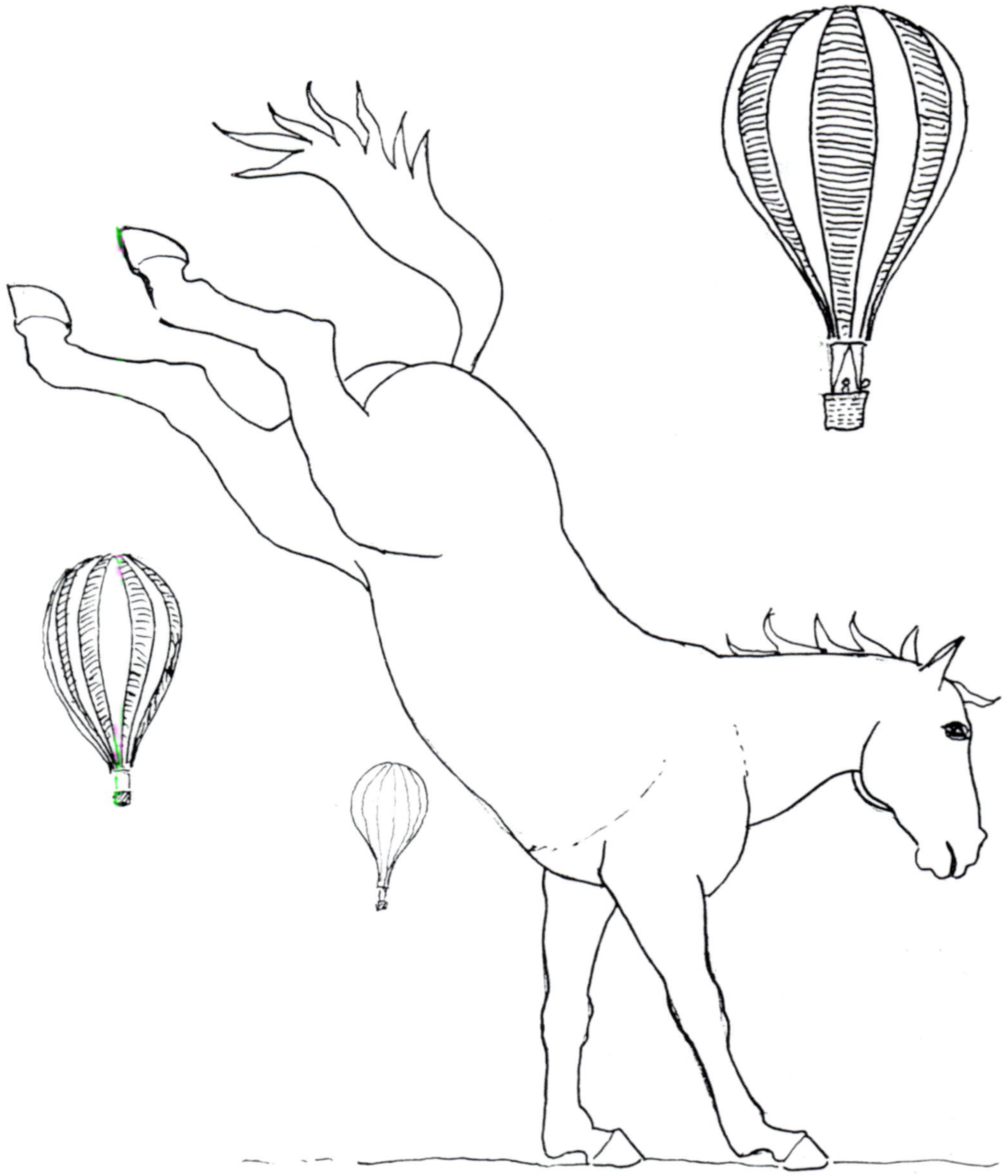

The Horse's Sensitive Skin

The skin of the horse is sensitive and thin and is easily torn on barbed wire and sharp protrusions. Because they are typically overfed and under-exercised, nervous horses run about for no good reason and contrive to tear this delicate skin which needs to be stitched up by the attentive vet. I have seen a paddock full of grazing horses go mad and career about with utmost abandon because half a dozen gas-filled balloons drifted across overhead. The horses' keen hearing picked up the hissing sound of the gas long before I would have heard it and they would not settle down until the balloons were out of sight.

This could be an instance where one man's seemingly innocent hobby could cause damage of which he is completely unaware. I heard of a group of disabled riders being led along a quiet lane when suddenly, great consternation was caused by a crop-spraying helicopter appearing over a hedge, scattering the ponies and terrifying the riders.

Animals Often Treated Better Than People

There is a *Royal* Society for the Prevention of Cruelty to Animals but only a *National* Society for the Prevention of Cruelty to Children. Being of a somewhat cynical nature, I have often wryly remarked that animals were better attended in sickness than people.

Doctors in our area were almost always most reluctant to make a house call to sick members of my family, preferring to prescribe over the phone or insist on a feverish child having to brave the elements to wait a turn in a draughty waiting room. And everyone knows you must not be ill at weekends or on public holidays! By contrast, I had nothing but praise for the prompt service of my local veterinary practitioners. I could ring the vet at any time of the night or early morning regarding an animal in distress, and almost before the phone was back on the hook, his car headlights would be piercing the darkness as he tore across our field road.

Vet Richard Gooch became a very good friend of ours.

It is the hope of reward that sweetens labour. It may be that the doctor got paid on a headage basis whether he laboured or not, while the vet was paid for actual work he was called out to deal with, and he had to defend his reputation for turning out promptly.

I well remember a conscientious old vet in his late sixties coming out at 11pm on Christmas Eve. Though snow was on the ground, he stripped to the waist, put on his gown and lay on the floor in the calving pen to deal with a mal-presented calf. Without being asked, he came out again on Christmas morning as a follow-up to see that mother and baby were both doing well. Here was an instance of devotion beyond the call of duty which enhanced his reputation and, I hope, earned him a few celebratory tots of whisky!

In the days when the local telephone was controlled by Mabel, if you rang through an emergency call for the vet, she would say, "'Tis no use calling his number, he's gone to old Ebor Hankin's farm at Willey half an hour ago. I'll put you through there". That way she saved valuable time and mileage and maybe an animal's life.

'No Time to Lose'

We were always amused by one of our veterinary friends who arrived at top speed in a cloud of dust and as he descended from the car, grabbing his bag, would bark out, "Where is she now, lead me to her quickly, no time to lose". Hardly appearing to listen to the symptoms, he would jab in a hypodermic needle injecting penicillin and vitamins, close up his bag and walk swiftly to the kitchen ostensibly to wash his hands, having spent barely two minutes with the patient. Once in the kitchen, Elizabeth would offer him a coffee. "Just a quick one then," he would say, as he sank into a chair. Half an hour later he would still be there recounting all the local gossip! Then he would suddenly straighten up, stride to the car and disappear in a cloud of dust - no time to lose!

Room for Sentiment

Animals are looked at in a different light from humans when one comes to consider sickness, injury and old age. The vet may recommend the local knacker man or fell-monger who will come and humanely despatch animals for whose condition there is no cure. Where there are livestock there are sure to be dead stock and commercial considerations are paramount. However, I have known farmers to keep retired old cows and work horses to live out their natural lives for no logical reason. For sentimental reasons, I brought my 'retired' grey Fergy tractor to live in my suburban garden shed!

My little grey Fergie

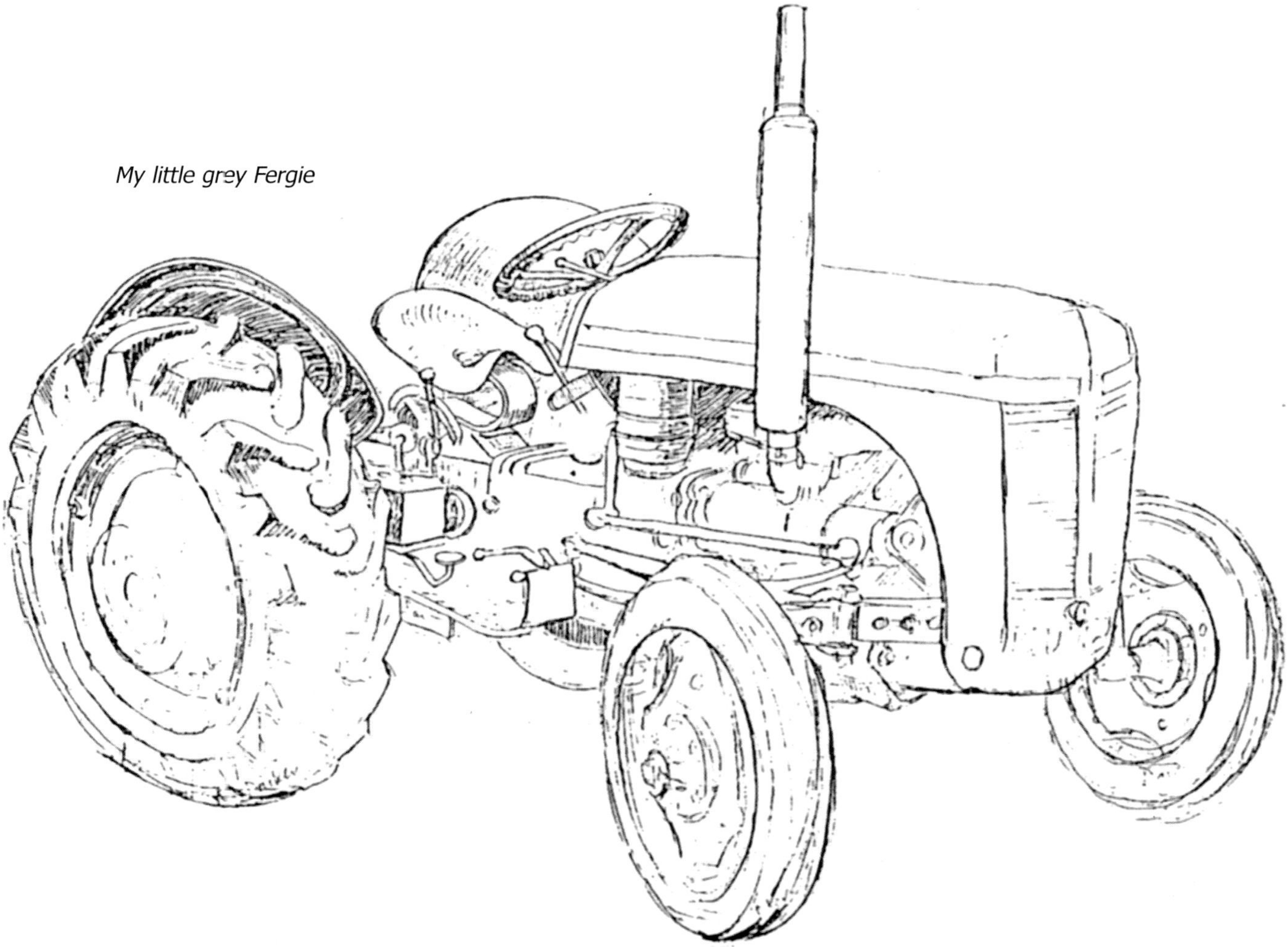

Our second son, Richard, showed mechanical aptitude from an early age - he subsequently became apprenticed with Massey Ferguson which carries with it the honour of being a Freeman of the City of Coventry

De-horning the Dairy Herd

When one thinks that the average veterinary surgeon is better qualified than your usual general practitioner, it seems incredible that they must spend such a disproportionate amount of time engaged in crude, physically-taxing occupations one would have thought more suitable to a butcher. Cleansing retained afterbirths, dealing with a prolapsed uterus in a cow or sheep, castrating horses and cattle are but a few of the unpleasant jobs a vet may be asked to do.

The most spectacular visitation was when the vet came to de-horn our dairy herd. An anaesthetic injection having been placed at the root of each horn, he attacked the gracefully curving appendages with a tenon saw. This caused blood to spurt in all directions, so that subsequently the cow-byres had to be whitewashed all over. More recently I have seen improved results by the use of an instrument resembling a long-armed bolt-cropper!

Use of a Metal-Detector

In the days when hay and straw bales were tied with wire it was fairly common for cattle to swallow short lengths of rusty wire, with dire consequences. Vets made use of a metal detector to confirm the diagnosis before carrying out an expensive operation to remove the wire.

It used to be thought that livestock had an optimum stocking rate which, if exceeded, would lead to the operation of a law of diminishing returns. Each animal would become its neighbour's worst enemy in competing for available resources. Resistance to disease would diminish as natural immunity became impaired due to overcrowding. However, pharmaceutical invention and veterinary practice have combined to counteract the inevitable results with additives to food stuffs and vets are kept busy doing routine dosing and injection of the livestock at risk.

Nature Tends to Get Her Own Back

If cattle were to see a dead sheep in their field, they would give it scant attention and it certainly would not occur to them to eat it! However, men, in their wisdom, include undetectable parts of dead sheep in the cow's ration so that she has no option but to eat it. Then follows an outbreak of bovine spongiform encephalitis (mad cow disease) with far-reaching, devastating effects, which like the salmonella scare with poultry, keeps many vets very busy for years ahead inspecting and testing.

Notifiable Diseases

A vet must be especially careful not to become infected accidentally by the diseases of animals, many of which are transferable to man - brucellosis, salmonella, tetanus and anthrax come to mind. The last two diseases lurk in the soil for many years and can be quite lethal. I once saw the agonising death of a Shire horse from tetanus, and I knew an old man who told me he had come very near to death with anthrax in his youth.

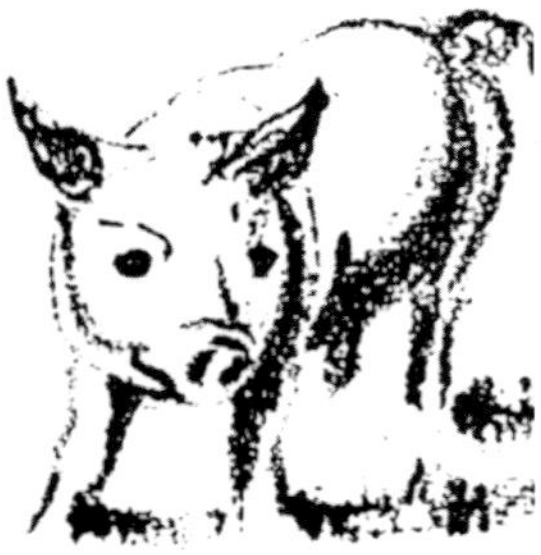

If a farmer has an animal which dies in suspicious circumstances, it must be inspected by a vet for such notifiable diseases as foot and mouth and swine fever; if cleared, it can be collected by the knacker man, fellmonger or the hunt kennels who perform indispensable services in disposing of fallen carcasses.

Vets Eat Their Patients

Pigs can be immensely strong and savage. I heard once of a vet who had been badly bitten by a sow. The doctor who had come to attend to the wound was said to have remarked, "I knew that vets, unlike doctors, eat their patients. *This pig must have been attempting to get its own back!*"

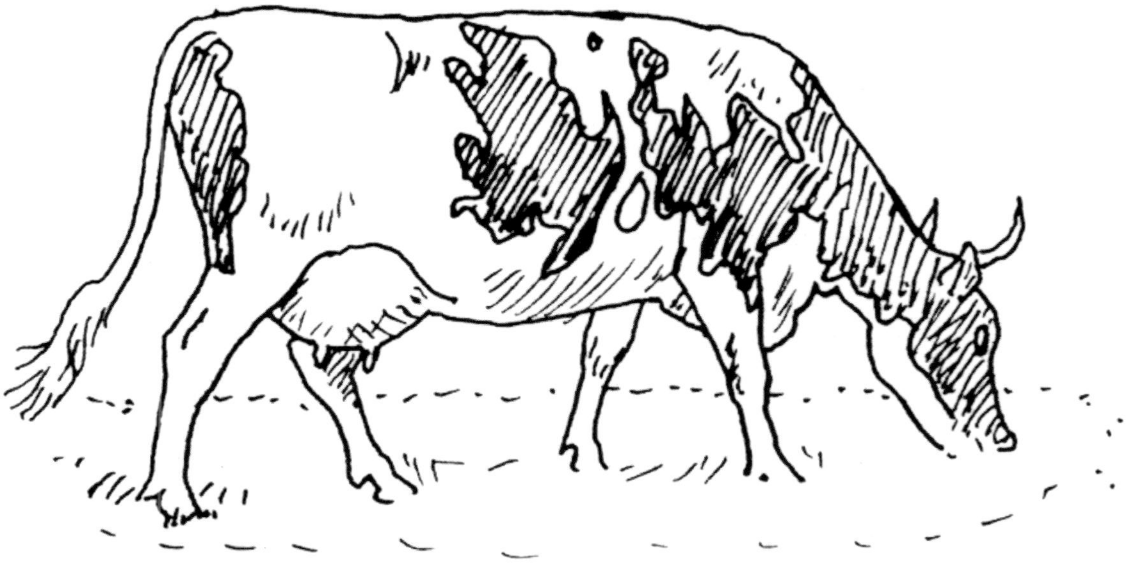

Chapter NINE

Field Work and Threshing

Invention of the Reaper and Binder

For thousands of years, sheaves of corn were tied by hand with back-breaking toil and twists of straw. Then McCormick and Massey Harris, on the plains of Canada, invented the reaper and binder which could cut and tie a sheaf with a knot of twine. These machines could be pulled by two strong horses on a flat field, but often a third trace-horse was added in front. I spent many happy days as a young boy perched on the leading horse, controlling him as we turned the corners.

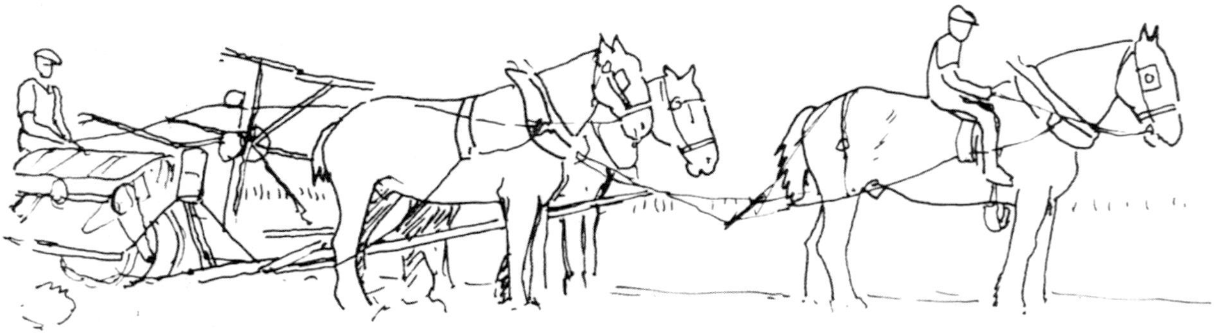

Christopher riding the trace horse pulling the binder

After the war, tractors were available to pull the heavy 'binder' and I fitted a carrier for the 12-bore so that rabbits bolting from the standing corn could be shot on the move. Towards evening, when the final acre was to be cut, as if by magic, men with guns and with sticks would appear to take part in the sport, as game and vermin bolted for freedom. Quite often there would be a fox's lair, a flattened area filled with chicken bones and feathers. I was always amazed that the fox invariably positioned its lair within yards of the true dead centre of the field.

There are many local names for the shortening runs made when finishing a triangular piece of fieldwork. In Somerset, they are 'batts', in the Midlands, 'pikes', and I have heard the term 'gore', which is also used in dressmaking to denote a tapering piece of material.

A REAPER & BINDER C1884

Made by A. Harris Son & Co of Brantford, Kingston, Ontario.

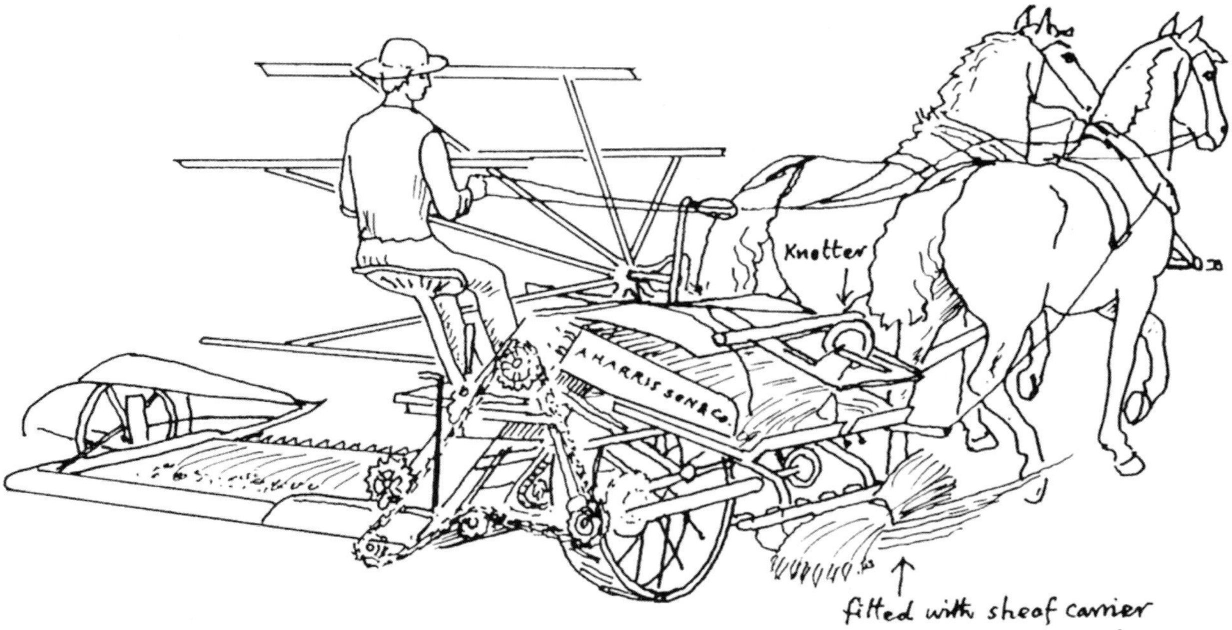

Daniel Massey, a successful farmer, began manufacturing simple farm implements in 1847 at Newcastle Ontario. The business was joined in 1891 by Alanson Harris, a skilled mechanic & competitor, to form Massey-Harris Ltd. With the Harry Ferguson merger in 1953 the Company became Massey-Harris-Ferguson; this was shortened in 1957 to Massey-Ferguson Limited.

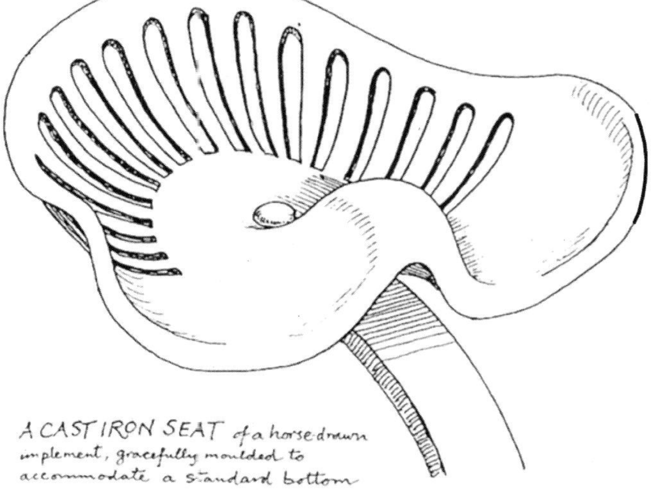

A CAST IRON SEAT of a horse-drawn implement, gracefully moulded to accommodate a standard bottom

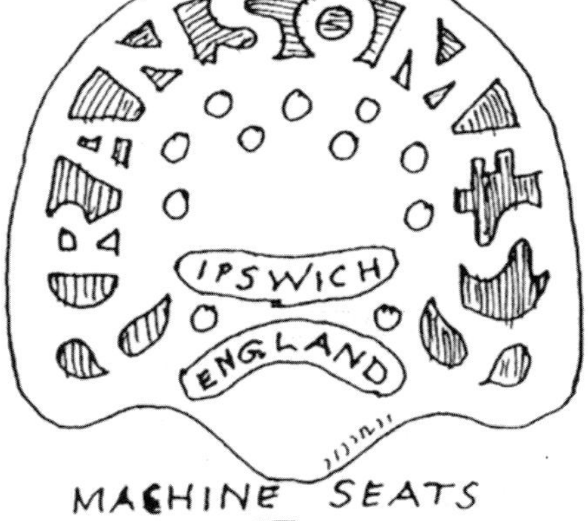

MACHINE SEATS

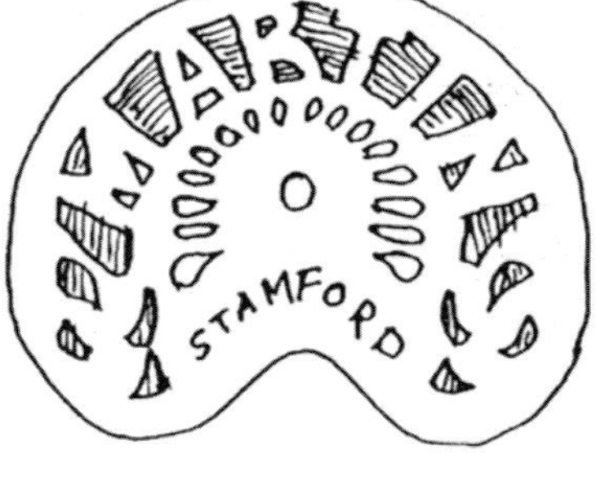

Stooking the Sheaves

When the corn had been tied into sheaves, these were arranged into 'stooks' or groups of six. These were placed in neat rows about five yards apart to allow pitchers to load from each side of a wagon driven up these 'aisles'. The stooks might be left out to dry for ten days or more, so they had to be well constructed to withstand the wind and rain.

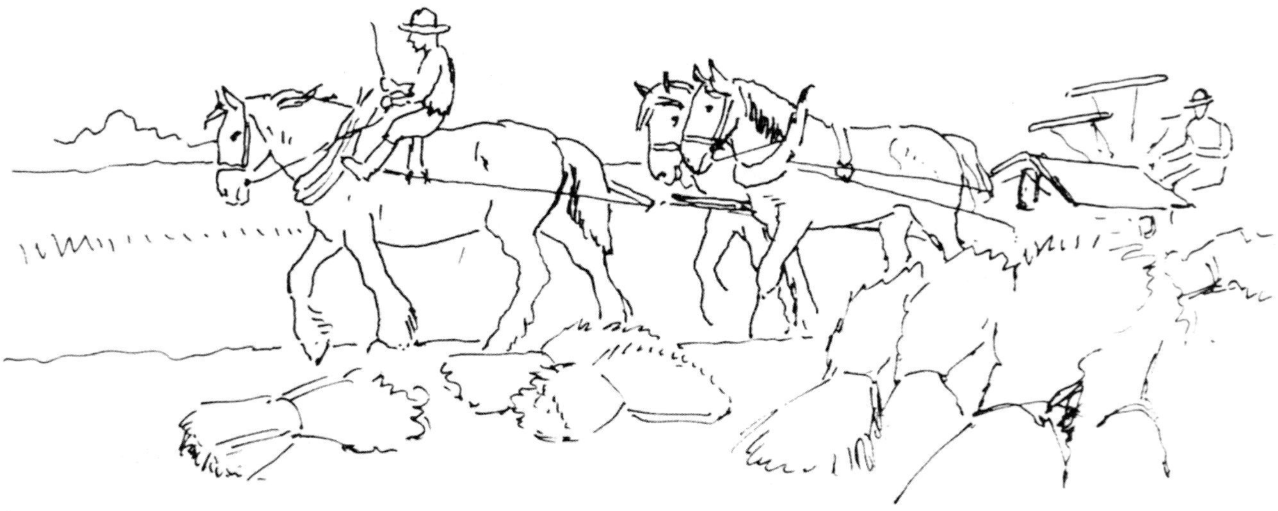

Hauling or Leading the Corn to the Stack

When hauling the sheaves from field to rick, it was common practice for the carter to build the load standing on the wagon, carefully placing each sheaf and binding it in a certain pattern so that it would withstand the bumpy ride across ridge and furrow and over ruts in gateways. This wagoner would then be responsible for steering and leading this great galleon, pitching and tossing on its way to the stackyard, where he would offload his own load by forking it up to the men on the rick. After a quick sup at the cider flagon, he would have a little respite as he drove the return journey. There might be three, four or five wagons following this cycle according to the distance from field to rickyard. Some of the older wagons were especially difficult to steer as they were made to half-lock or quarter-lock; that means that the front wheels were so enormous that they would not pass under but rubbed on plates at the sides of the wagon when turning. This made it necessary to steer in a wide arc when aiming for a gateway.

'Hermaphrodite' Wagon

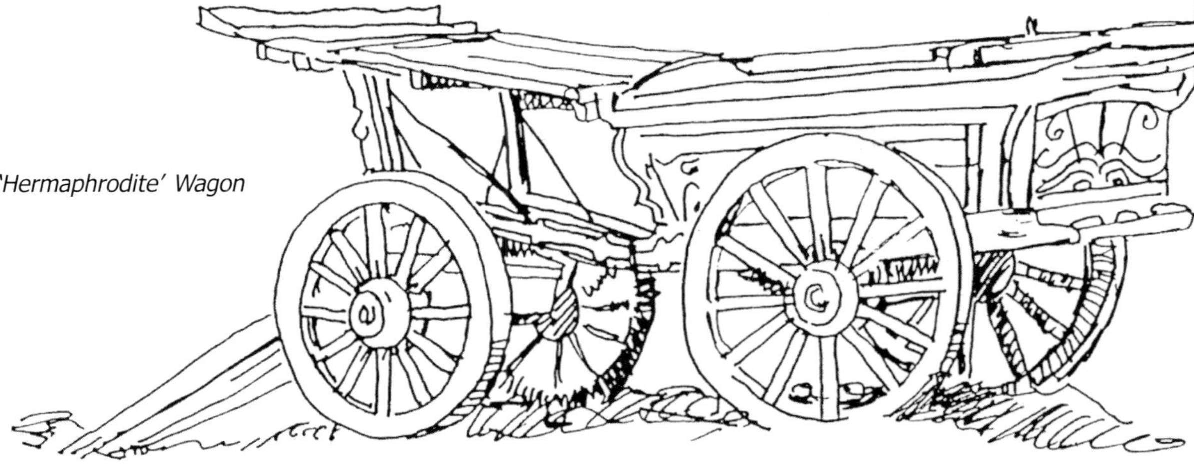

In some places, the ubiquitous two-wheeled tipping cart was turned temporarily into a harvest wagon by the addition of an open frame and a pair of front wheels on a turntable. This queer-looking vehicle was known as a 'mophrey' (hermaphrodite) - neither one thing nor the other (neither cart nor wagon!)

It is always a satisfying privilege to be part of a good team. At times such as harvesting and threshing, there was much evidence of teamwork and common purpose, each person striving for the success of the enterprise with little thought of direct financial reward.

Small wooden roller for trailing close behind rear wagon wheel when going up the hill.

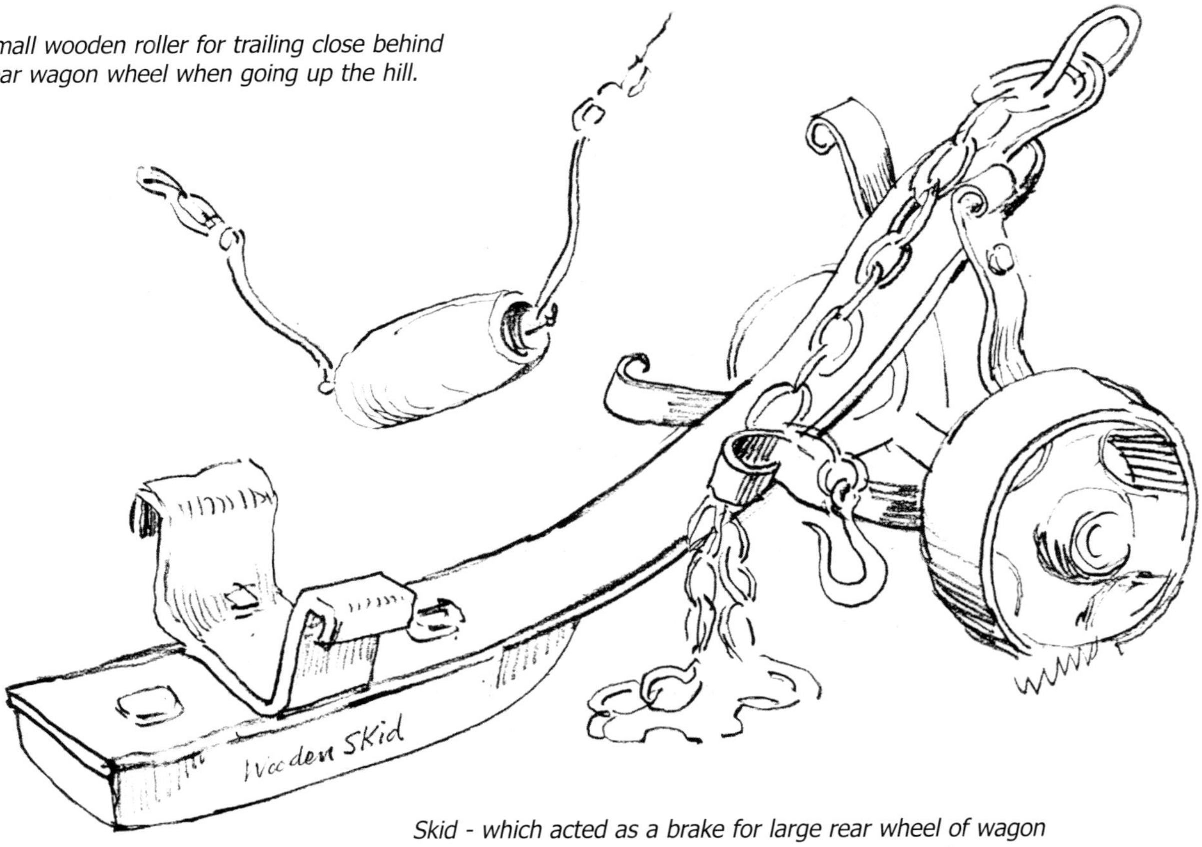

Skid - which acted as a brake for large rear wheel of wagon

Picnic Dinner in the Cornfield

Each man relied on the support of his wife and children to make things run smoothly. With the long hours of heavy toil and massive output of human energy, food and drink were much in evidence. Promptly at dinner hour, I have seen the farmer's wife and daughter appear over the horizon, laden with baskets covered by white napkins, which contained a sumptuous repast such as one would have had in the farmhouse kitchen - rabbit pies and pasties rich in gravy, scotch eggs and chicken legs, freshly baked bread and cakes, home-made butter and jam, all washed down by ale and home-brewed cider. Not, one would have thought, the best preparation for an afternoon's arduous toil in the hot sun! There was all the festive excitement of a picnic, with dogs and children romping in the sun, while adults rested in the shade, some puffing on pipes, others seeing to the needs of the patient horses and machines.

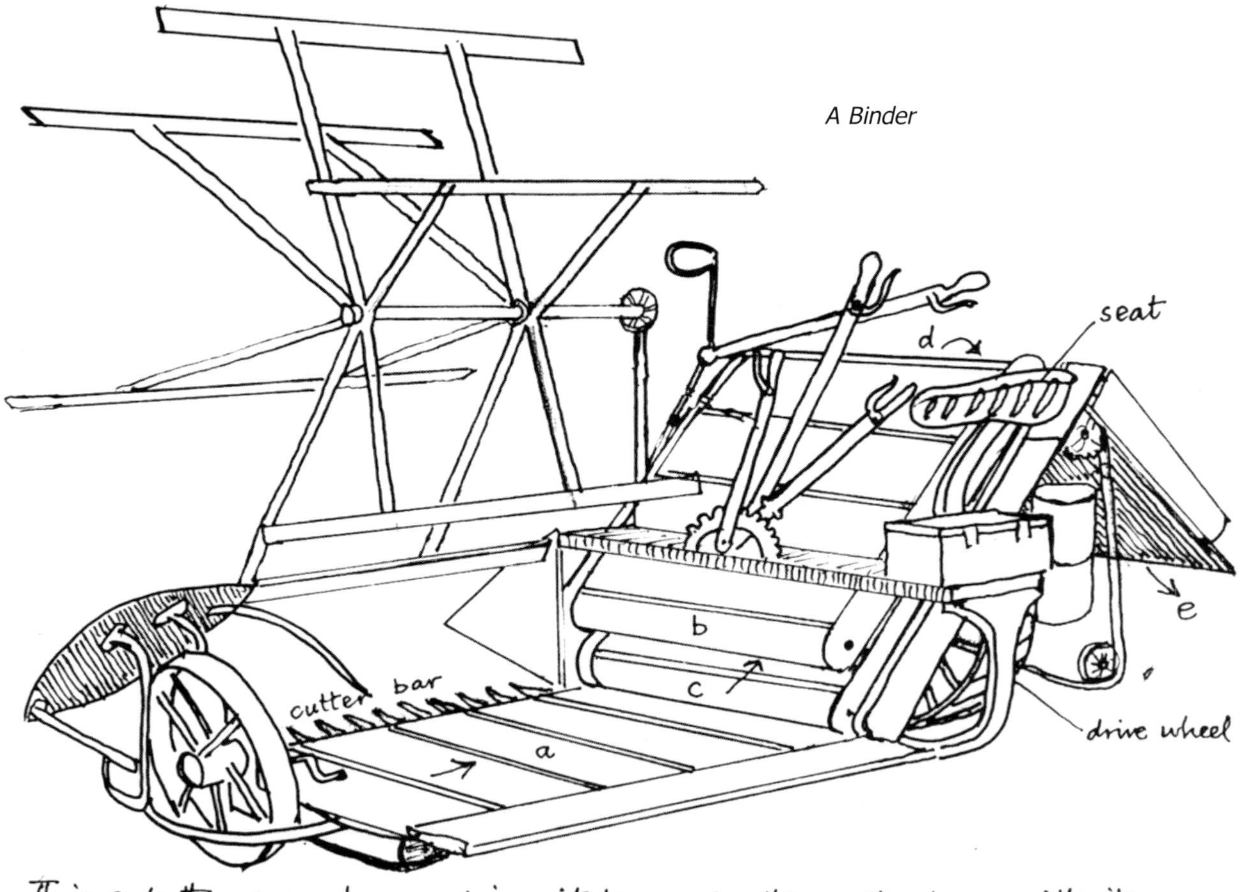

A Binder

This cut the corn by pushing it towards the cutter bar with its revolving sails so that it fell onto the moving platform (a). It was then carried upwards sandwiched between wide canvas belts (b & c) onto the downward slope (d) to be collected into a sheaf & bound with twine It was then discharged at (e) for the stookers to collect.

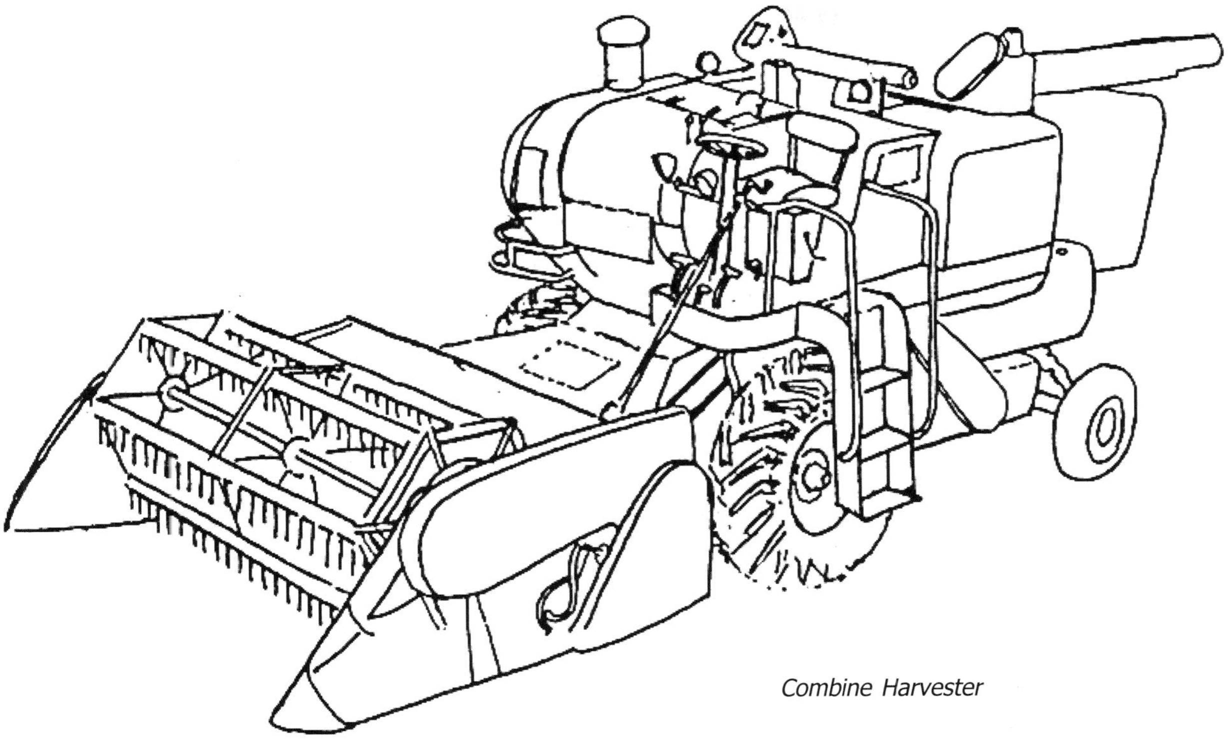

Combine Harvester

Wisdom of a Joint Decision

As chief stakeholder and leader of his worthy team, the farmer had to make far-reaching decisions as to timing and fitness of the crop for cutting or stacking and the future weather prospects. If he was wise, he would consult with each senior member of the team and contrive to make his proposals seem to be a joint decision, otherwise there might be grumbling dissension. There is nothing worse than, "I told 'ee so", when the haystack goes on fire or the wheat is flattened by a thunderstorm.

An anxious farmer proposing to lead in the stooks of oats too early was reproved by an old wagoner - "Thou's let the Almighty have 'em seven months, why not let 'ee 'ave 'em jist four more days?"

I have always found it better not to ask a man to do something against his will. He must be convinced of its wisdom or he will do it badly. If he refuses, someone has to lose face. The leader also has to know the idiosyncrasies of a team that might include neighbouring small farmers; Bill might hate Sam's guts and they'd be better kept far apart from each other; one to pitch in the field and the other to build the stack.

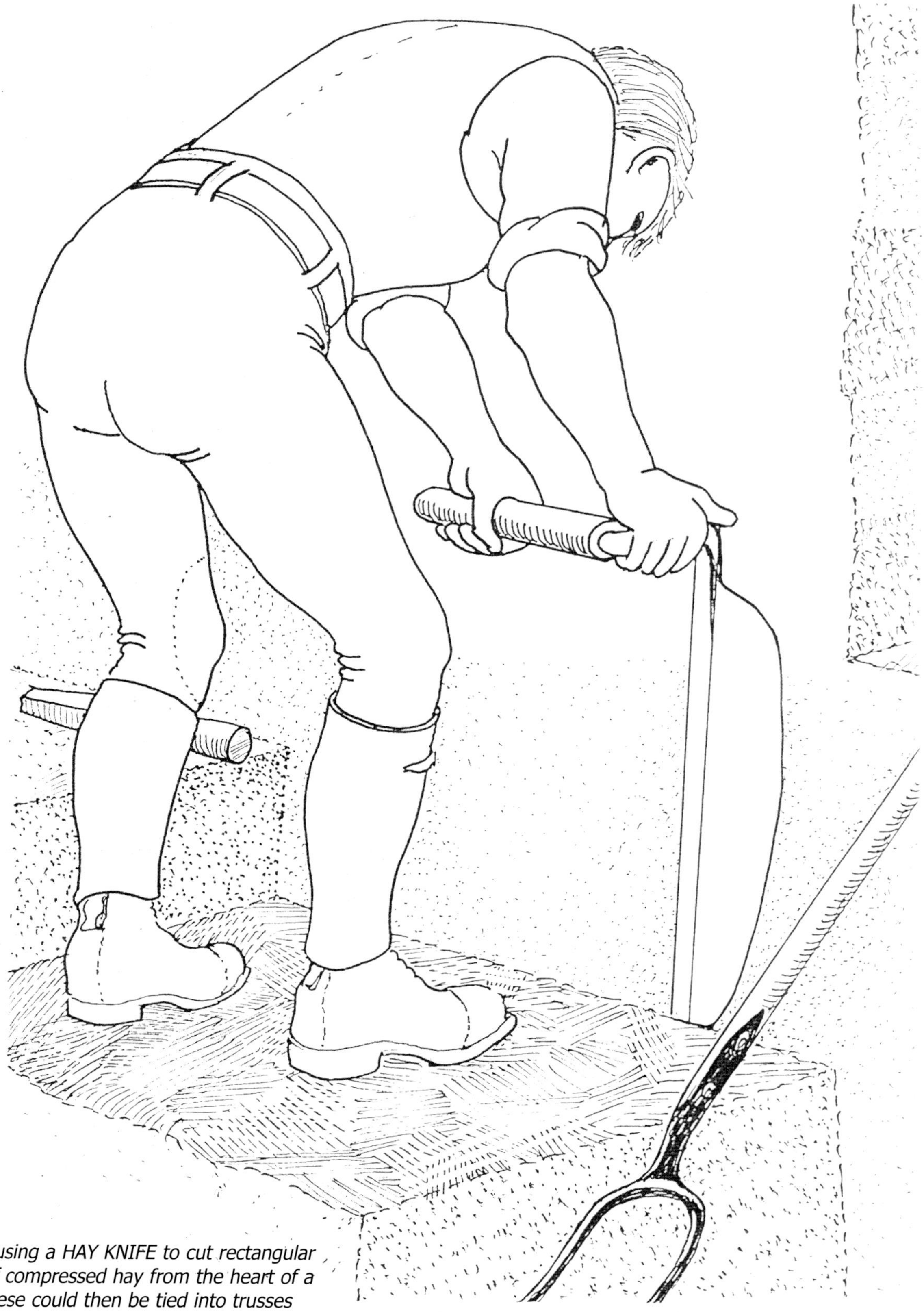

A man using a HAY KNIFE to cut rectangular wads of compressed hay from the heart of a rick. These could then be tied into trusses for transport to stables and cattle byres in far distant places. This knife was also often used for cutting silage and deep farm yard manure from a heap or yard.

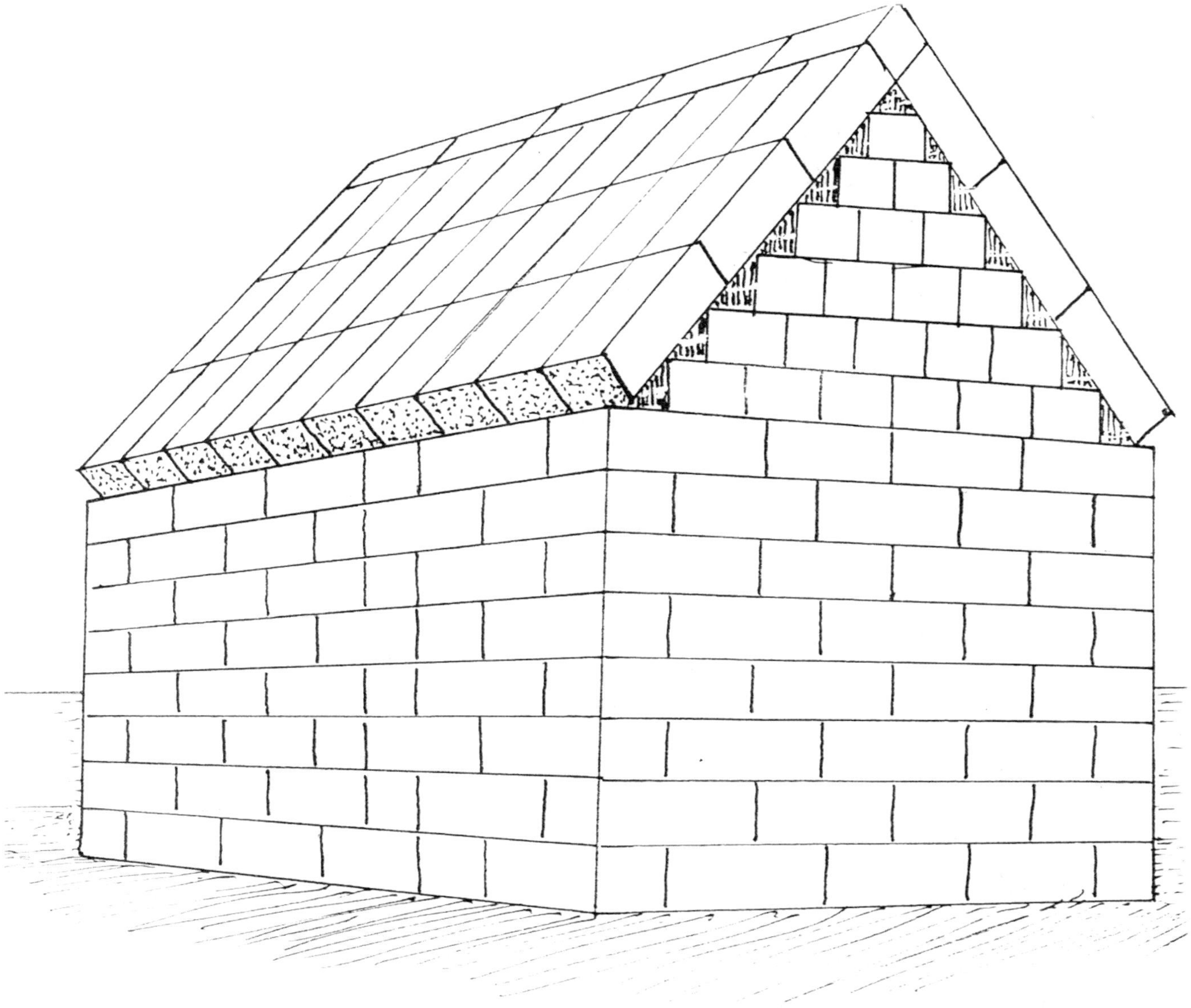

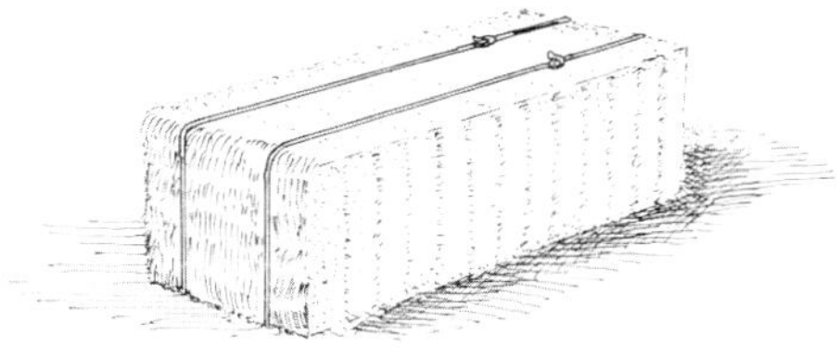

This is the method I used for building a stack of small rectangular bales of straw or hay each weighing 4 stones or 56 lbs.
The bales were made by a machine called a pick up baler, towed behind a tractor and powered by a flexible shaft from the tractor's engine.
This picked up the hay or straw and fed it into a compression chamber where it was tied with two bands of thick twine before being ejected at the rear.

Rick Building

The ricks might be built in pairs with just enough room for the threshing drum to come between them. Building the stack was a highly skilled job reserved for a man of great experience, usually the farmer himself. The sides would slope ever so gently outwards like a bread tin, turning at the eaves to either a hipped or a gabled roof of great height. As it was constructed in only a few hours, considerable settlement took place. If the rick had been made by an inexperienced builder, hastily placed props might be needed to give it stability, and scorn appear among the onlookers. Each sheaf, whether on rick or load, had to be placed with exactitude.

A Gruesome Find

In hay-stacks, a chimney or two might be made from base to ridge to help disperse the heat. This could often cause fires by spontaneous combustion if the hay were to be insufficiently cured. I have heard of men coming in the winter to cut a hay-stack and finding in the centre the body of a tramp. The unfortunate man had supposedly climbed the ladder and fallen into a deep, inebriated sleep, and been buried the next morning by the first forkfuls of hay to fall off the elevator. Although a rick might have a life of only six or eight months, great care and pride was taken in its appearance and it was finished off with the careful craftsmanship of the thatcher.

Variety of Thatching Materials

Hay-stacks and corn ricks had endless variety in shape and form according to local custom and the climate prevailing. In wet, misty places semi-dry hay would need smaller stacks with thick, effective thatch. In windy places the thatch would need to be especially well secured. Thatch would be contrived from whatever materials were readily available. The most common was stiff wheat straw, but rye, river reed, meadow rush, fern and even corrugated iron sheets have been seen. For the base of a hay-stack, a bed of straw, faggots or brushwood would be laid out to keep the damp from being drawn up and cause the hay to go mouldy. Corn, faggots and brushwood would assist the penetration of rats and mice, the only safe protection being the familiar mushroom-shaped staddle-stones. However, this had the serious disadvantage of making the rick three feet high before any sheaves were unloaded. Great care would have to be taken subsequently not to leave any props or ladders against the sides. Otherwise, vermin would climb up into the stack like rats gaining access to a ship by way of the mooring rope.

In pre-war years, the thatcher's craft was threatened by the increasing use of Dutch barns made of corrugated iron and asbestos. Good thatchers were not very common, so I was privileged to be taught by one who took pride in his work and who would add the ornamental finishes distinctive in the locality. As a young man, I could run up a ladder with a forkful of yelmed straw, hardly needing to put out a steadying hand to the side rail.

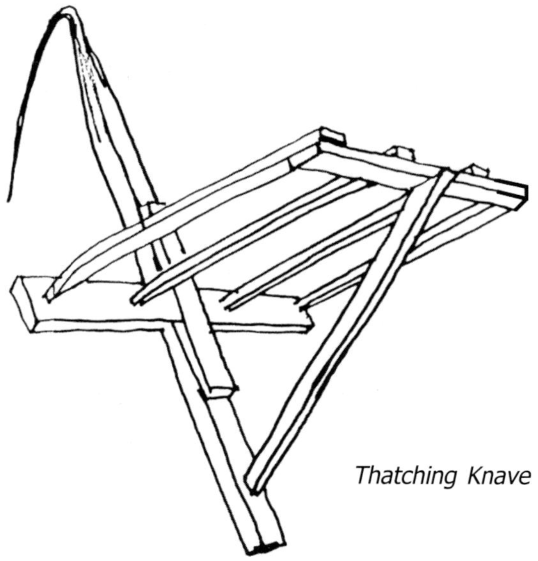

Thatching Knave

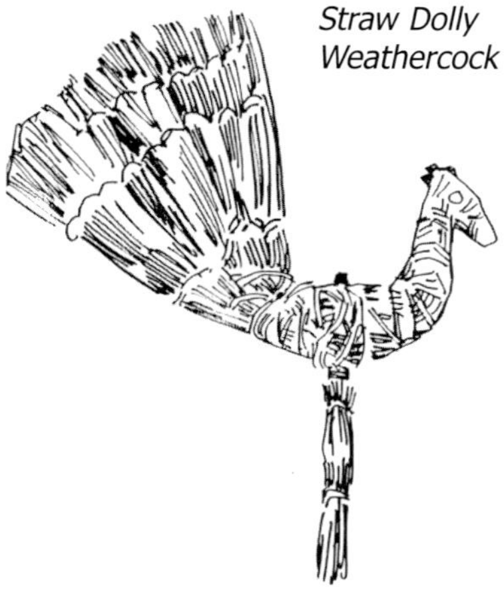

Straw Dolly Weathercock

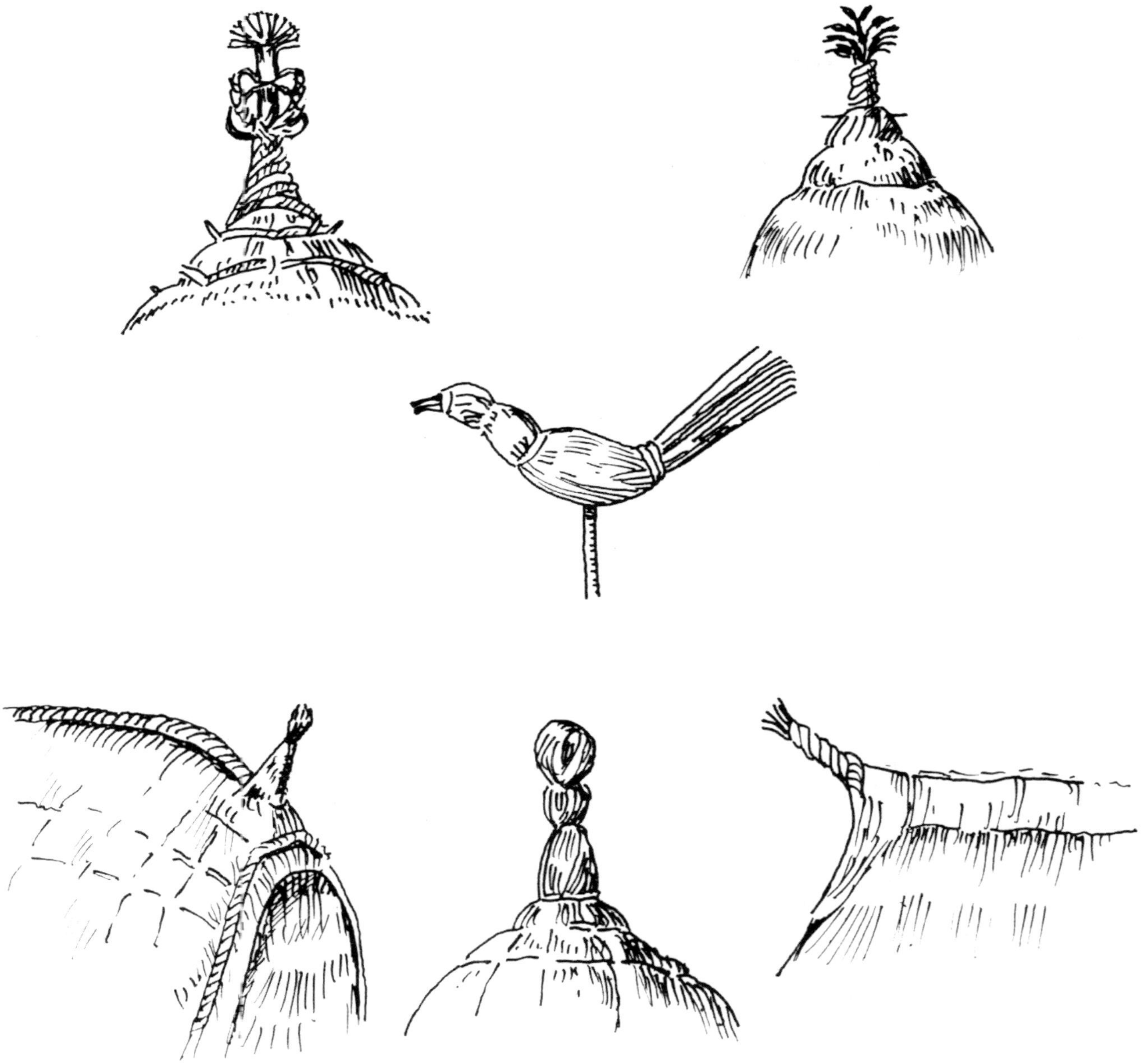

STRAW ORNAMENTS

It used to be a fairly general custom to decorate ricks and stacks by way of completing the work of thatching with some thing of a flourish. One of the prettiest seen in Norfolk was to set an unthreshed sheaf of wheat on top of the rick for the birds. Some thatchers would spend the midday hour weaving a bird round a piece of board cut to shape. Sometimes they would make a working weather cock mounted on a stick which would revolve in the neck of a bottle.

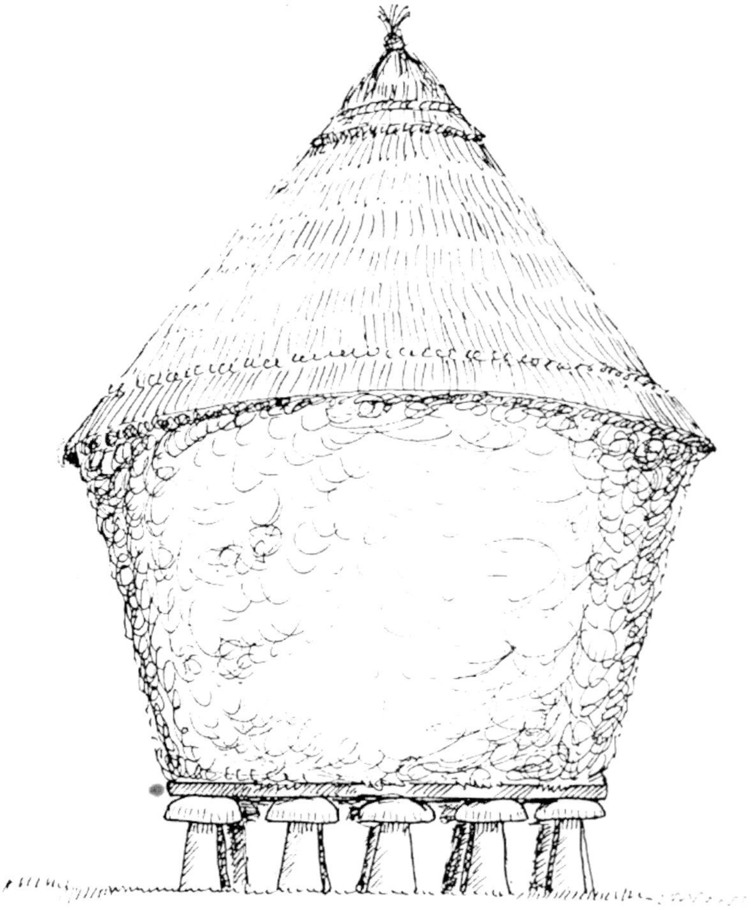

A CORN STACK was built on stone staddles. Their mushroom shape protected the corn from rodents which could not climb up the overhanging tops

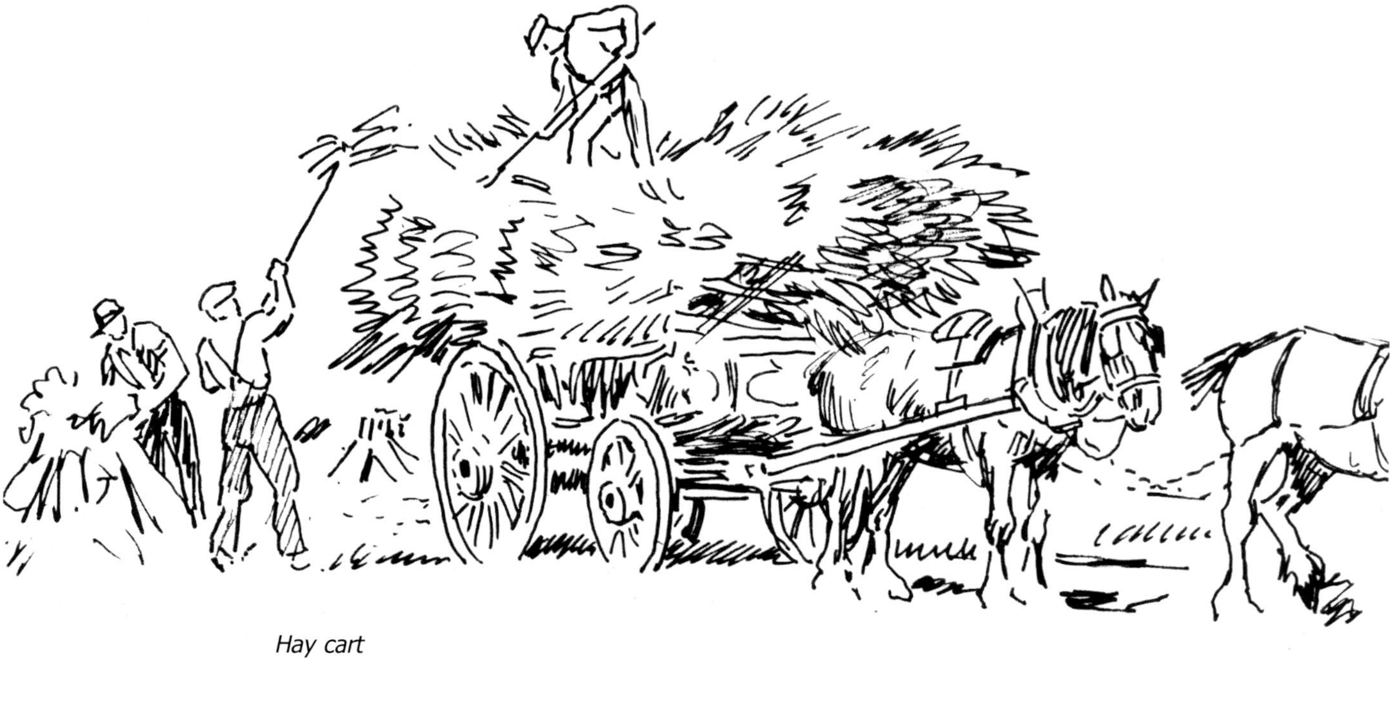

Hay cart

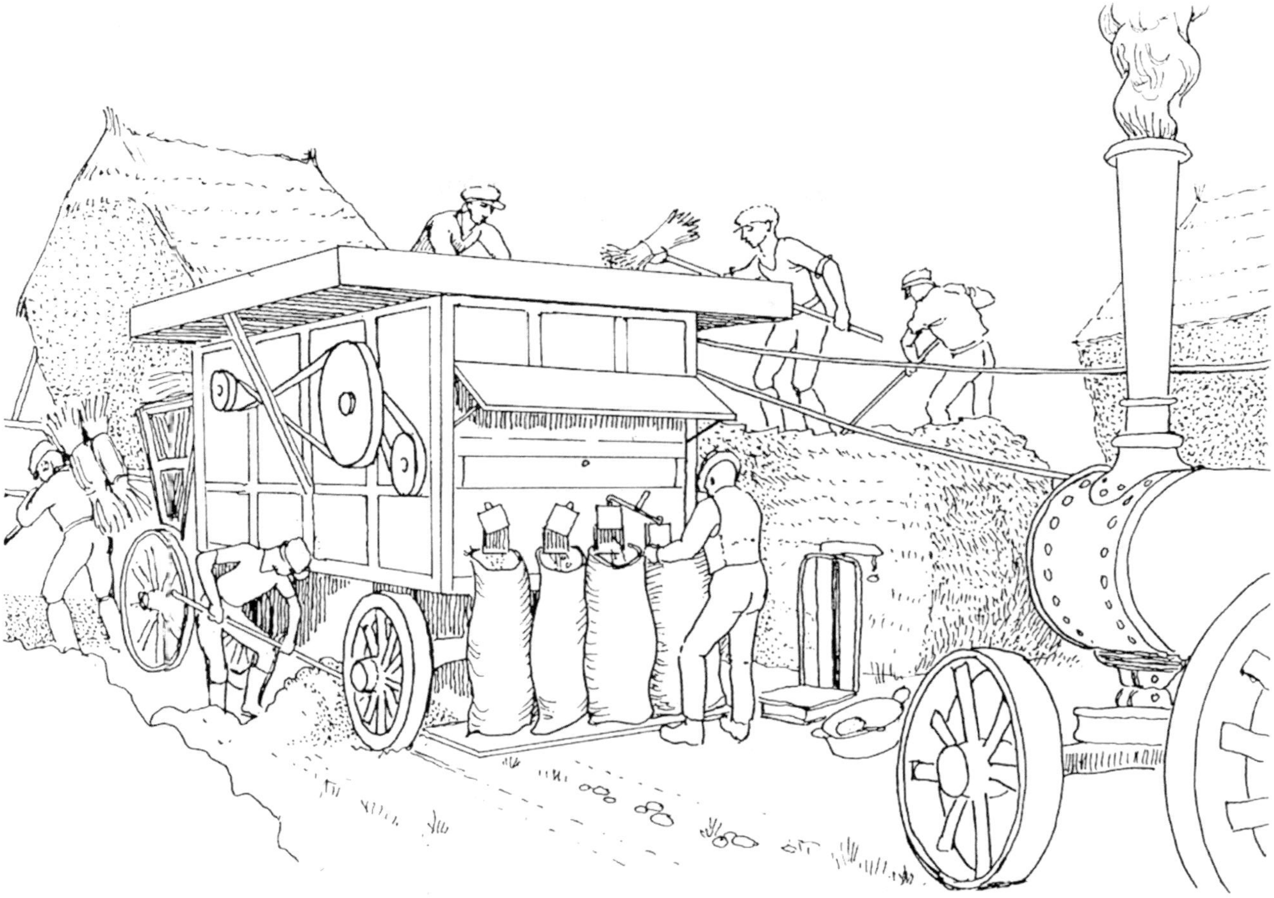

'The Arrival of the Threshing Drum'

Before the days of combine harvesters which cut and thresh the grain whilst on the move, the arrival of the threshing machine caused great activity. Friends and neighbours were alerted to help form a team; some casual labourers used to travel with the 'drum' to work on a daily basis.

The machine itself might weigh over four tons and, being on iron-shod wheels, needed, if possible, a metalled road. Trailing behind it might be a heavy baler and behind that, in convoy, a trusser for the straw. This complete outfit was often pulled by a steam traction engine which demanded a supply of coal and water to feed its insatiable needs. A tractor, which subsequently did the same job, needed to be exceptionally large and powerful and fitted with a pulley to drive by means of a belt this complicated machinery, which hummed away all day long with only a short break for dinner.

The risk of fire from the traction engine's sparks was always a considerable hazard with all the straw and chaff about.

After stripping the thatch, the sheaves were pitched to the men cutting the bands and feeding them continuously into that aperture leading to the swiftly revolving drum against its concave adjustable surface. This would knock the individual grains out of the ears. Chaff and cavings, weed seeds and awns would be separated by fans and riddles and ejected at various points, along with clouds of dust. Straw would be shaken along walkers to be thrown out at the back into a baler or a trusser. This machine tied it with two strings into suitable bundles which were carried away into stacks.

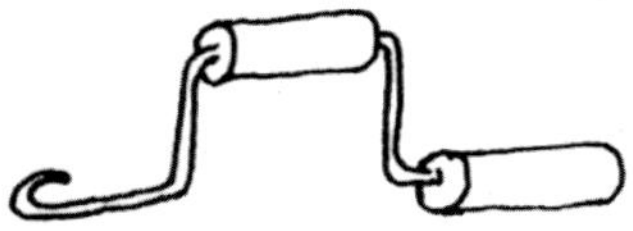

WIMBLE for twisting straw or hay bonds and rope

SHEAF-KNOTS

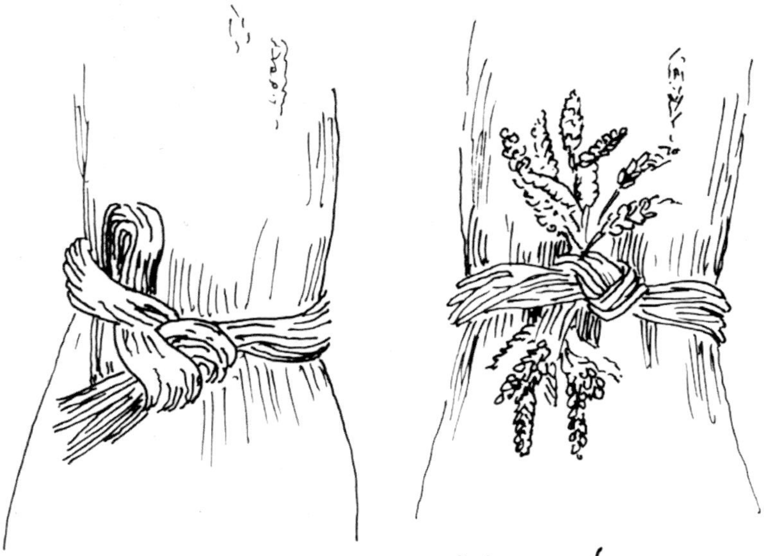

Romney Marsh

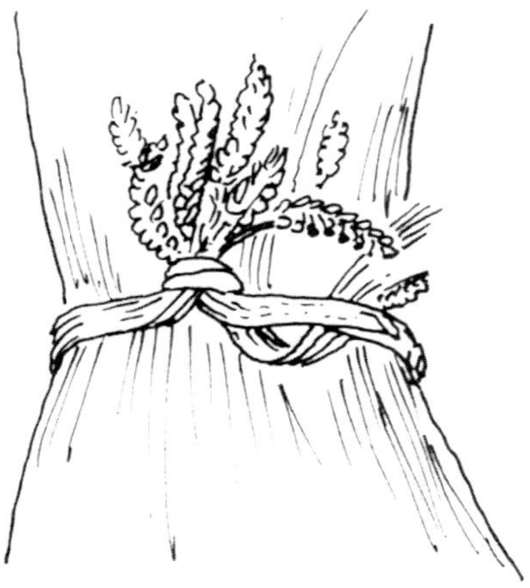

Dorset

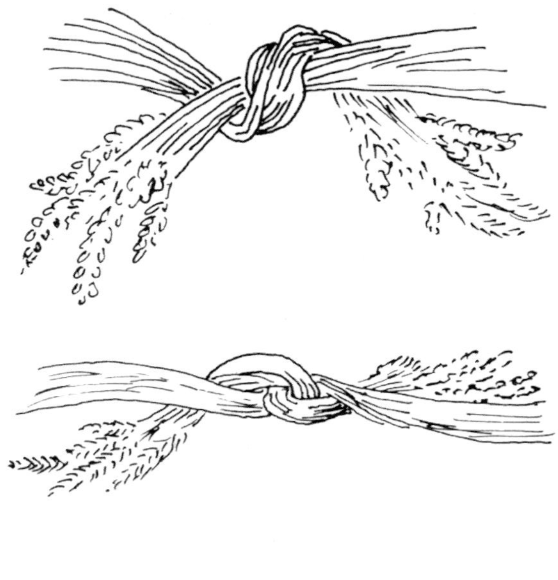

Offley, Herts.

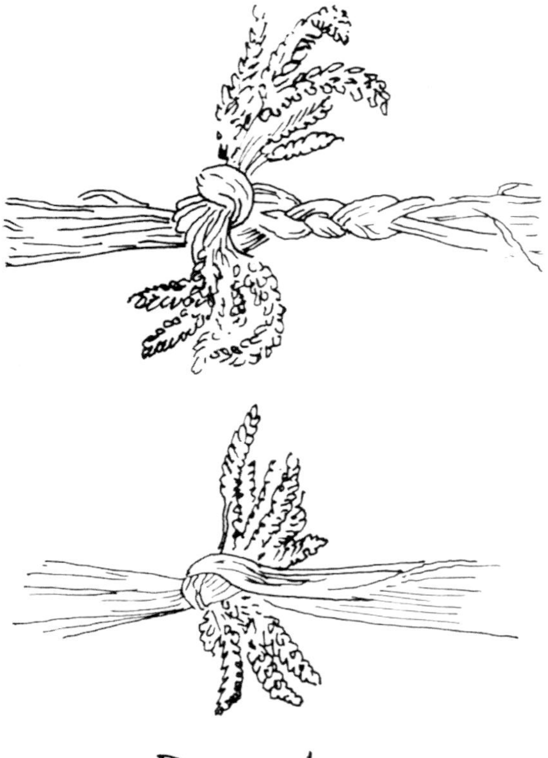

Dorset

Sheaf bonds are of two kinds; single in which one length of straw encircles the whole sheaf; and double in which two lengths are joined by the heads and their butts united on the other side of the sheaf. Harvesters could tie them with inimitable rapidity and deftness and were always totally incapable of explaining the process in words.

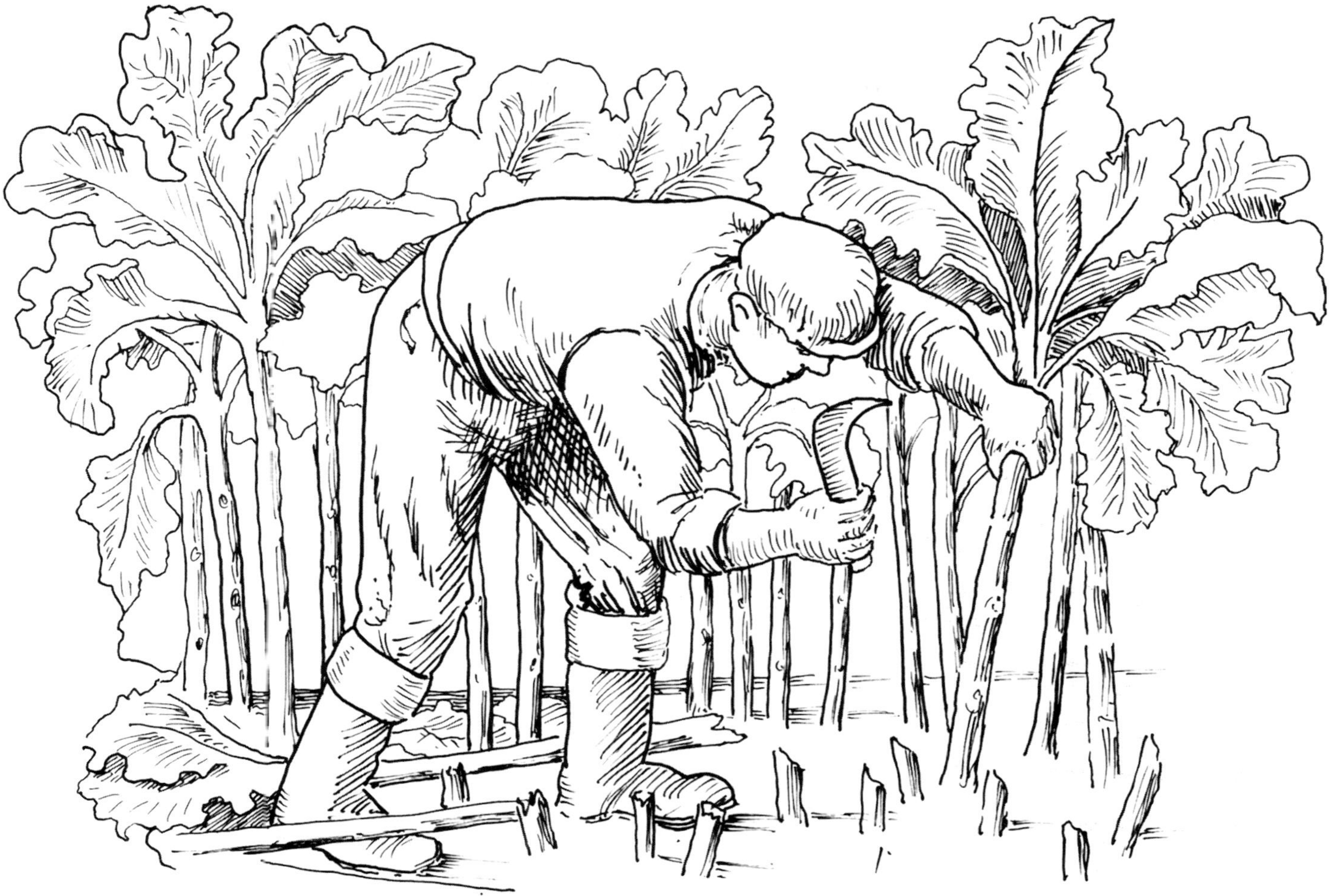

Marrow Stem Kale is cut by hand and carted to cattle

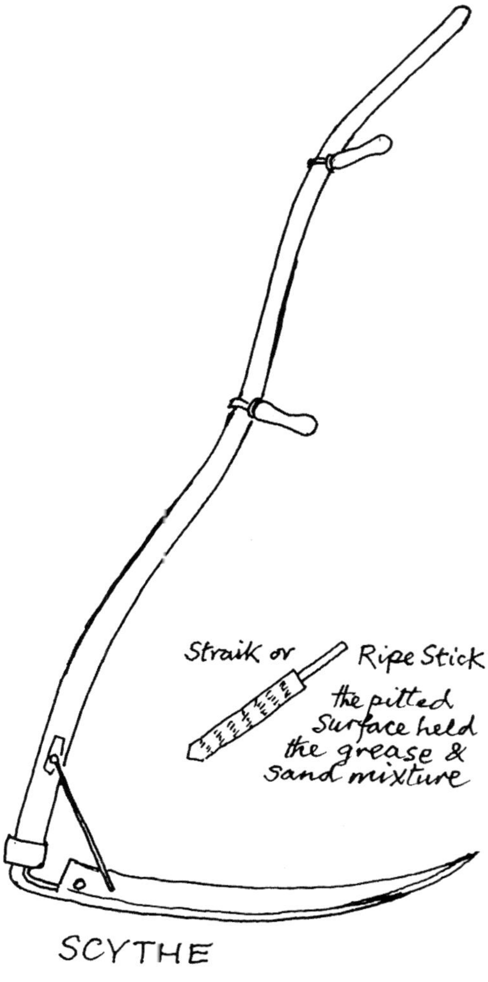

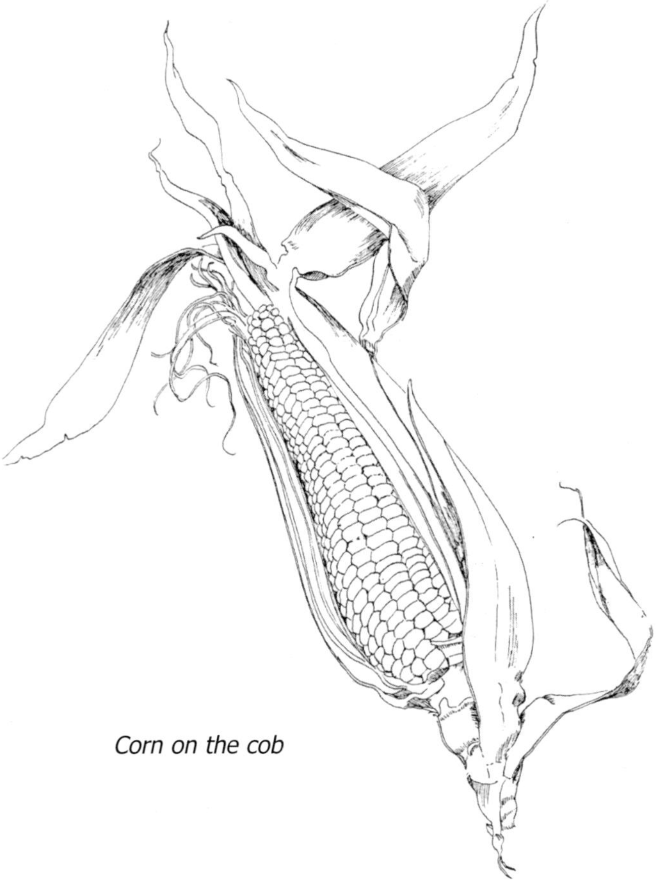

Corn on the cob

The Iniquitous Four Bushel Sack

The corn, after being subjected to various treatments, would cascade out of spouts with shutters at the end of the machine. Here, hooks were positioned to hold the man-killing four bushel sacks, made by prisoners and hired from the railway company for the occasion. When full, it took a mighty effort to remove one of these onto the weighing machine and from thence by sack barrow into the barn where they would be stacked, two high on boards, to await collection.

The customary weights for four bushels would be,

- Wheat, $2\frac{1}{4}$ cwt or 18 stones (114kg)
- Barley, 2 cwt or 16 stones (102kg)
- Oats, $1\frac{1}{2}$ cwt or 12 stones (76kg).

There would be a galvanised bath full of grain and a scoop to enable the contents to be correctly weighed. Then the sack would be safely tied with twine and removed, by which time the next sack might be running over from the relentless flow of grain, hour after hour.

This task required the individual attention of a very strong man while lesser mortals, even children, could help with the other jobs, such as removing chaff and cavings, weed seeds and broken tail corn.

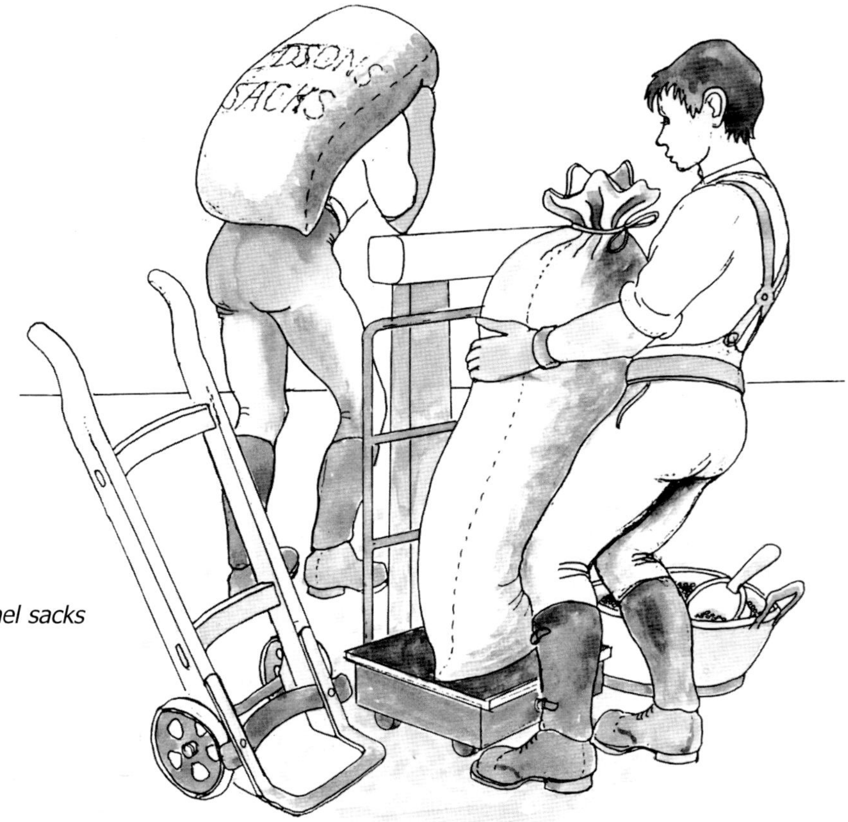

Weighing up four bushel sacks

The One-Armed Driver

The driver would be constantly attending to the health of the lethal, fast-moving machinery with oil-can, grease-gun and spanners. I knew one such man who had had his arm wrenched off by the unprotected main drive belt.

The farmer would be taking small samples and looking critically at the quality of the grain. A premium could be paid for seed wheat or malting barley and these small samples were scrutinised by the buyers at the corn exchange in the nearest town. Once a price had been agreed verbally and a deal struck, which might amount to many thousands of pounds, neither party would dream of welshing on the deal. It was a point of honour.

Sacks Much Too Heavy

The four bushel sack must have been invented and promoted by the railway companies and the corn merchants because it suited their machinery and methods; certainly by people who never had to move them. These, and the 18 gallon churn, must have been responsible for numerous strained backs and ruptures incurred by those poor workmen who were forced to handle them. It was certainly a daunting task to load a 10 ton lorry with 100 sacks of barley weighing 2 cwt (16 stones) each with nothing but muscle power. Sulphate of ammonia fertiliser sacks also weighed 2 cwts (102kg) and often they were set like a lump of stone and had to be broken with a sledge-hammer before they would pass through the distributor.

The Farm is a Factory

When analysed, farming often amounts to moving vast quantities of heavy material about from one place to another. Every move adds considerably to its cost, without necessarily adding significantly to its value. Time and motion study is just as important for profitable efficiency on a farm as it is in factory production. The farm can be thought of as a farmer's factory - ramblers cannot wander at will through a car manufacturer's production lines! 'The chore-route factor' can be the subject of much scrutiny to save wasteful journeys when feeding stock.

St. Vitus and the Primitive Dance

As I made my way home from visiting some outlying stock in distant pastures I was intrigued to espy on the horizon a middle aged man in heavy boots performing some kind of syncopated tap dance around a small area used for corn stacks.

When I drew nearer it became evident that there was a smouldering fire of chaff, cavings and broken straw and his frenzied dance was to step on and extinguish the sparks as the rising wind coaxed them back into flame!

In my youth it was common to hear reference to those afflicted with a dancing mania known as St. Vitus' dance - a nervous disease which causes irregular jerking movement through involuntary muscular contractions. It is now known as chorea (Latin for 'dance'). Hydrophobia was also a disease I was taught to dread, a morbid fear of water, (nothing to do with childish lack of cleanliness), following a bite from a rabid animal. I am told this will almost certainly become more widespread as European frontiers are abolished and there is free movement through the channel tunnel.

Women's Land Army to the Rescue

During the Second World War, fit young women were recruited to join the Women's Land Army. They wore a smart uniform consisting of brown felt hat, green woollen jersey and fawn breeches and stockings with strong shoes. As they were inevitably short on skills, farmers were quick to invent ways of making their work more effective. For thatching ricks, someone perfected a machine for weaving straw into what resembled unbroken lengths of stair carpet and there was soon invented a thatching needle for fixing it onto rick roofs in horizontal overlapping rows to keep the rain out.

For teaching them how to milk, a four-legged frame like a table with no top was equipped with a rubber udder and teats to be filled with white liquid which was 'milked' into a galvanised bucket. Luckily, the frame could not be made to kick and shuffle, stand on your toe and beat you round the ears with its filthy tail!

A similar frame idea is in use today when agricultural students are being shown how to deal with difficult births of sheep and cattle, except that this one would be equipped with a rubber uterus.

A Touch of Gaiety

Tribute must be paid to the WLA for all the sterling work their members did in helping to secure food for our rations in time of need. There would inevitably be flirtations and even a bit of hanky-panky in the hay barn, but they brought a touch of gaiety and feminine beauty to many arduous tasks of back-breaking toil. An old man's eye would flash as he offered his gnarled hand with quixotic courtesy to the young lady descending from the wagon load of sheaves she had built to his pitching, and his plodding step would quicken as he opened the gate for her to go through.

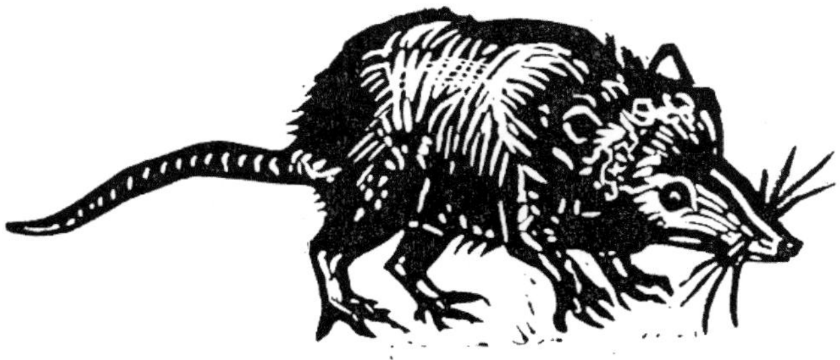

Pygmy shrew linocut

A SEED-BARROW

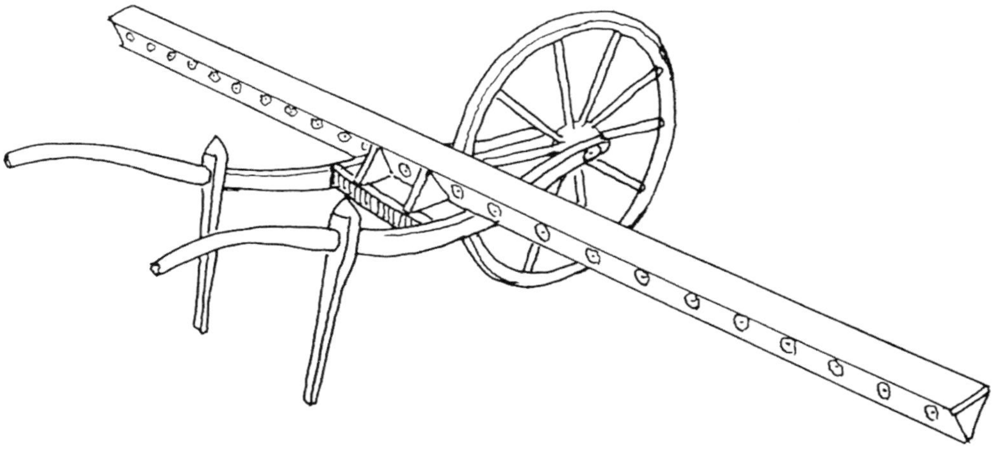

A tyrannical machine for sowing grass and clover seeds with a large narrow-rimmed wheel and carrying a trough 15 feet long. This is divided into sections which are filled with seeds and as the barrow is pushed a gear from the axle turns a spindle which runs the length of the box; on this are mounted brushes which as they revolve sprinkle the seed regularly out of small holes along the trough. In my youth I have spent many days pushing this exhausting machine up & down hilly fields; a truly back-breaking task.

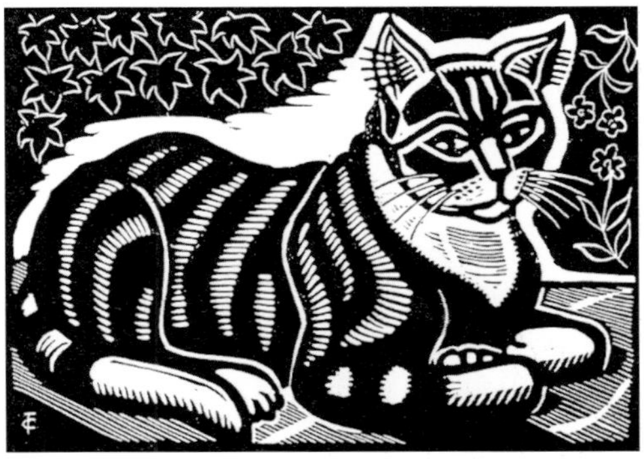

Bartholomew
Linocut

Gangs of Migrant Workers

In the immediate post-war years, most of my neighbours organised their work so that with a staff of two or three, who lived in tied cottages on the farm, they could keep on top of it. There might be a short period in the spring when the fodder crops of mangels, swedes and kale were singled and hoed by casual migrant workers. Sometimes there would be Romany gypsies who would park up their barrel-roofed horse-drawn vans nearby. At other times, the seasonal work might be done by gangs of Irishmen who came over from their small-holdings for the season, living rough in special buildings equipped with a fireplace, known as bothys.

Usually the negotiations were done by the leader or 'ganger', a man elected by the others to strike a deal for them with the farmer as to the piece-work rates. Then the areas would be measured out and allocated to individuals. These were usually men with muscles of iron, big rangy frames, a mighty capacity for back-breaking work and likewise a thirst to match it.

I have seen one of these hoers work steadily up a row of 300 yards (275 m), turn at the end and come back without once looking up to rub his hands and ease his back. His sharp hoe would be darting back and forth cutting away the weeds and surplus plants to leave singles to grow about one foot apart. Some experienced hoers had taught themselves to work equally well ambidexterously with the hoe either side in order to rest their bodies while continuing to work without interruption.

Before the invention of machinery to replace them, these same gangs would return in the autumn to lift the mangels, swedes and sugarbeet and to harvest the potatoes. My experience led me to think that a properly managed team of school children with a few adults were the most efficient and cost effective for lifting potatoes, partly because they have sharp eyes and are nearer to the ground.

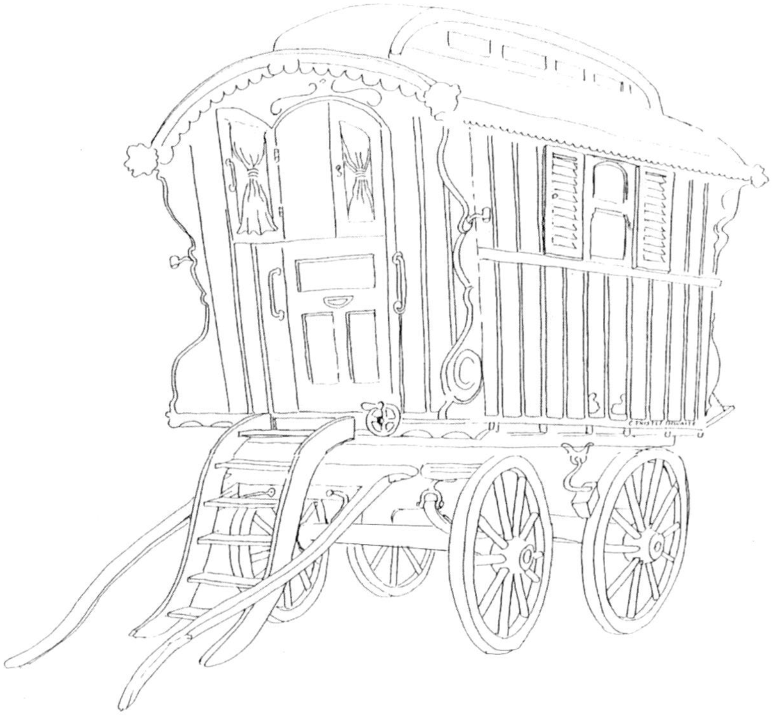

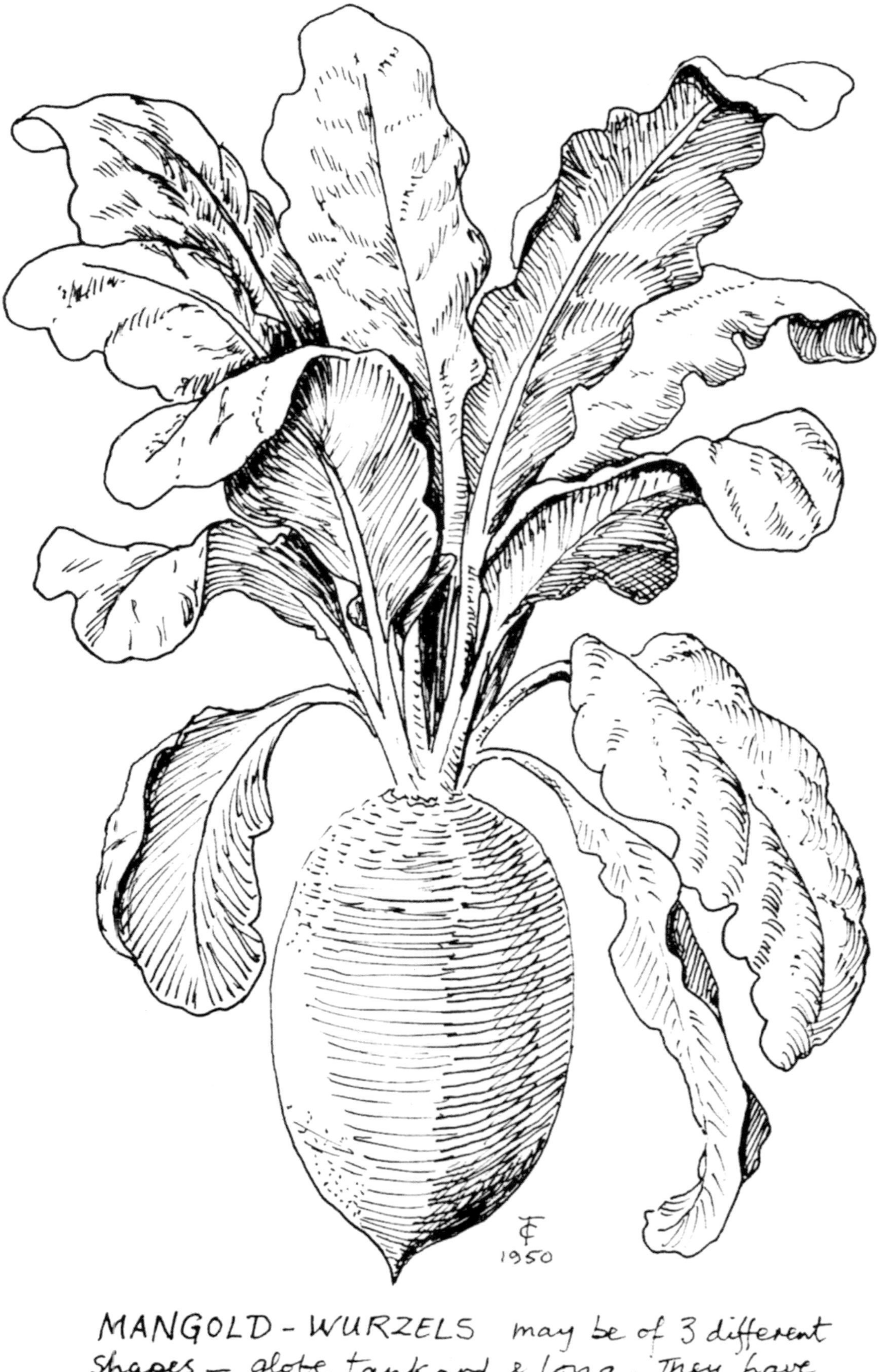

MANGOLD - WURZELS may be of 3 different shapes — globe, tankard & long. They have large, wavy and glossy dark green leaves and they may be 3 different colours — red, orange & yellow. These roots, which grow bigger than a man's head, were often pulled, heaped and carted to a clamp by teams of itinerant labourers, often Irish men.

If You See a Boy, Hit Him

Some people still think, like Dickens' Mr. Squeers, that if you see a boy you should hit him because if he has not just come from doing something reprehensible, he is just about to commit some misdeed! Many of my school teachers gave the impression of bullies who found that, because children are smaller, it makes them easier to hit, patronise or ignore. One of these used to conduct his Latin class as if driving a coach and four, reaching out to smite the miscreants in the far corners of the room with long reeds he had plucked from the osier-beds! He had been a victim of shell-shock in the trenches at Vimy Ridge, and our cruel ploy was to divert him from the lesson to war stories, watching his reactions as he graphically described the carnage and the rats.

Potato Picking Gangs

In early October, the village schools would close for a week's half-term break so that the children could earn some cash helping with the important work of potato picking. Usually I would rely on a village lady to act as 'ganger' and assemble a team of other women and children to wait at an assembly point to be collected by car and trailer. The rows would be paced out in lengths of 20 or 30 yards for each person and the tractor-drawn spinner would start lifting the tubers, leaving them revealed on the surface to be picked into buckets and bags. It was essential to have a reliable machine with plenty of spare parts as, if it broke down, one was very conscious of having to pay for the pickers to sit there doing nothing while it was being repaired. As soon as the bags were filled, strong men would lift them onto the slow-moving carts to be taken and unloaded at the clamp.

Liquid refreshments would be brought round by my wife who also kept a tally of the names and ages of the children so that they could be paid according to the number of hours worked. In addition, each woman would take home a large bag of specially selected spuds that she had shamelessly 'nicked' as a perquisite.

One old lady would insist on being collected separately and would come to the front door in her best hat and coat so that the neighbours, who were peering through the net curtains, would not know the true purpose of her excursion!

I have heard of people deliberately scratching with their feet to cover potatoes with soil, so that they would be employed for an extra day or two to find them again!

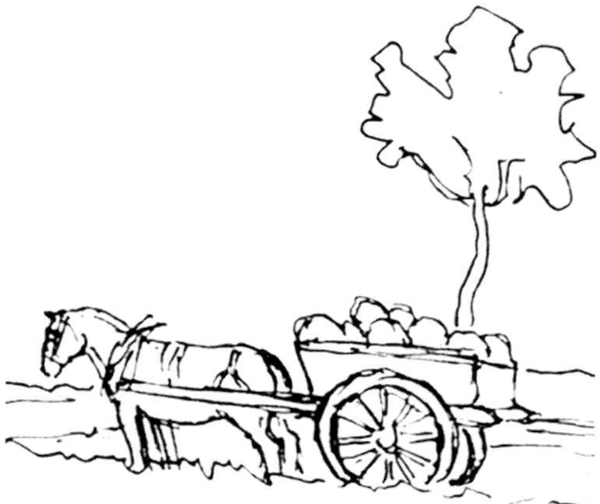

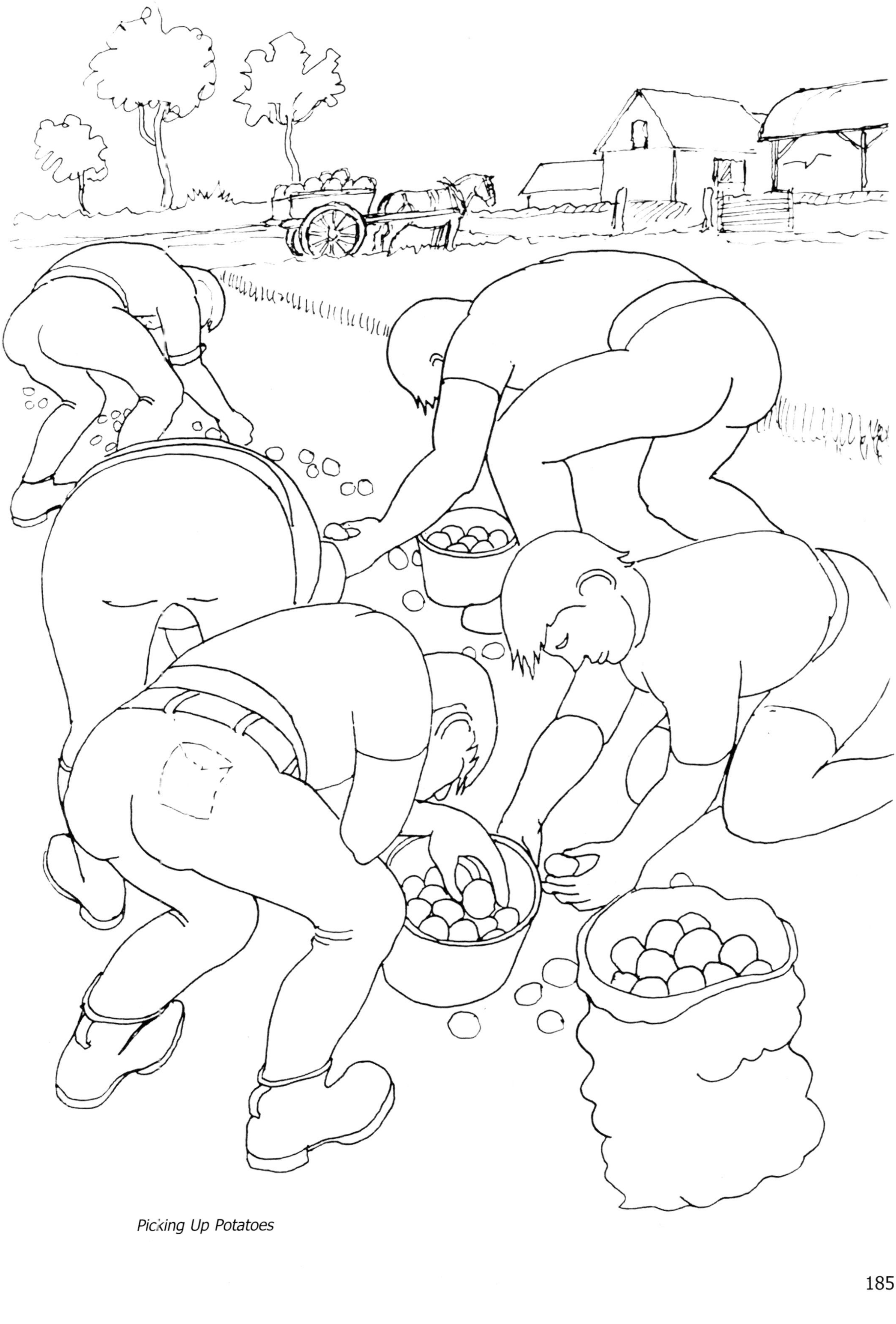

Picking Up Potatoes

Herculean Labours and the Dangers of Piece Work

In the days when the physical efforts of man and horse were the main source of power to get the various farming operations done, there was an unspoken challenge to achieve an acceptable norm. A youngster with the enthusiasm of youth would gladly accept the challenge of a Herculean task with whole-hearted application of rippling muscles, skill and sweat, labouring for long hours to have the satisfaction of viewing the results which were evident for all to see.

In each area there existed a system of attainable targets, often rewarded in the form of piece-work rates on larger farms. The gaffer would have to watch for the occasional scamp who would try to cheat the system, like the carter who threw a pile of loose straw in the cart and then packed it round with manure to make it look like a full, heavy load. Or the inexperienced shearer whose sheep appeared without wool and almost devoid of skin too, so badly had they been lacerated by his inept handling!

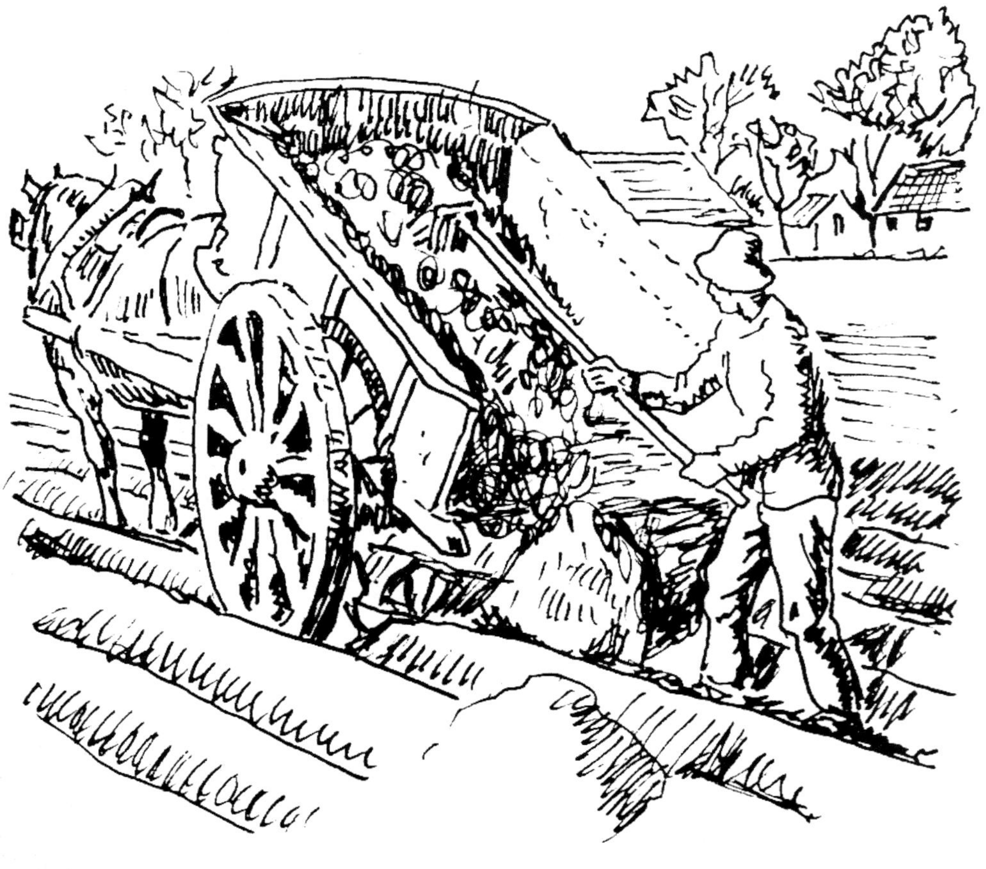

Muck Spreading

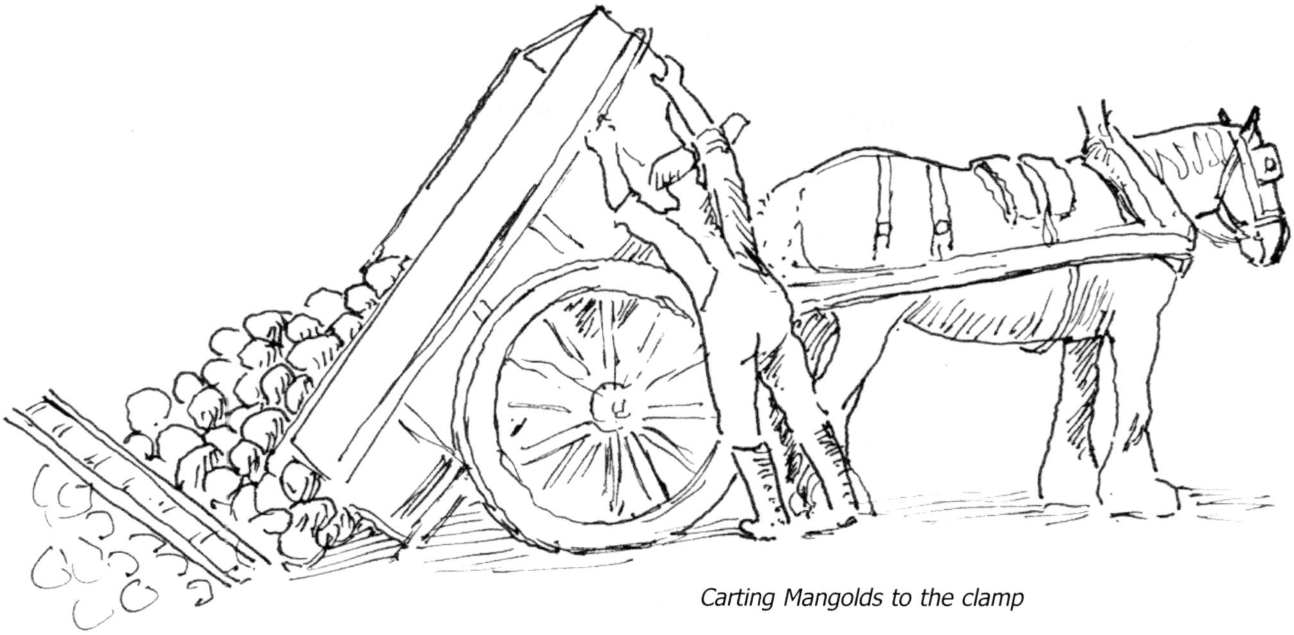

Carting Mangolds to the clamp

Keep the Home Fires Burning

When working in the fields at a lonely job, one kept a weather eye on noteworthy happenings near and far. The cowman hoeing swedes or mangels, kale or potatoes would take the passing of the 3:45 train to the nearest town as a signal to fetch the dairy cows in for the evening milking. There was a single track branch line on the farm controlled by a signal box, and a staff, like an enormous key, was given by the fireman to the signalman as the mineral train joined the main line. This staff was part of a safety device so that two trains could not simultaneously use the single track. There was a regular stopping-place and the bored train crew would set snares for the rabbits that lived in huge numbers on the undisturbed embankments. I have heard that those who lived near the tracks in shunting yards would set bottles and cans on top of the walls to encourage the fireman to throw lumps of coal to dislodge them, thereby gaining free-of-charge much needed fuel for their home fires.

The signalmen did long shifts with little interruption from scheduled trains. As a side-line, one would cut our hair and another mend our boots, thereby caring for both ends!

Bus drivers and postmen on country rounds would perform errands for their isolated clients, keeping them in touch with events in the outside world. I have seen a sharp-eyed bus driver stop his vehicle and run 100 yards to lift a ewe, cast on her back in a depression in the land. She would have died within a few hours if left on her back.

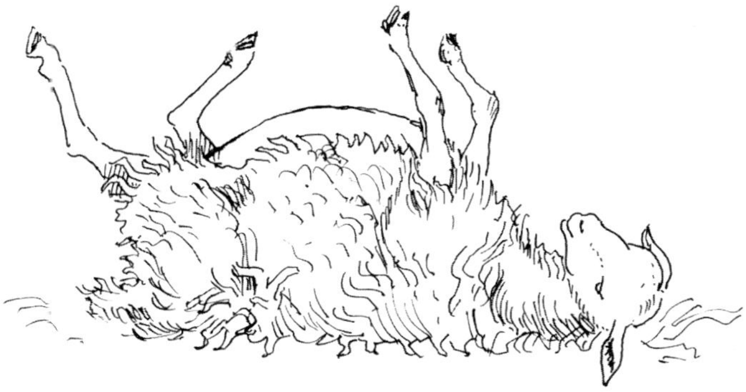

Warm weather makes sheep itchy, and to scratch their backs, sheep roll over.
If they get cast in a hollow, they sometimes cannot get to their feet without help. Within a few hours, they would be dead with a belly as tight as a drum, distended with gas from fermenting grass.

Lester Mawby of Ashby Parva, who was born on a farm in Canada.

When he sold up the Canadian farm during The Depression, his farm stock value was less than the auctioneer's fees.

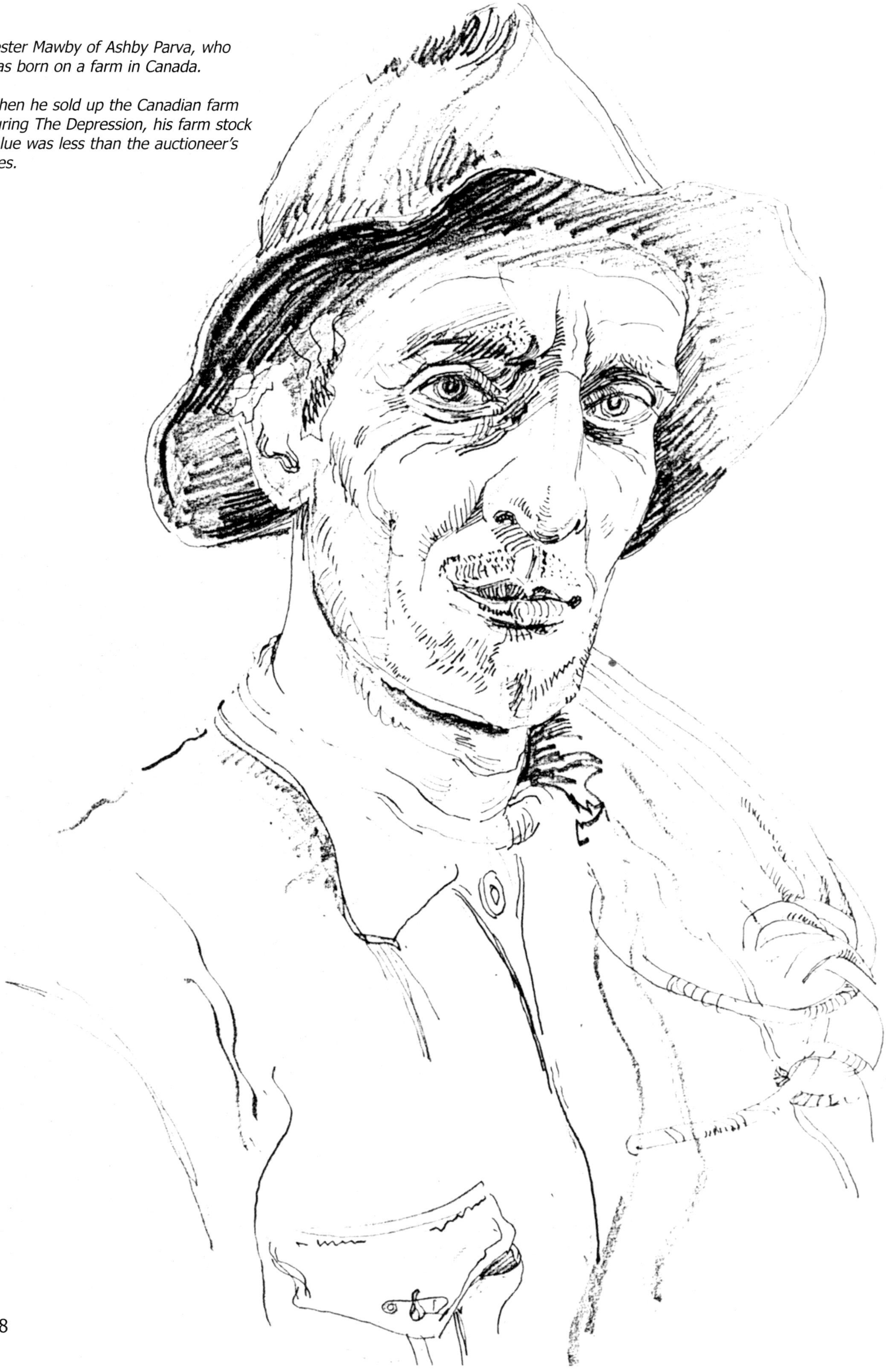

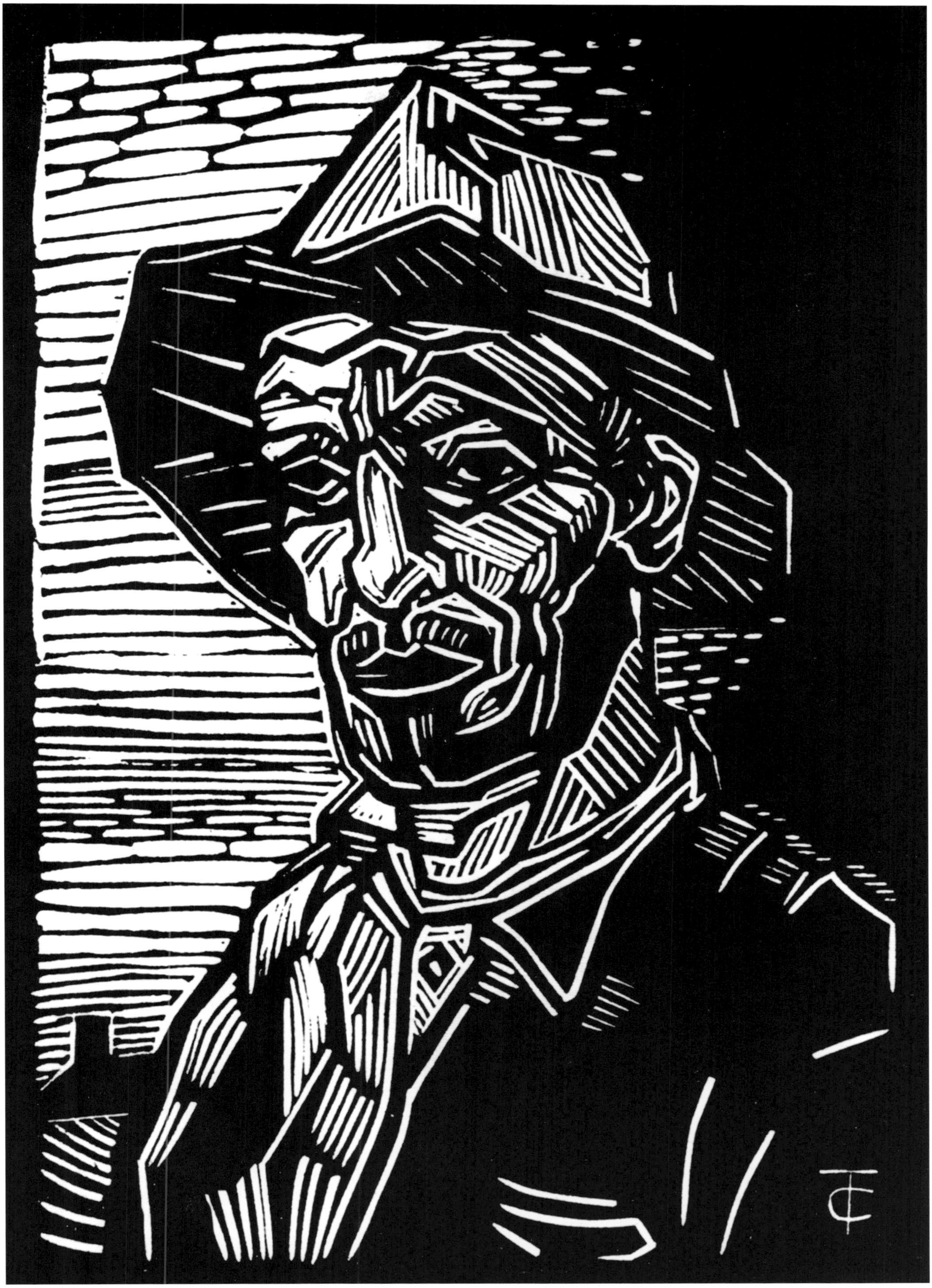

Lester's daughter, Zilla-Mae, was for many years our poultry and dairy maid. Being a conscientious worker, she too was a great asset to the farm. (See page 90 for sketch)

Lester Mawby Linocut

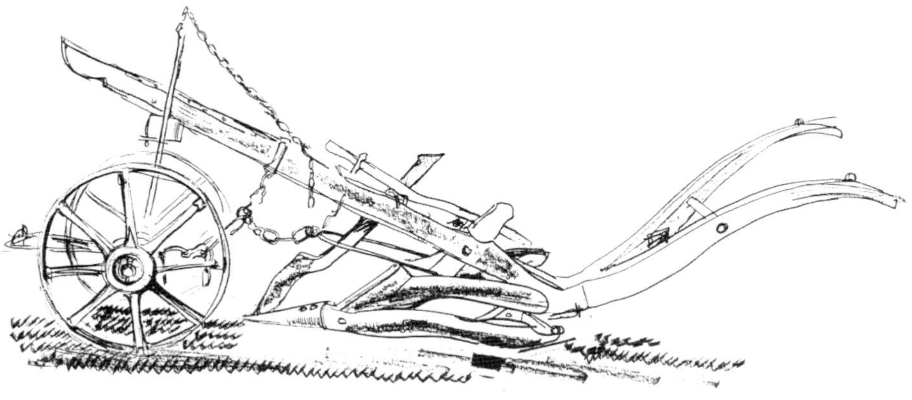

Bill's Broken Plough and the Good Neighbour

We are admonished by the Bard: "Neither a borrower nor a lender be". There is a tale about a man named Bill whose plough had broken when he still had ten acres to finish. So he decided to walk across to his neighbour, Fred, who lived a mile away to enquire whether he could borrow his plough for a few days. On the way, he began to reason with himself. Perhaps the neighbour will not have finished his own ploughing. Perhaps he would be afraid of it getting broken. Perhaps he has already lent it to another neighbour and so on. By this time he had reached the other's farmyard and the man appeared and said, "Hello Bill, it's a lovely day." "Oh, keep the bloody plough", said Bill, ignoring the friendly greeting as he turned on his heels and walked away!

One of the biggest and best farms in the village was run by a kind and considerate man, always helpful and obliging. He had a well-kept, up-to-date set of implements to carry out all the cultivations needed for his enterprises. He used to complain bitterly, however, that when he himself had need of the tackle in a hurry to catch the weather, he had to rack his brains and send his men scurrying all around the parish to retrieve his useful machinery from clumps of nettles in the farmyards of all his feckless neighbours, who had borrowed them long ago and not had the decency to return them promptly in good order.

Temperamental Tractors and Drivers

A friend's tractor, though otherwise in good condition, had a series of ugly indentations along the bonnet. His brother told me, rather sheepishly, that they were caused by blows from the starting handle if it refused to start on a cold morning!

Most of the early tractors seemed to be very temperamental about starting in the morning. As it was quite common to spend an hour or more pulling on the starting handle, there was a certain understandable reluctance to stop the machine once it got going! This called for a relief driver to appear on a bicycle in the field at meal times to continue with the cultivation. As the tractor tank would need replenishing in a twelve hour day, the cyclist carried a five-gallon drum of tractor vaporising oil (TVO) in a hessian sack slung over his shoulder, quite an acrobatic feat over rough tracks!

It was unusual to see a rubber tyred tractor. Iron wheels fitted with large spade lugs meant they were excluded from road work and had to be driven to the work place along the grass verges. Some people kept large sacks filled with straw to place on the road at crossing points!

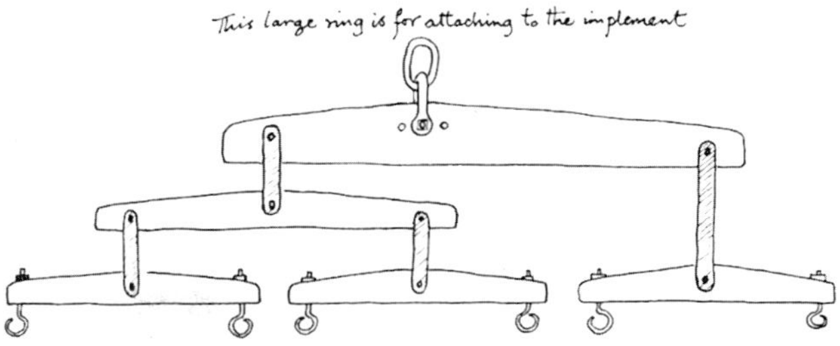

Ploughing by Moonlight

If the work was behind, sometimes we would decide to plough until 10pm by the light of the moon. It was a cold and lonely task straining to see that you were doing a fair job. If the moon was obscured as you turned on the headland, a miscalculation could easily find you in the hedge or ditch. One day someone took pity on my chapped hands and lent me some gauntlet gloves. One fell off the tractor and got ploughed under in the dark. Luckily it reappeared the following year not much damaged!

I remember once looking back to see a £1 note disappearing between the furrows. It had worked out of my hip pocket. Wouldn't it be a miracle if currency propagated and multiplied in that fashion!

An old farm worker who noticed the clergy assembling from all over the diocese for a synod in the cathedral city was heard to remark, "Parsons be like muck. Spreaded about the land, they may do a power o' good, but all together in an heap they be no use to man nor beast!"

'Let us Spray'

The burden of decision-making lies with the farmer day and night and some carry it more lightly than others. These days there are many professional consultants who help the larger farmer to decide on seed varieties, fertilisers and sprays. They are regularly walking the fields, testing and sampling to see what is going wrong. No doubt, some of these may say six times or more in a season, "Let us Spray", and it is done according to their word.

The layman might be forgiven for thinking that having sown and harrowed in the seed the farmer shuts the gate and forgets about the crop until he goes in many months later to harvest it. At this time, nothing could be further from the truth.

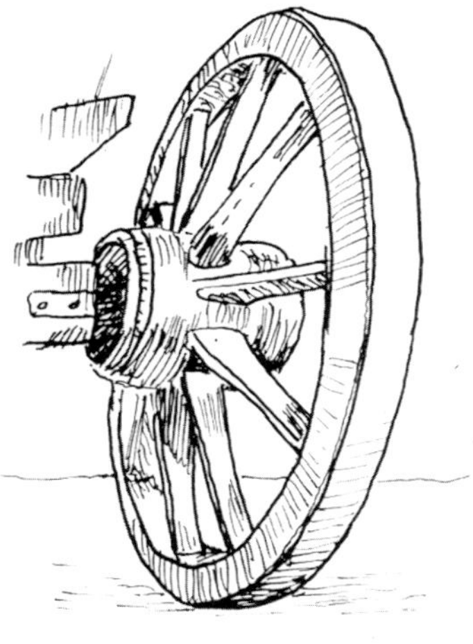

Dish of a wagon wheel.

Elm for the Hub,
Oak for the Spokes,
Ash for the Felloes.

A Pattern Non-Existent 30 Years Ago

Even while he is drilling the corn, he is preparing for the inevitable spraying in the time to come by leaving 'bare tramlines' at regular intervals which coincide with the width of the spray boom, leaving a pattern across the land which was non-existent 30 years ago. In the early days of spraying, it went very much against the grain, in more ways than one, to have to drive a tractor into a crop of standing corn. Apart from the weeds that compete with the crop, there are many soil and seed borne diseases such as, fusarium, leaf stripe, mildew, rusts, loose smut, covered smut, net blotch and rhynchosporium. In biblical times, one had to see that an enemy did not 'oversow cockle in the wheat'. Today's farmer has to be constantly vigilant against diseases, blights and insect invasion.

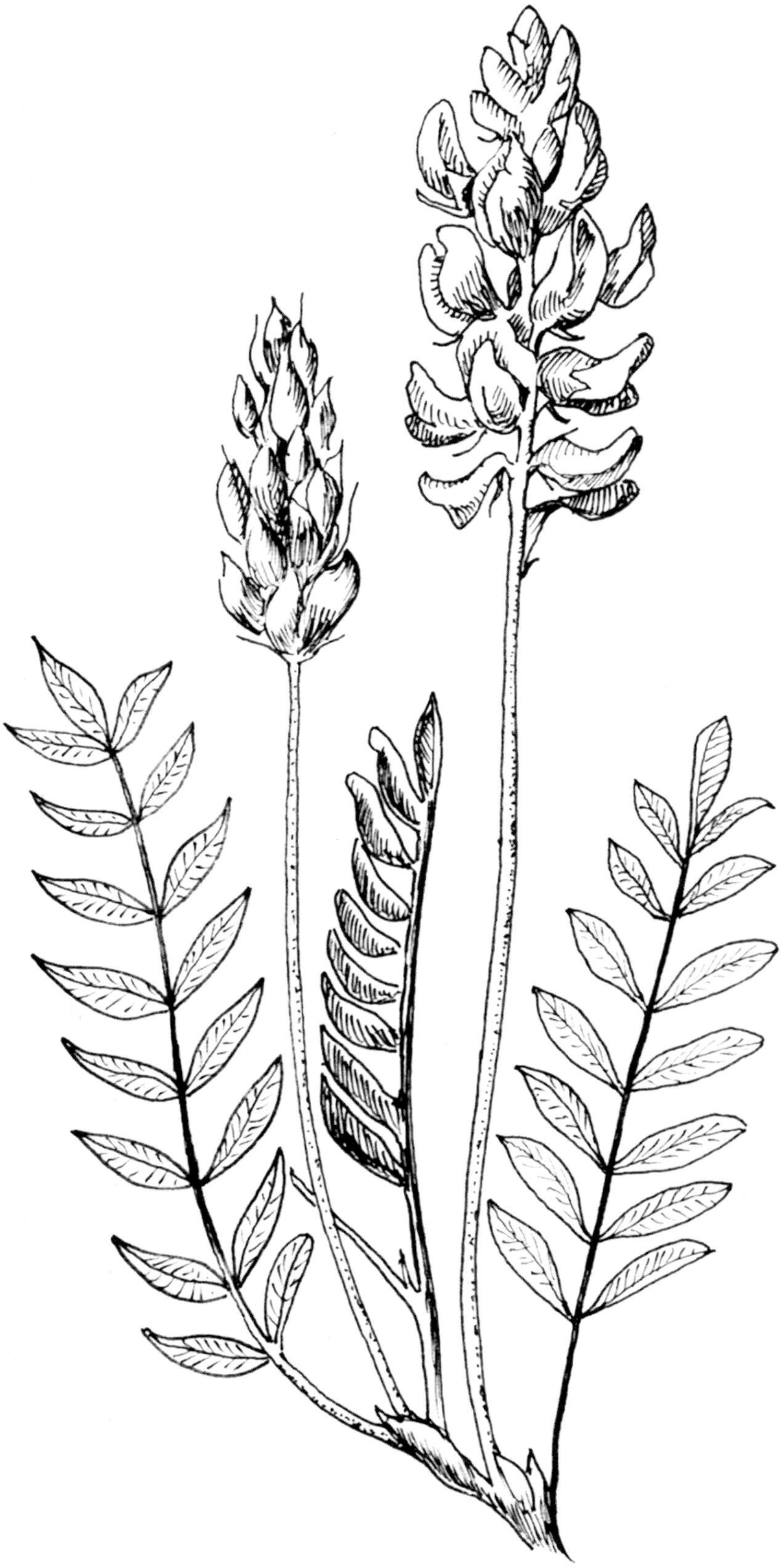

SAINFOIN Whereas sainfoin has a conspicuously pink blossom, Lucerne, whose roots penetrate down as far as 30 feet has a handsome dark blue or violet flower. They are both useful as crops to be made into silage.

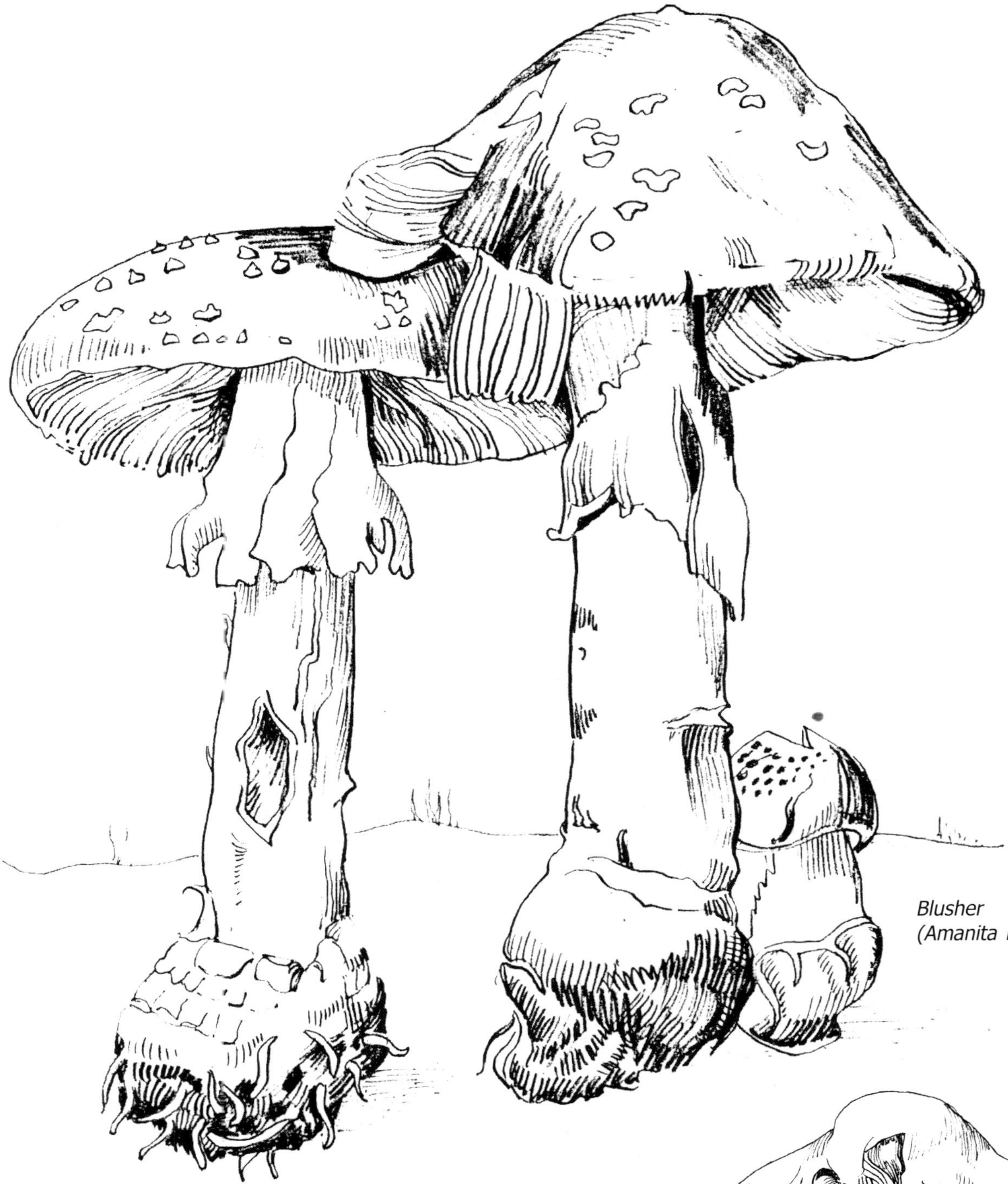

Blusher
(Amanita rubescens)

Fly Agaric (Red)
Poisonous, can be deadly.

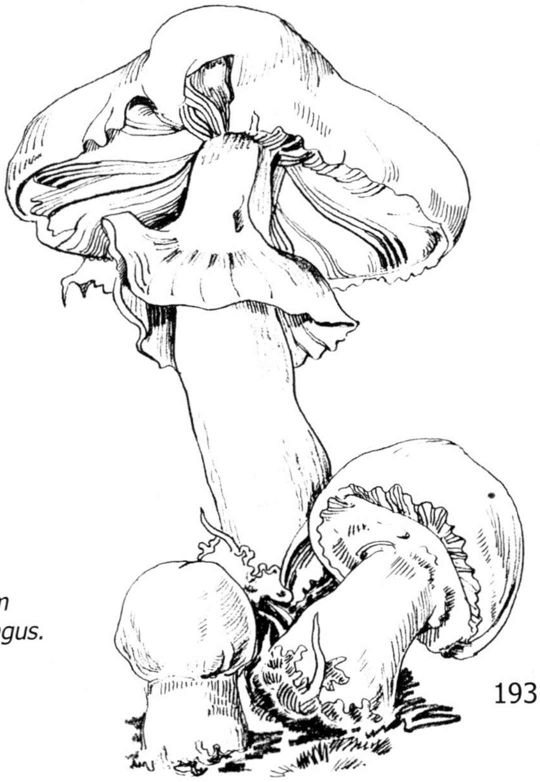

Horse Mushroom
Edible white fungus.

Chapter TEN

Agricultural Shows and Rural Ramblings

Nothing Left to Lose

"For what availeth the plough or sail or land or life if freedom fail?"

Thus said Ralph Waldo Emerson (1803-1882). Living in a land addicted to slavery, he should have known what he was talking about from a gentleman's point of view - but the hobo's song goes, "Freedom's just another name for 'nothing left to lose' ". A farmer's freedom can be a largely illusory thing. Like any other business, his freedom is hedged around with restraints, regulations and returns. After a busy day in the fields doing real productive work, to come home to a couple of hours of form-filling does not enhance his view of bureaucracy.

It is a commonly held belief that farmers are happy only when they're complaining - but for myself I always tried to accept, in a philosophical way, the trials and tribulations of nature and the elements as being intrinsic to the job, and common to all who labour in the open with livestock and crops.

Monarch Of All He Surveys

As he admires the beauty of the landscape he has helped to create, it is easy for a farmer to have a fleeting fantasy that he is Robinson Crusoe and monarch of all he surveys. Then he remembers that Man Friday will soon be knocking on the door for the wages, the insurance and the VAT.

In general, it was the politicians and their attendant train of bureaucrats who brought out the worst in me. How on earth is a man to keep track of all the legislation brought in under EEC rules, the CAP, GATT, etc. For anyone who lived through wartime shortages and with the training and potential to produce high yields at the lowest cost of production, in a world where most people still go to bed hungry each night, how can one be happy with 'quotas' and 'set aside' putting a brake on production? Set aside might mean that 15% of one's land must be left to grow weeds. The country's fishing fleet has been told it may work only 1½ days a week. The small farmer might easily find that he is free to work for the landlord or the bank or hire purchase company, leaving very little for himself and his workers. It often seems that the people with power don't want responsibility and the people with the responsibility haven't got the power to change things for the better.

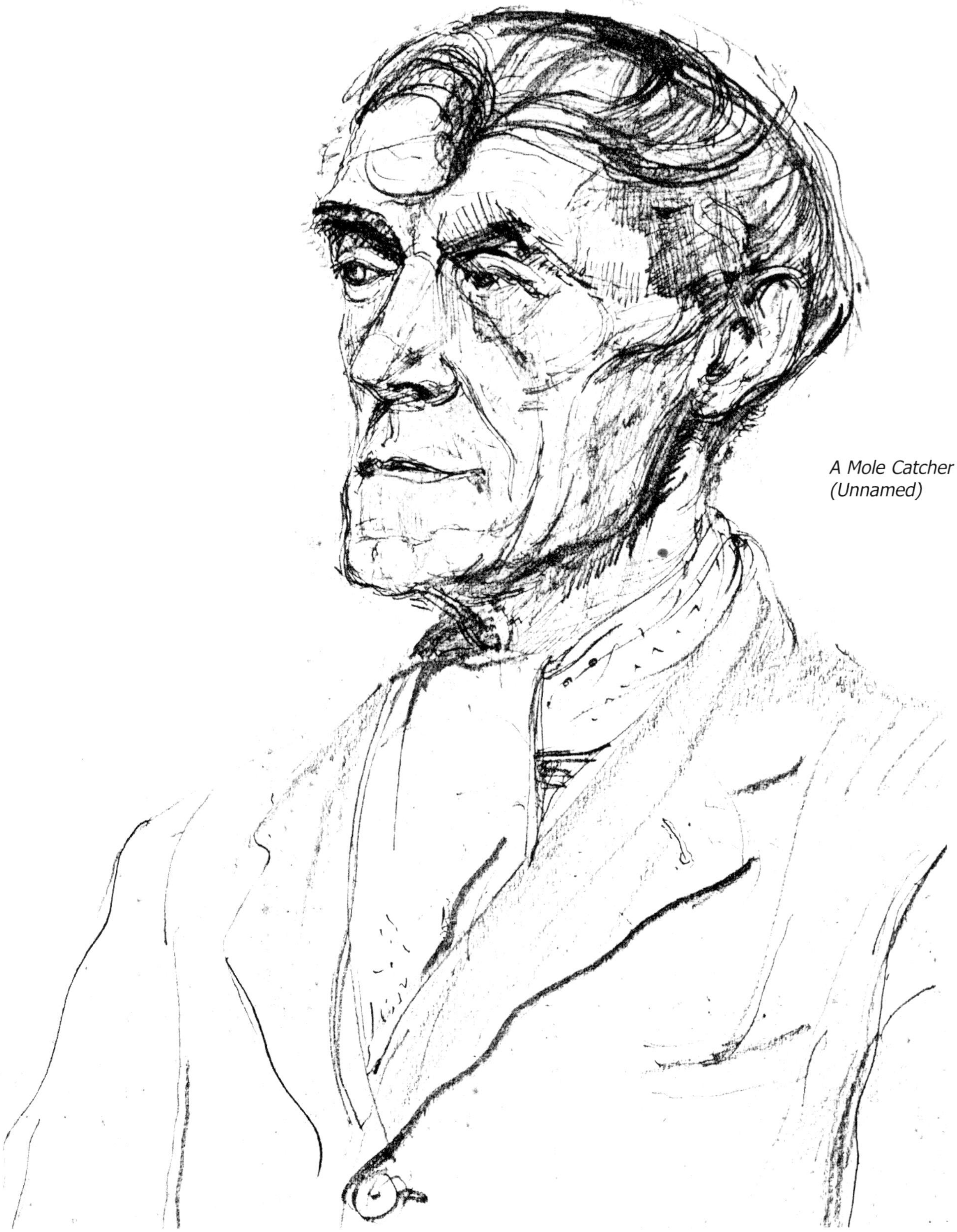

A Mole Catcher
(Unnamed)

Where are the yeomen, the yeomen of England,
Stained with the ruddy tan God's air doth give a man,
Free as the winds that fan the broad breast of England?

- from Merrie England

Agricultural Shows

Some may have felt free to go to a show, a ploughing match, a steam fair or a gymkhana. Each year, some of us farming folk will elect to go to an agricultural show for an educational and enjoyable day out. We need to keep aware of new developments in machinery, gadgetry and techniques, for improving efficiency in our roles as custodians of the countryside. There are experimental plots for crops and live exhibits showing the latest methods of housing and feeding livestock.

There are elaborate stands to promote this and that product or a vast array of expensive machinery. As the work of twenty men 50 years ago now has to be done by one, some people say that if it can't be done from the tractor seat, it does not get done at all! This cannot be strictly true as there are still husky young men competing in skilled handicrafts such as sheep shearing and shoeing horses; there may be craftsmen in wood making hurdles and trugs. Stonemasons and dry stone wallers ply their trades along with thatchers and saddlers making elaborate sets of harness for the mighty draught horse turn-outs.

Most of the trade stands offer hospitality by way of much-needed refreshments in recognition of the business exchanges done with the farmer over the past years or in the hope of generating new business through the good will shown to him. Our serious eating and drinking was usually done at the expense of the bank to offset against charges and overdraft interest incurred over twelve months!

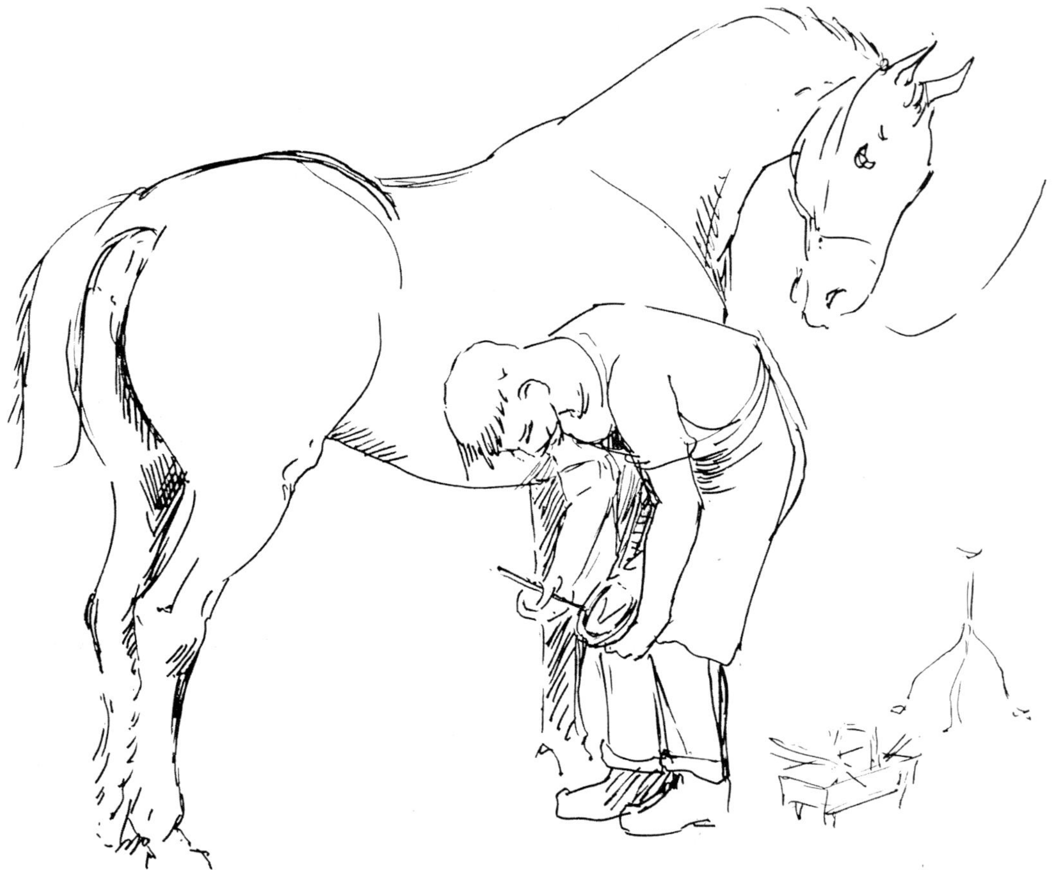

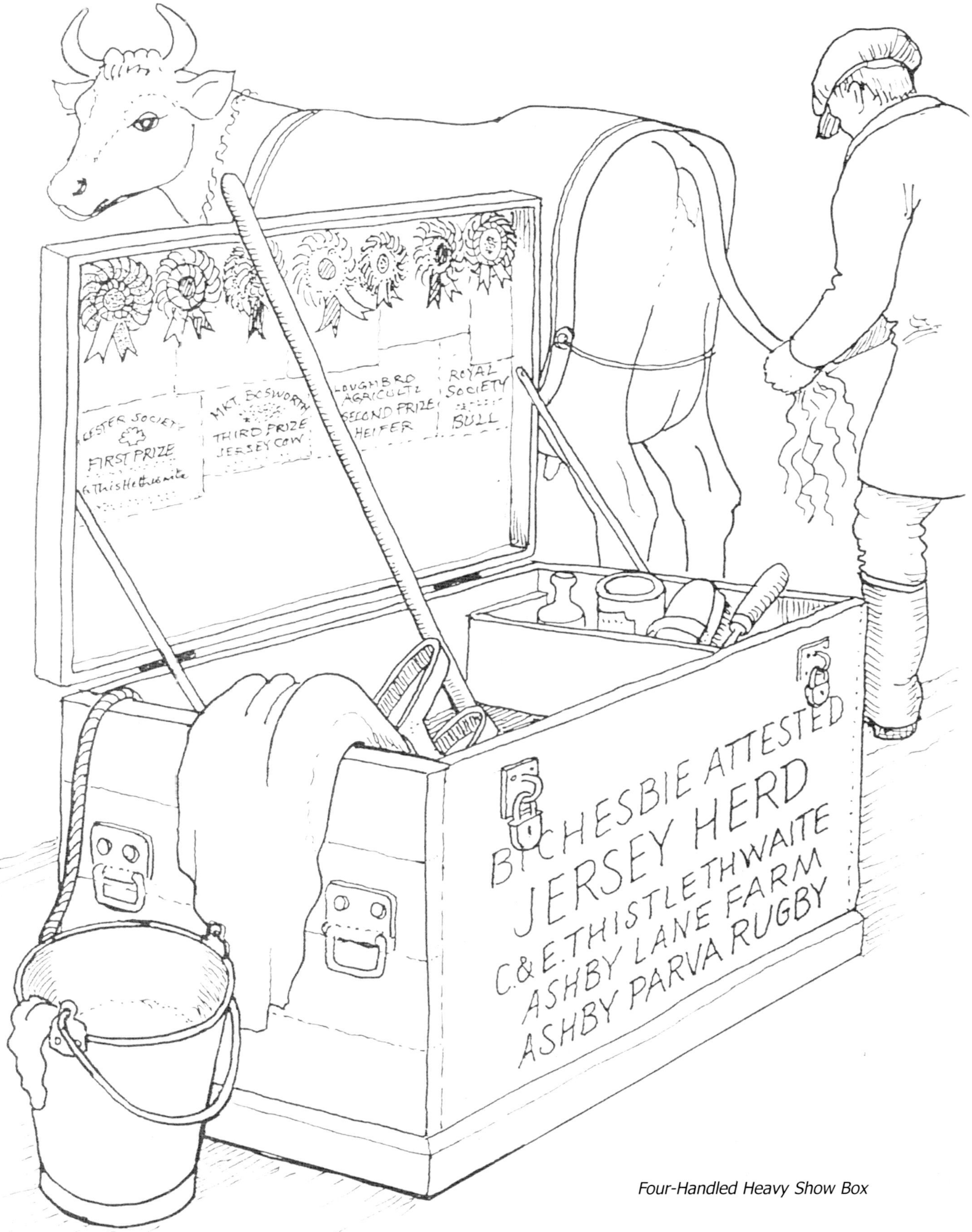

Four-Handled Heavy Show Box

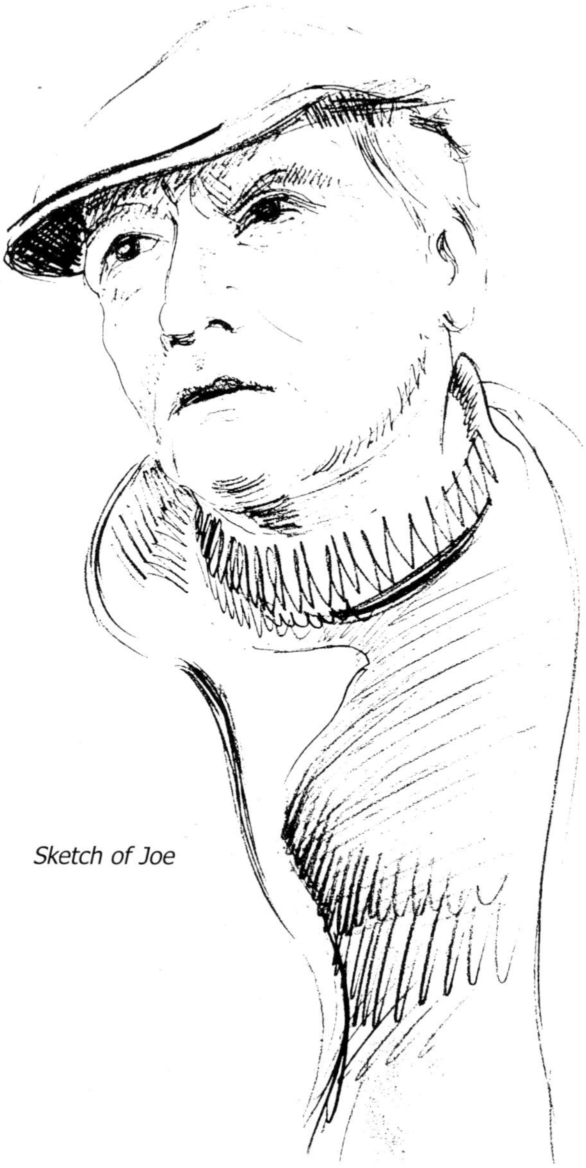

Sketch of Joe

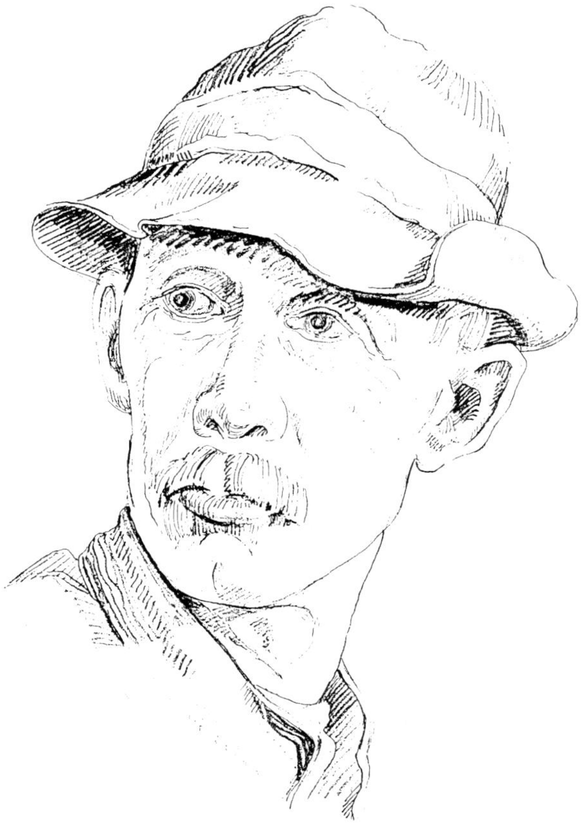

"Son of the Soil"

Three of the farm helpers, part of an excellent team of workers.

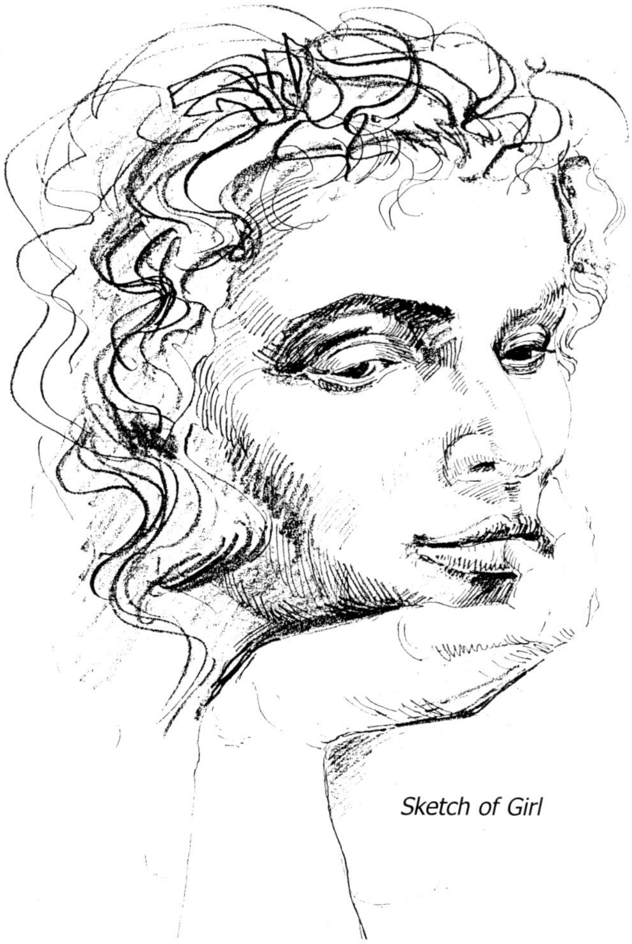

Sketch of Girl

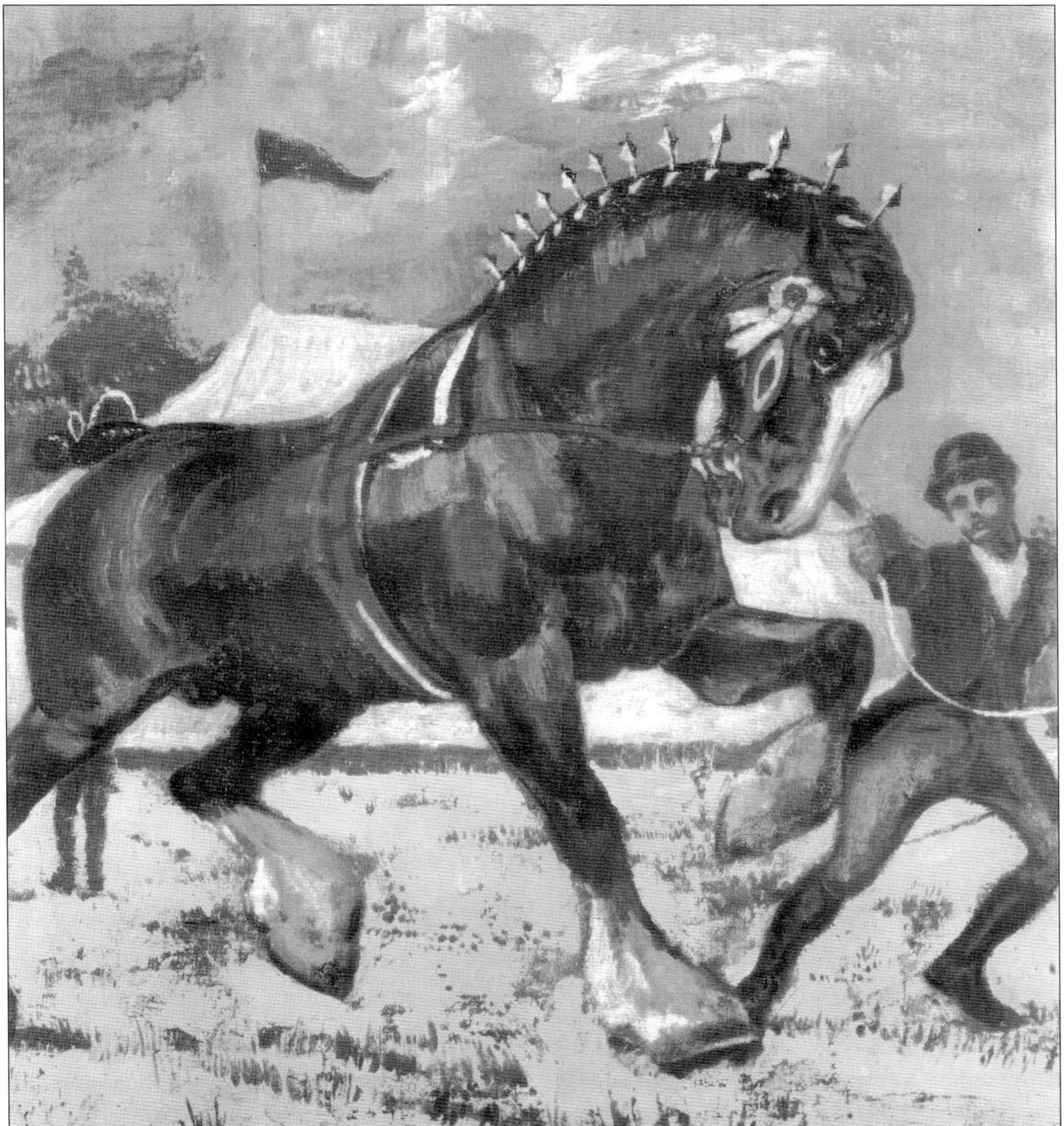

Shire stallion at agricultural show

It Pays to Advertise

Some people will say that the returns don't warrant exhibiting at shows. Maybe it depends if you win prizes or not. It surely must pay to advertise your stock and services. You may have a wonderful pedigree strain of cattle, sheep or pigs back at the farm, but if no-one knows about them, you will not reap the benefit from competition of buyers beating a path to your yard to part with their cash for your stock.

It pays to advertise by keeping your product before the eyes of the purchasing public. For the stock farmer, by winning rosettes, show cards and trophies at local and county shows, one gradually makes progress to the more prestigious shop windows for agriculture at the Royal Show at Stoneleigh, the Smithfield Show at Earls Court and the Dairy Show at Olympia.

Having been persuaded to take part in the showing of pedigree dairy cattle, I quickly found out that there was a considerable outlay in time and equipment: special leather halters with white ropes attached to lead them into the show ring; a heavy show box with lettering thereon proclaiming the herd's name and address. This contained all the grooming paraphernalia, and inside the lid, which stood open, were stapled all the show cards and rosettes. Rugs for the animals had to be purchased and insignia to be embroidered or appliquéd by my wife, who often drove the animals to the show in a horse-box along with the herdsman and his wife.

As this left a sizeable hole in the farm staff, I would be required to stay home like Cinderella doing all the milking and the chores while others took the accolades! The inevitable disruption to the smooth working of the farm meant that, apart from one excursion to the Royal Show where staff were away for a whole week, we restricted our participation to one day events in the county.

The stockmen and women have to display great enthusiasm and stoicism, as they have to endure considerable discomfort, living and sleeping in makeshift accommodation adjoining their charges. The pampered animals are waited on hand and foot with much grooming, clipping, shampooing and polishing. Each stockman for each class of animal has his own mystique in show preparation, jealously guarded from one generation to the next, and one would do well to pander to his every whim at this time if rosettes are to be won!

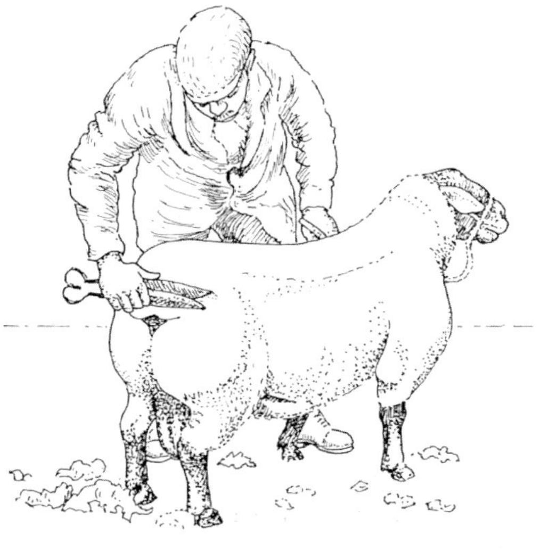

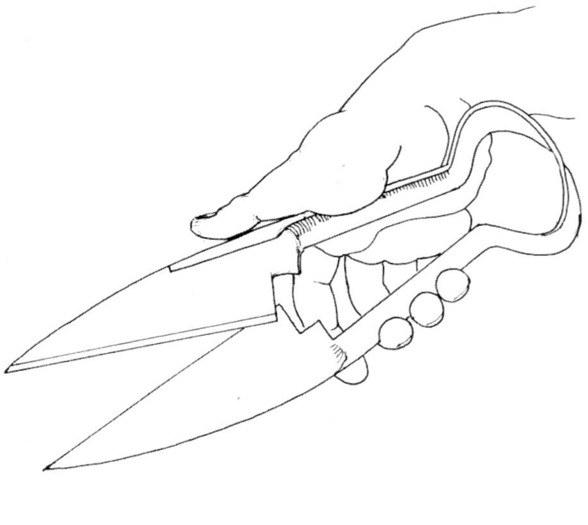

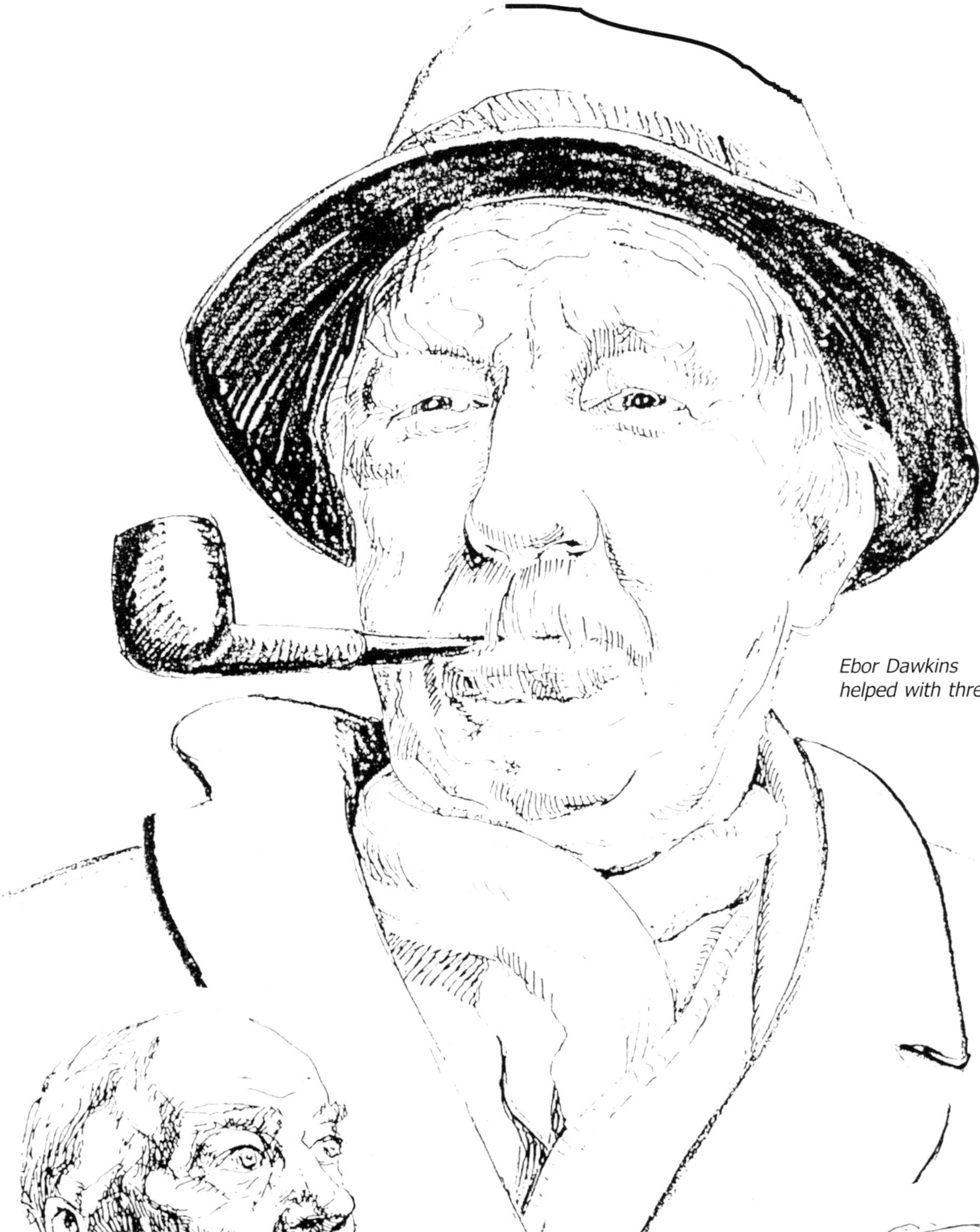

Ebor Dawkins
helped with threshing

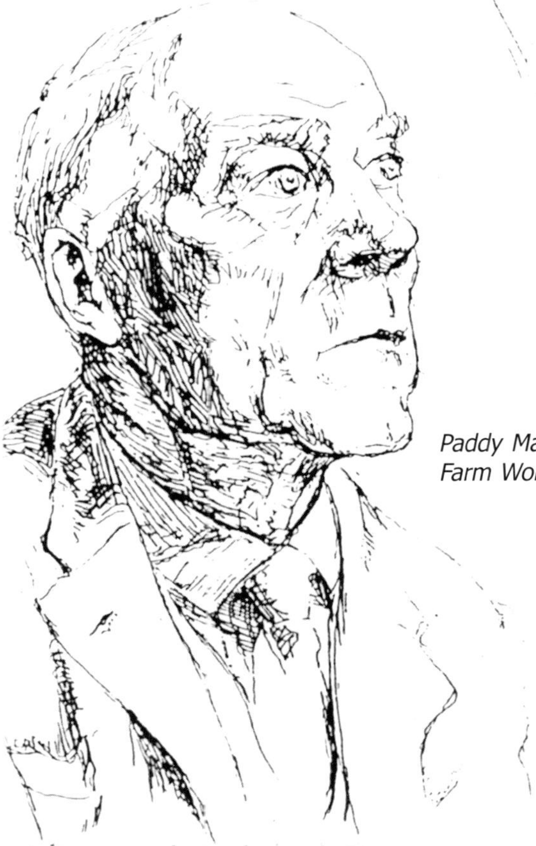

Paddy Malone
Farm Worker

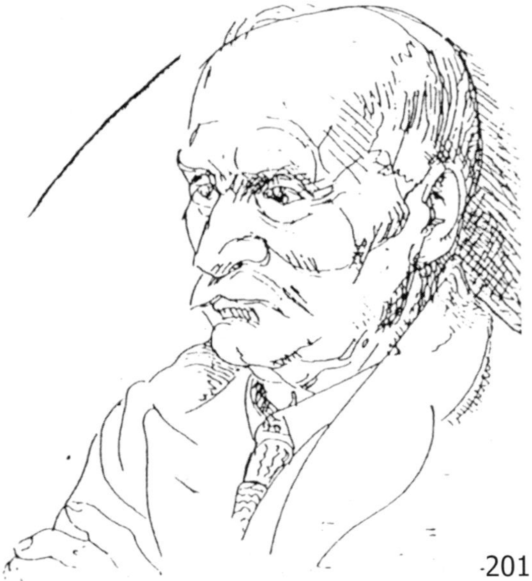

'The Gaffer'
Harry Hickman - The Hedger
First etching by Christopher, circa 1938

Stock Lines are Like a Lady's Boudoir

Sheep are washed, brushed and carded out and subjected to very careful clipping to enhance their natural shape. Pigs are oiled to ensure a scab-free skin texture, shampooed and treated with white wood flour. The stock lines appear like a lady's boudoir with lacquer, hair dryers and talcum powder giving off exotic aromas.

Once in the ring, there are all manner of wily ways for catching the judge's eye and every time you and your animal have to stop and stand still, an attitude must be struck and held: head high, ears pricked, back straight; in fact one is inevitably reminded of the traditional pose adopted by trapeze artistes and beauty queens with one knee flexed coyly across the other!

Stirring Sight of the Grand Parade

There are few more stirring sights to a stock farmer than the grand parade of stock in the ring at the Royal Show. Here we may see the finest examples of man's co-operation with nature by careful breeding and selection to produce a multiplicity of stock, each eminently suited by its special traits to the varied conditions of its environment and commercial requirements of the buyers.

The harness horse classes exemplify the uses to which this tractable animal has been put in the service of mankind: from the high-stepping hackneys to the trotters' buggies, from the stagecoaches with their four-in-hand Cleveland Bays to the magnificent Shires and Clydesdales, Suffolks and Percherons moving round with their brewers' drays and farm wagons.

At the larger shows, one may see impressive parades and performances by the latest models of tractors and newly invented machines which have relieved our farmers of back-breaking toil and contributed to making them some of the most efficient in the world.

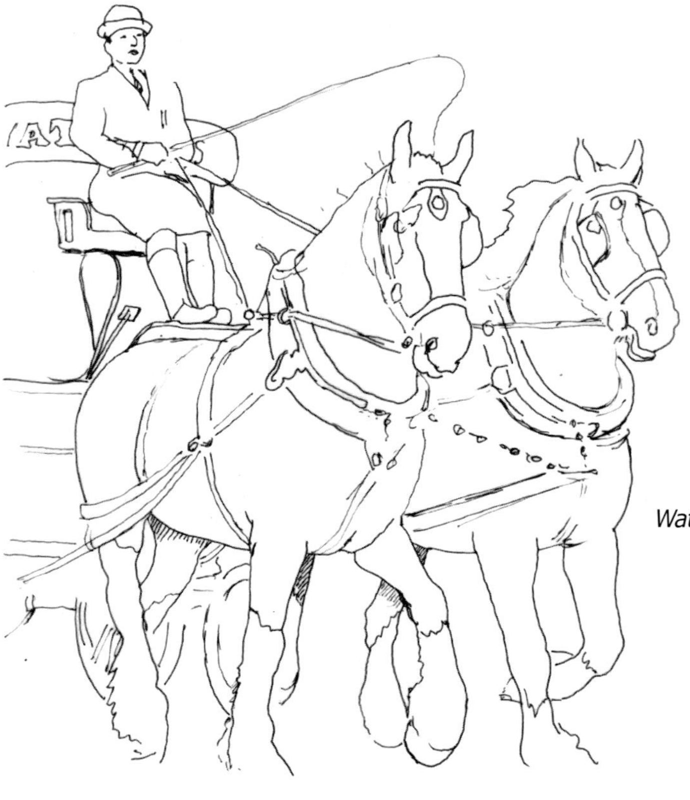

Watneys Brewers dray

Civilisation's Roots Lie Deep in the Soil

"When Adam delved and Eve span, who was then the gentleman?" said Wat Tyler during the peasants' revolt.

Scholars and men of learning would do well to remember that the sweetest, fragrant, most sophisticated rose is grafted onto the humble briar whose wild roots, lying deep in the soil, impart to it vigour and sustenance without which its very existence would be in doubt. The National Farmers' Union motto is:

By the labour of the farmer, the citizens shall flourish and prosper. By being emancipated from the obligation to hunt for, or to grow food for themselves, men and women are granted the opportunity and time to develop the arts of civilisation.

As Brutus said,

Lowliness is young ambition's ladder whereto the climber upward turns his face; but once he doth attain the utmost, round looks in the clouds, scorning the base degrees by which he did ascend.

Proud of Humble Origins

It is well-known that Bernard Wetherill, Speaker of the House of Commons, kept a thimble in his pocket to remind him of his humble tailoring origins. Likewise, I keep a horse-plough in my suburban front garden to remind me of those days when I was wresting an honest living from the soil, striding out behind a team of horses, covering 15 miles a day over rough terrain, clod-hopping through lumps as big as your head.

'Miles on the Clock'

I have a theory that those years of clod-hopping have left me with an advantage over my smooth-walking fellows which persists to this day. Along with the gout, I have a kind of sight-sense in my big toes, so that when all around me are twisting their ankles and stubbing their toes, I very rarely trip or stumble, the relief map of the route immediately ahead being imprinted in my subconscious mind! Furthermore, my theory postulates that we are born with a certain number of 'miles on the clock'. As I evidently used up many more than usual walking over fields in my youth, there are now fewer left, so I must be excused unnecessary walking and be allowed to ride even short distances in my old age!

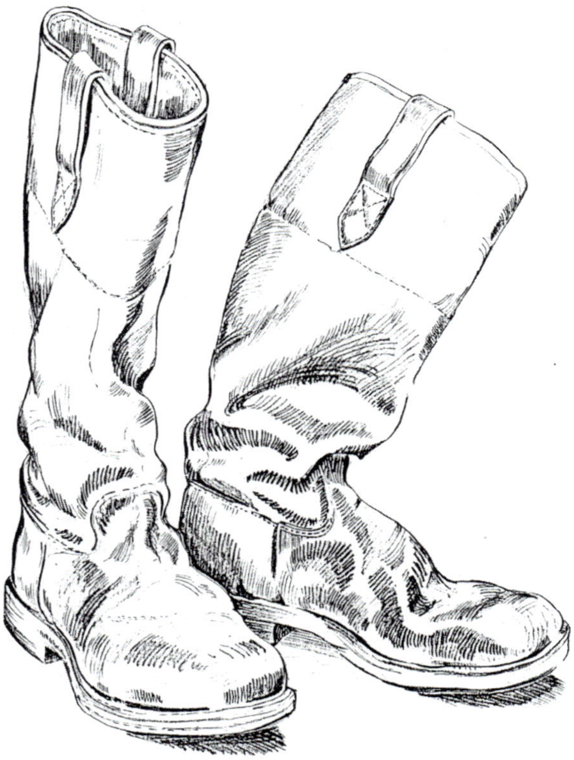

Black Market in Food

I well remember when during and after the war, the country was on short rations and farmers enjoyed a popularity previously unknown. The rich and arrogant drove their Bentleys over rough tracks to fill humble stone-flagged farm kitchens with cigar and whiskey fumes, while they persuaded the peasants to part with their flitches and hams, butter and eggs at black market prices beyond belief.

Those sufficiently affluent could acquire farms of their own, install a farm bailiff and continue to live, safe from the law and bombs, on the fat of the land. One local Justice of the Peace who had an isolated farm used a remote building as a slaughterhouse for illegally killed meat. However, he fell out with one of his key employees, who promptly ensured that his employer's brother magistrates sat in judgement on him and meted out a suitable punishment for his misdeeds.

Temptations of the Unjust Steward

The businessman who employs a bailiff-manager to run his farm lays himself open to exploitation in numerous ways. Whenever the bailiff appears at market to buy and sell stock, he will be subject to the blandishments of wheeler-dealers ready to buy him whisky galore to befuddle his mind and weaken his resolve as they suggest wicked schemes by which he can cheat his master. Back-handers and perquisites will be offered fraudulently to manipulate the prices, the quality and the quantity of the animals being traded that day.

The situation is particularly dangerous if the bailiff has his own holding nearby. How is the dude farmer to know that a wagon-load of hay bales or fifty sacks of wheat took a wrong turn when they were being hauled off his land?

I have even heard of bunches of cattle being driven through the villages in the early hours, rustled under cover of darkness, never to be seen again!

It is rather puzzling that the unjust steward in the New Testament (Luke 16:1-13) was commended by the Lord of the Manor for making friends of his Lord's debtors by reducing their bills when he was dismissed. I would have thought that this was one of those occasions when connivance would be considered tantamount to complicity!

Welsh 'Invasion' of the Midlands

During the period of scandalous neglect of British agriculture between the two world wars, there was a Welsh invasion of the Midlands by farmers from less favoured areas across the border and well accustomed to a lower standard of living on the hills. I am told there was more Welsh than English to be heard at Rugby market in those days. English landlords were grateful to have anyone willing to occupy their farms at subsistence level on the dog and stick principle

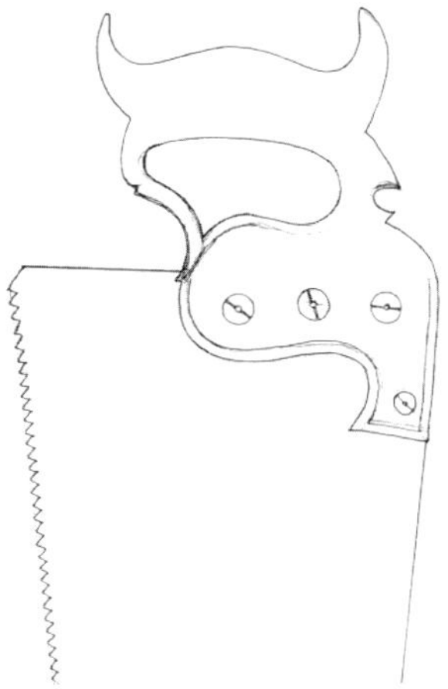

and at very low rents. Such men were typically under-capitalised, and had little stomach for the more sophisticated arable techniques foisted on them by the edicts and requirements of the War Agricultural Committees who had power of eviction over those considered not to be pulling their weight in food production.

Hard-Headed Men Showed Compassionate Care

One such man was a much-loved, courteous, generous soul, who nevertheless would have trouble getting 2 out of 10 for management skills! His stock was poor, his farm neglected; crops stunted and weedy, gates and fences broken. Then word got around among his neighbours that the powers that be were coming soon to inspect and probably to evict him. Without being asked, all his neighbours came together to help him. Within a few days, miracles were performed as his farm received a complete facelift.

Manure was removed and spread; pens white-washed and gates creosoted and re-hung. Weedy pastures were topped and scruffy cattle spirited away and replaced by well-matched sleek ones. It was a touching example of normally hard-headed men showing compassionate care for a neighbour. The inspectors were agreeably impressed and the situation redeemed until things slipped back to normal.

A Difficult Man to Help

Later, when his crop of barley was ready to cut and he showed no signs of getting on with it, one of his neighbours decided to offer his help as it was a fine day. He arrived at nine o'clock and, after some discussion, went out to start the tractor. This couldn't be done as there was no fuel, so they would have to go with the pony and float to fetch some in five-gallon tins from the merchant in the nearest town four miles away. They then went out to catch the pony. It had a loose shoe. When that was fixed, they found that the harness was broken and had to be mended. Only two tins could be found so they had to call at the garage for four more. When they got back with the fuel the tractor wouldn't start. The plugs had to be taken out and cleaned. When it was fixed to the binder, one of the canvasses was broken and the knife had to be repaired and sharpened. It was now time for afternoon milking and not worth starting today. Next day it poured with rain! And so on and on. You cannot help men permanently by doing for them what they could and should do for themselves.

Due to the state of his gates and fences, his unthrifty cattle, sheep and pigs would roam the village unattended in search of better grazing. Rather than fetch posts and rails to mend a fence, he would tie a sheepdog in the gap.

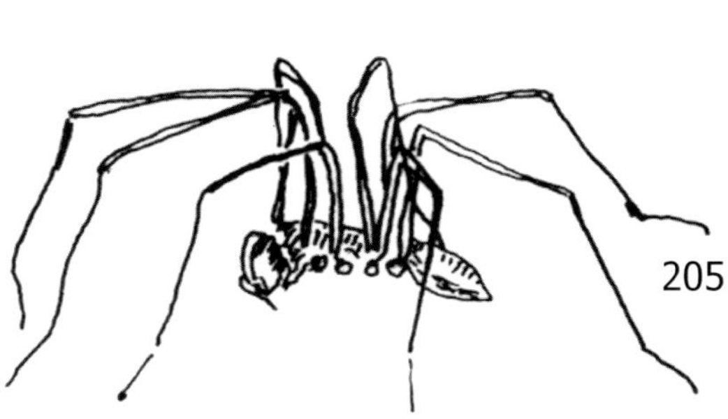

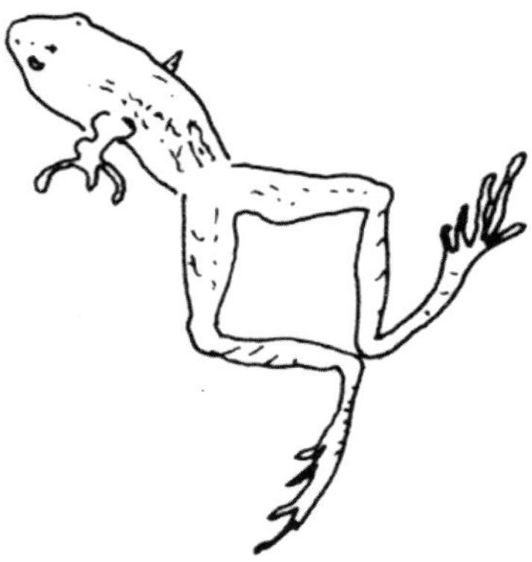

Campers and Caravan Visitors

Our lives were constantly enriched by virtue of the fact that I had the farm listed in various books as an overnight stop for campers and caravanners. People from many countries and different walks of life made their way to our farm to share with us the delights of the English countryside. A chief constable might share a paddock with the producer of the Antiques Road Show. A professional footballer might bottle-feed a lamb while a D'Oyly Carte singer looked on. Blonde beauties on motorbikes from Finland would crack a bottle with Aussies in a motorised recreational vehicle from the outback.

A district surveyor would help me to install a drain for which I had no planning permission and an electrician would help to move the electric fence! A publisher helped us to build a tree house for our children. By picking their brains and enlisting the help of complete strangers, I found myself conducting, quite naturally, an experiment in social engineering to further the cause of the Brotherhood of Man and the League of Nations! And I think it gave the townsfolk visitors some insight into the problems of mixed farming.

If I was not too busy I would, for a small fee, sketch the portraits of children between five and fifteen years of age. Visits were organised by Scouts, Guides, Cadets, Duke of Edinburgh Award seekers, The Woodcraft Folk, various schools and disadvantaged children from London.

Tents Resembled a Mediaeval Battlefield

More formal, highly-organised rallies were held by the Caravan Club, the Caravanners Club and various camping clubs. The field, resplendent with gaily coloured tents and flagpoles, resembled the preparations for the battle of Agincourt.

I could almost hear my neighbours saying, "That be the best crop he do grow and it don't take nothing out of the ground, look you!" But the VAT man wanted his tithe, though I challenged him to show me what article had value added to it! I was rather peeved that no discount was allowed to host farmers when we in turn wanted to join the club. Being skilled myself at reversing trailers, I was always amazed at how few caravanners had learned what I would have considered that necessary art! And why are caravans not all painted green to blend with the countryside?

When the motorways were being constructed nearby, I was glad to be able to help two worthy families by accommodating their mobile homes, thus enabling the men, who worked impossibly long hours on the giant scrapers, to have some semblance of normal family life, with the children going to the local school.

This man came to do some plastering for us.
He kept raptors (birds of prey) in his back yard.

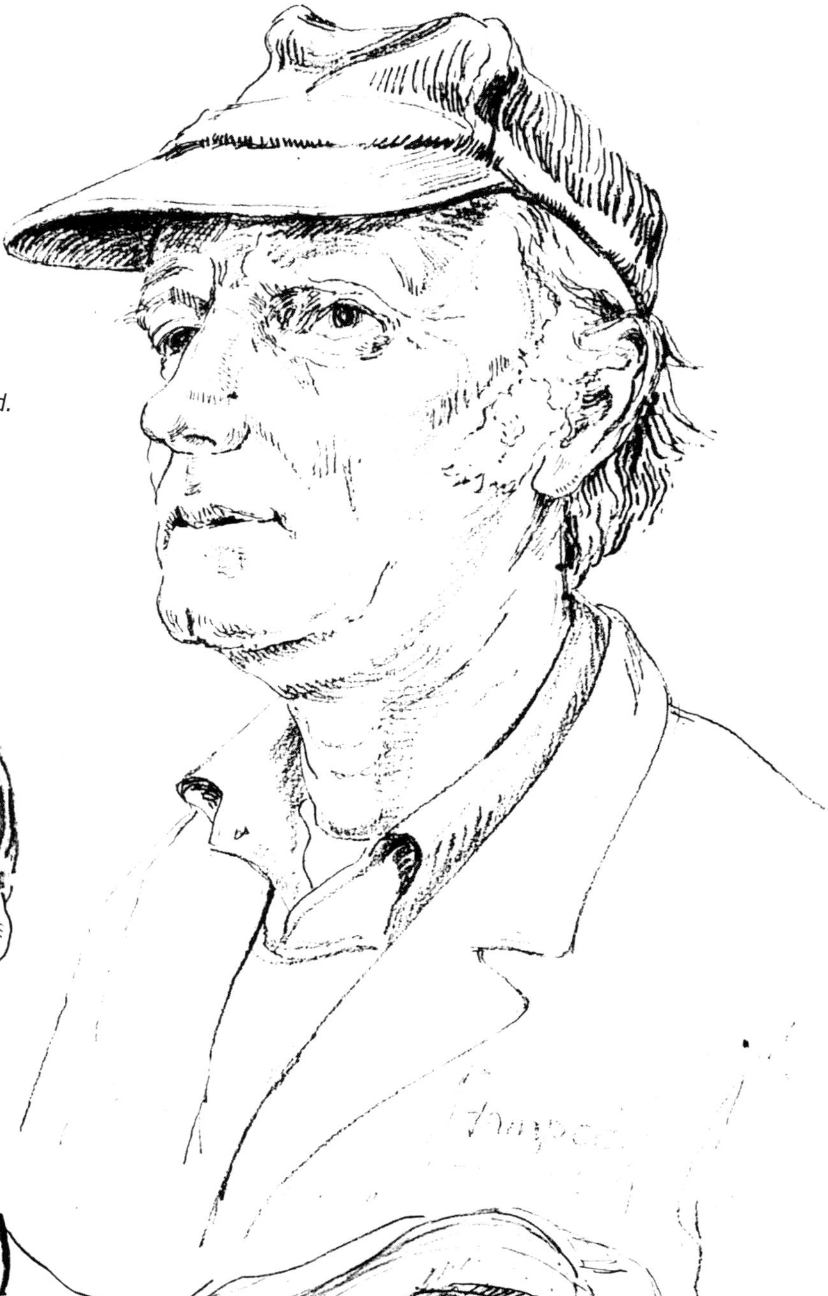

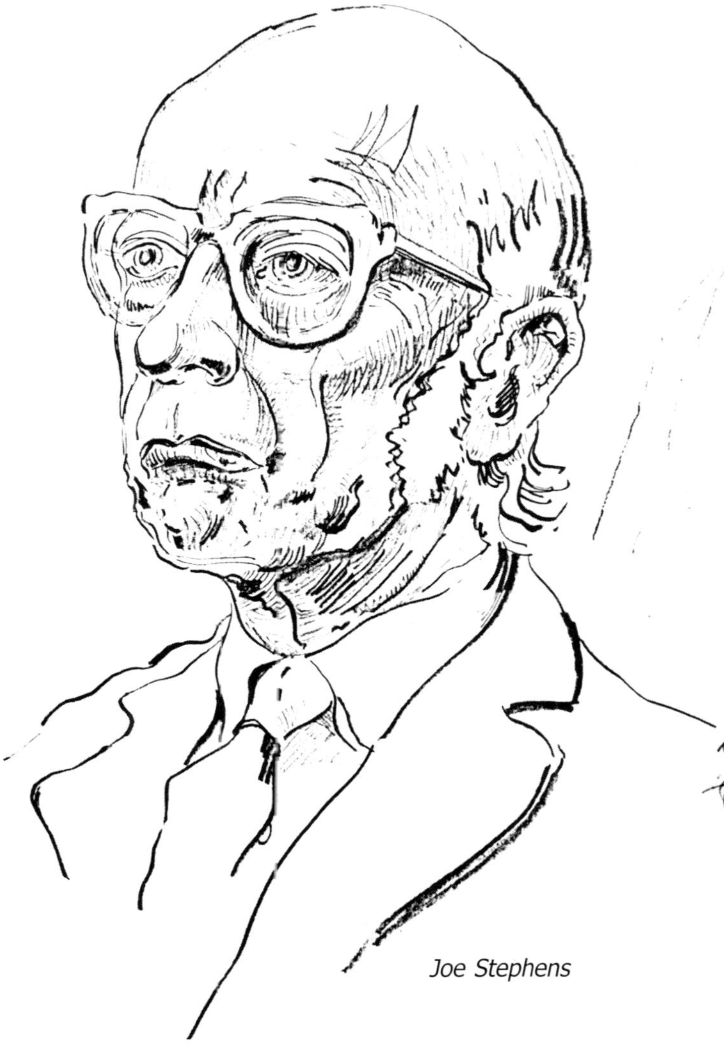

Joe Stephens

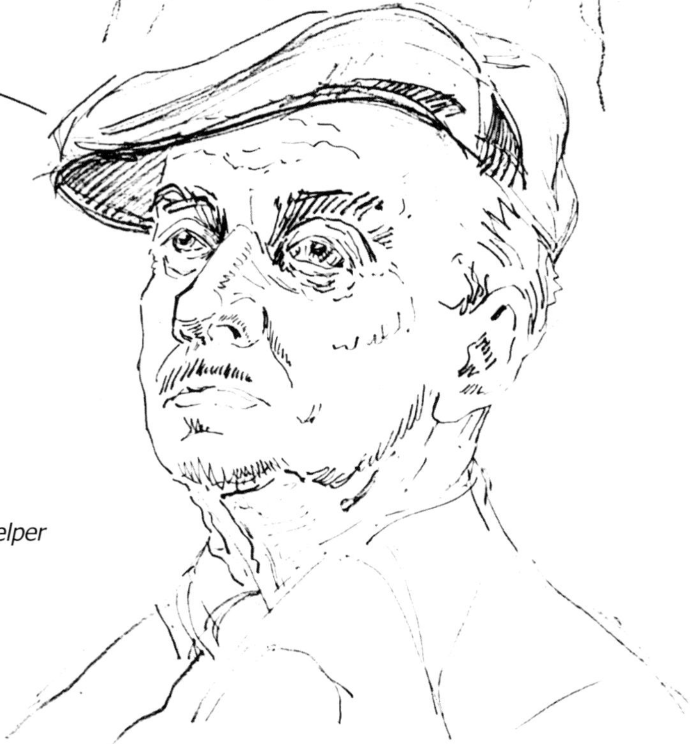

A farm helper

Somerset Banks

I spent a year helping a friend establish a small farm in the Quantock Hills. On this Somerset farm the fields were small, steep and sandy, surrounded by banks six feet high and ten feet wide, surmounted by a few beech and sycamore saplings which were intended to serve as a hedge to contain the stock.

In fact, they served more as a home to innumerable rabbits and rats, such that the corn was cropped short for a distance of fifty yards all around the perimeter of these tiny fields, leaving very little to harvest in the centre. I have seen the trappers come into the farmyard day after day with hundreds of rabbits slung between their shoulders on a pole. It was said that some farmers at that time made more from the rabbits than they did from their depleted crops!

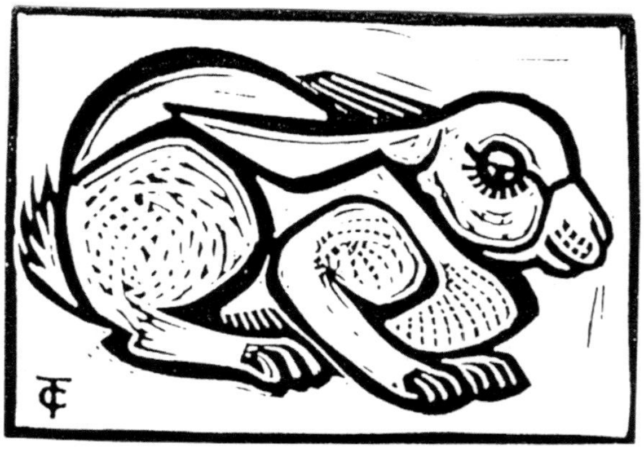

One myopic trapper went to release what he took to be a rabbit from his trap. It happened to be a live rat which bit his arm. The wound turned septic and he was dead within a few days!

Steep, Light and Hungry Land

The beautiful deer from Exmoor would invade and devour the grain and root crops until the hunt drove them back onto the hills. The land was light and hungry and constantly on the move. A deluge would be capable of washing inches of good top-soil out of the gateway, depositing it on the road, from whence it would have to be carted back!

Ploughmen had to use one-way Huxtable turnover ploughs wherever possible, turning the soil back up the hill to counter the effect of erosion. The lanes were so narrow and steep that a carter would need a second trace horse if he proposed to carry more than half a ton. It was very hard land to farm.

During my year in Somerset, I was constantly amazed at how different were the methods of carrying out the same task that I had become accustomed to in Warwickshire.

Local Terminology

Even the terminology was vastly different from that commonly used in the Midlands. A pitchfork was a 'pick', a pick was a 'peck' and a mattock was a 'bisky'. A two-wheeled tipping cart was named a 'putt'. Whereas in the Midlands, a horse's collar and harness was inverted and pushed over his head as you harnessed him, in Somerset the collars were opened at the top and the hames undone at the bottom. This seemed an unnecessarily time-consuming refinement to achieve the same result!

Most farmers made their own cider from the apple orchards adjoining the farmyards. Visiting workers were generously plied with this scrumpy brew, often with dire results! It was said that a beer drinker did not need to eat much as it took away his appetite, whereas the cider-bibber still loved to attack his food with a mighty zest. After a hard day's ploughing, so tired was I that I have been known to help myself from a cleaning soda pan and eat it in the mistaken belief that it was gravy!

One year we grew cabbages which were to be planted by hand. I rolled the area with a flat roller and then had to mark out the field with dead straight lines using a horse-hoe frame like a chequer board both ways, leaving two foot-squares marked on the ground. The small but hardy cabbage plants were then dropped at the intersections. They were picked up and planted at incredible speed by men walking doubled up with small mattocks or biskies in their hands, with which they made the holes for the cabbage roots. As the rows were accurate both ways, they could be horse-hoed and cultivated much more effectively, and there was visual pleasure to be had from looking along the diagonal rows.

Ferret Fiasco

It was quite common for groups of men and children to go rabbiting in their spare time with ferrets and nets. The nets having been fixed over the exits to the burrows, the ferret would be introduced into the warren to make the rabbits bolt out into the nets. Sometimes a line-ferret would become lost underground and this called for some serious digging, often among tree roots, in order to get him out.

Ferrets are fed on chunks of butchers' offal which reminds me of an occasion when a young man was relieving himself against a tree with a ferret in his other hand. Someone called out to him and, as he swung round to answer, he let out a howl of anguish as the hungry ferret fastened onto his morsel of meat!

He used to blush for all the world like a Victorian virgin on hearing her first four letter word. Imagine then, his blushes as he was being treated by the young nurses in the casualty department of the local hospital! He was not allowed to forget this incident for a long time. It is remarkable how much people delight in the downfall or discomfiture of their fellows!

Chapter ELEVEN

Crop Blessing and Miscellaneous Musings

What is this life if, full of care
We have no time to stand and stare?
- W. H. Davis

It is almost impossible to farm in this country without becoming aware of the deeply religious significance of so many of our customs and beliefs. Farms generally change hands and rents become due either at Lady Day (The Feast of the Annunciation) - 25th March, or Michaelmas Day (The Feast of St. Michael the Archangel) - 29th September.

In addition to rent and rates, a tithe was levied annually. Originally, this was based on the principle that a tenth of the land's produce would be given towards the upkeep of the church. A portion of land attached to a clergyman's benefice was (and sometimes still is) called the glebe.

The three days before Ascension Thursday are called Rogation Days and the Litanies of the Saints were sung in procession on these days as the people walked round the boundaries of the parish. This is still known as 'beating the bounds'. When these boundaries were clearly defined for all to see, the obligation for supporting the poor of the parish could be seen to have its just limits.

Superstition is not to be confused with faith. On Rogation Days, in keeping with the traditions of the Christian faith at that time, we admit our dependence on and give thanks to Almighty God the Creator for all the gifts of the natural world and ask that blessings may continue to be bestowed upon the property in our care, and especially for fertility in the crops and livestock. It was our custom to invite the parish priest and congregation to the farm, where we would have a service in the cleared-out and decorated barnyard. Token animals would be appropriately penned there, the male animals being noticeably absent for the needs of safety and decorum! Holy Water would be sprinkled liberally as a sign of the blessings. Our spirits being suitably uplifted, we would then retire to refresh our human frames with tea, cakes and ale.

I well remember one energetic parish priest from the Emerald Isle who insisted on setting foot in every field, byre, barn and dwelling on a 500-acre spread, sprinkling with such abundance as would counter any drought! Frequently we had to stop and replenish the water from one container and our flagging spirits from another!

Faith in the Future

Aside from any religious ritual, it is my contention that no farming would be done without *faith*; belief in the future outcome of what you labour to do today; that the chicks you rear will lay eggs and the calf one day will give milk. It seems most improbable that the small grain of wheat you bury in the cold, unpromising clay in November will have grown by next August into golden straw carrying ears bursting with nourishing grain. Look at the eight-foot constructions built by gardeners in their vegetable plots as they bury a little bean at the foot of each pole. They have confident faith that one day soon a plant will emerge, grow to the top and provide a crop of beans to sustain them. The wonder of it all!

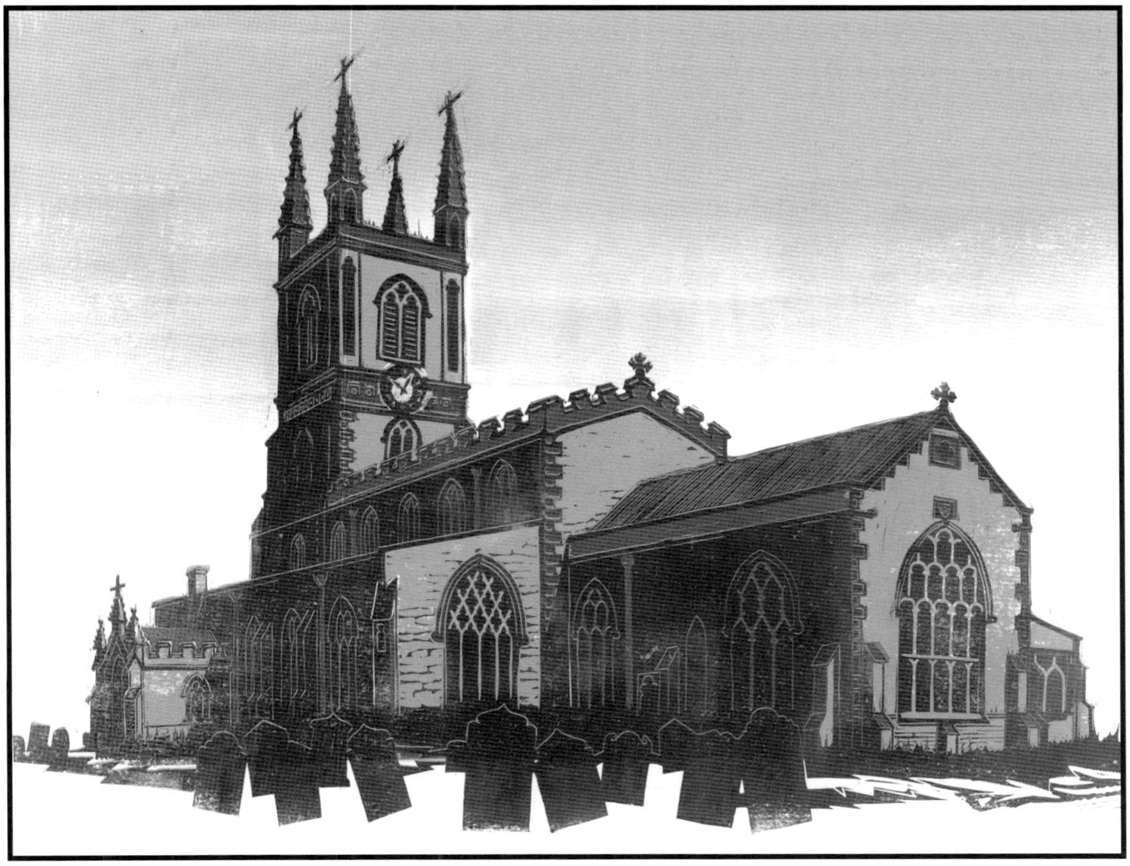

St. Mary's Church, Lutterworth, Leicestershire - whose Rector was John Wycliffe (circa 14th Century) - The Morning Star of the Reformation - first translated the Bible into English.

"Christ and His Apostles spoke unto the people in the language of the people.
Why should we not now so do?"

May Queen and May Pole Dancing

Robert Herrick wrote in the 17th Century,

There's not a budding boy or girl this day
But is got up and gone to bring in May.

A garland for crowning the Queen of the May was an essential element in the pagan ritual hallowed by the Church, so that a chaplet of roses was used to crown the statue of the Virgin Mary by the prettiest girl in the village.

Every year around the beginning of May our children at the village school were seen to be weaving intricate traditional patterns as they danced around the maypole to the strains of a violin ably played by the village school master.

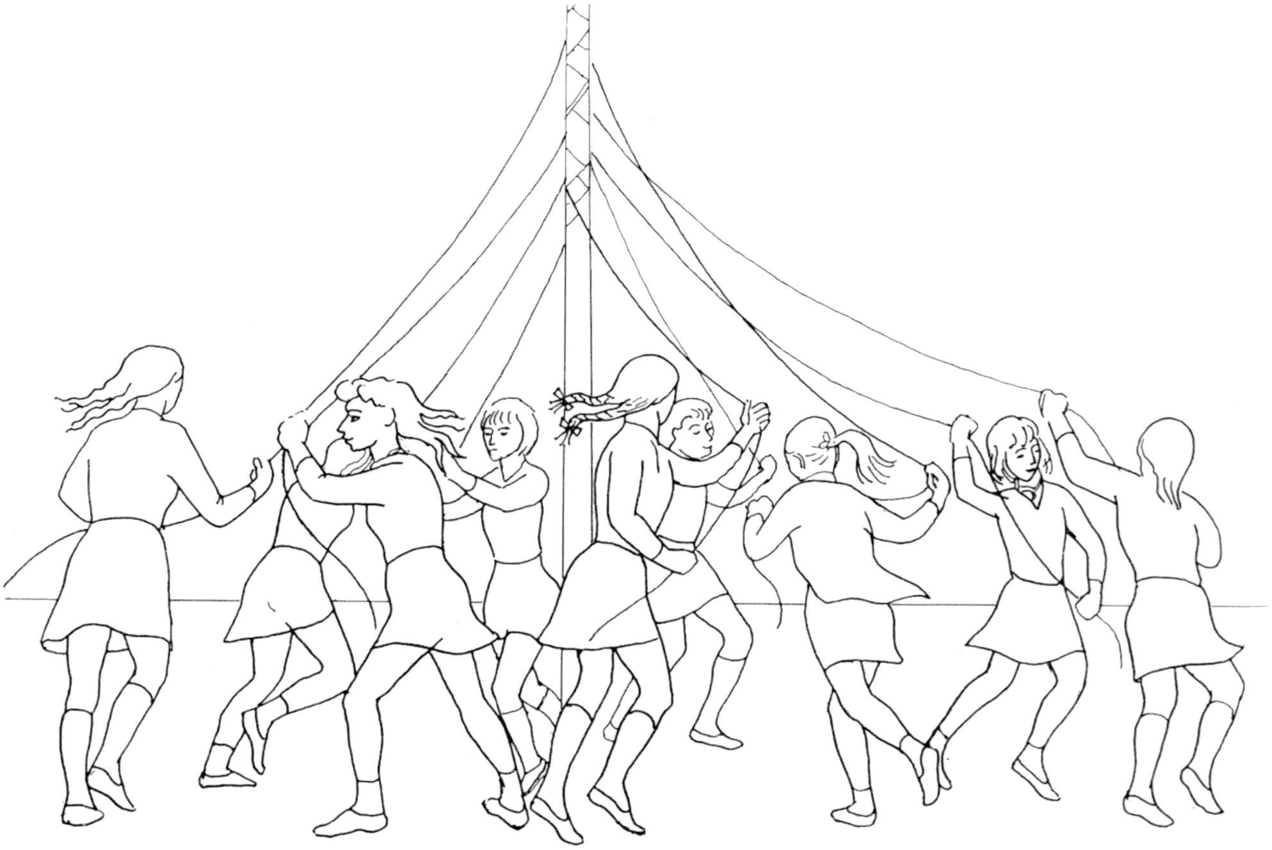

Dancing round the Maypole

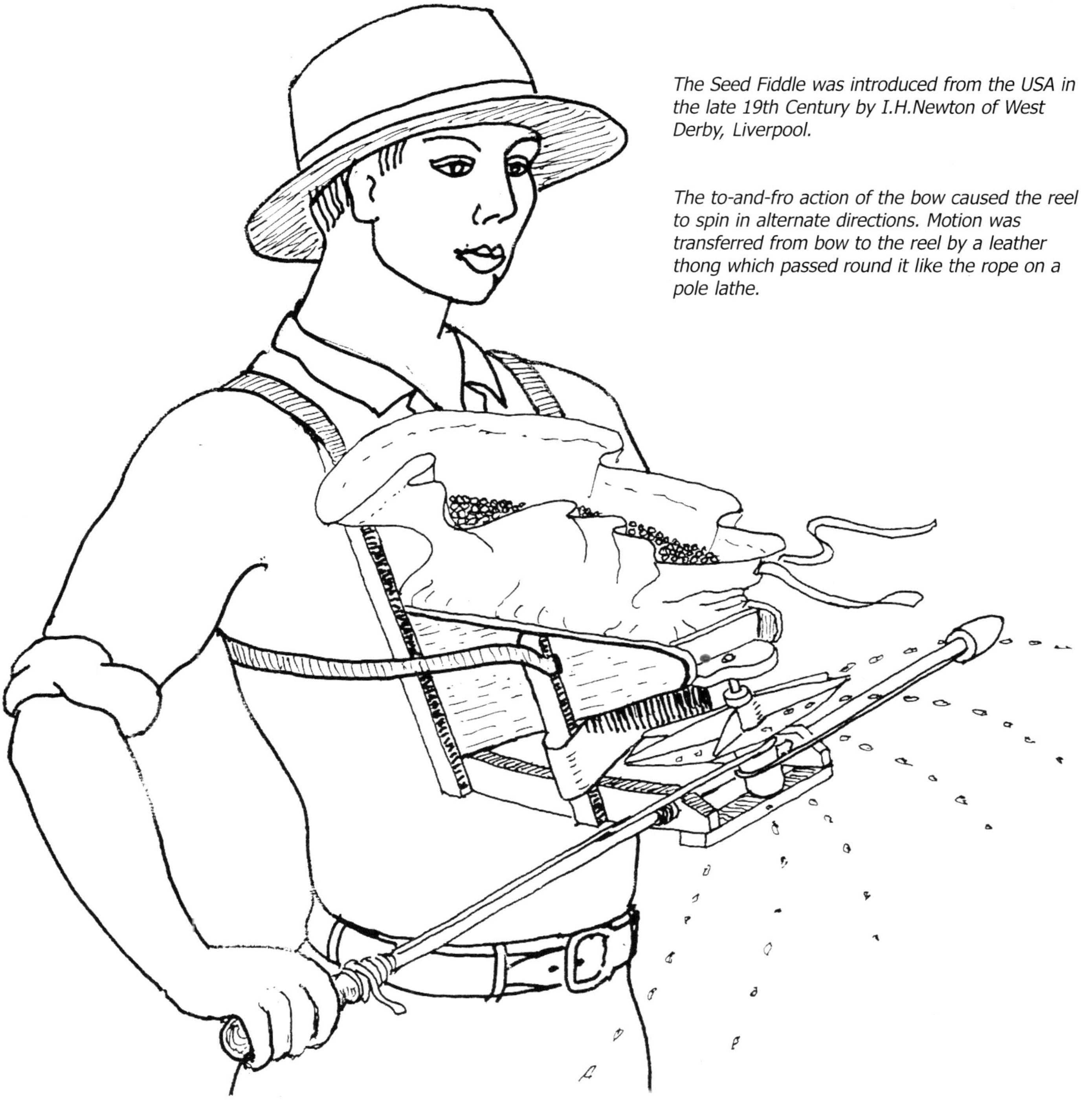

The Seed Fiddle was introduced from the USA in the late 19th Century by I.H.Newton of West Derby, Liverpool.

The to-and-fro action of the bow caused the reel to spin in alternate directions. Motion was transferred from bow to the reel by a leather thong which passed round it like the rope on a pole lathe.

The Fiddle Drill

The sight of a violinist always reminds me that seed was sometimes broadcast by a fiddle 'drill' which emitted no musical sound. The man walked and kept his stride in time with his arm, using the bow which operated a spinning flanged wheel upon which the seed was made to trickle from a crumpled bag.

A man leaning on the gate watching me striding up and down sowing grass seed held his hand to his ear and dryly asked, "What ditty are you playing today, young man?"

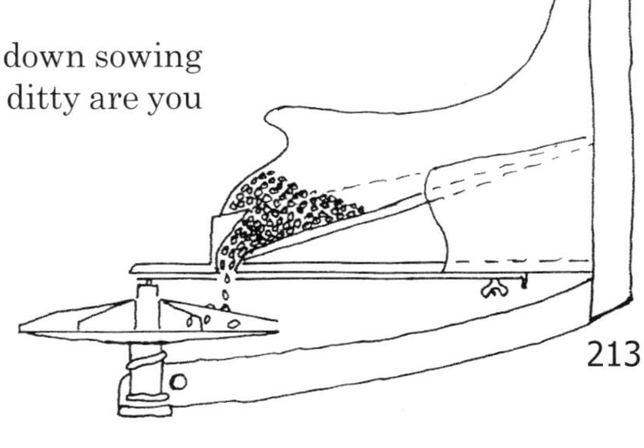

Section through Fiddle Drill

Scarecrows

An old bachelor friend needing to make several scarecrows put a small advertisement in a local paper for 'old ragged clothes'. He was truly amazed at the response. Not only did he receive enough garments to keep himself warm for a decade, but also he was embarrassed to be given tins of biscuits, cakes and pies by warm-hearted well-wishers who obviously thought he was in dire straits and likely to die of starvation if hypothermia did not get him first!

Excuse to do a Good Turn

I have often observed that people who do a good turn for a neighbour feel it necessary to make some excuse, such as "I was going that way anyhow", whereas people require no excuse to be unkind as if it were normal behaviour! Sometimes people given to criticism fail to make the welcome observation that 90% of the subject under scrutiny is of excellent quality before wading in with the shortcomings.

Part of our farm boundary consisted of a mixed deciduous and conifer spinney about 15 yards wide and half a mile long, amounting in area to about three acres. This had been planted 100 years ago to beautify the environs of a stately home and to provide cover for game birds. As regards hard-headed commercial modern farming activities, this was a total liability as it required constant attention, fencing, lopping, thinning, etc. carried out more or less assiduously by myself over a period of thirty-six years.

"I Think That I May Never See a Poem Lovely as a Tree"

Things are not appreciated until they are under threat to be withdrawn.

All my neighbours enjoyed the amenity value of the beauty of these trees as they enhanced the journey from one village to another, yet *not once* in all that time was I approached by anyone who wished to congratulate me on my years of unpaid service in contributing to the visual harmony of the scenery. No positive credit was given at any time. If, however, as I was then quite entitled to do, I had ordered in the chainsaws and sold the timber for a goodly price and added 3½ acres of good arable land to the farm, I would have been £15,000 better off, but what a public outcry there would have been! There is certainly a case to be made for farmers being paid as park-keepers in these circumstances.

Our children and their young friends loved trees and would often come with me to get firewood, looking under up-turned logs and bark for the myriads of insects, voles and fungoid growths to be found there.

I have found that children have little fear of creepy crawlies, even of snakes and spiders until adults set the fear upon them, along with fierce instructions like "wipe your nose", "keep your hands clean" and "don't do that!". On a cloudy day, I overheard a child telling his little friend that it was the trees waving energetically in the breeze that were driving the clouds across the sky!

Tree House

It was someone's happy inspiration to build a tree-house in a forking sycamore. There was great enthusiasm as we assembled the tools and materials and carried them to the site. After half an hour of chopping and sawing, my friend and I stopped for a rest and looked round. To our amazement, all the children had vanished, because of our failure to involve them sufficiently in the work. Nevertheless the tree house was a source of much pleasure as they used it frequently for a den and a picnic place, until it was destroyed by mindless vandals ten years later.

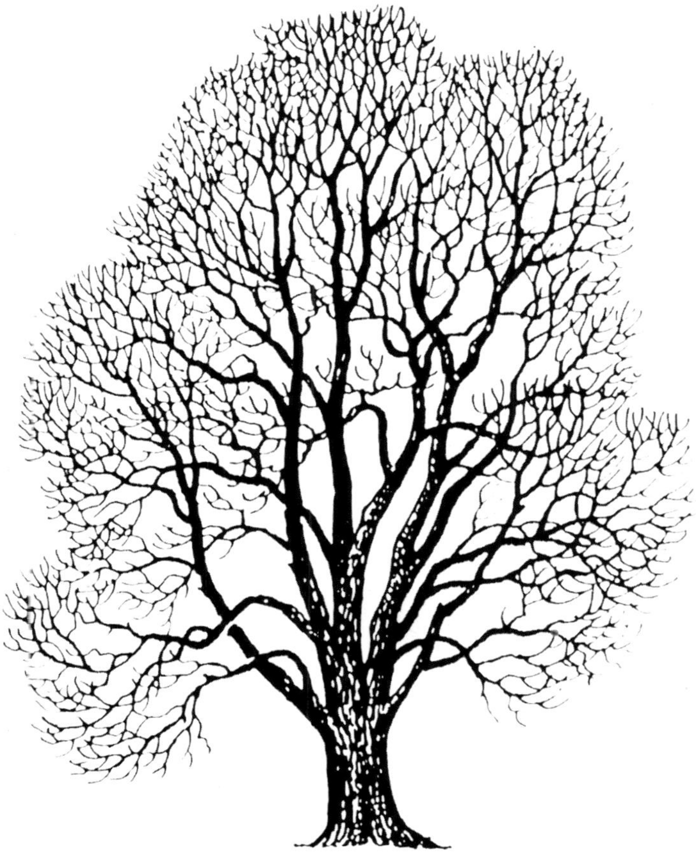

And now in the grass behold they are laid,
and the tree is my seat that once lent me a shade
- Wm. Cowper (1731-1800).

A Completely Unselfish Action

There must be few more completely unselfish things a man can do than plant a hardwood tree. He has no possible hope of profiting from it for it will mature long after he has died. When one day the great Husbandman - Designer of the Universe - calls me to account for my misdeeds, I will have to admit that I did not visit him in prison, (as I thought they might keep me there!); however, I will respectfully point out that a few sturdy trees stand to my credit, planted about this sceptered isle with no thought for personal gain.

This was how I could move quite big saplings. In the Autumn, having found an appropriate site, I would excavate a large hole, then take the tractor and fore loader to a self-sown young tree in the spinney, dig around the base to loosen the soil, fix a chain to grip the foot of the trunk and wrench it up by hydraulic power bringing out most of the roots in good order. The tree could be in the ground again within a few minutes.

Difficulty of Growing Small Trees

Small trees are some of the most difficult things to grow on a farm as everything militates against their survival. Farm animals and machinery will get them even if they are not smothered by weeds or nibbled by rabbits.

A girl rode up to visit us on a pony and I noticed that as she sat in the saddle chatting, her mount, on a slack rein, quickly dropped its muzzle down the wire netting tube protecting a tender chestnut tree and chewed up the growing buds. She was so absorbed in conversation that she was completely oblivious of the destruction. Trees should be lopped, trimmed and cared for like any other crop and when they come to maturity there must be an optimum time for felling them for timber. However, few sights are as dismal as the land laid waste in the wake of the chainsaw.

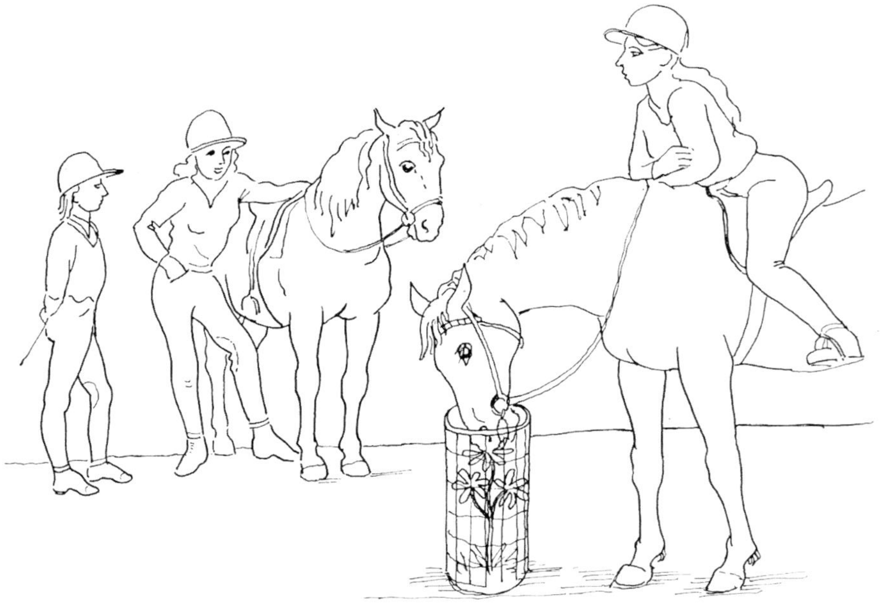

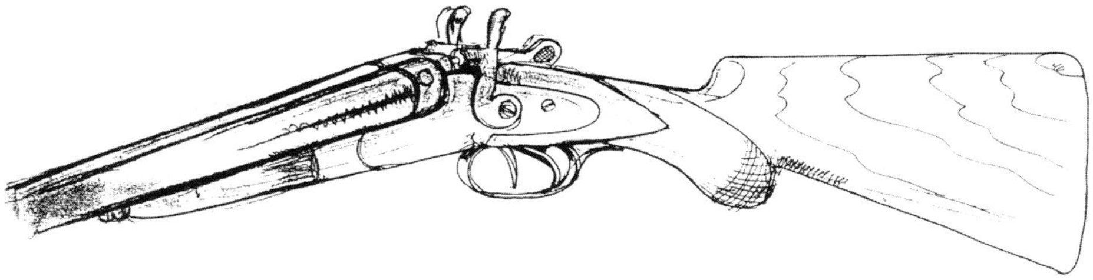

Peat Warms You Thrice

It is said that peat warms you thrice; once when you cut it, once when you carry it and once when you burn it.

With the advent of Dutch elm disease, as I could not bear to see dead trees around the farm, I installed a wood burning stove and bought a chainsaw. I soon discovered that the heat generated in producing the logs was greater than the calorific value of the logs in the grate! Chainsaws are tools to be treated with great respect as any accident incurred is a serious one. I thought I had stopped the tractor amply far away but the falling tree missed it by inches! Another day I was actually on the phone telling my son of our trimming activities when the line went dead as a helper laid a small elm across it!

Blizzard and icy conditions can cause electric power lines to fall and make a power cut, which can do untold damage to modern livestock farms. For such an eventuality, there must be installed a standby generator or petrol motor. The animals and birds may need heating, ventilating, feeding and pumped water. The lighting and machinery are vital to the proper functioning of a modern farm. I used to keep a petrol engine adjacent to the vacuum pump of the milking machine, and that too had to be kept in working order or it would refuse to start when needed in an emergency.

Albert Schweitzer said, "If a man loses reverence for any part of life, he will eventually lose reverence for all life".

I would use the gun only to protect my crops and livestock or to put some injured creature out of its misery. "Where the body lies, there will the vultures be gathered together" (Luke 17:37). A weak and sickly animal can often be found by observing the movements of magpies and carrion-crows. Rabbits and hares and the odd pheasant make a welcome addition to the farmer's menu. When mowing with a tractor, in spite of a sharp lookout, gruesome accidents are sure to happen. Animals and birds stay too long on the lair or nest, mother-love outweighing fear of the lethal reciprocating blades. Several times I have known a team of horses stop in their tracks and refuse to proceed at the word of command because of the camouflaged nest of some ground-nesting bird, invisible to the driver walking six yards behind!

A fairly good case can be made for the operations of shooting syndicates, apart from the fact that they provide social and sporting occasions of well-earned relaxation for local country folk. Vermin are kept under control and game-birds reared in large numbers far in excess of those shot, resulting in more protected and conserved wildlife for all to see and enjoy.

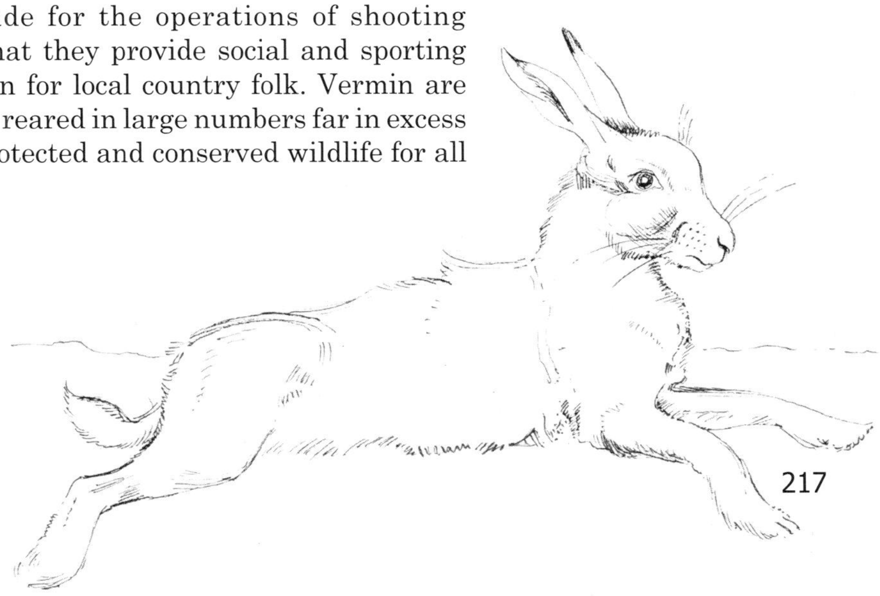

A Privilege Demanded as a Right

Try as one may to be a good, considerate neighbour, human nature contrives to put obstacles in one's way. In the matter of rights of way, I have found that what is conceded as a privilege is soon demanded as a right. A townsman came to live as a neighbour and soon he telephoned to see if I would permit his aged wife to walk across two of our fields to catch the bus. As this would cut her walk to one quarter of the normal route, I felt it would be churlish to refuse the request. I reasoned that, as she was on foot, she would be able to open and close the three gates on the route, which I am sure she intended to do. However, before long, her husband and all and sundry visitors and tradesmen were using the route in their cars and vans and constantly leaving the gates open, thereby rendering two ten-acre grass fields unusable by stock. When I politely pointed out that I could not be expected to stand the loss of two fields and would therefore have to padlock the offending gate, he flew into a great rage and became most abusive, threatening to cut the chains, which he did, as he was now claiming the route as a right of way over our land.

Untold Costly Trouble

Gates left open or thoughtlessly unsecured by hikers, ramblers, riders and even hunting folk, can cause untold costly trouble to the farmers concerned long after the culprits are miles away and safely tucked up in their beds.

By unplanned mixing of stock for even a few hours, years of work can be ruined by mismating, fighting and even spread of disease. Cattle and sheep carefully selected for market and segregated the previous day to await collection by the cattle lorry at 5am will have got mixed together and a vital sale missed.

A Spudder used for digging out deep rooted weeds

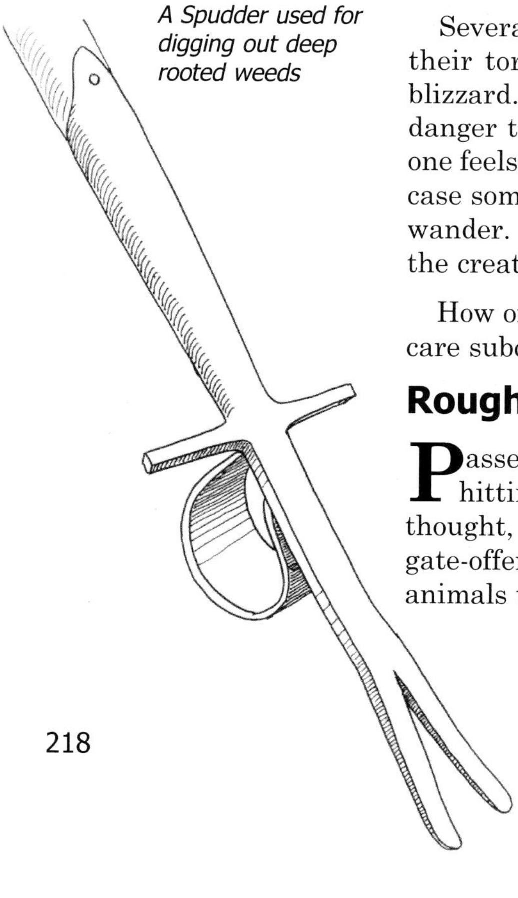

Several times, I have had policemen knocking on the door and shining their torches at my bedroom window, usually at 2:00 am and in a blizzard. They say that there are cattle loose on the turnpike and a danger to motorists. As the police are not able to describe the beasts, one feels obliged to pull on one's gumboots and anorak to investigate in case some courting couple have left a gate open to allow one's stock to wander. This is part of the 24 hour, 365 day-a-year responsibility for the creatures in one's charge.

How often does a townsman think of that ongoing load of continuing care subconsciously on the farmer's mind?

Rough Justice

Passengers in a speeding car can be killed or severely injured by hitting a half-ton bullock or horse in the dark. One might have thought, uncharitably, that it would be rough justice if the trespassing gate-offenders had a punishment to fit the crime by running into the animals they had let out previously that day.

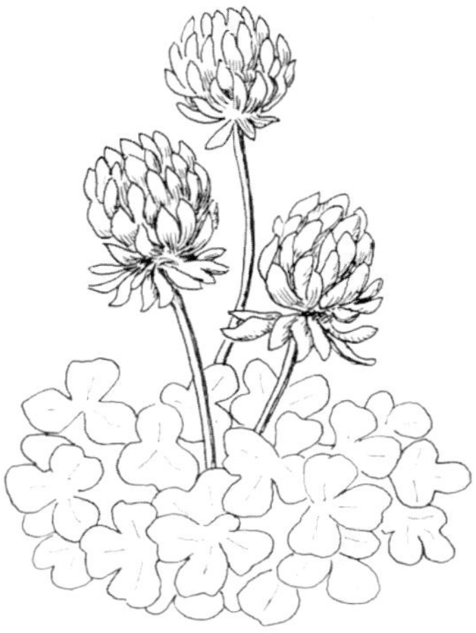

One early morning, after a rainy spell of weather when the fields were waterlogged, I noticed a locked saloon car stuck fast in a wet patch just inside the gate of one of our pasture fields.

The scene was not too difficult to reconstruct: an amorous couple on the way back from the pub decide to pull into our field for a bit of nookie. During their intimate encounter, the car was settling ever more firmly into the mire so that it defied all attempts to move it, mud flying in all directions from the spinning wheels. A long cold and wet tramp home had no doubt dampened the ardour of the middle-aged man who shamefacedly presented himself later in the day to ask for a tow with my tractor.

In Flagrante Delicto

Of course a charitable chap like me encountering a victim *in flagrante delicto* wouldn't dream of exploiting the situation with thoughts of blackmail and an exorbitant tractor hire fee!

This thoughtless, selfish Romeo would have been just the type to drive out of the field in the middle of the night, too flushed with conquest to alight in the mud to secure the gate after him, thereby letting our valuable stock escape to cause damage to themselves and others.

The Rhythm of Life

Coming home late across fields from the farrowing pens on a misty night it was quite easy to lose one's bearings and travel in a circle. On one such occasion I spied a distant light sending out more or less rhythmic signals which I could not recognise as Morse code. On close inspection it was discovered that the blinking message came from a loosely connected side light on a scruffy 'banger' van being used as a love nest by a neighbour's amorous son and his dusky lover. They were completely oblivious of the fact that their particularly energetic 'rhythm of life' was being broadcast far and wide for all to see!

If people out for a day in the countryside would approach the owners and politely ask for permission to picnic or pick berries, they would invariably be welcomed and given instructions as to where to go and what hazards to watch out for. Flattened mowing grass is hard to cut and animals are naturally inquisitive of picnickers!

A Veiled Threat

People in search of blackberries and elderberries may be directed to further fields, leaving those nearby for the farmer's wife and family. Trespassers tend to break down weak places in the hedges and fences to gain access. One young man, when challenged as he was picking laburnum in our spinney, replied that he had every right as he had just fought for his country in a war, adding that he had learned to shoot people to get what he wanted!

Each year at Christmastide there would be a nocturnal invasion of shady characters in small vans and pick-ups to strip the holly, ivy and laurel bushes for sale in shops and markets. With predators like that about, turkeys and cockerels were clearly at risk. I have known a plucky chained sheepdog to be killed by a couple of heartless thugs as it bravely tried to prevent them from stealing a few sacks of his master's potatoes.

Gypsies and scrap dealers would plunder the hedges for wood for their fires. Their horses would be tethered by night in secluded pastures while their lurchers searched the fields for hares and rabbits for their pots.

Farm Machinery Tends to be Noisy and Lethal

Machinery tends to be very noisy. A farmer I knew got his arm in the archimedean thread of a mill and mixer in the barn. His cries for help could not be heard as his cowman was sawing logs on a saw bench nearby. I went into a noisy workshop at a grass dryer on an aerodrome where I was making hay. The foreman was sharpening a knife with a faulty electric grindstone. The current going through him was such that he could not leave go the tool or reach to switch it off. He was far gone with exhaustion and I was able to save his life by throwing the switch. He had very nasty burns from the electric current. Never was he more pleased to see anyone, as he thought his hour of death had come.

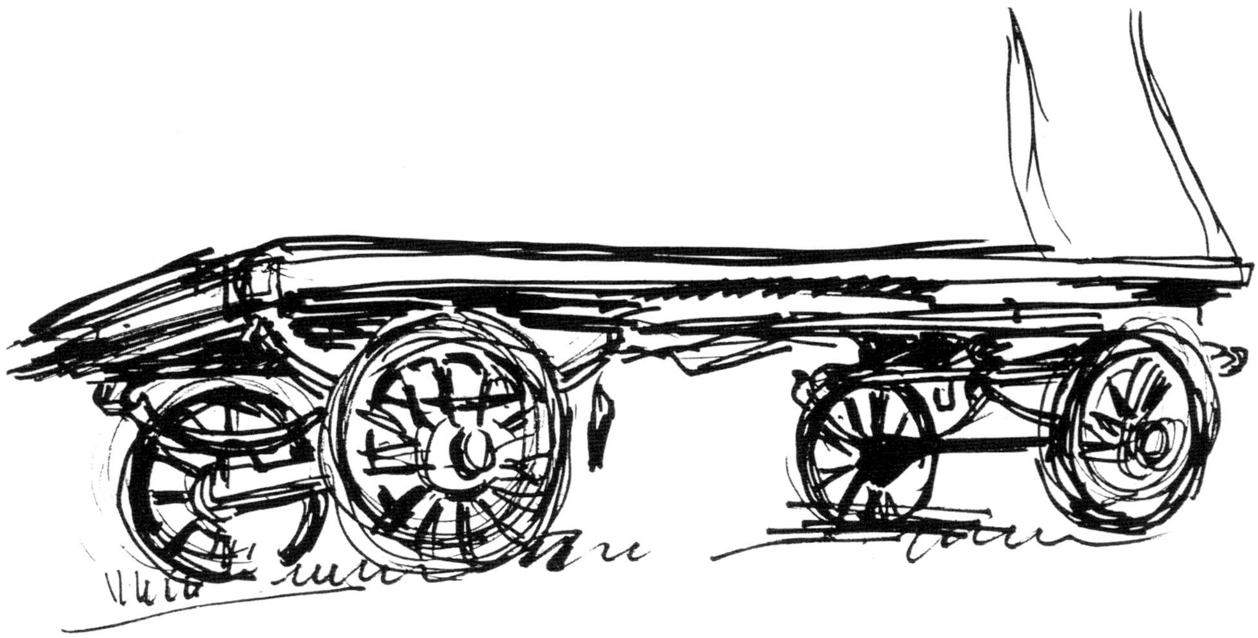

Euston Station, Four-wheeled dray, 1914

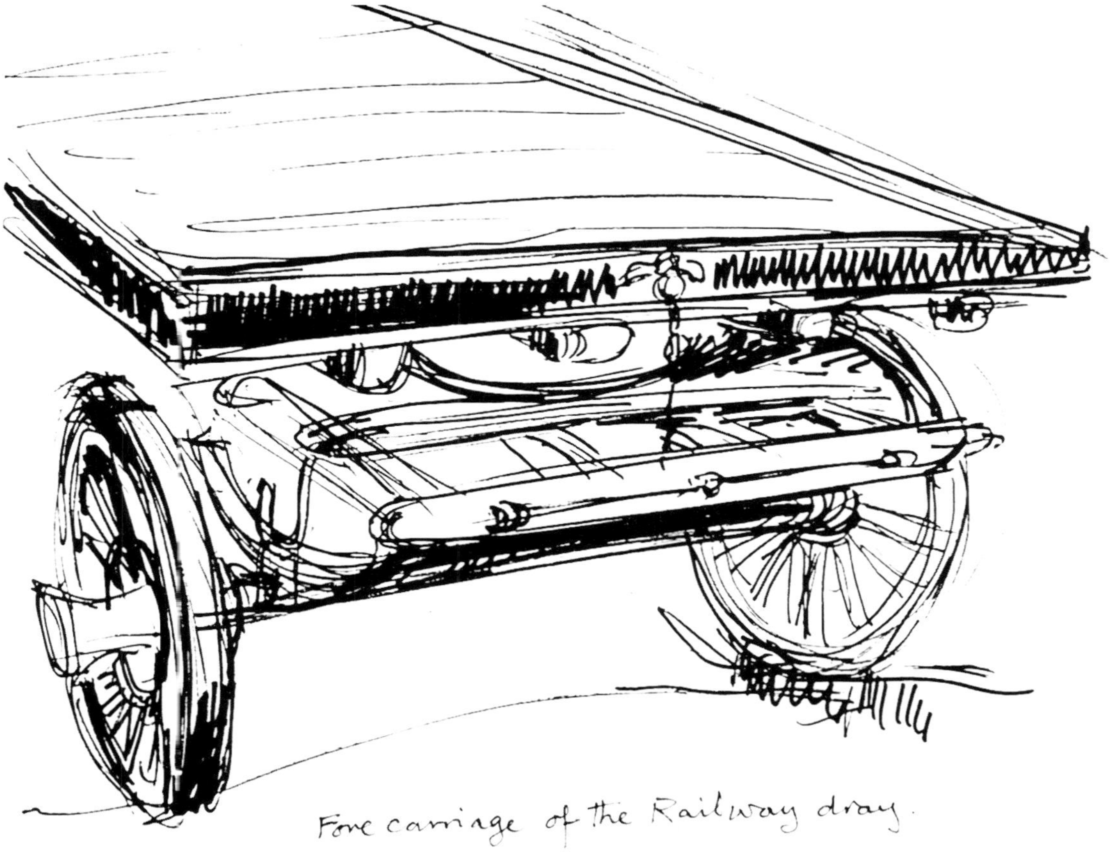

Fore carriage of the Railway dray.

Cast-Offs From Other Industries

Small farmers, being typically under-capitalised, were forced to be resourceful in making good use of the cast-off rejects of other, more prosperous industries or enterprises such as the railways, or the Army or the General Post Office Telephones Department. In pre-war years, it was quite common to see cut-down cars and vans in use in the fields pulling mowing machines or pushing hay sweeps.

For £5, I bought a four-wheeled dray, marked Euston Station 1914, fitted with a tractor draw-bar instead of shafts; it could bring in 100 bales of straw if the ground were hard. Next I bought a 22-foot long semi-trailer from the railways and had the local blacksmith fit a jack and clevis for a tractor. This would carry 160 bales on its rubber tyres. Another four-wheeled trailer I constructed myself on the chassis of a Bren gun carrier, while the armour plating was used to reinforce the doors of the bull-pen against the thudding attacks of the animal's mighty head and horns.

My children will hardly believe me when I tell them I remember the Birmingham buses going on solid rubber tyres. The driver had no windshield to protect him from the weather, just a macintosh sheet suspended over his hands and knees! His maximum speed was only 20 miles per hour, quite enough over granite setts.

Rogers Bros. Wheelwrights of Lutterworth, Leicestershire would adapt our carts.

Advantages of Pneumatic Tyres

Any builder who has used a pneumatic-tyred wheelbarrow after toiling with solid-tyred barrows appreciates its ease of travel. Just so were farmers quick to recognise the advantage of such tyres over the old iron-shod wheels on all sorts of farm vehicles. This was especially true when it came to hauling produce off the land. Carts and wagons at first looked a little incongruous perched on makeshift axles borrowed from cars and lorries. Apart from the occasional puncture, they were vastly more efficient. Owing to post-war shortages of the correct type, a pair of aluminium aeroplane wheels with smooth tread were fitted to one of my carts. They were much too light and thin and were constantly being punctured by thorns, so I had to replace them when more suitable ones became available.

Fetching a Goods Wagon Body

For £20 I bought a double-skinned hardwood-covered goods wagon, the body weighing about five tonnes. There were double doors half way along each side. I set it on blocks so that the floor was at lorry height where it proved invaluable for unloading fertilisers, seed and feeding stuffs, as it saved lowering these heavy sacks to the floor and lifting them later for transport about the farm.

To collect it, I took a large ex-Army flat bed trailer to the goods yard ten miles away where the body was jacked up, the buffers and wheels having been removed. The trailer was reversed under it and the wagon body lowered into position. I then began seriously to wonder about the two low bridges, the inclines on the route and whether my tractor brakes could cope in an emergency! It must have presented a very strange sight indeed to anyone in a roadside field who happened to look up and notice a railway truck making its way along the country lanes!

As this indivisible load was far too heavy for our equipment, I had to hire a small crane lorry from a garage to unload it sideways into position.

Younger people will not remember, but not so very long ago all major roads and railways lines had sturdy poles set at fifty yard intervals alongside the way, festooned with masses of telephone wires which carried our more or less important messages from place to place. When it was decided to bury the wires underground, forests of these peerless poles became redundant and lay in heaps at the roadsides. Never one to miss a bargain, I filled up a tender form from the GPO and to my amazement found I had purchased about eighty poles situated in a lay-by seven miles away.

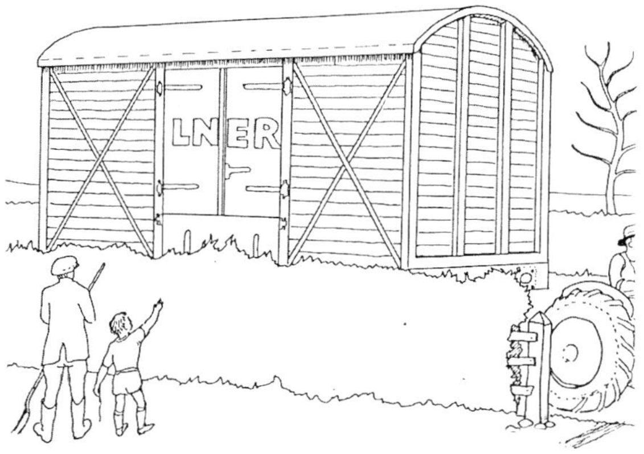

Viewed from behind tall hedges, the strange sight of a railway truck proceeding as if under its own steam along the country lanes.

Telegraph Poles Purchased for Dutch Barns

As there were more than I needed, I sold half of them to a farmer who lived a few miles further off. We met at the site with two trailers apiece and used the tractor's fore loader to lift them onto the trailers. We must have presented a strange site as we made our journeys home for nearly all the poles were still equipped with footsteps, crossbars, stays and insulators! When these had all been removed, I selected ten of the longest and sturdiest to go in the ground as uprights for the five-bay Dutch barn I was about to build. The remaining thirty were taken to the local sawmill to be ripped down into purlins and timbers for triangular roof trusses. When the hay was ready, it was stacked between the uprights, thus providing a useful safe platform to walk about on as we subsequently fixed the roof trusses, purlins and covering sheets on our fine new barn. Whatever else may be said about its aesthetic qualities, it was an extremely cost-effective way to keep our hay and straw safe from the elements.

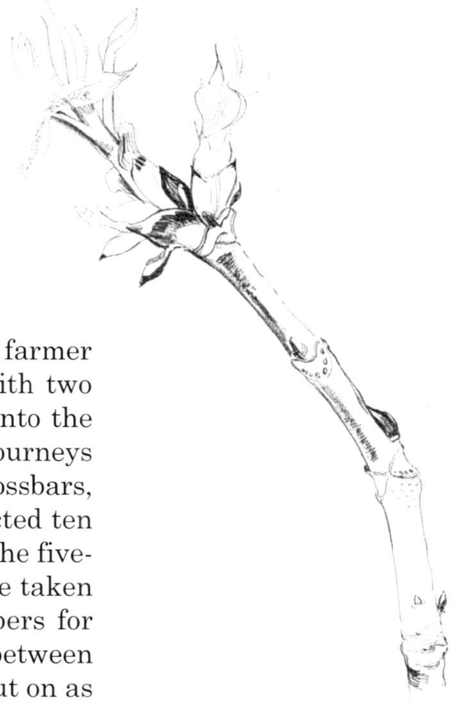

The Darling Bud of May

The Tail Wags the Dog

There are often situations in life where you might say that "the tail wags the dog". I have heard of people buying a movie camera to record events in their forthcoming holiday; on the face of it a very reasonable idea but quite soon they find that the machine rules their lives. Their whole holiday is dominated by its demands, down to the colour and shape of the clothes they wear. Each arrival and departure has to be done twice and the choice of hotel dining table is the subject of much acrimonious discussion, so that it may be in the best possible light and with a suitable background.

It is quite common for people to take up gardening as a hobby. Some may be persuaded to buy a greenhouse as a seemingly suitable adjunct to that activity, and place of refuge in inclement weather. I suspect that some are secretly surprised by how much extra expense and regular attention is demanded by this innocent looking tyrant, which almost certainly adds considerably to the sum total of gardening work!

Mixing Machine Actually Created Work

Farming, being the business of efficient food production, presents a different attitude as one is always looking for labour-saving devices to streamline the operation. I was once sweet-talked into the purchase of a feed mixing machine which was to save several pounds a ton over buying balanced rations from a merchant. I soon came to recognise this dangerous contrivance as a malevolent taskmaster that kept me working alone late into the night amidst noise and dust pollution. Far from saving work, this machine actually created toil of a particularly tedious kind while contributing nothing to my health, temper and family bliss.

Good, Bad and Sticky Weather

It has always seemed to me a little strange that the official forecasters, instead of describing the weather in an objective way, refer to "good" and "bad" weather as if there were something malevolent about the rain which, after all, is responsible for England's green and pleasant land. There is a new term, 'sticky weather', used by some weathermen. The townsman, largely insulated from the weather in his double-glazed house, office and air-conditioned car, would be the first to complain if there were no water for his bath or swimming pool and if his lawns and putting greens turned brown!

Our habit of changing the clocks to British Summer Time is vastly inconvenient to those who work on the land and who, I suspect, are not consulted over this childish device to make the townsman get up earlier! As the dew does not lift until noon instead of an hour earlier, farmers cannot work at haymaking or corn harvesting. This tiring work goes on till late at night, but the men have to be up at 5.00 a.m. to get the milking done in time for the early milk lorry as usual. Men and women become accident-prone when they are over-tired.

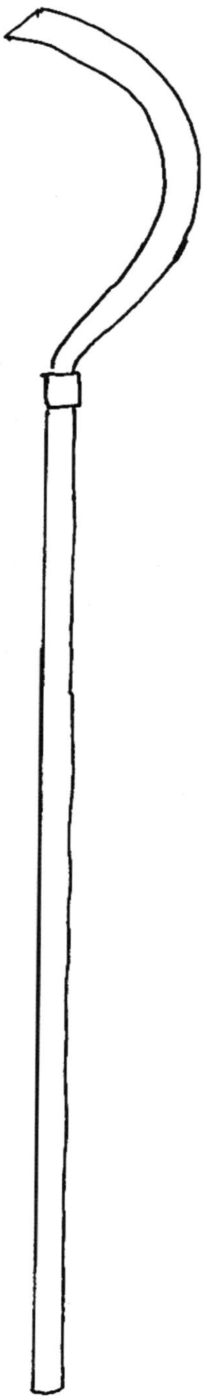

SLASHER

Disillusioned Ex-Servicemen

In the immediate post-war years, I came across several ex-servicemen such as colonels and squadron leaders who, being vaguely attracted to farming as a way of life, had bought small farms and were rapidly becoming disillusioned. Their romantic dreams and fond hopes were being dashed on all sides, and their bank balances were rapidly diminishing.

Eating homely fare in haste in the farm kitchen surrounded by steaming, smelly socks, sweaty gum boots and the odd cade lamb warming on the oven top could hardly compete with the privileged life in the officers' mess, where all one's wants were supplied by an ever-faithful, uncomplaining batman.

These people were learning that an idle worker could not be put on a charge or that a cheating dealer was unafraid of the glasshouse. Wayward pigs and cretinous cattle do not jump to attention when bawled at. Plans have to be infinitely adaptable. U-turns have to be made as distant goals fade out of sight.

It is rare for hope to triumph over experience.

Someone Should Have Told Them

It would have been a kindness if someone could have convinced these naïve town dwellers that their efforts were predestined to failure. Their minds and bodies were not attuned to the rigours of country living, much less to the relentless grind of inordinately long hours of physical labour involved in wresting a living from the land in all weathers.

Such a man could be seen drinking spirits with his wife in the local hotel at midday while his neglected stock back on the farm bawled in vain for their breakfasts. Ignorant people like this were an easy prey for unscrupulous charlatans and vicious vagabonds, who would take them for all they could get.

Never confuse information with knowledge. It is difficult to see why men so charming and gifted in other ways had allowed themselves to be misled into thinking that, without any training, they could manage a complex and arduous business, as though they were taking up golf in retirement!

Oliver Goldsmith wrote in 1770 in *The Deserted Village* - "A bold peasantry, their country's pride, when once destroyed, can never be supplied".

An Endangered Species

Once we were told small was beautiful - now it is inconvenient. A man who once thought of himself with some justifiable pride as a small farmer, then became a grasping peasant; now he recognises himself to be an endangered species. The suicide rate among farmers has soared to become twice that of other small businesses. He often lives a lonely life in glorious isolation and he may well ask himself why a farm, which had hitherto supported his ancestors in modest comfort for many generations, has now suddenly become, under his management, no longer viable. He loses his self-respect. A run of unfortunate incidents, each quite small in itself, may have a cumulative effect of inducing a deep depression and a feeling of guilt that he cannot control things any more. He has no-one at hand in whom he feels able to confide and the gun hangs on the wall...

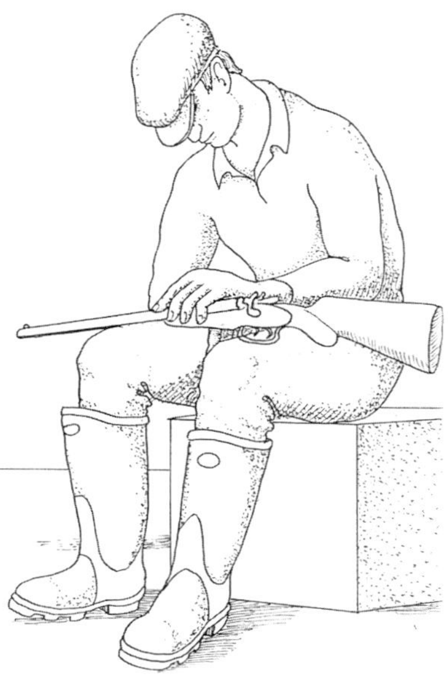

Depressed farmer

Conflicting Requirements

There would seem to be two irreconcilable conflicting desires at work in the mind of the consumer regarding the countryside. The inexorable movement towards vast prairie-like arable farms and the accompanying trend to gigantic units of factory-produced livestock. These are the inevitable results of consumer demand for cheap food regardless of the consequences. Organic produce accounts for only a very small percentage of the total market.

However, wearing his other hat, the consumer, as he drives about the countryside, complains at the lack of small fields and hedgerows, and the enormous, ugly, factory-like sheds that house the livestock that give him cheap meat, milk and eggs.

Large farms get larger and ever larger as the smaller farmers go out of business and leave the land in droves.

Old Barn, Malham

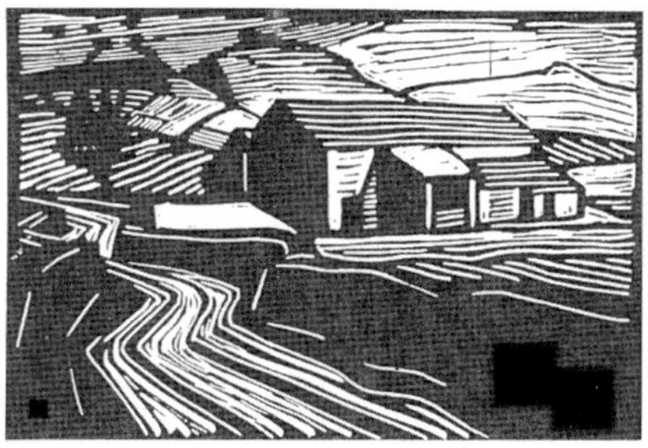

Dormitory Villages

Isolated old farmhouses, cottages and buildings fall into disrepair and are deserted as they are no longer viable and would be difficult to modernise. The few remaining farm workers cannot afford to live in villages near their work and migrate to the towns.

Cotswold villages are bought by stockbroker millionaires from Birmingham and become dormitory places, no longer requiring a school, a shop or a post office; so that those who formed the heart of village life are dismissed, to be replaced by the flower arrangers of the Mother's Union at the local church.

Never Criticise a Farmer with your Mouth Full!

The Black Horse car park is arrayed with Mercedes and Jaguars of the latest registration, while the bars resound with their owners' nasal voices as they consume their prawn cocktails, shepherd's pies and ploughman's lunches to the yuppie talk of takeovers and asset-stripping. One suspects that if a real shepherd or ploughman were to venture inside, he would be patronised, ridiculed or at best frozen out by his agricultural inferiors who wouldn't know a coulter from a mould board, a ewe from a wether, or wheat from barley!

Maybe in the distant past, one of these former public schoolboys may uneasily remember having to construe the lines from Cato: "The best citizens spring from the cultivators", or maybe recall reading the assertion of Xenophon, the Greek, that "Agriculture, for a high-minded man, is the best of all occupations".

I remember as a little boy at prep school having to write in perfect copper-plate hand with a scratchy, flexible nib, pithy maxims to elevate the mind or deter the would-be wrongdoer: "Unity is strength, Vice brings ruin" and "Sweet are the uses of Adversity". I did not know what they meant then but I think I do now!

Sweet Are The Uses of Adversity

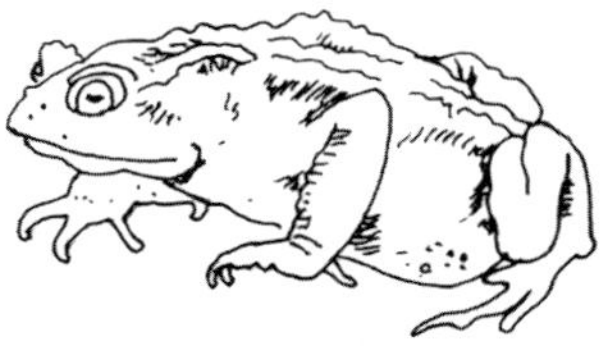

Few of us would deny that having to wait and struggle, even a little, for our heart's desires makes us appreciate our good fortune more when it finally arrives. In small luxuries, self-denial strengthens character and there is often more pleasure to be had from giving than from receiving.

In small-scale farming there are many jobs that require the co-ordinated effort of two or more people. This need for unity of purpose overrides personal animosity and creates a lasting bond in the purposeful struggle against adversity. In my lifetime, I have seen a dramatic decline in the ethic of hard work and unselfish fortitude, which has been displaced by an ethic of personal fulfilment and the pursuit of happiness.

They say that money can't buy you love or friends - only a better class of enemies! Happiness is not to be relentlessly pursued; rather it occurs, as the flower by the wayside, in the most unlikely places. In my experience, jealousy and envy of another's power and possessions does not make for happiness. The grass always looks greener on the other side of the fence.

Strangely some people are suspicious of gracious treatment. They feel uneasy if kindness seems to come to them with no strings attached. But *some of the most precious gifts in life come this way.* You cannot purchase a sunset or earn the aria of a song-thrush. There is no harm in shining up your neighbour's halo. Often there is a kind of echo-principle at work. A good deed or kind word passes on and it returns like a boomerang to the hand of the sender.

A Good Place to Rear Children

In this country, in spite of the risks, a small farm is still a good place to bring up young children under both parents' watchful eyes. Even grandparents can grow old gracefully doing useful jobs around the homestead. I am sure that a child reared in the poverty of a small third world subsistence farm is better able to meet the challenge of life than one running wild amidst the squalor and vice of a shanty town.

With children at school, one was often presented with a dilemma such as whether to bring in the hay or attend the school sports. I have been known to visit the lambing pens during the interval of our local opera performance in which my family were involved! Small unwelcome guests would find their way into our bed after such night-time visits to lambing and farrowing pens, where, scorning my own tough hide, they would cause consternation on my partner's sensitive skin!

Delightful Sense of Achievement With Nature

"The newborn lambs in rustic dance nimbly ply their feeble feet."

The antics of young animals as they cavort about in unruly gangs is a sight to gladden the heart of any stockman, who will look with satisfaction and contentment on the fruits of his labour.

The farmer and his workers shared the delightful sense of achievement when admiring a yard full of well thatched ricks or a neatly cut and laid hedge.

The field workers showed their skills not only in the ploughing but also in the sheer accuracy of the straight patterns of alternate light and dark green as they drove their harrows and rollers over the meadows and growing corn.

At harvest time, the rows of stooks were kept as straight as the proverbial gun barrel, as were the rows of hay cocks and heaps of manure, mangels and swedes. Everywhere on a well run farm was a sense of order and discipline which made for visual harmony and mental contentment.

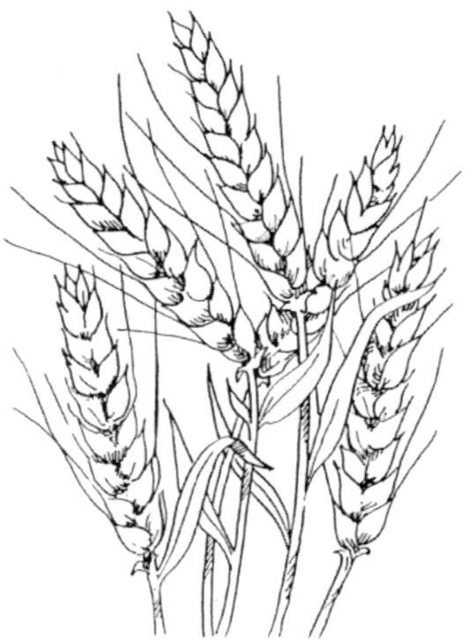

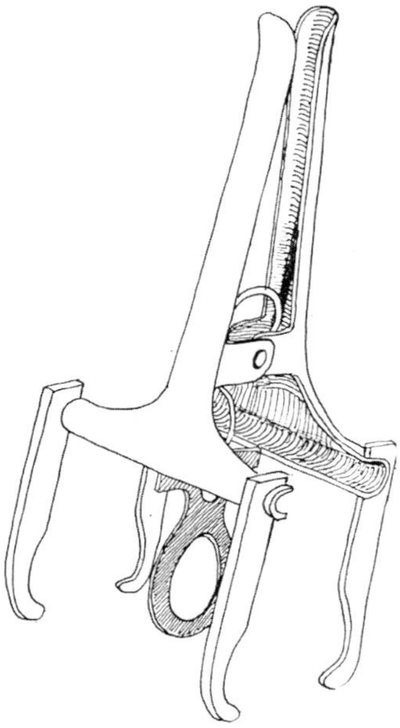

Mole Catcher in 'set' position.

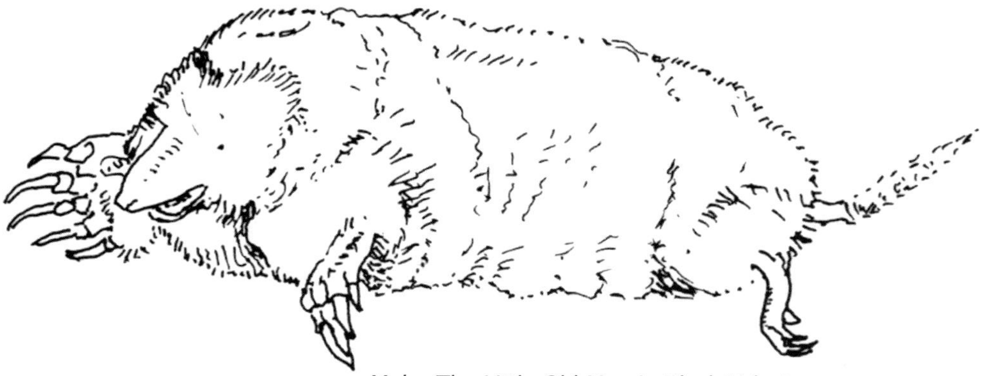

Mole: The Little Old Man in Black Velvet

Even game-keepers and mole-catchers showed their prowess by displaying their grisly trophies in neat rows along the fences of the spinneys and coverts.

There is one unfortunate animal (it could be a camel or a duck-billed platypus) said to have been designed by a committee.

Committee meetings have a propensity for generating hot air in great quantities, and sometimes little else! I have noticed that no gas or steam drives anything until it is confined and channelled. No movement ever grows great until it is focused, dedicated and disciplined into a worthy cause.

Unresolved Paradox

There would seem to be some paradox in the thought, so often commended by the worldly wise, of continuously working towards some distant worthy goal without distraction and deviation. However, I have observed the manifest advantages of seizing opportunities as they present themselves, keeping one's options open and being infinitely adaptable to changing circumstances. How can the two concepts be reconciled?

Dogged persistence and rigid adherence to a set of rules can be perceived as reactionary resistance to inevitable change. Whereas an unseemly readiness to jump on the swings and roundabouts of fashion shows a reprehensible lack of stability. It is often much easier to emulate the Vicar of Bray and sit on the fence, being all things to all men until it is seen 'which way the cat will jump!' For myself the precepts instilled by my loving parents and teachers when I was as a small child have acted as a guide book and beacon to aim for along life's journey. My conscience is informed by the Ten Commandments, although my wayward instincts prompt me to wish they came accompanied, like examination questions, with instructions to attempt only seven at any one time!

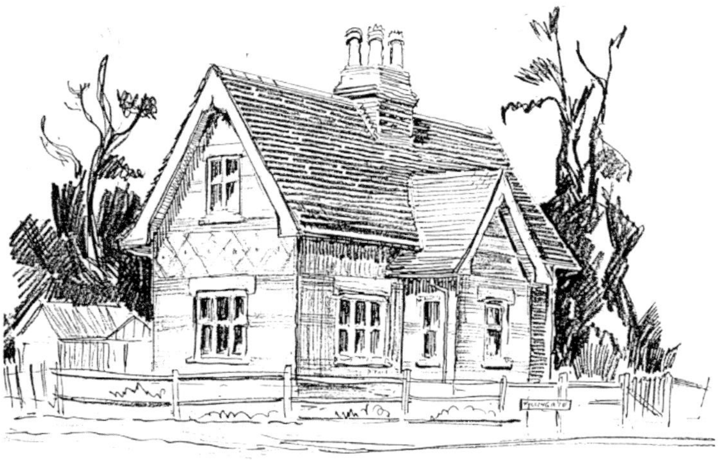

An Agricultural Worker's Tied Cottage

In Conclusion

In this account of my life as a farmer, I fear I may have given the impression that it was more varied and hilarious than it actually was. In reality, much of the time was occupied with dull, routine chores, and it is only the highlights that are memorable. Few things can be more monotonous than hoeing swedes; but seeing the lightning set fire to an ash tree, or watching the whirlwind sweep up the hay are wonders of nature not given to be observed by many people. The tedium of milking cows twice or thrice a day is relieved at regular intervals by the miracle of birth at calving, which induces the cow to produce an abundance of milk for our consumption.

* * *

My ancestors in the Yorkshire Dales suffered great tribulation in 1752, when an avalanche of snow and enormous rocks descended on their farmstead.

Those who fled from Harborgill at the time of the avalanche were as follows:- William Thistlethwaite our common ancestor aged 70 years, his son Thomas Thistlethwaite aged 28, his youngest son Timothy Thistlethwaite aged 26, his grandson Richard Thistlethwaite aged 9, and his housekeeper Elizabeth Atkinson, aged 27. The fleeing inhabitants of Harborgill in Dentdale had but 400 yards to traverse in a direct line to John Thistlethwaite's at Leayat, yet spent more than two hours upon the journey.

They lost all their peats, fleeces, wool, three horses, and husbandry gear to great value. The next morning they heard

"...the melancholy and affecting news that Thomas Stockdall's whole family to the number of eight persons were all Buried in Ruins by the Like misfortune [at a neighbouring farm]. Even in a moment they were surprised by Death, and was no more. This gave us fresh cause to be thankfull to heaven for his wonderfull protection in so manifest dangers."

A rather similar disaster struck our farm and homestead on 17 March 1947, when we found ourselves in the direct path of a hurricane or tornado. It was only five months after we had become owners of the property, and it was heartbreaking and frightening to see it being pounded and smashed by the elements.

The storm cut a swathe across our section of the county, destroying buildings and uprooting trees by the thousands. We lost 150 large trees, oaks, elms, ashes, sycamores, Douglas firs and Scots pines. All our roofs sustained massive damage. Slates, tiles corrugated iron and asbestos sheets were blown off, some of them landing a quarter of a mile away. We untied and let out all the terrified indoor stock to chance their luck with the storm and flying objects, and then we struggled inside and battened down the doors and windows. As we prayed for deliverance we could hear the howling of the wind and the crashing of the failing masonry. The force of the wind actually shook the brickwork of the walls with powerful gusts.

It was thought that the snow which had lain for the previous six weeks had begun to thaw, loosening the soil around the roots of the great trees. This loosening had been aided, no doubt, by the burrowing of innumerable rabbits who had taken up residence in the spinneys.

The next morning I surveyed the scene of desolation, and with a feeling of resigned, peasant-like resolution began to salvage what materials I could from the chaos. We had very little money, but with the optimism and resourcefulness of youth we proceeded to patch and repair our very large roof areas.

We bought a tractor-driven sawbench and ripped up some of the pine trees into laths and rafters, and where the roof had blown off the house, used the opportunity to lower into the roof space a very large, galvanised water tank. Later this proved to be invaluable.

The cordwood was cut into logs which we bagged up to sell to our customers. I took a trailer to a local brickworks and brought back a load of tiles to patch a roof where the force of the gale had lifted out an area about five yards square.

You will gather that farmers had perforce to become more or less expert jobbing builders, capable of coping with plumbing, electrical and drainage emergencies, to say nothing of the need for some mechanical engineering and veterinary knowledge. A typical jack of all trades and master of none!

Tributes to Friends and Family

When I look back over my years of farming, I realise how much credit should be given to those alongside whom I have worked. Employees, friends and neighbours have been conscripted and shamelessly exploited to help me in times of crisis. They have always shown remarkable forbearance in overlooking my shortcomings whilst offering assistance with formidable tasks. It is only too easy for a farmer to earn the reputation of being a slave-driver; for example, when dusk approaches, he may drive his willing helpers to bring in just one more load of hay, anxious to clear the field in case it might rain in the night. The requirements of the work must often take precedence over personal convenience.

Similarly, tribute must be paid to our four children, Jeremy, Richard, Anthony and Julia, who from an early age worked uncomplainingly, without thought of reward, when asked to help with some essential task on the farm. We are proud of the way they have all shown sturdy independence and distinguished themselves as they progressed along their chosen ways of life. They say that a child follows in his father's footsteps, but in our case it is in Mother's footsteps they must have trodden, following her example and precepts. Her devotion to the care of her family is second to none, and her down-to-earth wisdom and sterling values were imparted to her offspring with their mother's milk. They all display a caring concern for the welfare of their ageing parents and a willingness to help in practical affairs when necessary.

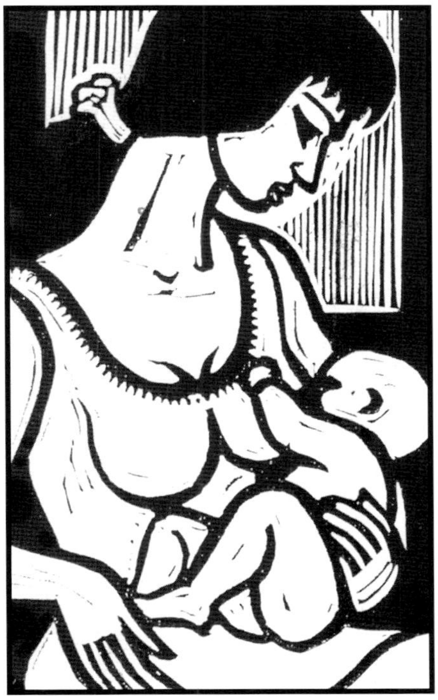

The greatest tribute must go to my loving wife and partner for half a century, Elizabeth, who has smoothed my path along life's way, supporting and caring for me in sickness and in health. She has taken selfless pride and pleasure in providing a loving, peaceful and beautiful home with nourishing, home-cooked meals for hungry people. And there is no appetite like that created by hard physical work. Each year she used to enjoy singing and acting with the local opera group. When the children were old enough, she returned to her former vocation, teaching art, craft and calligraphy, and has now returned to painting pictures of considerable merit. Eleven of them are hanging in the Leicester City Art Gallery at the moment.

I am also grateful to those who encouraged me to persevere with the compilation of these memoirs, the progress of which has suffered from long periods of inertia over the past five years. Also, many thanks to Maria Giblin and Julie Malik for their typing services, and to my good friend Daniel King for helping with the preliminary editing.

With these tributes I will draw the work to a close.

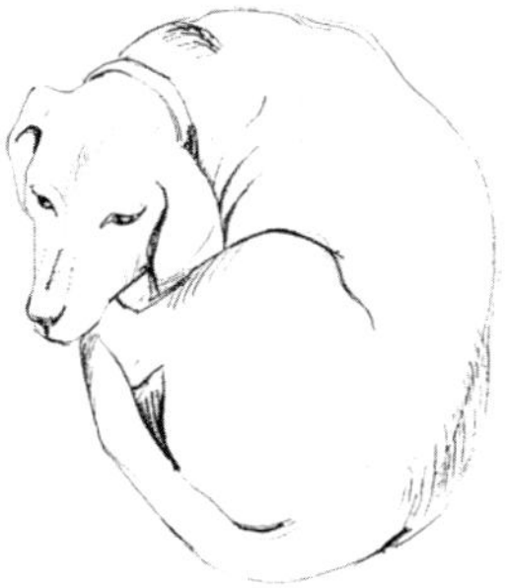

Christopher Thistlethwaite

I was born in 1920 in Buxton, Derbyshire, my Thistlethwaite ancestors were yeoman farmers in Dentdale, North Yorkshire.

In 1928 my father's work took him to Cadbury's at Bournville, so I spent my youth in the nearby suburb of Harborne where I lived in the family home while studying Fine Art at the Birmingham College of Art in Margaret Street. It was here that I met my late wife Elizabeth.

In 1940 I was directed into agriculture and I acquired considerable skills in the arts and crafts of agricultural practice, and developed, with Elizabeth, the ambition to buy and work our own farm in Leicestershire, where we would have a Pedigree Herd of Jersey Cattle.

Although leading a very busy life as a farmer, I always had a sketchbook to hand where I sustained my interest in drawing which, as Ingres said is "nine-tenths of painting".

In 1962 I was awarded the Art Teachers Diploma (ATD) and obtained a Certificate of Education from Leicester University. During 18 years as Head of Art and Crafts at a large Comprehensive School in Coventry, I developed printmaking among the students and Elizabeth, likewise, developed a traditionally high standard of Calligraphy.

My own work has been influenced by the German Expressionists, Fernand Léger, Matisse, Picasso and, of course, Edward Bawden and Eric Gill.

I have shown work in the Royal Academy's Summer Exhibitions, and three large works have been purchased for the Leicester City Art Gallery's permanent collection.

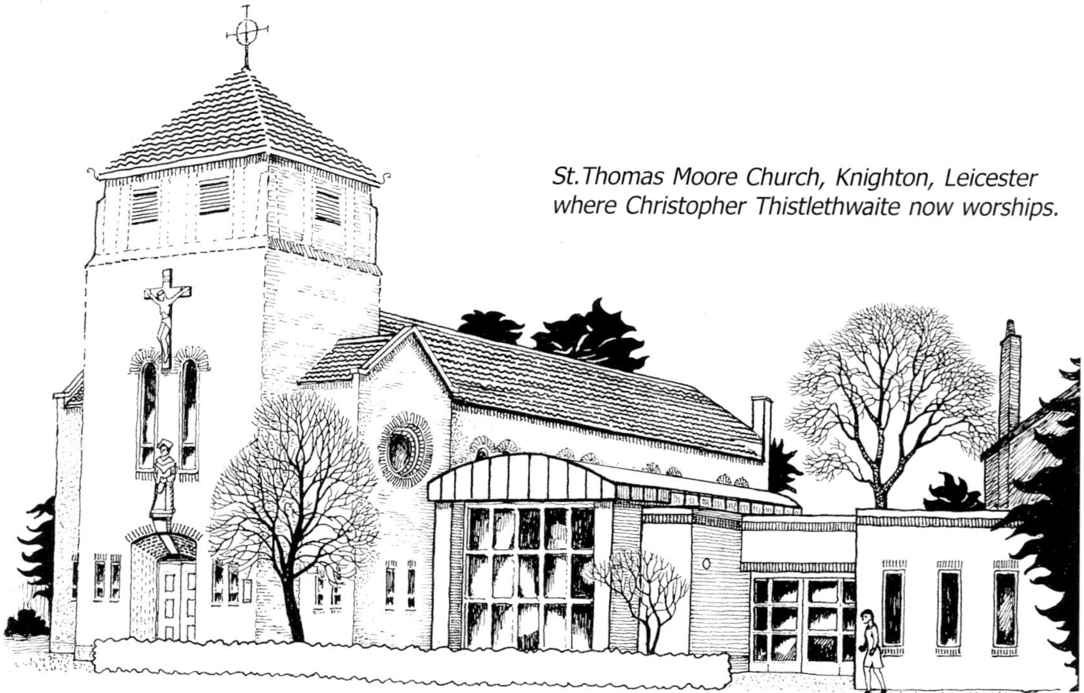

St.Thomas Moore Church, Knighton, Leicester where Christopher Thistlethwaite now worships.